BEST PRACTICE CASES IN BRANDING:

LESSONS FROM THE WORLD'S STRONGEST BRANDS

BEST PRACTICE CASES IN BRANDING:
LESSONS FROM THE WORLD'S STRONGEST BRANDS

Kevin Lane Keller
Dartmouth College

Upper Saddle River, New Jersey 07458

Acquisitions editor: Wendy Craven
Associate editor: Melissa Pellerano
Production editor: Carol Zaino
Manufacturer: Technical Communication Services

ISBN 0-13-1141133-0

10 9 8 7 6 5 4 3 2

BEST PRACTICE CASES IN BRANDING:
Lessons from the World's Strongest Brands
Table of Contents

Preface

Biography

BEST PRACTICE CASES IN BRANDING:
Lessons from the World's Strongest Brands
Preface

The brands and companies spotlighted in this book represent some of the most successful brands and companies in the world over the last decade or so. The marketers behind these brands and companies have all made noteworthy accomplishments to our understanding of the strategic brand management process and how to best build and manage brand equity. These cases highlight these achievements while also suggesting some of the opportunities and challenges they currently face.

The cases cover a lot of ground in terms of industries, geographies and brand management issues. The cases range from fast-moving consumer goods to high-tech and on-line brands and from durables to service brands. The cases often provide detailed descriptions of the global landscape for the brand and how it was received in different markets. Two cases are primarily set in Europe (Nivea and Red Bull). Finally, a host of brand management topics are addressed in the cases that will help the reader understand how to:

1) Brand a new product (even if it is a commodity or ingredient);

2) Employ new marketing approaches to build brand equity and brand loyalty;

3) Expand a brand into new geographical markets and channels;

4) Establish a brand hierarchy and introduce brand extensions;

5) Manage a corporate brand;

6) Keep a brand strong over time;

7) Revitalize a brand that gets into trouble; and

8) Change a brand name or reposition a brand.

Collectively, these cases provide a comprehensive overview of the strategic brand management process and corresponding best practice guidelines. Each of the 12 cases also yields valuable specific lessons into how to build and manage brand equity.

As good as the marketers have been with these brands, however, marketing is never perfect. As these marketers themselves would probably readily admit, sometimes mistakes have been made and opportunities have been overlooked. If given another chance, they might have done some things differently. So as the reader studies these cases, it is important to do so with a critical eye to properly discern the key lessons in strategic brand management. What did these brands do well? What was their formula for success? What could they have improved on? What might you have done differently? Finally, in looking forward, what kinds of things should be done so that the brand flourishes? The discussion questions at the end of each case pose additional questions for your consideration.

Acknowledgements

I would like to acknowledge some of the many people that helped to create this casebook and develop associated teaching materials. First, many thanks to all the companies profiled here whom, directly or indirectly, provided valuable input or feedback. In particular, I would like to extend special thanks to the following individuals who provided important assistance when they were associated with companies that were studied: Scott Bedbury, Jerome Conlan, Howard Behar, Howard Schultz, Jim Alling, Thomas Yang, and Oren Smith (Starbucks); Liz Dolan, Bill Zeitz, David Kottcamp, Steve Miller, Nelson Farris and Trevor Edwards (Nike); Jamie Murray, Barbara Pandos, Scott Nelson, and Cheryl Gee (DuPont); Dennis Carter, Pam Pollace, Sally Fundakowski, Karen Alter, Ann Lewnes, and Ellen Konar (Intel); Rolf Kunisch, Norbert Krapp, Ann-Christin Wagemann, Inken Hollmann-Peters, and Franziska Schmiedebach (Beiersdorf); Steve Goldstein, Robert Hanson, James Capon, and Bobbi Silten (Levi-Strauss); Jeff Manning (CMPB); Jim Murphy, Teresa Poggenpohl, Charles Teeter, and Brian Harvey (Accenture); Michael Weinstein, Ken Gilbert, and Jack Belisto (Snapple); Norbert Kraihamer (Red Bull); and Anke Audenaert and Murray Gaylord (Yahoo!).

At Prentice-Hall, Wendy Craven spearheaded the effort with ample assistance from Melissa Pellerano, but a number of other people there provided guidance and help for which I am thankful, specifically, John Roberts, Jeff Shelstad, Danielle Serra, and Anthony Palmiotto.

Finally, I would also like to thank my case writing assistants who helped to research and write these cases over the years: Leslie Kimerling, Sanjay Sood, Peter Gilmore, Greg Tusher, Emmanuelle Louis Hofer, and Eric Free. I would like to express special thanks to my research assistant for the past few years, Keith Richey, who was involved in writing or updating every case in this book. An incredibly gifted writer and natural-born marketer, his contributions were immense.

Dedication

This book is dedicated to my wife, Punam Anand Keller and my two daughters, Carolyn and Allison with much love and appreciation.

Kevin Lane Keller
Hanover, NH
June 2002

BIOGRAPHY

Kevin Lane Keller is the E. B. Osborn Professor of Marketing at the Amos Tuck School of Business Administration at Dartmouth College. Professor Keller received his B.A. in Mathematics and Economics from Cornell University in 1978, his M.B.A. from Carnegie-Mellon University's Graduate School of Industrial Administration in 1980, and his Ph.D. in Marketing from Duke University's Fuqua School of Business in 1986. At Dartmouth, he teaches an M.B.A. elective on strategic brand management and lectures in executive programs on that topic.

Previously, Professor Keller was on the faculty of the Graduate School of Business at Stanford University, where he also served as the head of the marketing group. Additionally, he has been on the marketing faculty of the Schools of Business Administration at the University of California at Berkeley and the University of North Carolina at Chapel Hill, been a Visiting Professor at Duke University and the Australian Graduate School of Management, and has two years of industry experience as Marketing Consultant for Bank of America.

Professor Keller is acknowledged as one of the international leaders in the study of strategic brand management and integrated marketing communications. He is currently conducting a variety of studies that address strategies to build, measure, and manage brand equity. His advertising and branding research has been published in three of the major marketing journals -- the Journal of Marketing, the Journal of Marketing Research, and the Journal of Consumer Research. He also sits on the Editorial Review Boards of those journals. With over forty published papers, his research has been widely cited and has received numerous awards.

Actively involved with industry, he has worked on a host of different types of branding projects. He has served as brand confidant to marketers for some of the world's most successful brands, including Disney, Ford, Intel, Levi Strauss, Nike, Procter & Gamble, and Starbucks. Additional brand consulting activities have been with other top companies such as Accenture, AC Nielsen, Beiersdorf (Nivea), General Mills, Goodyear, Kodak, Mayo Clinic, MTV, New York Knicks, Nordstrom, Shell Oil, Unilever, and Young & Rubicam. He is a Senior Marketing Consultant for Knowledge Networks and an academic trustee for the Marketing Science Institute. A popular speaker, he has conducted branding seminars to top executives in a variety of forums.

An avid sports, music, and film enthusiast, in his so-called spare time, he helps to manage and market one of Australia's great rock and roll treasures, The Church. Professor Keller lives in Etna, NH with his wife, Punam (also a Tuck marketing professor), and his two daughters, Carolyn and Allison.

LEVI STRAUSS & CO.:
CREATING A SUB-BRAND[1]

INTRODUCTION

In the spring of 1985, Levi Strauss & Co. (LS&Co.) was flush with success in the blue jeans market. The company's star campaign, called "501 Blues," had recently brought new vitality to the company after several failed expansions into other apparel market segments in the earlier part of the decade. Confident in the wake of 501's success, the company was contemplating next steps when research revealed a decline in jeans purchases by LS&Co.'s core customer base of baby boomers. In short, the company's "bread and butter" customer for the last 30 years -- the American male teenager -- was now 25-49 and was moving out of the jeans market at an alarming rate. To retain these customers even as their jeans purchases slowed or stopped, the company introduced Levi's Dockers casual pants. Dockers, as the name was later shortened to, was one of the most successful new product introductions of the 1980s in the clothing industry. Consumers responded to the product design, which utilized the comfort and casual feel of cotton, and by purchasing enough Dockers to make it a billion-dollar brand by 1993.

Over the course of the 1990s, LS&Co. enjoyed phenomenal success from its Dockers sub-brand. The Dockers brand achieved record sales growth in 1998 and *Fortune* magazine estimated in 1999 that 75 percent of American men owned a pair of Dockers and that the average customer owned 3.8 pairs. That year, the total number of Dockers owners exceeded 40 million. However, the company noticed at this time that younger consumers began to lose interest in Dockers, with many dismissing the pants as something their fathers wore. In the late 1990s, Levi Strauss developed new advertising campaigns and introduced new Dockers sub-brands to counter-act this trend. Sales of Dockers remained over $1 billion through 2000, but sales growth was slowing. Many questioned the brand's long-term relevance. Would Dockers be able to keep up with changing consumer tastes and shifting fashion standards? Could the brand maintain a loyal customer base while adapting to new styles?

THE ORIGINS OF LEVI STRAUSS & CO. AND LEVI'S 501 JEANS

In 1849, a poor Bavarian immigrant named Levi Strauss landed in San Francisco, California at the invitation of his brother-in-law, David Stern, owner of a dry goods business. This dry goods business would later become known as Levi Strauss & Co. Strauss quickly learned that the gold miners were seeking a durable pair of pants that could withstand their rugged lifestyle. To meet their needs, Strauss designed a pair of pants from a heavy brown canvas-like material -- the world's first pair of "jeans". Levi's pants quickly became an indispensable part of the miner's uniform, gaining a reputation for being as tough and rugged as the people who wore them. Strauss called his pants "waist high overalls." The miners called them "those pants of Levi."

Strauss soon switched to a sturdier fabric called serge de Nimes, made in Nimes, France, to make his pants. The fabric name was later shortened to denim, and indigo dye was added to give the jeans their blue color. In 1873, rivets were added to strengthen pockets, which had been unable to hold up under the weight of the miners' gold nuggets, along with the patented double arcuate pattern sewn into the back hip pocket -- America's first apparel trademark -- and the "Two Horse Brand" leather patch. By the 1890's, the popularity of LS&Co.'s jeans and other dry goods had spread, and to keep better track of the expanding product line, LS&Co. adopted a new inventory system. Levi's jeans were assigned the lot number "501" and given that number as their name.

Sales of Levi's 501 jeans grew through the 1900s. During the 1930's, Levi's jeans' popularity burgeoned as Western movies began to glamorize blue jeans, establishing 501's Western mystique. Levi's jeans became an even more valuable product during World War II, when the government declared them as an essential commodity available primarily to defense workers. In the 1950's, appearances by teen-age idols James Dean and Marlon Brando wearing jeans in the motion pictures *Rebel Without a Cause* and *The Wild Ones*, respectively, captivated an entire post-war baby boom generation. LS&Co. abandoned the wholesale dry goods business and concentrated exclusively on selling their own brand of clothes to a generation that represented millions of potential customers. By 1959, Levi's sales volume totaled $46 million. The love affair with Levi's jeans continued into the 1960's as students started to wear 501's as a form of self-expression. By the time of the Woodstock rock festival in 1969, Levi's jeans were the essential fashion for the emerging baby boom generation. What had originally been a tough pair of pants had become a symbol of freedom, adventure, and independence. Levi's 501 jeans were now an icon, and the Levi's brand name became synonymous with jeans.

DIVERSIFICATION: 1970-1984

For nearly 30 years after World War II, LS&Co. serviced a seemingly "bottomless" jeans market. Through the 1950s and 1960s, the company doubled sales every three to four years. By the end of the 1960's, the company's operations included jeans, cords, slacks and sportswear for men, as well as a range of apparel for women and children. In 1968, new operating divisions for youth wear, sportswear and accessories were created. The Levi's for Gals marketing unit was expanded into a full-fledged women's wear division. In addition, Levi Strauss International was formed as a subsidiary, enabling the company to parlay its legendary "All-American" image to foreign consumers eager to own a piece of Americana. With all this growth activity, LS&Co.'s worldwide sales in 1969 totaled some $251 million.

The rapid expansion necessitated further capital. In 1971, the company was taken public with an initial public offering of $47.50 per share. LS&Co.'s sales continued to experience rapid growth as baby boomer teens entered college. By 1975, sales had reached $1 billion, and rose to $2 billion in 1979. During this time the company's flagship product -- 501 jeans -- remained its top-selling product, and LS&Co. continued to hold nearly a third of the U.S. jeans market. Production expanded locally and abroad to meet continuing demand. Nonetheless, given the slow growth among its primary market -- the 12 to 24 year olds -- cash rich LS&Co. considered alternative actions to hedge against an expected decline in the jeans market in the 1980's.

In the early 1980s, LS&Co. adopted a strategy to expand beyond the core jeans lines to utilize the Levi's name on non-jeans. "We are not going to forget the gal we brought to the dance," explained Robert Haas, then Executive Vice-President and COO and great-great grand-nephew of the company's founder. "We want to reemphasize our central nature. But we want to bring out flanking products in our basic industries, to make them more exciting."[2] LS&Co. introduced new product lines, covering a broad range of family clothing needs. Many of these came from within the company's existing divisions. Product lines included denim and corduroy jeans for men, women and children; Action Suits and Tailored Classic blazers and slacks for professional men and Activewear for sports participants -- skiers, tennis players and the general outdoors person. Counting colors, styles and sizes, the company was offering thousands of different pants, skirts, vests, shirts, blazers, shorts and blouses -- even maternity jeans and jumpers.

An acquisition strategy was also implemented to provide for further growth. LS&Co.'s 1979 acquisition of Koracorp Industries, a $185 million California clothing manufacturer, immediately doubled Levi's women's wear sales. Koracorp businesses included: Koret of North America women's wear, Byer-Rolnick hats, Oxxford men's suits and a European-based children's wear division. Other LS&Co. acquisitions included Resistol hats, Rainfair industrial clothing and Frank Shorter running gear. The company also established numerous licensing agreements for products including casual shoes and socks bearing the Levi's brand, as well as with designers, including Perry Ellis America, Alexander Julian and Andrew Fezza, to broaden LS&Co.'s scope of business into more fashionable clothing segments. The new internally generated labels -- David Hunter men's sportswear division and the Roegiers' Tourage SSE collection of men's casual wear -- were the only lines that did not carry the Levi's logo. As a result of this vigorous diversification and acquisition strategy, LS&Co. owned apparel businesses that offered products to suit almost any lifestyle.

LEVI STRAUSS & CO.'S COMMUNICATIONS STRATEGY

Historically, LS&Co. advertisements had focused almost exclusively on the quality of Levi's jeans for men. The ads, whether print or TV, had emphasized the quality, durability and timeless nature of Levi's jeans for men. Western gold miner themes dominated the tone of the early ads. Beginning in the 1970s, however, LS&Co. shifted it advertising strategy to reflect the company's change in product focus. LS&Co. largely replaced its traditional western, miner or prospector image with more contemporary, psychedelic, "hip" imagery of the day. With the help of its long-time advertising agency, Foote, Cone & Belding, the company adopted the "alteration of reality" creative technique and developed a series of animated ads produced with the use of state-of-the art, computer-generated imagery. In an effort to leverage the Levi's brand name and quality image, these ads emphasized the diversity, variety and fashionability of Levi's non-jeans products. Ad tag lines included: "Levi's don't have to be blue -- they just have to be good"; "Quality never goes out of style" and "We put a little blue jean in everything we make." At the same time, even though they were diversifying dramatically, the company also wanted to ensure that American men understood that LS&Co. still sold its traditional jeans as work clothes for men. Consequently, the company produced some ads that focused exclusively on men's jeans, retaining the traditional emphasis on jeans as a quality, good-value pant for hard-working American men.

When LS&Co. reorganized its corporate structure in the early 1980s, each division became responsible for its own advertising strategy. As a result, the focus of the company's ads shifted to target specific groups rather than selling products across divisions. Ads were created to address multiple audiences simultaneously, and multiple product lines often were promoted in one commercial. Many of the men's jeans ads targeted Levi's jeans and cords, emphasizing the variety of colors and styles available. These ads moved away from the psychedelic imagery of the early 1970s to a high-tech, "space age" feel. Regular denim jeans continued to focus on the basic qualities associated with Levi's jeans in an effort to reach working men.

Although LS&Co.'s advertising focused primarily on selling to men, expansion of its women's wear and youth apparel lines resulted in more advertising dollars being allocated to these two consumer groups. To sell its array of new apparel lines, LS&Co. expanded its advertising budget dramatically beginning in 1978. By 1982, the advertising budget had grown to $100 million.[3] In addition, the mix of advertising media significantly changed, with national media spending rising from $6.4 million in 1976 to $19.7 million in 1978 and $28.7 million in 1980. Network TV as an advertising medium grew the most dramatically, from $1.8 million in 1976 to $15 million in 1980.[4]

BACK TO BASICS

Initially, LS&Co.'s diversification efforts produced promising results. Starting in 1980, however, LS&Co. began a three-year earnings decline. Between 1980 and 1982, LS&Co.'s sales fell 10 percent and net income dropped 76 percent. Although sales and earnings rebounded in 1983 as a result of expanding retail distribution to include Sears and J. C. Penney, they slipped again in 1984.

Many of the company's non-jeans lines struggled in the face of more established competition. Concern arose that the failure of a number of non-jeans products could adversely impact the cachet associated with its jeans. LS&Co. management had learned that while the Levi's brand was the company's most powerful asset, it also had its limitations in terms of the products with which it could be identified. With the decline in sales, the company began to consider further expanding its distribution to accounts like Wal-Mart and K-Mart. Reflecting back on the years, Robert Haas described the situation as follows:

> We had diversified too much. We produced everything from hats to $2000 suits,
> but we no longer stood for anything. We had lost our focus on our core products.
> Our retail relations had sunk to a point of hostility.[5]

In October 1984, Tom Tusher, president of Levi Strauss International, was named Executive Vice-President and Chief Operating Officer. At the employee meeting in which his appointment was announced, he indicated his first decision -- LS&Co. would not expand its distribution, but would rather concentrate on changing product focus and rebuilding relations with its department and specialty store accounts. Thus, under Tusher's direction, the company instituted plans to:

1) Improve relations with its retailers and

2) Re-focus the Levi's brand name and image to bolster sagging sales.

For Tusher and Haas, LS&Co.'s main objective was to preserve the company's "important values and traditions." To achieve this objective, LS&Co. planned to move away from non-core products and re-emphasize its basic jeans and corduroy lines, which comprised almost two-thirds of revenues, as the company's mainstays throughout the 1990's

4

and "to grow the company from the bottom line - through greater efficiency, penetrating market segments more effectively and through cost savings."[6]

STRENGTHENING THE BRAND IMAGE

Next, LS&Co. focused its marketing efforts on strengthening the Levi's brand. In mid-1985, after reporting a $114 million loss, the company was taken private through a $1.65 billion leveraged buyout, the largest LBO ever at the time. The strategic direction outlined by Tusher in late 1984 -- shifting the focus back to the core product businesses -- began to be implemented. Consistent with the core product focus and as a means to pay down debt, non-core businesses were sold or discontinued: Rainfair in 1984, Resistol in 1985, Koret of North America Oxxford and Frank Shorter all in 1987. LS&Co. also discontinued its licensing arrangements with Perry Ellis America and Andrew Fezza in 1986. The company closed 40 factories and streamlined staff, reducing LS&Co.'s payroll from 48,000 employees in 1980 to 36,000 employees by 1986.

LS&Co. also set out to reinvigorate the company's core products. At this time, the company faced both increased competition and shifts in fashion trends. In the early 1980s, there had been a proliferation of new products in the apparel market. Within the jeans market, competition had intensified at the same time that consumer demand began to fall. The well-defined urban image of Lee jeans and western image of Wrangler jeans, in addition to the high priced, fashion image of Calvin Klein, Bill Blass and Gloria Vanderbilt designer jeans, posed a serious threat to the loyalty of the traditional Levi's 501 jeans buyer. Moreover, LS&Co., whose historic franchise had been in the Western U.S., found their sales failing to meet expectations in the Eastern U.S., particularly in major metropolitan areas and among their key target market of 18 to 24 year olds. This slump in sales was due, in part, to the company's failure in product development to keep pace with changes in the jeans market. LS&Co.'s products remained "non-washed" long after designer jeans and LS&Co.'s own international markets had begun to rinse and bleach their products for sale to the customer.

501 BLUES

The $36 million "501 Blues" advertising campaign set out to create an image for 501 jeans consistent with LS&Co.'s corporate philosophy and values. The ads featured a variety of real people "being themselves" by wearing 501s as part of everyday life in a series of urban East Coast settings. The ads' audio focused on Levi's unique, personal "shrink-to-fit" and "button-fly" attributes and blended blues-style music with free association verbiage. The hope was that the campaign would remind existing customers of the uniqueness of 501 jeans and how comfortably they fit into their everyday lives -- both in a physical and social sense -- as well as introduce the company's flagship product to a new generation of adults. The award-winning campaign helped 501 sales double in 1985, despite the fact that overall U.S. denim sales for the year declined, and placed 501 jeans in a firmer footing nationally.

NEW CHALLENGES

By the beginning of 1986, management was confident it was on the right track. The 501 jeans campaign had proved extremely successful among its target 12-24 year-old urban audience. Not only had it re-invigorated jeans sales, but had also brought the Levi's brand back to its core values. Plans were to continue with the "Blues" campaign for the near future. The 1986 advertising budget was $70 million.[9]

A per-capita jeans purchases chart prepared by the LS&Co. Menswear research department, however, revealed a troubling fact: 25-49 year old U.S. males purchased an average of one to two pairs of jeans annually, as compared to an average of four to five pairs for 15-24 year olds. In 1980, there were 36.8 million men in the United States between the ages of 25 and 49; by 1990, this figure was expected to be 47.5 million, nearly half of the adult male population. Although these baby boomers had grown up with Levi's jeans and had developed tremendous loyalty to the Levi's name, they now sought a different kind of pant. Because baby boomers viewed themselves as distinct from their parents' generation in tastes and lifestyle, as they had proven by adopting jeans as kids, they wanted their clothes to be a break from tradition. Fashion assumed a far greater role for these males than for previous generations. While these men had aged chronologically, they still had a driving need to be active, involved, fashionable and comfortable. Rejecting the artificial fabrics traditional to the Menswear business in the past, they preferred more natural fibers. At the same time, in the traditionally formal work environment, many companies were relaxing their dress codes to allow employees to dress in more casual attire.

For these reasons, male baby boomers needed a pant that combined style, versatility and comfort that would be appropriate for both professional and leisure activities. This need was reflected in the change of emphasis on 100 percent cotton and cotton blends in the product mix in men's departments at retailers.

DEVELOPING A MARKETING STRATEGY

LS&Co. recognized that the casual pant market represented an enormous opportunity. Between 1981-1985, jeans retail volume had decreased by 11 percent (25m units), while slacks volume had increased by 19 percent (21m units). Slacks as a percentage of bottoms sales (jeans plus slacks) grew from 33 percent in 1981 to 40 percent in 1985, and the trend was certain to continue. Between the summer of 1985 and the summer of 1986 alone, slacks sales grew by 20 percent.[10] Yet merchandising of slacks was uninspired, and consumers found the slacks department one of the most boring areas in the store. Moreover, brand fragmentation was more prevalent in the dress slacks category than with jeans, and there was no dominant brand leader. LS&Co. had been in the dress slacks market since the mid-1950s (its first non-jeans diversification effort), but the top three dress slacks brands (Levi's, Haggar and Farah) accounted for 25 percent of the U.S. market, and the top five brands accounted for only 35 percent of the market. In contrast, the top three jeans brands (Levi's, Wrangler and Lee) accounted for 66 percent of the U.S. men's market, and the top five brands accounted for 75 percent of the market.[11]

In addition, natural fibers and blends were replacing the traditional 100 percent polyester slacks. Research indicated that 100 percent polyester slacks were expected to account for 33 percent of sales volume in 1986 -- down from 59 percent in 1980 -- compared to 50 percent for 100 percent cotton and cotton blends. Certain designer menswear, such as Paul Smith and Ralph Lauren (Polo), did offer full legged, tapered bottom trousers that were cotton/cotton blend trousers.[12] Although these pants were often found in the Main Floor Men's department, they were sold as "Better Sportswear" with a price tag of $60-$80.

LS&Co. was determined to maintain the brand loyalty of the "Levi's jeans generation"-- who were about to enter into their peak earning years -- even if they were no longer buying traditional jeans. These men had been the cornerstone of the company's success and key drivers of apparel trends for over 20 years. The company hoped to appeal to the traditional, older Main Floor Men's customer as well as to the new, younger crossovers. As the overwhelming brand leader in the men's jeans market, LS&Co. hoped to capitalize on the changing demographics and consumer tastes in two ways through a new line of casual slacks and a new line of re-styled, loose fitting jeans.

INTRODUCING "NEW CASUALS"

The Menswear division -- led by Robert Siegel, President; Steve Schwartzbach, Vice President of Merchandising; Steve Goldstein, Director of Consumer Marketing; and Jerry Maschino, Vice President of Sales -- decided to first address opportunities in the casual slacks market because it was felt that existing product lines did not sufficiently satisfy the needs of the 25-49 year old male customers. LS&Co. identified its challenge as follows:

> To increase our slacks brand share, Levi's must aggressively market and support trend-right products to create a leadership position in a market that is growing and has no category owner.[13]

The image that the Levi's brand had earned from its jeans business was thought to have already contributed in a limited way to its current slacks image - namely, that Levi's slacks were considered to be more contemporary, less conservative and more casual than other leading slacks. However, its Action Slacks line (made of 100 percent polyester) did not address the fabric shifts in the slacks market, nor did it reflect the core values that the recent 501 jeans campaign had so successfully established. As one LS&Co. executive explained, "We feel as though we've got the power of the Levi's brand which is significant and carries with it all the mystique to be influential in the marketplace. But we recognize that we need to segment from a marketing/advertising perspective because there are so many market types."[14] LS&Co. needed a new product that motivated the customer to remain within the Levi's brand franchise, but that was different from anything they had sold before. Perhaps with some reservations, LS&Co. was moving away from jeans again. In this case, however, rather than de-emphasize its jeans business, the company was determined to simultaneously continue its strong core jeans focus.

To meet the needs of its customers, and to establish LS&Co. as the market leader, the Menswear team believed a bold strike was necessary. They decided to create essentially a new product category -- new casuals -- that would position the new pants to men as more formal than jeans and less casual than dress slacks. To LS&Co., new casuals satisfied an unfilled need in the men's pants market. They were designed to appeal to the baby boomers' fashion demands: casual and comfortable, yet stylish; the right pant for a variety of occasions and, of course, meeting LS&Co.'s high quality standards. The basic pants design was a 100-percent cotton, pleated, washed fabric with a "reverse silhouette" design -- wider at the top and narrower at the leg opening -- available in a variety of stylish colors. LS&Co. hoped that its new casuals, the first line to bring the full-leg, tapered-bottom trousers of "better sportswear" to the main floor of department stores, would give men a way to ask for a pair of loose, unfitted pants. LS&Co. wanted this new pant to become the standard for the new casual pant category. In an effort to make this new pant accessible and affordable, it was priced in the moderate to upper moderate price range, retailing, on average, for $32.

BRANDING NEW CASUALS

To brand this new line of casual pants, the Menswear team needed to choose a name, logo and other important brand elements. To attract the "baby boomer" shopper, the idea was to package the product with a memorable, trademarked name; a unique, permanent, on-garment logo; and a colorful pocket flasher. The team knew they could not simply call this new product "Levi's Pants." The strategic marketing positioning of the company's very successful 501 jeans campaign had defined Levi's as jeans. Somehow the name had to establish its independence and leverage the Levi's brand name in a way so as to maintain a link to the Levi's name and heritage, but not detract from the Levi's core jeans focus. At the time the team was contemplating a name for these new pants, Sue Kilgore, a Menswear merchandiser, returned from a trip to Japan with a pair of twill pants sold by Levi Strauss Japan named Levi Docker Pants. LS&Co.'s Japanese group had adopted the moniker from a Levi's pant sold in Argentina. Both Japan and Argentina had positioned the product to their younger age consumers, but with only limited success. The team liked the Docker name, but knew Americans would never say "Levi Docker Pants". The question became how to shorten the name to something Americans would say. In the end, the team decided to add an "s" to Docker and shortened the name to Levi's Dockers. The team liked the Dockers name because, although it did have some nautical connotations, for the most part it was considered a neutral, empty basket that the company could fill with imagery that was relevant to its broad target audience.

The logo that was chosen blended the Argentine and Japanese logos found on their versions of the pants, and consisted of interlocked wings and anchors. In order to qualify for co-op advertising -- now considered a key ingredient for establishing brand awareness -- it was necessary to integrate the brand's name with its symbols. Working with a local San Francisco firm, Goldstein and the Menswear team adapted the Dockers logo and tag. The pocket flasher, attached to the back of all pants, consisted of a woman who was being led off a ship by a formally dressed man but whose attention was focused on a relaxed, casually dressed young man standing on the dock. Finally, to establish an understated association with the Levi's name, the Levi's moniker was incorporated in the Dockers' winged logo.

INTRODUCING NEW CASUALS TO THE RETAIL TRADE

Levi's Dockers pants were marketed to the retail trade as a major fashion statement -- an alternative to jeans -- and the driving force in the "new casuals" category. Based on the changing demographics of the U.S. male population, Levi's projected "new casuals" to grow from 28 percent of the total bottoms business to 34 percent by 1989, with contemporary dress slacks increasing from six percent to 28 percent and traditional dress slacks decreasing from 38 percent to 21 percent over the same period.[15]

In an effort to establish its Dockers new casuals line, LS&Co. concentrated distribution in department stores and chains where the majority of 25-49 year old men did their shopping and where one-third of all slacks were sold. The company worked closely with retailers, from J. C. Penney to Bloomingdale's, to generate excitement and support for its new pants. The company courted retailers nationwide -- including those department and specialty stores who had previously curtailed business with LS&Co. in the early 1980s -- with extensive presentations, sell-in brochures and swatch books. They provided sales support in a variety of ways including sales kits that provided a "road map" for retail based marketing, cooperative advertising and sales promotion programs. In addition, the company offered supplemental financial support (RAP) for advertising and promotional activities to important high image department stores. Funds (RAP plus co-op) available to retail for 1987 totaled $1.6m.

A critical component of the company's marketing effort to concentrate attention on the new line was the establishment of Dockers shops within Main Floor Men's areas of major department stores. The traditional main floor men's department was changing, reducing its emphasis on dress slacks and shifting to 100 percent cotton and cotton blends that were targeted to the more youthful customer. This trend was expected to continue as the baby boomer market segment increased as a percentage of the main floor customer base. Retailers were showing greater interest in innovative merchandise techniques.

In recognition of these trends, LS&Co. introduced the first in-store concept shop for the men's main floor area. A test version was constructed for display at MAGIC (Men's Apparel Guild in California), a key trade show, to introduce Dockers casual pants to retailers. The Dockers in-store shop sought to create a friendly, accessible environment, prominently displaying the sporty Dockers logo, linking consumer advertising with point-of-sale signage and posters and making trial as easy as possible. Fixtures and tables were installed that allowed for displaying the pants folded, similar to the experience of buying jeans, and distinctly different from the rows of hanging slacks. Testing of the concept proved very successful, generating twice the sales of pants that were just hung on racks. In stores where shops were not possible due to space or financial constraints, LS&Co. planned to establish point-of-sale displays.

The company's product positioning and marketing strategy was able to overcome the initial reluctance of retailers, and ultimately generated an exceptionally high level of pre-promotion excitement. The company successfully placed Levi's Dockers in all of the Menswear Division's top 50 accounts and in another 50 accounts across the country. Retailers saw Levi's Dockers as the leader in the new casuals category and moved the pants ahead of its primary competitors, including Gallery by Haggar, Savane by Farah, "M" by Bugle Boy and Tivoli by American Trouser. With the retail trade behind them, the Menswear Division turned its attention to the development of an effective communications program focused on the consumer.

LAUNCHING DOCKERS TO THE CONSUMER

It quickly became apparent to the LS&Co. Menswear Division that in order to establish Levi's Dockers as a major brand in men's casual sportswear, a focused, comprehensive consumer marketing effort beyond the available resources of the Menswear Division would be required. Given the market opportunity for casual pants, the Menswear Division believed that a high impact consumer marketing program would accelerate the growth of the Dockers line and generate consumer support that could be leveraged to effectively influence trade awareness and interest. The Menswear Division management team convinced Tom Tusher, who had established an advertising reserve for special marketing opportunities, that investment in the required marketing effort to launch Dockers would produce the requisite

9

pay-back to the corporation in terms of revenues, profits and long-term brand ownership of the crucial baby boomer segment. With the entire LS&Co. organization behind them, the Menswear Division set out to establish a clear proprietary position for Levi's Dockers in the men's bottoms market.

ADVERTISING STRATEGY

The advertising challenge was to build product and brand awareness for Levi's Dockers so that they would be seen as an unpretentious alternative to traditional dressing for almost every occasion. Thus, advertising had to achieve two goals: 1) because there was no consumer terminology for Dockers-type pants, the ads would have to educate its audience about the new product itself and create brand awareness; and 2) an image for the new product had to be created that leveraged the positive Levi's brand associations, but also established a certain amount of autonomy or distance to signal the inherent product differences.

The target audience for their advertising was defined demographically as white collar working men between the ages of 25 and 49 who lived in major metropolitan areas in the U.S.[16]

These target men were expanding their wardrobes to include more casual apparel made from natural fibers that were suitable for a range of informal occasions. Working with Mike Koelker of Foote, Cone & Belding, LS&Co. conducted a series of focus groups with men in their target market. The men were shown pictures representing a variety of leisure situations and asked to select the pictures that best described when they were "most comfortable and relaxed." The most common scenes chosen included a man sitting on top of a hill alone, two men walking together on a golf course and a group of men hanging out and laughing on the beach. Even though many of the men said they did not tend to partake in these events once they were older and married, they still thought fondly in reminiscing about them.

Based on the results of the focus groups and the marketing objectives for Dockers, Koelker and LS&Co. decided that the ads should create an image for the brand based on an emotional appeal. The ads were to create a singular, appealing and relevant image for the brand that elevated Dockers above all other possible alternatives. Given the target customer, the attitude of the advertising needed to be contemporary. It was important, however, to ensure that the styling of the pants be perceived as timeless and classic. The men wearing Dockers were to be real, approachable and attractive, but not fashion models. The ads were to show Dockers as appropriate attire for a variety of occasions -- for work and for weekends. They wanted Dockers to be seen as a way to be comfortable and casual in any setting. Therefore, the advertising was to emphasize the sociability of men wearing the pants. It was also important for the ads to convey the high quality of the Dockers pants line and maintain the link to the Levi's brand name and heritage. The Levi's name would help give the new pant credibility and capitalize on the tremendous loyalty of the target group to the Levi's brand. Finally, the ads would use the "reality-based advertising" style and imagery begun with the 501 Blues ads that LS&Co. wanted to continue. Management hoped that men would view a Dockers' commercial and say to themselves, "I like those guys. They're like me. And I like the way they look in those pants."

Advertising Executions

Based on this strategy, LS&Co. and Foote, Cone & Belding developed a $4.5 million television campaign for Dockers consisting of three 30-second ads of men in their 20s, 30s and 40s having informal conversations about life. The situations were varied to include both casual weekend and work-related settings. The audio in the ad consisted of natural, unscripted dialogue while the camera worked like an eye, moving around the group and using extreme close-ups. The ads carefully sought to exclude any "yuppie" talk or yuppie accessories (e.g. Rolex watches). The focus was on the waist down, and no faces were shown at any time. The tagline ran: "Levi's 100 percent Cotton Dockers. If You're Not Wearing Dockers, You're Just Wearing Pants". As Koelker explained, "using '100% cotton' provided a tangible bridge to the Levi's jeans heritage."

Media Strategy

The company planned to introduce Dockers® through a multi-dimensional, high impact regional program aimed primarily to consumers and secondarily to the trade. The consumer advertising was to provide a positioning and image umbrella for both the consumer and trade markets. The Dockers ads were slotted to run in Fall 1987 and Winter 1988 in 11 major regional markets where Dockers pants were sold. The markets were selected on the basis of retail placement of Dockers, potential for volume growth and geographical dispersion. The 11 markets were New York, Columbus, Cincinnati, Minneapolis, Houston, Washington D.C., L.A., Miami, Dallas, Charlotte and Denver. Of the 11 target markets, New York City -- the largest consumer market accounting for eight percent of the national TV viewing population -- was considered the key market for a successful introduction. New York was the center of the men's apparel industry and tended to set fashion trends for the whole country. In addition, buyers from major stores across the country were influenced by what they saw placed in New York.

The Dockers media strategy used spot TV in all eleven targeted markets. Spot TV was considered the most effective medium to communicate Dockers' "attitude" since it provided an intrusive and impactful means of delivering the message to a broad target audience quickly and efficiently. The company chose to air its commercials during selective "showcase" prime time, sports and late night programs. To increase overall effectiveness of the effort, the company planned to show multiple commercials in a single program. In key late night shows, the commercials would be aired each night of the week. Commercials were aired in sports events that included local target market teams. In New York City, TV spots were supplemented with subway signs and mobile billboards located primarily in and around the city's garment district.

Additional Promotion Activities

In addition to TV, LS&Co. targeted consumers through co-op advertising with retailers. Dockers Shops and point-of-sale displays provided in-store visibility. Sales promotions, e.g., gift with purchase programs, were planned during kick-off and key seasons to create in-store excitement.

Concurrent with the initial airing of the Dockers commercials, LS&Co. organized an advertising kick-off party in New York City for buying groups, trade press and key retail executives. In addition, a publicity campaign targeted key market influencers with talk show fashion presentations and press kits. As a follow-up to its initial marketing to retailers, LS&Co. planned a series of visits to key retail accounts by designers, merchandisers, marketing personnel and senior management.

Initial Results

Success for Dockers came almost overnight. Department stores ordered so much of the product during its first season in 1986 that LS&Co. experienced difficulty filling all the orders. But since other brands like VF Corporation's Lee Jeans chose not to introduce casual pant lines of their own, Dockers continued to draw customer and retailer demand. Following the success of the initial "butt-cam" advertisements, as they came to be known, LS&Co. updated the campaign to make it more stylish. The new ads showed Dockers pants being worn for specific occasions, either at work or at play. These spots featured the tagline "Relax. You're Among Friends." They ran from 1986 to 1990. By 1991, Dockers was a $500 million business and the brand enjoyed 90 percent awareness in the target market of men between 25 and 44 years of age. From this group, 40 percent owned at least one pair of Dockers. The average Dockers customer owned 2.5 pairs of the pants.

Seeking to retain its current customer base while attracting new customers, LS&Co. devised a new advertising campaign in 1991 that attempted to broaden the Dockers image beyond plain khakis. The campaign, titled "Nobody Does Colors Like Dockers," used vibrant color schemes to convey this new image. Each ad in the series showcased a different color offered by Dockers. For example, one ad used only gray tones and featured the tagline: "Gray. What Black Would Look Like if It Lightened Up."

A BILLION-DOLLAR BRAND

By 1993, annual Dockers sales topped $1 billion. That year, Dockers accounted for 50 percent or more of casual pant volume in stores where the line was sold. During 1993, LS&Co. attempted to promote full-time casual office environments by mailing a four-page newsletter entitled "Casual Clothing in the Workplace News" to over 40,000 human resource managers at corporations nationwide. The newsletter contained information about implementing dress-down policies, as well as articles about corporations that adopted casual dress codes. According to the company, 19 percent of the corporations that received newsletters responded, including 81 of the *Fortune* 100 companies.

The year 1993 also marked Dockers' move into European markets. LS&Co. established the Dockers Europe subsidiary in Amsterdam and launched the brand with pan-European advertising designed by Swedish agency Garbergs. Posters designed by the agency appeared in metropolitan centers across Europe throughout the following year.

LS&Co. introduced a Dockers brand extension during the summer months of 1993. In the hopes of attracting a younger and more style-conscious breed of customer, the company unveiled its Dockers Authentics brand that summer. LS&Co. applied the new Dockers Authentics label to pants and shirts cut more stylishly and made of more sophisticated fabrics than the 100 percent cotton used for Dockers. The company allocated about 20 percent of the overall Dockers advertising budget, or $5 million dollars, to a campaign for Authentics. Dockers Authentics occupied roughly 20 percent of Dockers' department store floor space. In addition to a 500,000-piece direct-mail introduction, Dockers Authentics received support from a series of print ads appearing in male-oriented magazines such as *Esquire* and *Outside*. One ad showed a model fitted with the product and the words "authentic khaki" on the first of two pages. The opposite page contains a picture of World War II soldiers and the text "minus three years active duty."

WRINKLE-FREE COMPETITION

LS&Co. also encountered a challenge to its market dominance in 1993. Companies like Haggar and Farah developed "wrinkle-free" cotton pants that looked like the standard Dockers khaki pant, but contained a special fabric treatment that eliminated the need for ironing. Consumers responded positively to the wrinkle-free pants, but LS&Co. ignored the trend in the belief that the pants "[were] too formal for Dockers."[17] Other pants manufacturers gained ground on Dockers, causing the brand to experience slowed sales in 1993 and its first drop in sales in 1994. In the latter year, Dockers' share in the men's khakis market at department stores dropped to 29 percent from 42 percent the previous year, as a host of look-alike and wrinkle-free competitors drew consumers away from Dockers. Wrinkle-free pants had grown from two percent of all pants sales at the beginning of the decade to as much as 15 percent at some stores in 1994. Dockers' competitor Haggar held a staggering 73 percent share of the wrinkle-free segment. LS&Co. realized that in addition to losing current customers, the Dockers brand was failing to attract new customers. Research showed that men in their 20s had little interest in the brand. The company needed to ensure that Dockers remained relevant to the existing customer base while attracting new customers.

A first step in the domestic revival of Dockers was to catch up to the wrinkle-free trend, which LS&Co. did by launching wrinkle-free Dockers in November 1994. The launch was supported by a $40 million advertising campaign that began in April. In addition to a new tagline – "Don't just get dressed. Get Dockers" – the campaign included four humorous television spots and a retail promotion linked with the U.S. Open golf tournament. The TV ads showcased the wrinkle-free properties of the pants in scripts that sought to appeal to baby boomers. One ad featured a situation that many men were likely to identify with -- appearing in court to fight a traffic ticket. Another ad, titled "The Red Eye," showed an airline passenger executing various contortions in order to get comfortable. Throughout the elaborate maneuvers, the pants remain free of wrinkles. LS&Co. continued to expand aggressively into the wrinkle-free market, and by 1995 almost all Dockers pants were wrinkle-free.

Since many consumers had just assumed Dockers offered wrinkle-free pants before the line was launched, LS&Co. took a more noteworthy step -- from the consumers' point of view -- that same year with the development of the sex-soaked "Nice Pants" campaign. The focus of the ad series was a distinct departure from the male bonding scenes characteristic of the original Dockers ad series. The television spots turned up the sex appeal by featuring an ordinary-looking male actor -- the Dockers-wearing archetype -- pursued by a stunning female. A bout of somewhat awkward eye contact led up to the commercial's climax, when the woman admired the man's pants aloud by remarking, "Nice pants." The advent of Dockers Wrinkle-Free combined with the "Nice Pants" campaign contributed to the reversal of Dockers' sales decline. In one major department store chain, sales of Dockers rose 10 to 15 percent per year in 1995 and 1996, compared with growth of less than five percent in 1994. By 1997, Dockers represented 80 percent of all men's casual pants sold at the chain.

CREATING ANOTHER SUB-BRAND

Levi's Move Into Business Casuals

Office workers in the late 1980s witnessed the widespread acceptance of "casual Friday" by the corporate world. In the latter half of the decade, many companies slackened their dress codes even further by instituting a "business casual" standard that banished suits for the duration of the work week. Just as Levi's Dockers capitalized on the surge in popularity of informal casual wear for Fridays and weekends, the company positioned its Slates brand to capture what it predicted would be a burgeoning office casual market. At the time of the launch, however, the strategy seemed like a risk. LS&Co. introduced the Slates line in August 1996 into a market dominated by dress pants makers Haggar Clothing Co., which dwarfed Levi's 14 percent dress pants market share with 30 percent of the market. Additionally, the dress pants market had experienced a recent sales slide, from $2.0 billion in 1994 to $1.9 billion in 1995. In spite of the competition and the ailing category, LS&Co. executives felt that "there was room in a man's closet for a third brand."[18]

For the twelve months before the launch, LS&Co. conducted extensive market research to determine the "Slates" name, the pants' pre-tailored cut, the in-store shop style and the advertising content. After the Sausalito, CA naming consultant Lexicon created the name, LS&Co. tested it on mock clothing labels and in fake news and magazine articles to gauge customer reaction to the name in print. Consumer testing revealed that double pleated pants were the favored among men, as were hemmed and cuffed pants that did not require additional tailoring. Believing that odd-numbered waist sizes provided a better fit off the shelf, LS&Co. offered Slates in sizes such as 35 and 37. The company tested in-store displays with focus groups in New York and San Francisco. Over 240 retailers nationwide featured the Slates displays -- mahogany detailed circular affairs -- upon the launch. The company spent more advertising dollars launching Slates than it did on the Dockers' introduction, spending $20 million on a similar introductory campaign involving both extensive television and point-of-purchase advertising.

RETURN OF THE KHAKI

Accompanying this move into business casuals was an overall increase in demand for khakis. By the end of 1997, sales of men's khakis had risen 21 percent from 1995 to $2.8 billion. The success of khakis sharply contrasted a decline in the men's jeans market, which experienced a 6 percent decrease in growth rate from 1996 to 1997. Dockers began facing increased competition from The Gap in 1998, when that company introduced a $20-million TV, print and outdoor advertising campaign to promote their own khakis. According to figures released by LS&Co, The Gap had a lot of ground to cover, however. Dockers claimed 26 percent of the khaki market in 1998, more than double its closest competitor. Additionally, Dockers more than doubled The Gap's ad expenditures that same year, launching a $50 million consumer marketing campaign.

A healthy portion of the 1998 marketing budget – 65 percent – went to Dockers' "urban networking" program. The program, begun in San Francisco, functioned as a sort of cultural outreach, where Dockers sponsored parties, dinners, film festivals, concert series and khaki giveaways in urban centers across the country. In order to coordinate these efforts within a city, the company created the position of "urban networker." The Dockers urban networker worked from street level to promote the brand to the city's "visionaries." The networker's liberal expense account funded everything from intimate dinners at posh restaurants and rounds of drinks at popular nightspots to extravagant themed parties and independent film festivals. One reason for the large investment in the elaborate urban networking program was the fact that a sizeable portion of Dockers wearers lived in metropolitan areas. According to Amy Rosenthal, senior marketing specialist for Dockers, one-third of khaki sales came from the top 10 urban markets in the States. Believing also that the consumer public took their fashion cues from the trendsetting urban population, LS&Co. sought to establish Dockers as a desired brand among the urban "critical influencers."

FACING NEW CHALLENGES

Khaki Competition

As khakis climbed in popularity, so too did Dockers competitors. Khakis had been attracting a following in the youth market, and these more youth-oriented brands such as The Gap, Polo, and Tommy Hilfiger appealed to teens and twentysomethings in a way Dockers -- with its history of targeting ageing baby boomers -- could not. Research revealed that the young generation of khaki buyers was inclined to think of Dockers as pants that belonged in their fathers' closets. Companies like The Gap, which in 1998 launched a $20 million TV, print and outdoor ad campaign for its Gap Khakis, began massive marketing efforts to attract these younger buyers. The Gap Khakis television spots featured young khaki-wearers dancing, singing and skateboarding to background music that varied depending on which of the themes from among "Khakis Rock," "Khakis Swing" or "Khakis Groove" was highlighted. Dockers countered the popular Gap ads with a youth-themed ad of its own, using the tagline "Khakis with a blue jeans soul" to connect Dockers with the Levi's brand. That same year, LS&Co. added another tagline to its advertising, dropping "Nice Pants" in favor of "One leg at a time." The new ads, which targeted 25-34 year olds, debuted on television during the 1998 NCAA basketball season.

In early 1999, LS&Co further modified its Dockers marketing approach to make the pants more appealing to young consumers. A first step was to make the link between the Dockers name and the popularity of khakis obvious by rebranding the line of pants "Dockers Khakis." Additionally, the company increased its mass media advertising budget 12 percent from the previous year. The centerpiece of the new Dockers Khakis campaign was a series of slick and sexy television commercials that were in complete contrast to the original Dockers spots that featured men relaxing amongst friends and "being themselves." One ad, entitled "Nightclub," features a Docker-wearing man dancing at a stylish nightclub. Women everywhere were drawn as if by magnetism to him, or, more specifically, his pants. Each time he finishes dancing with one, a different woman aggressively caughts hold of his waistband and pulled him toward her for another dance. Upon leaving the club, the man entered a taxi driven by a woman, who leered suggestively at him. The spot ended with a shot of the man smiling while a female voiceover intones, "Durable, authentic khaki. You'll wear out before they do." The ad also marked the return of the "Nice Pants" tagline, which appeared at the end of the spot. LS&Co. also sought to attract the attention of retro fashion fans by introducing the classically influenced yet cutting-edge styled unisex Dockers K-1 Khakis. The K-1 Khakis were made from throwback fabrics styled after military-issue khakis from the early 20th century.

Levi's Business Woes

The success of Dockers represented one of the few positive aspects of LS&Co.'s business in the late nineties. As well as the company understood the tastes of its ageing baby-boomer consumer base, LS&Co. failed when it came to anticipating what the 13-24 year-old segment of the market would demand. As jeans designs for the youth market became increasingly dissimilar to the traditional straight-legged Levi's template, young buyers began abandoning the classic denim look in favor of baggy pants with big pockets fashioned from synthetic fabrics. LS&Co. resisted changing with the styles at first and subsequently fell out of favor with the teen market. The collective disfavor took its toll on the company's business. After achieving record sales in 1996, the company experienced a sales slide and a market share drop for each of the next 4 years, a period in which the overall jeans market grew four percent annually.

The company dumped their ad agency of 67 years -- Foote, Cone & Belding -- and after a thorough review of their $90 million jeans ad account in late 1997, LS&Co. chose the agency TWBA/Chiat/Day. In spite of the fresh creative ideas offered by TWBA/Chiat/Day, LS&Co.'s overall sales dropped 13 percent to $6 billion from 1997 to 1998. Their market share dropped below 17 percent in 1998, nearly half of their 30 percent share at the beginning of the decade. By comparison, the Lee and Wrangler brands, owned by VF Corporation, combined market share rose from 17 percent in 1990 to 26 percent in 1998. Additionally, private-label jeans brands like J.C. Penney Co.'s Arizona label market segment climbed from a mere three percent of the market in 1990 to 20 percent in 1998.

LS&Co.'s string of losses prompted the company to drastically reduce its domestic work force by closing half of its remaining 22 North American manufacturing plants and laying off 30 percent of its 19,000 employees in 1999. Company spokeswoman Linda Butler explained at the time, "To maintain a large number of owned-and-operated plants is simply not feasible in this competitive market."[19] In 1999, LS&Co. lost $207 million as sales dropped 14 percent from the year before to $5.1 billion. More drastic was the 95 percent dive in LS&Co.'s net profits, which fell to $5.4 million from $102.5 million in 1998. Worse, Levi's jeans market share continued to hover near 17 percent.

E-commerce Troubles

Contributing to the company's woes was the fact that LS&Co. did not enjoy the same success with e-commerce that many other firms did. Reluctant at first to offer products for direct-order online for fear of angering retail partners, the company eventually allowed customers to purchase clothing from its web sites beginning in November 1998. Each brand -- Levi's, Dockers, and Slates -- had a separate web site with information about seasonal lines and retail locations as well as an on-line ordering feature. The Dockers site also featured an interactive fashion adviser that supplied ensembles for different occasions. The company touted its e-commerce venture with $5 million of web advertising on more than 20 prominent sites, including America Online and Yahoo! According to the company's director of e-commerce and retail marketing, Kevin McSpadden, the Internet advertising effort met with minimal success directing traffic to Levi's.com. When the company abandoned its on-line advertising scheme, McSpadden lamented, "We dumped a lot of money into the Internet. It didn't pay out."[20]

Instead of on-line marketing, LS&Co. returned to the more traditional media mix of print, radio and TV ads to enliven sales at Levi's.com, with similarly little success. The company operated the commercial site for 15 months, but never made it profitable. Customers at the site typically spent between $56 and $120, but these numbers could not offset the costs of operating the site and delivering the products. At first, LS&Co. prohibited web sites run by its retail partners from selling jeans and other LS&Co. products on-line. When the company repealed this restriction before the 1999 holiday season and allowed JCPenney.com and Macys.com to sell Levi's products, the retailers' sites sold 60 percent more merchandise than LS&Co. did at its own site. The e-commerce features of the company's web sites were ultimately removed in January 2000.

WHAT NEXT FOR DOCKERS?

The question remained, however, whether Dockers could continue to stimulate growth in a nearly saturated market. With every major clothing brand offering its own interpretation of the classic khakis, Dockers no longer single-handedly filled the hole between jeans and formal pants. To expand outside the now-crowded khakis market by attracting more "fashion-forward" customers, LS&Co introduced the Dockers Recode brand extension in the spring of 2000. As a line of business-casual tops, bottoms and outerwear offered in a range of colors and made from stretch fabrics, Dockers Recode bore a greater resemblance to Slates merchandise than the original "100% Cotton" Dockers. Dockers and Slates president Bobbi Silten viewed Dockers Recode as a natural bridge between original Dockers and Slates, remarking of the new line, "These are not basic basics. Nor do they interfere with our Slates message. This is where we can play with fashion a bit."[21] This latest fashionable upgrade for the Dockers brand was accompanied by a print and television advertising campaign.

In 2001, Levi Strauss introduced the Dockers Mobile Pant, a pair of fashion-forward Dockers that featured additional pockets for technological gadgets. An advertisement for the Mobile Pant displayed the pant's features using a spy-movie premise. In the ad, a woman uses X-ray spectacles to spy on a Dockers-wearing man. She notes that his pants conceal mobile devices such as a cellphone and a PDA, which are invisible to the naked eye. The Mobile Pant was a high-volume seller for Dockers in 2001. Net sales for Dockers declined in 2001, however, and analysts wondered if new styles would be enough to reinvigorate the brand in the coming years. Though still a billion-dollar brand, Dockers sales in 2001 were hovering near the mark set in 1993. Levi Strauss needed to find ways to make the brand relevant and interesting to new consumers.

DISCUSSION QUESTIONS

1. How would you characterize Levi's branding strategy in general? What are the positive aspects? Are there any negative aspects?

2. Analyze the Dockers' communication strategy at the time of the launch. How did it fit in with past Levi's advertising efforts? How did it contribute to brand equity?

3. How would you characterize the Dockers brand image? What makes up its brand equity?

4. Describe some of the changes in the Dockers marketing strategy from its debut. Has LS&Co. maintained a consistent enough marketing message? Are they well-positioned strategically and tactically to maintain their strong leadership status in the coming years?

REFERENCES

[1] This case was made possible through the cooperation of Levi-Strauss and the assistance of Steve Goldstein, Director of Marketing, Men's Jeans, Levi-Strauss & Co. Leslie Kimerling and Gregory Tusher prepared this case with research assistance from Keith Richey under the supervision of Professor Kevin Lane Keller as the basis for class discussion.

[2] *Business Week*, October 23, 1983.

[3] *Business Week*, March 8, 1982.

[4] *Media and Marketing Decisions*, Spring 1982.

[5] *San Francisco Focus,* October 1993.

[6] *Forbes*, August 11, 1986.

[7] *San Francisco Focus*, October 1993.

[8] In 1993, Macy's began to sell Levi's products in its stores again.

[9] *Forbes*, August 11, 1986.

[10] Internal Company Sources.

[11] Internal Company Sources.

[12] Internal Company Sources.

[13] Internal Company Sources.

[14] *Bobbin*, November 1990.

[15] *Daily News Record*, January 6, 1988.

[16] Internal Company Sources.

[17] As quoted in *The San Francisco Chronicle*, July 19, 1997.

[18] As quoted in *Brandweek*, "Levi's New Dress Code," August 19, 1996.

[19] As quoted in *Advertising Age*, June 1999.

[20] As quoted in *Advertising Age*, June 1999.

[21] As quoted in *DNR*, January 26, 2000.

INTEL CORPORATION:
BRANDING AN INGREDIENT[1]

INTRODUCTION

Intel's corporate branding strategy, which many credit for the company's unparalleled success in the microprocessor industry during the 1990s, stemmed from a court decision. On March 1, 1991, U.S. District Judge William Ingram ruled that the 386 designation used by Intel for its microprocessor family was a generic description and therefore did not represent a trademarkable name. Intel had been confident that the judge would rule in its favor, and the unexpected court decision effectively invalidated Intel's current branding strategy. This decision would allow a host of competitors to use Intel's established naming scheme, which would be potentially disastrous.

Intel responded by developing a trademarkable name for its processor family, the now-familiar Pentium, and launching a corporate branding campaign designed to make Intel the first name in processors. Both moves proved to be enormously successful. Intel became one of the leading companies in the PC boom, enjoying virtually unchallenged market leadership through the 1990s. However, potential problems arose as the PC industry slowed in the early years of the new century. Intel was facing a future in which the PC, which represented the core of the company's microprocessor business, was no longer the essential tool for the Information Age. Wireless telecommunications devices, for which Intel was not a leading supplier, were becoming increasingly popular. Intel realized that it had to expand its business into new technologies and product segments. The company had spent over three decades building the most recognizable brand in the PC microprocessor industry. The challenge at the turn of the century for Intel was to extend into new categories while maintaining equity in the brand and in its microprocessor leadership position.

COMPANY BACKGROUND

Intel Corporation was founded in 1968 by Robert Noyce and Gordon Moore (later to become Chairman of the Board). Soon thereafter, Andy Grove (later to become President and Chief Executive Officer), joined the firm. Intel's initial focus was the integration of large numbers of transistors into silicon chips to make semiconductor computer memory.

In 1978, Intel introduced the 16-bit 8086 processor followed by the 8088, the 8-bit version of the 8086, in 1979. These microprocessors were the first of the Intel "x86" line of microprocessors. At the time, Intel faced competition from a number of companies, the most serious being Motorola with its 68000 microprocessor. In response, Intel launched a campaign to make the 8086/8088 architecture the standard in the emerging microprocessor market. A critical step in this process was IBM's selection of the 8088 in 1980 as the exclusive microprocessor architecture for its first personal computer. The success of the IBM PC placed Intel at the center of the personal computer revolution and established Intel's x86 microprocessor architecture as the de facto industry standard.

Intel continued to produce chips with improved performance over the next decade. In June 1988, Intel introduced the Intel 386SX microprocessors, which became the backbone of IBM's and clone manufacturers' growing PC lines, and positioned Intel for its explosive growth over the next five years.

In April 1989, the company introduced the first of its next generation microprocessor, the Intel 486 processor. The i486, a 32-bit processor like the i386, held 1.2 million transistors on a single chip and ran typical PC programs two to three times faster than i386-based machines. In 1990, Intel sold approximately 7.5 million 386 and 486 microprocessors.[3] Intel's 1990 revenue from 386 microprocessor sales alone was estimated to be approximately $850 million.[4] As of year-end 1990, Intel was a $3.9 billion company, representing a 360 percent growth in 10 years. Net income over the same period grew 570 percent to $650.3 million. Intel microprocessors were found in almost 80 percent of all IBM and IBM compatible machines. The company, one of the largest semiconductor manufacturers in the world, was recognized as the undisputed microprocessor industry leader.

The Microprocessor Industry in the Early 1990s

Since 1986, Intel had been the only supplier of 386 technology, and since 1990, the only supplier of 486 technology. Between the second half of 1990 and the first quarter of 1991, however, a number of competitors had announced intentions to market their own versions of Intel's 386 and 486 microprocessors. The most serious threat came from Advanced Micro Devices (AMD) who in October 1990, had announced its own version of Intel's then hottest product, the i386 SX, called the AM386. Volume shipments were scheduled to begin in March 1991. In January 1991, two small semiconductors firms, Chips and Technologies and NexGen Microsystems, had announced their intentions to introduce 386-compatible chips within the year. Many of these competitors claimed that their 386 microprocessors would rival certain configurations of Intel's i486 chip. Whatever their true technological capabilities, Intel knew these chips could be named "386" or "486" and that they could do nothing to prevent such naming.

As of January 1991, Intel offered over a dozen versions of the Intel 386 and 486 microprocessors. In 1991, the company was expected to introduce another six new versions of the i486 microprocessor, including an i486SX, a lower priced, stripped down version of its 80486 microprocessor. By 1992, revenues from Intel 486 CPU sales were expected to surpass Intel 386 CPU revenues. That year, Intel planned to announce availability of its 586-generation microprocessor, internally named "P5" until the name under which it was to be marked was decided upon.

BRANDING ISSUES CONFRONTING INTEL

In the late 1980s, there was a significant shift in the general focus of the personal computer industry toward the mass-market, non-technical business and home PC users. Recognizing this shift, Intel moved from more of a "push" strategy to more of a "pull" strategy and began to re-direct a portion of its advertising efforts away from computer manufacturers to actual computer buyers. Until this time, the consumer's choice of a personal computer was based almost exclusively on the brand image of the manufacturer, such as Compaq, Dell, IBM, etc. Consumers did not think about the components inside the computer. By shifting its advertising focus to the consumer, Intel hoped to create brand awareness for Intel and its microprocessors, as well as build brand preference for the microprocessor inside the PC.

Intel still considered the MIS community to be its primary buyer, but also recognized the growing importance of the retail or "Circuit City"[10] buyer as a significant market segment and wanted a message that spoke directly to them.

As the market and technology leader, Intel was always the first to introduce a new generation of product and to establish the name and value of the new technology in consumers' minds. With competing products carrying the same or similar names, however, it became increasingly difficult for Intel to differentiate its products from those of its competitors.

Competitors had used Intel's numerical sequencing to name their products since the introduction of the 286. In the case of the 286 and earlier generation microprocessors, Intel had licensed its technology to several vendors who manufactured Intel's technology under their own name. Intel had not licensed its 386 technology, however, so the use of the same numerical sequence did not necessarily reflect Intel's architectural standard as it had with the earlier generation microprocessors. As a result, what one competitor called a 386 chip may or may not have had the same product characteristics as an Intel microprocessor with the same name. Not only were consumers confused about who made a particular generation of microprocessor, but also what level of performance to expect from a particular product. In the end, consumers were confronted with a product "alphabet soup" that made establishing a point of differentiation, and a distinct brand identity for Intel products increasingly difficult.

In June 1989, the company experimented with its first print campaign targeted to the consumer. The $5 million campaign promoted Intel microprocessors through their numbers -- the 286 and 386. The initial ad was an oblique, but attention-getting print ad and outdoor billboard that mimicked graffiti by spray painting over 286 and inserting 386SX. The tag line read, "Now, get 386 system performance at a 286 system performance price." Within months, buyers began asking for personal computers with the Intel386 SX chip, promoting computer companies to expand their production. In 1991, the 80386 SC became Intel's best-selling chip ever, shipping approximately 8 million units.[11] Intel's graffiti ad campaign had successfully introduced the microprocessor to the consumer, and market research indicated that an increasing number of consumers identified with 386 and 486 microprocessor technology.

EVOLUTION OF THE INTEL INSIDE BRANDING STRATEGY

During Fall 1990 and Winter 1991, Intel was involved in a trademark case with AMD to prevent their use of the 386 name in a new microprocessor that AMD planned to introduce in Spring 1991. Observing testimony in the 386 trademark case, Dennis Carter, Vice President of Intel's Corporate Marketing Group (CMG), became concerned about the potential impact that a negative verdict would have on Intel's branding strategy. The proliferation of competitive products using Intel's numerical sequencing was already an issue impacting Intel's current branding strategy. A loss in the trademark case would only exacerbate the company's problems in addressing the growing market confusion among product offerings. A negative verdict would mean that in the future any competitor could market its products under the same marks used by Intel. It would also mean that any computer maker could call a machine 386, without regard to the manufacturer who supplied the chip. Concerned about the possible negative verdict, and feeling a general need to clarify strategy, Carter began developing an alternative branding strategy, although he planned to wait until the court's ruling to decide whether or not to implement it.

In March 1991, Intel did in fact lose the 386 trademark case. This ruling cleared the way for AMD to sell its new AM386 microprocessor under the 386 name when it began volume shipments later that month. Given the court's decision, it was clear to Carter that Intel needed to change its branding strategy. Knowing that AMD would begin selling its own version of the 386 microprocessor within the month, and that other competitors would soon follow, created a real sense of urgency to make the change quickly. Within a few days Carter proposed a new processor branding strategy to Intel's executive office. The strategy recognized Intel's status as an ingredient supplier to PC OEMs and consisted of three elements: 1) the use of a logo based around the words Intel Inside to represent Intel processors used in PCs; 2) the use of MDF funds to share PC OEM advertising expenses and 3) and an Intel advertising program to build equity in this new brand. The strategy was accepted and Carter immediately established a task force whose sole mission was to implement this new branding strategy. In the interim, Intel would refer to its microprocessor as the i386 and Intel386, both Intel trademarks.

The first action of the task force was the introduction of a new ad using the "Intel: The Computer Inside" slogan. This ad, focused primarily on raising awareness of the Intel name, asked the reader, "Quick, do you know the first name in microprocessors?" showing a blank line in front of the numbers 486, 386 and 386SX. Turning the page, the blanks were filled in with the word "Intel". With the ad, Intel put the company's name directly in front of the consumer. In addition, Intel 486, Intel 386 and Intel 386 SX microprocessors were all trademarked names. The ad copy sought to assure the reader that purchasing a personal computer with an Intel microprocessor inside was a safe and technologically sound investment, providing "the power and compatibility to take you into the future." At the bottom of the ad was the Intel corporate logo with the slogan, "The Computer Inside" below it.

Despite not having a detailed pre-set plan, the task force established the fundamentals of a new branding strategy within a month of the court decision. The primary focus of the new strategy was the establishment of Intel as a brand, transferring the equity of 386 and 486 microprocessors to Intel, the company. Much of the brand equity Intel had at that time was in the numbers. Given the court decision and the increasing level of product confusion, Intel rejected a product-based brand strategy in favor of a strategy that focused on establishing the company's brand image. Establishing a unique identity for Intel was considered the best way not only to distinguish Intel products, but also to communicate the depth of Intel as a corporation with respect to its competitors. Intel wanted to sell the whole company, not just microprocessors. While the majority of the company's revenues were derived from sales of microprocessors, the company offered a broad range of products for the computer industry, including microprocessor peripherals, multimedia products, microcontrollers, flash memory, OEM modules and systems, supercomputer systems and PC enhancement products. Dennis Carter explained:

> We wanted to brand the whole company, but in a way that was clearly focused on processors. An initial proposal that I rejected early on that Intel Japan was proposing to do within Japan – was to brand all components. That would not,

however, solve our current problem. The branding program had to carry the Intel name and image, but focus on selling processors.

At the heart of the new strategy would be an advertising campaign that, according to Carter, would "cut the 'utter confusion' clones bring to the marketplace [and] drive the premium-brand message home to PC buyers."[14]

Critical to the establishment of Intel as a brand was the need to reverse perceptions of Intel as an impersonal, unfriendly technology company. If Intel was to gain the consumer's trust for its products, Intel knew the consumer had to feel good about the company itself. Intel wanted to establish a brand that offered the promise of "safety" and "technology" to the consumer. By convincing consumers that a computer with an Intel microprocessor inside was a safe investment in leading edge, software-compatible technology, Intel hoped to establish its microprocessor as the premium product and thereby command a premium price. The consumer would not necessarily need to know exactly who Intel was or what it made as long as he or she could be convinced that a personal computer powered by the "creator of microprocessors" was preferable. Intel also believed that if they could gain consumer confidence in Intel as a brand, they would be able to use the Intel name to help move the market forward into new generations of microprocessors and transfer the equity of the Intel brand to new products and technologies.

CHOOSING A LOGO

Since Intel's products were always inside the computer, unseen by the average purchaser of a personal computer, the company wanted to make the consumer believe that what was inside the computer was as important, if not more important, than the company that assembled the components and placed them inside a box. Intel's "The Computer Inside" campaign had not been explicit enough in linking Intel's name to the microprocessor inside the computer. The company needed a slogan, logo or some other means that more explicitly identified an Intel microprocessor as the essential ingredient when purchasing a computer.

Carter had previously wanted to use "The Computer Inside" campaign in Japan. Intel's agency in Japan, Dentsu, believed that the slogan too complex and recommended modifying it to "Intel In It" instead and presenting it in a logo form. Japan adopted this logo and began using it for all Intel products, not just processors. Needing a logo for processors fast, Carter, as part of his recommendation to the executive office, suggested using this logo form as the basis for the new microprocessor logo. In order to keep continuity with "The Computer Inside" tag line being used elsewhere in the world, Carter changed the phrase to "Intel Inside" which clearly conveyed to the consumer that there was an Intel microprocessor in the computer. For a number of executional and trademark reasons the Japanese logo form was modified. The new logo -- a swirl with Intel Inside -- placed the company and its name directly in front of the consumer.

COMMUNICATIONS STRATEGY

Essential to executing its new branding strategy and establishing awareness of its Intel Inside logo was getting the support of the OEMs who used Intel microprocessors in manufacturing their products. The most important group of OEMs were the personal computer manufacturers who purchased the vast majority of Intel's microprocessors. Intel's first priority was to get these manufacturers to include the Intel logo in their print ads. In addition to this "push" strategy, the team planned Intel-sponsored advertising and promotions to build equity in the logo and create a "pull" preference among consumers for Intel products. For this pull strategy to work, however, it was also important to make it possible for consumers to easily recognize that a computer had an Intel microprocessor at the point of purchase.

Enlisting Support of OEMs

To enlist the support of OEMs for their Intel Inside program, Intel developed a cooperative advertising program available to all computer manufacturers who used Intel microprocessors. Intel offered computer manufacturers rebates to include the Intel Inside logo in the print ads for their products. Negotiating with a broad range of OEMs in June 1991, Intel found much positive reaction among OEMs to the idea. In particular, the smaller, third tier manufacturers loved the idea. They had no brand name of their own and promoted their products primarily on the basis of price. Print was their main medium of communication, so any advertising subsidy was considered very beneficial. In addition, adding the Intel logo to their machines gave an assurance of quality to their product, and they proved eager to sign on.

The first and second tier OEMs were more skeptical. Many of these OEMs were afraid that the Intel campaign would dilute their own brand equity, weakening their points of differentiation from one another. According to Kevin Bohren, a Compaq vice-president, Intel's campaign "was leveling the playing field," thereby making Compaq's efforts to differentiate its PCs from clones harder.[15] However, it was this group that Intel needed most to ensure the success of their strategy.

The Intel Inside Program

Intel officially announced the launch of its Intel Inside program in November 1991. Specifically, the company announced its intention to spend approximately $125 million during the next 18 months on a combination of print, billboard and spot television advertising. Of this total, $15.2 million represented direct expenditures by Intel[16]. Intel also announced that 240 customers had agreed to participate in a cooperative advertising program and to carry the new Intel Inside logo on their packaging. For participating in the program, Intel offered to rebate 30-50 percent of the cost of any print ads that included the Intel Inside logo, up to a maximum of three percent of the cooperating company's Intel microprocessor volume. Dennis Carter described the program as "trying to create a brand image for products that fall under the Intel Inside umbrella".[17] As one reporter described the campaign, "The 'Intel Inside' campaign... is aimed at changing Intel's image from a microchip-maker to a quality standard-bearer."[18]

All advertising that included the Intel Inside logo was designed to create confidence in the consumer's mind that purchasing a personal computer with an Intel microprocessor was both a safe and technologically sound choice. All elements of the Intel Inside program focused on reinforcing those two key associations -- "safety" and "technology" -- whenever and wherever consumers saw the Intel Inside logo -- in an Intel TV ad, a computer manufacturer's print ad, or at the point-of-purchase in a store. By successfully creating consumer "pull", the competition would not only have to create their own distinct image with consumers, but also supply some reason for an OEM to use their product in the absence of any consumer demand.

Intel planned to focus its own ad campaign on products where it was the sole supplier, such as its 80486 line. According to David House, an Intel senior vice president of microprocessor products, "Intel hopes to encourage users to skip the i386 and go right to computers using i486 chips."[19]

OEMs and the Intel Inside Program

IBM was the first major OEM to use the Intel Inside logo. With the introduction of its first 486-based PC in April 1991, IBM offered to use the new logo – still in draft form. Intel faxed IBM a rough drawing for their use in the ad. IBM would not tell Intel where on the ad it would be located, and all the marketing task force could do was hope for prominent, highly visible placement. In fact, the Intel Inside logo was clearly visible in the ad layout. After running this ad, however, IBM did not use the Intel Inside logo again for nearly a year.

By December 1991, over 300 OEMs had signed cooperative advertising agreements with Intel, up from 240 the previous month, including first, second and third tier manufacturers. Over 100 of these companies featured the Intel logo in their ads, including Zenith Data Systems, Everex Systems, NCR Corp., Dell Computer and AST Research.[20] Nevertheless, at this time the largest first tier computer manufacturers -- including Compaq and IBM -- still were not using the Intel Inside logo in their ads.

Intel's Ad Campaign

Simultaneous with the development of its OEM co-op advertising program, Intel developed its own Intel Inside ad campaign. The first ad using the Intel Inside logo was a print ad that ran in July 1991. This ad, affectionately called the "measles" ad, showed the Intel Inside logo splashed across a page. The headline read: "How to spot the very best computers". At the bottom of the page, was the tag line: "Intel: The Computer Inside." The primary objective of this ad was to get the new Intel Inside logo in front of consumers and get them familiar with the Intel name. The ad text promoted Intel as "the world's leader in microprocessor design and development," and reassured the reader that "with Intel Inside, you know you've got unquestioned compatibility and unparalleled quality. Or simply put, the very best computer technology." The ad ran in both computer trade publications and consumer magazines such as *National Geographic* and *Time*.

In November 1991, Intel launched its first TV ad, dubbed "Room for the Future". In this ad, Intel sought to move the market to i486 technology. The ad stressed consumer investment protection by emphasizing both the affordability of Intel486 SX technology and the added feature of "built-in upgradability". The ad, developed by Intel's ad agency, Dahlin Smith White (DSW), used special effects designed by Lucas Arts' Industrial Light and Magic Co. to take the viewer inside the computer, giving them a whirlwind tour of the inside of a microcomputer showing how the Intel486 SX chip streamlined computer upgrading. At the end of the ride, a flashing "Vacancy" sign indicated where the faster chip of the future might go -- either a math coprocessor or the soon-to-be introduced OverDrive processor. Careful not to use any "technospeak", a friendly voice-over said, "Something's waiting inside the powerful Intel486 SX computer. We call it... room for the future. Check into it. From Intel. The Computer Inside." Complementing the TV campaign was a print campaign launched one week after the initial airing of the TV ad. The print ad headline read: "The affordable power source for today's software." The two-page ad ran in *The Wall Street Journal, Business Week, Fortune, PC Week, Infoworld, PC Magazine* and *Time*. A version of this Intel486 SX processor ad was placed on billboards in Los Angeles, San Francisco, Chicago, Toronto and seven other metropolitan markets.[22] Finally, the company prepared a small booklet describing in detail capabilities of the Intel486 SX microprocessor. Two pages of text were devoted to describing each of the following product attributes: upgradability, power, affordability, compatibility and the experience of Intel.

The "Room for the Future" ad was Intel's first experiment with television as an advertising medium. Dennis Carter explained, "We thought it might be an interesting cost-effective way of reaching a broader audience more effectively – a more impactful way to augment the print advertising campaigns that we do."[23] Consumer research indicated that most viewers of the commercial remembered the Intel name, rather than the product (the Intel486 SX) being advertised. Intel's print ads, on the other hand, proved much more successful in educating the consumer on specific product attributes associated with the Intel486 SX.

In March 1992, Intel introduced its second television ad. The "Power Source" ad promoted the Intel486 processor as a mainstream computing solution, emphasizing its power and affordability. In October 1992, Intel began a two-month run of its third Intel Inside TV ad. The "Library" ad promoted the compatibility of Intel-equipped personal computers with leading software packages. Once again, the ad first focused on the outside of a personal computer with the Intel Inside logo. The voice-over said: "This symbol outside means you have the standard inside that an entire library of software has been written to." The ad then took the viewer inside the computer through a library of software, including Microsoft and Lotus products. The trip ended with the camera focused on a microprocessor stamped with the Intel Inside logo. The voice-over continued: "Check out computers with Intel. To run an entire library of software, look for this symbol. The Intel microprocessor... think of it as a library card."

Intel Inside Program in 1992

By December 1992, over 700 customers were participating in the program, up from 400 in April 1992, primarily consisting of second and third tier OEMs.[26] According to Dennis Carter, by July 1992, at least half the computer ads in personal computer magazines included the Intel Inside logo.[27] Participating OEMs were pleased with the results of the co-op program, and many claimed that the Intel Inside logo had boosted their advertising effectiveness.

> The Intel Inside program has been a good program for us. It has helped add some credibility and enhancements to our messages, says Bill Saylor, manager of U.S. advertising for NCR. The advertising manager with another leading computer maker says the logo communicates a quality message... You know our product is a quality product because it has an Intel chip in it.[28]

BRANDING P5

Intel had been working on its next generation processor -- code-named "P5" since 1989 -- and expected to introduce it sometime after the fall of 1992. However, unlike previous processors though it was not obvious what Intel should name the P5, or how it should be branded in light of the developing Intel Inside program.

The Intel Inside program had generated a lot of awareness for Intel and made the company and its chip program newsworthy in the eyes of the general and business press. The existence of the Intel Inside program also meant that any branding strategy developed for the P5 would have to work in conjunction with the Intel Inside program. The heightening competition over the last year within the microprocessor industry had generated unusually keen interest in the P5, and both the technical and business markets were looking for information on the product, its capabilities, its expected introduction date *and* its name.

A critical event occurred on March 24, 1992 when Cyrix announced plans to introduce a 486SLC processor -- targeted to the notebook market -- in mid-April. The financial community reacted with a $2 per share drop in Intel's stock price that day. Six weeks earlier, Intel had begun to market its own chip targeted to the notebook market. The Intel 386SL chip was an integrated chip designed to minimize power consumption, a problem specific to the notebook market. The company had developed a series of ads designed to build brand equity in the SL name and get the SL name linked specifically to notebook computing.

Though the Cyrix chip was essentially 386 generation technology, naming it 486SLC gave the impression that the Cyrix product was a 486 generation product and, hence, more advanced than Intel's own i386SL. By positioning the product as 486, Cyrix negatively impacted Intel's i386 SL branding strategy and forced the company to review the possibility of altering the chip's name. After much deliberation, Intel concluded that it could not change the i386 SL name given that the product was actually selling in the market, but the episode significantly influenced Intel management's thinking concerning naming strategies.

Because of these and other events, the team knew they would have the attention of the public whenever they were ready to tell their story. However, the heightened interest in Intel and its new generation processor meant that it would be critical to manage the communications process and information flow carefully to ensure that the correct story was told.

NAMING P5

Carter appointed Karen Alter to manage the P5 naming process. She formed an ad hoc team whose first concern was choosing a name for this new processor. The team wanted a name that would stand on its own, as well as indicate the generation of the new chip. Clearly the court's decision that numbers were not trademarkable and the recent experience with the i386 SL made the choice of 586 a risky one. In a June 1992 interview with an AP reporter, Andy Grove was quoted as saying: "Over my dead body will this new product be name 586." This quote was picked up by newspapers around the world, thus laying the issue of a numerical name to rest once and for all.

With the 586 option eliminated, the team decided to use the name P5 as an opportunity to re-define the industry language for microprocessors. Naming P5 offered Intel the opportunity to create a new brand with a clean slate that could acquire equity of its own over time and make it more difficult for other CPU suppliers to get a "free ride" from Intel's equity.

In specifying criteria for the choice of a name for the "P5", the team decided that it was necessary that the name: 1) be difficult for competition to copy; 2) be trademarkable; 3) indicate a new generation of technology that could effectively transition from generation to generation; 4) have positive associations and work on a global basis; 5) support Intel's brand equity and 6) sound like an ingredient so that it worked *with* Intel's partners' brand names. In selecting the name, the team's primary target audience was the retail consumer. While a key objective was to establish credibility for the new product with early adopters -- industry technology experts -- they knew this group did not really care that much about the actual name of a microprocessor per se.

Intel's sales force surveyed a broad range of customers during a two month period to get their reaction to the planned naming concept (e.g., to not use a numerical name). Some customers told Intel that changing the industry language by not using "586" was not possible. They argued that the industry moved too fast, that the market was already on a level playing field and that the product was too complicated to "re-educate" the consumer. Others, particularly the technologically sophisticated OEMs, liked the idea as a way to differentiate Intel technology. A distinctive name would allow them to distinguish their products from lower tier manufacturers in the PC market, as well as from their competition in the workstation and server markets.

Inside of Intel, the managers viewed this naming process as a major strategic move. As Karen Alter explained:

> Here we are – a company that spends $2 billion a year on capital and R&D. Every 2-3 weeks we would get together with the senior executives who *wanted* to be locked into a room to talk about this issue. Everyone had come to believe that technology was moving so fast that communicating to the end-users and getting them to buy the right technology was critical. It would be a huge competitive advantage for us if we got it right. Even though it's a little name, we had to get it right the first time because we wouldn't get a second chance.

NAME SELECTION

Intel undertook the most extensive search in its history to find a name for the P5. In addition to hundreds of names generated from the task force's own brainstorming sessions, Intel hired Lexicon – a naming firm – and ran a company-wide naming contest in which over 1200 Intel employees worldwide participated. Some of the more humorous entries submitted included, "iCUCyrix, iAmFastest, GenuIn5 and 586NOT! *Computer Reseller News*, an industry trade publication, even held its own contest! In all, the selection process generated 3300 names. Karen Alter described the process that followed:

> Compared to 586, every name sounded terrible because it lacked the familiarity of the x86 naming scheme. It appeared that there were no exciting protectable names, but we knew we had to get over it. We divided the names into three concept categories: 1) closely linked to Intel; 2) technologically "cool" – e.g., naming an architecture; and 3) completely new with some generational concept embedded.

We then discussed the pros and cons of each concept category and selected ten alternative for extensive review and testing.

The company conducted a very detailed global trademark search to insure that each name on the list could not be copied, as well as a worldwide linguistic review to ensure the name would be effective in all languages. Certain that each name on the list was trademarkable and linguistically correct, the company then tested each name and its related concept with MIS and end users in the U.S. and Europe to determine how well each name met the established goals. In particular, the team asked the participants to evaluate each name for negative and positive associations, memorability, willingness to use, appropriateness for the product and ability to merchandise. In addition, the team got internal input from its Asia Pacific and Japanese counterparts.

The task force discussed pros and cons for each of the 10 tested names and selected one name from each of the concept categories to present to the top management executives for a final name selection. The final three name options for the respective concept categories were: InteLigence, RADAR1, and Pentium[29]. Finally, ten days before the planned announcement of the official name, the company's top executives and the members of the task force met to make the final name selection. Grove led the meeting, asking each participant to choose from the three alternatives and to tell the group what he/she liked about that name and why. Grove and Carter did not give their opinions, saying that they would make the final decision after the meeting was over. Once the meeting was over and a name was chosen, Grove told the group, the topic would never be discussed again.

Not surprisingly, the members of the task force were almost evenly split across the three names. The public relations members of the task force liked the InteLigence name because it was the easiest name for them to explain to the public. The technically-oriented members liked the "techie cool" name, RADAR1. The sales/marketing-oriented members were partial to the Pentium name because it was new *and* represented the cleanest break. As a result, they felt that it would be easier to sell to OEMs and other customers. After everyone had given his or her opinion, Grove and Carter thanked the group and went into Grove's office to make a final decision.

COMMUNICATING THE NEW NAME

Since the name would not be chosen until the last possible moment, the task force had to decide on a communications strategy without knowing exactly what name they would be communicating. Consequently, they developed a communications timeline for introduction of P5 -- from name announcement through products and systems launch. The task force planned to release information so as to create a "crescendo" effect by the time the product was actually introduced into the market and available for sale. A key question was how to announce the name -- during a speech, press conference, television program, etc.? A primary objective of the task force was to capture the attention and interest of the press so that by the time the new chip was shipped in volume, everyone would know the name of the new chip and no one would even think about 586. The name would not be officially announced until October 1992. However, by September 1992, Intel's public relations efforts had effectively decreased mention of the 586 name in published press articles to 17 percent of press articles worldwide, from 55 percent in February.

When the naming options had been narrowed to three choices, the task force considered the impact of each name on the multiple audiences -- press, OEMs/dealers, competitors, and employees -- to whom they would have to communicate the decision. Without question, many people would react negatively to any name that was not 586 and Intel wanted to counter this reaction as quickly as possible. In preparation for the name launch, the task force developed a series of presentations for customers to keep them informed of the naming process and timing of the product's introduction. The company made formal presentations explaining the company's intentions and asking for "help and understanding in launching the new name, even before it was made public."[29] Intel hoped the computer companies would market the name to users as a key product ingredient, much like Nutrasweet, Teflon and Goretex. As one Intel spokesperson explained, "The market is changing and with other people (competing chip makers) introducing a key ingredient, you don't know what part you're getting inside."[30] Intel also hoped the computer companies would market the name to users as a way to convey the power and efficacy of its fifth generation processor family.

LAUNCHING THE PENTIUM PROCESSOR

Intel officially announced the name of the new chip on Monday, October 20, 1992. Grove, in New York City for the 10th annual NY PC User Society convention, made the announcement during an exclusive interview on CNN at 7:30am eastern standard time. CNN provided Intel the ability to make a live official announcement on a worldwide basis. Andy Grove announced that the name of Intel's fifth generation microprocessor was Pentium and said the company would begin shipping production versions of the chip in early 1993. In describing the choice of Pentium for the name, Grove explained, "the name should suggest an ingredient. The "Pent" of Pentium, from the Greek meaning five, alludes to the fact that the new chip is the fifth generation of the family. The "ium" was added to make the chip sound like a fundamental element." The company coined the name because it conveyed the positive attributes such as quality, state-of-the-art technology, software compatibility and performance that its OEM customers wanted their brands to be associated with. Grove explained the rationale for not using a number as a name, "We can't count on another number. It's so much cleaner to designate a name that's protectable."[31] In the interview, Grove said that the company expected to ship "hundreds of thousands" of Pentium chips in 1993 and to reach a manufacturing rate of a million Pentium processors in 1994.

Immediately following Grove's announcement on CNN, the Pentium processor marketing team launched a full scale effort to ensure the Pentium name was quickly adopted into the every day industry vernacular. Intel's PR department phoned all leading individuals who wrote about the industry to let them know the new name. A not uncommon response was, "I can't believe this name. This is the most ridiculous name I've ever heard." Intel's PR department carefully monitored all press for references to the Pentium processor, and if they found anyone using 586 or P5, they immediately sent the author a letter correcting the error. Within one month after the naming launch, over 90 percent of press mentions used Pentium instead of 586.

Before Grove's announcement on CNN only six people inside Intel knew the name -- Grove, Carter, Rick Giardina (the Intel attorney in charge of trademarking the name), two

PR people and Karen Alter. Alter described the scene inside Intel following Grove's announcement:

> Our microprocessor team had to convert over 20,000 documents. It wasn't like anyone really liked the name, but they just did it. We all converted everything rapidly – all the trademark documents, all the internal communications, e-mail, product material – you name it, we did it. The people preparing for Comdex had banners they were just waiting to place the name in. For two days we gave interviews non-stop. The press picked up the name more and more. Our European team loved the name because they thought it was a global name with a historical root. That got picked up favorably in the European press. The name began to grow on people. They felt better about it. We had this massive organization to handle the situation while it was still in our control.

THE PENTIUM PROCESSOR PRODUCT ANNOUNCEMENT

On March 22, 1993 Intel announced the company had begun shipping production versions of the Pentium chip. No pricing plans were disclosed. Sales by personal computer makers would not begin until May in order to give Intel time to build up inventories of the chip to meet expected initial demand.[32] Andy Grove said Intel planned to push the Pentium processor early in its life as a mainstream microprocessor and not as an expensive high-end chip by pricing the new chip "aggressively".[33]

On May 10, 1993, one week before the Pentium processor-based PCs would officially be available for sale, Intel introduced its first ad for the Pentium processor. The four page magazine insert, the first in a year long "technology briefing" campaign, positioned the Pentium processor at the elitist end of the market, saying "all but the most demanding users" should use personal computers with Intel486 chips. The insert, describing in some detail how the Pentium processor made PCs run faster, was a shift away from the simpler, consumer-style advertising Intel had done since 1989. As one Intel spokesperson explained, "In the olden days, we would do very "techy", spec-driven ads in engineering books, and then we got very end-user (focused) without much meat on the bones. Now we're going a little bit back to our roots."[37]

Although Intel expected to ship only "tens of thousands" of Pentium chips in 1993, the company, as with previous generation microprocessors, began advertising the new product early to create demand and stay ahead of clones of its old products.[38] "It's the eat your own children theory," explained on Intel spokesperson. "We have to do it before someone else does it to us."[39] The insert was scheduled to appear initially in computer titles and then *Business Week*. International Data Corp. Estimated that 80,000 Pentium processor machines would be shipped in the U.S. by year-end 1993, rising to 640,000 in 1994, 2 million in 1995 and surpassing the 486 by the end of 1996.[40] The prices of Pentium processor-based desktop computers were expected to cost around $5,000 in 1994, and to drop to as little as $2,000 within three years.[41]

INDICATIONS OF SUCCESS

Between 1990 and 1993, Intel had invested over $500 million in advertising and promotional programs designed to build Intel's brand equity. The Intel Inside campaign had constituted the bulk of this investment and plans were to continue with the campaign. The two pillars of the Intel brand message continued to be Intel's guarantee of safety -- both in terms of software compatibility and upgradability -- and provide the most advanced technology -- via the double clocked i486 DX2 and Pentium processors.

Within the industry, there was considerable debate about the effectiveness of Intel's "branded ingredient" strategy. AMD, for example, had publicly rejected adoption of a similar branding strategy. As one AMD spokesman explained, "You wouldn't find an 'AMD Inside' campaign even if we had the kind of deep pockets that Intel has. We don't think it's particularly effective to try to build brand awareness."[42] In contrast, Cyrix was scheduled to introduce a print ad campaign in June 1993 for its line of 486-like chips. The ads would initially run in computer publications.

In the last two years, the Intel Inside program had won a number of advertising awards, including the Marcom Award for best TV campaign at the computer industry's premier trade show, Comdex, in 1992.[43] Also at Comdex, Dahlin Smith White, Intel's ad agency, won the "Grand Marquis" excellence award for its "Power Source" commercial. In presenting the award, Donna Tapellini, editor of *Marketing Computers* magazine, explained, "This is not just for the best marketing program or campaign, it is for a work that has raised the standard irrevocably and made a difference. . . Not only have they moved the goal posts in terms of advertising values, but this campaign is a culmination of a brilliant 'Intel Inside' branding strategy. They have done for (computer) chips what Frank Perdue has done for chickens. They have set the standard and become the ones to beat in the industry."[44] In 1993, Financial World rated Intel as the third most valuable brand, behind Marlboro and Coca-Cola, with an estimated worth of $17.8 billion.

Intel's own market research, both in the U.S. and in Europe, indicated that end user awareness of the Intel brand name had increased significantly since the introduction of the Intel Inside program. The independent research, performed in June 1992, indicated that users worldwide viewed Intel as the technology leader versus such competitors as AMD and Cyrix and the overwhelming microprocessor of choice. Research in the U.S. also indicated that Intel had the strongest image on quality and compatibility attributes. Over 80 percent of those surveyed had seen the Intel Inside logo in personal computer ads and nearly half had seen the logo in store displays, product literature, or on a personal computer. Over 75 percent of those who had seen the logo said that it conveyed positive attributes, and 50 percent said they looked for the symbol in making their personal computer selection.

In Europe, two-thirds of business computer purchasers surveyed had seen the Intel Inside logo and understood that the logo indicated a CPU brand. However, among the non-sophisticated non-technical users, the "Intel" name and Intel Inside logo were often confused. The problem was particularly acute in certain foreign languages, like character-based Chinese, that did not link the Intel Inside brand with the Intel company name.

Pentium Becomes a Hit

The price of the original Pentiums targeted high-end consumers as well. At the time of their launch, Pentium PCs cost around $5,000, compared with 486 systems that cost as little as half as much. The prohibitive cost of the chip and limited availability prevented the Pentium from making an instant sales splash, and a year after the chip's introduction it accounted for only 10 percent of Intel's revenues. When the company increased production and began cutting Pentium prices, sales rose dramatically. In 1994, Pentium sales grew eight times faster than 486 sales did when that chip was new. That same year, the company shipped over 6 million Pentiums. Within two years after the company's decision to use the Pentium name for its P5 generation chips in 1992, Intel possessed roughly 90 percent of the world's PC microprocessor market and enjoyed exclusive relationships with several of the biggest computer manufacturers.

EVOLUTION OF THE PENTIUM

Intel's Microprocessor Genealogy

The company saw the Pentium sub-brand as an important part of its success, and extended the name in branding their next four PC processors. By 2000, Intel had unveiled the Pentium Pro, Pentium II, Pentium III, and Pentium 4 chips. In 1994, Intel's revenues rose 24 percent from the previous year to $11.5 billion on the strength of over 6 million Pentium processor shipments. Following the success of the Pentium chip, Intel decided to call its next generation P6 processors the Pentium Pro. The first Pentium Pro chips, released in December 1994, contained 5.5 million transistors -- almost twice the number of transistors as the original Pentium -- and ran at 266 MHz. Initially marketed for use with computers running high-end business applications, the chips eventually entered the PC market once advancing technology required more powerful processors. In January 1997, not long after Pentium Pro chips began appearing in PCs, the company introduced an enhanced Pentium processor that contained MMX technology. MMX stood for multimedia extension and referred to the unique chip design features that enabled it to process sound, video and graphics more efficiently than previous chips. The chip contained 4.5 million transistors and was capable of speeds up to 200 MHz. A hit with consumers from the time of its introduction, the Pentium MMX accounted for 13 percent of Intel's sales by March 1997.

Just five months after the Pentium MMX became available to consumers inside PCs, Intel launched its next chip, the Pentium II processor. The Pentium II incorporated the multimedia technology of the Pentium MMX while running 50 percent faster, at 300 MHz. The chip design made it incompatible with any of Intel's previous chips or any competitor's chips, a fact that required PC manufacturers to build new systems solely for the Pentium II. Nevertheless, the Pentium II launch in 1997 was the most coordinated in Intel's history up to that point, as IBM, Compaq, Packard Bell and Gateway all offered new PCs containing the Pentium II timed with the chip's release. But initial sales were slow; the Pentium II accounted for only two percent of total microprocessor sales three months after its release. In August, Intel offered its biggest processor price cuts in its history, discounting the Pentium II by up to 57 percent, well above the company's average 20 to 30 percent discount.

The next month, the company spent a record $100 million on an integrated marketing campaign to promote the Pentium II. The campaign included several high profile advertisements, such as a 1998 Super Bowl spot featuring the popular "bunny people" series. The "bunny people," first introduced during the 1997 Super Bowl in an ad for the Pentium MMX, were commercial versions of Intel technicians dressed in brightly colored contamination suits. In the ads, the colorful characters danced to a disco soundtrack while they worked inside a processor fabrication facility. The company felt that by taking the audience inside the fabrication plant where the chips were manufactured, the new TV spots remained consistent with the original Intel Inside TV ads, which had given the viewer a virtual tour of the interior of the computer. The ads aimed to capture the technological origins of Intel's products while, at the same time, revealed a fun-loving human side of the company. The "bunny people" ads always took place outside the PC, and Intel's first Super Bowl ad sent the "bunny people" as far as China on a fictional "road trip" promotional tour. Popular though the "bunny people" were, some felt that the lively spots strayed too far from Intel's core product placement, the inside of the computer.

Perhaps sensing that the "bunny people" marketing strategy had run its course, Intel shifted back to a more PC-centered campaign for the Pentium III, the successor to the Pentium II. When it was released in 1999, the chip's 9.5 million transistors enabled it to reach speeds over 500 MHz. The company positioned the chip as a tool to enhance home PC users' Internet experience. Intel nearly doubled its 1998 advertising budget to promote its new chip, spending $300 million on a global campaign that promoted the processor in nearly every available medium. The Pentium III marketing campaign used a theme reminiscent of the original "Intel Inside" slogan: a blue door bearing the Intel Inside insignia accompanied by the line, "This way in."

In October 2000, the company introduced a trio of spokespeople -- performance artists Blue Man Group -- that appeared in television ads for the Pentium III. The ads featured the Blue Man Group performing acrobatic and musical stunts that reinforced the number "III." In one ad, each blue man uses a catapult to launch paint on a wall in stripes that form the Pentium III logo. The third blue man pours paint on his head, catapults himself against the wall, and slides down to create the third stripe.

RENEWED PROCESSOR COMPETITION

In early 1997, Compaq unveiled a PC that retailed for $999 and was powered by an inexpensive Pentium clone. Compaq's computer featured a chip from Intel rival Cyrix chip and sparked a trend in low-cost computers. In 1998, Hewlett-Packard and Compaq chose to buy cheaper chips from Cyrix and AMD instead of buying certain Intel Pentium models. Intel executives initially ignored the discount PC market, noting that PCs priced at less than $1200 comprised only 27 percent of the total market in 1997 and did not sell well overseas. But as the cheaper PCs attracted American consumers who only needed a simple machine that would allow them to access the Internet, Intel re-thought its strategy. By the middle of summer in 1997, AMD and Cyrix had gained 20 percent of the overall U.S. retail PC market and Intel's share of the low-end PC processor market dropped below 30 percent. A research firm predicted that though PCs priced above $1,500 -- the market in which Intel had a virtual stronghold -- comprised 61 percent of the computer market in 1997, this figure would likely dip to 18 percent by 2001.

Intel realized that not only would it lose market share in the near term if it ignored the low-end PC, but a lack of products in that market could also erode its core business over the course of a few years. By not properly anticipating the surge in popularity of sub-$1000 PCs, Intel wound up fighting to keep from losing overall market share. To combat the increasing competition from AMD and Cyrix, Intel released the low-end Celeron chip in April 1998. The first Celerons, slower than comparably priced chips, drew unfavorable reviews and sold poorly. As a result of these sluggish sales, Intel's share of the sub-$1000

PC market dropped from 68 to 56 percent in the third quarter of 1998, while AMD's share rose to from 19 to 24 percent.

Competition from AMD

In the fall of 1999, AMD unveiled a 700-MHz version of its Athlon chip, which surpassed the latest Pentium in terms of performance. A few chipmakers, notably Cyrix Corp. and NexGen Inc. (which AMD subsequently bought), had claimed higher-performing products than Intel in previous years, but AMD was the first microprocessor manufacturer in almost a decade to offer a PC chip that surpassed the Pentium in terms of raw speed. The release of the 700-MHz Athlon put Intel in the unfamiliar position of trailing a competitor's technology advancements. Major PC manufacturers had been reluctant to buy AMD processors, however, and as of late 1999 none of the top PC makers used an AMD processor in its machines. "It's the same reason that people bought IBM for years and nothing else," said an executive with a computer reseller. "There's a sense that there is less risk in Intel."[45]

For much of 2000, AMD and Intel battled for the title of "fastest chip," which usually changed hands with each successive product release. The important issue for AMD was to keep pace with Intel's highest performing chips, a valuable point of comparison that helped AMD's stock rise 353 percent from 1999 to 2000. When AMD became the first chipmaker to produce a 1 GHz PC processor and reported a net profit of $65 million in the last quarter of 2000, its stock climbed to a record $60 a share. In April 2000, as AMD announced that profits for the first quarter had tripled from the previous quarter on $1.1 billion in revenue, the stock rose to $76 per share. In addition to their improved profitability, AMD was selling microprocessors to every major PC manufacturer by June 2000. Many industry analysts considered AMD's revitalized business to be a "serious challenge"[46] to Intel. Intel experienced a number of product flaws, shortages, and delays in 1999 and 2000, which critics partly blamed on Intel's push to beat rival AMD to market with faster processors. Intel's product delays enabled AMD to gain significant inroads in the PC microprocessor business. In 2000, AMD had a 17 percent share of the chip market, up from 13 percent in 1999. That year, nine out of the top 10 PC makers were using AMD chips in their computers. While Intel had to recall flawed chips in addition to its product delays, AMD was producing its Athlon and Duron processors with near-perfect performance records.

INTEL'S SEGMENTATION STRATEGY

The heavy competition prompted then-CEO Andy Grove to initiate an aggressive promotion of the Celeron, while admonishing his co-workers "if we lose the low end today, we could lose the high end tomorrow."[47] Intel quickly increased the processor speed on its Celerons and cut prices 30 percent during the holiday season. These counter measures precipitated an overall microprocessor market share drop for AMD from 16 percent to 13 percent from the third to fourth quarter of 1998. Intel's market share rose to over 80 percent from 75 percent over the same period.

The fear of "losing the high end" drove Intel to restructure its processor business by segmenting it into three price and performance categories. The top processor, the Xeon, was designed for servers and powerful networks and retailed for as much as $3,000. The

Pentium class targeted the performance-PC market and sold for roughly half the Xeon's cost. The Celeron retailed for as low as $63. The aggressive promotion of the Celeron eventually had the desired effect: Intel gained a 62 percent market share in the sub-$1000 PC category by the year 2000. Still, Intel made most of their profits from sales of the two upper-level processors, and designed their marketing strategy accordingly.

The Pentium II processor, released in 1998, received heavy marketing support across nearly every medium, from expensive TV spots to web advertising to print campaigns. The Celeron processor, on the other hand, got no TV time and was marketed using comparatively sparse print and radio only. The segmentation strategy helped Intel keep its average chip price above $200 dollars since the company could sell enough high-end processors to take up the slack from low-margin Celerons. In 1999, Intel revised its $800 million co-op advertising program to reflect the segmentation strategy. The company introduced scaled reimbursement rates that coincided with the level of product. PC manufacturers received 60 percent reimbursements for advertisements for the Pentium III or Pentium III Xeon processors, while ads featuring the Celeron chip earned 40 percent refunds. Previously, the co-op program involved flat-rate reimbursements of 60 percent.

NEW PROCESSORS

Itanium

Intel's next big processor development, the Itanium, was a 64-bit chip capable of performing advanced operations on complex data much more rapidly than the 32-bit Pentium family of chips. Various problems with the chip forced the company to repeatedly delay the Itanium's debut from its scheduled release date of early 1999. In July of 2000, the company announced though it had roughly 15,000 Itanium prototypes operating in some 5,000 systems, another delay would push the release back from the third to the fourth quarter of 2000. The company finally released Itanium chips in May 2001, two years after the original target date. Due to the lengthy delay, at the time of its release Itanium ran only half as fast as the latest Pentium 4. Consequently, sales expectations for the Itanium were low, as corporate customers appeared to be waiting for the next-generation chip due in 2002. Analysts worried that Intel would be unable to recoup the estimated $1 billion to $2 billion it took to develop Itanium.

Pentium 4

In 2000, Intel announced that their next Pentium-generation chip would be called the Pentium 4, and would be the company's first completely new desktop processor design since the 1995 Pentium Pro. The Pentium 4 was a major new weapon in Intel's processor speed battle with AMD. By July of 2000, Intel had unveiled a 1,100 MHz processor to top AMD's 1,000 MHz Athlon. The Pentium 4 performed at 2 GHz (2,000 MHz) during tests that summer with the aid of special cooling technology. Pentium 4 debuted in November 2000 in PCs starting at $2,000. The first commercially-available Pentium 4's ran at speeds of 1.4 GHz. Though the 2 GHz chip would not find its way into PCs before the end of the year, Intel's Pentium 4 processors soon became the fastest desktop processors on the market, outpacing AMD's 1.5 GHz Athlon.

Intel supported Pentium 4 with a $300 million advertising campaign -- Intel's largest outlay for a single chip -- that initially also featured the Blue Man Group. The company decided to keep the Blue Man Group, which also appeared in ads for Pentium III, in order to provide "continuity between the two chips as it phases out the older product."[48] Research found that the Blue Man Group ads scored high among Pentium 4's target audience of well-educated, middle- to upper-income PC consumers. The ads positioned Pentium 4 as a chip that enhances media and Internet applications with the tagline, "The center of your digital world."

At the time of the Pentium 4 launch, the domestic PC market was in less than ideal condition. The percentage of U.S. homes with PCs had stayed at 58 percent since 1999. Faced with a declining PC market, Intel cut prices on Pentium 4 chips by as much as 23 percent in January 2001, only two months following the chip's release. The Pentium 4 got off to a slow start, PCs containing Pentium 4 chips accounted for less than four percent of the U.S. retail market by April. Amidst slowing demand for fast processors, analysts predicted that Intel would sell fewer than the expected 20 million Pentium 4 chips in 2001.

INTEL'S NEW GROWTH VISION

Surviving In a Shrinking Market

After enjoying ten years of better than 30 percent compound annual growth, Intel executives looked toward the future from their market leader position in 1998 and saw the PC market declining in the years to come. Already, consumers in America bought cheaper computers than they had in previous years. These discount computers contained cheaper processors manufactured by Intel's competitors, which meant that expensive Pentium processors often sat in the top-of-the-line computers on store shelves. With sales of Pentium-based computers, which provided Intel with 70 percent margins, dwindling, Intel was forced to lower the prices of its chips during 1997 and 1998 in order to retain market share. As price drops cut into margins, Intel profits fell and its stock shed about 30 percent from its peak. The company recognized that the period of high growth and large margins in its PC processor business was ending, and determined that diversification within its processor lines and growth into other technologies would help the company weather the PC market decline. By broadening their business base, Intel aimed to increase the longevity of the company in the volatile technology sector.

In 1998, when then-chief Andy Grove stepped down, Intel appointed company president Craig Barrett as its new CEO. Barrett's vision for Intel's future included broad product offerings and technological developments for the Internet. He understood the limitations of a processor-dominated business strategy and declared "If Intel wants to continue to occupy a central position [in high tech], it's not just enough to build the hearts and brains of computers."[49] Broadening the company's focus seemed like a bold risk at first glance, since 90 percent of revenues and 100 percent of profits came from Intel's microprocessor business. But with the Internet technology sector growing 30 percent faster than the PC industry, and new technology like wireless communication increasing in popularity, Barrett knew that an expanded role on the net would be crucial in helping the company grow in the next decade.

From the start of his tenure as CEO, Barrett steered the company into a host of new businesses, such as consumer electronics, e-commerce and Internet hosting. He also revamped Intel's microprocessor offerings, expanding into chips for network utilities, information appliances and lower-priced PCs. The company supplemented its expansion by rapidly acquiring competitors and specialists in new growth areas. In 1999, Intel spent $6 billion acquiring 12 different companies, and in the two years since Barrett started as CEO the company invested in 25 communications-technology startups. Over half of the more than 250 companies Intel invested in from 1996 to 2000 were Internet-focused startups, including such ventures as on-line retailer E-Toys and web searching technology developer Inktomi.

Non-Pentium Growth

Another strategy was to boost sales in the networking chip division, which had previously been a sideline to sell more PCs, but was one of the fastest-growing chip categories. Intel's Network Communications Group, which manufactures chips found in modems, routers, switches and network interface cards, received large budget allowances for acquisitions, marketing and hiring in recent years. In 1999, Intel made its largest acquisition ever by buying networking chipmaker Level One for $2.2 billion and also bought net players SoftCom Microsystems, Netboost and the telecom chips division of Stanford Telecommunications. In September, 1999, the company unveiled a family of thirteen networking chips that featured a programmable network processor designed to speed and simplify network expansions. Though sales in Intel's network group exceeded $1 billion by 2000, the company remained a minor player at that time since the category featured prominent networking chipmakers Lucent, Motorola, and Texas Instruments.

New Product Categories

At the same time, Intel recognized the importance of extending its business beyond processors by developing other electronic products. Intel's first ventures outside processors flopped, however. The company introduced modems and videoconferencing equipment in the mid1990s, but these brand extensions went virtually nowhere. The company refocused its efforts to establish itself in consumer electronics by creating the Home Products Group in August 1998 that developed Internet appliances such as web-ready TVs, set-top boxes, PC cameras, a children's microscope and wireless keyboards. In 2000, Intel introduced two new digital cameras, the Me2Cam and the Pocket PC Camera. The company also unveiled a digital music player, the Intel Personal Audio Player. For children, Intel's Smart Toy Lab designed a Computer Sound Morpher that enables users to record sounds and mix and alter them on a computer. Said John Middleton, marketing manager for Intel's consumer products, "These products extend the business and the brand and they make the Internet more fun."

In 1998, CEO Craig Barrett established the New Business Group, a division aimed at growing Intel's business opportunities outside processors. The group worked on small projects, each one of which was treated like a start-up, with "venture capital" coming from Intel's cash reserves. As of 2000, the company had spent $50 million on over 20 new projects, including an effort to install 3,000 terminals on seats at Madison Square Garden that sports fans could use to access information about teams and players and a start-up called Vivonic that built handheld computers designed to enable users to monitor their diet and fitness.

WILL INTEL'S EXPANSION WORK?

Intel CEO Craig Barrett remained highly optimistic about the benefits of his company's brand extensions. In 2000, he announced that within five years he expected that every new business Intel grows into would generate revenues exceeding $1 billion. Barrett also anticipated that by that time, Intel's new ventures would be fueling 15 to 20 percent annual growth, compared with 8 percent compound growth between 1998 and 1999. This optimism helps explain the dramatic shift in focus represented by Intel's aggressive growth outside the microprocessor business. Others outside the company foresaw profit contributions from Intel's various brand extensions. One analyst predicted in 2000 that within a year, a quarter of Intel's revenues would come from products other than processors. In fact, one-fifth of Intel's revenues came from non-processor products in 2001.

Not everyone believed that Intel's expansion strategy would yield success, however. While the Internet remained the hottest place for new business growth, Intel was not a proven player in the Net economy and faced stiff competition from established Internet powerhouses and earnest startups. Additionally, some investors and analysts worried that Intel's rush to develop, in the words of the company's New Business Group head Gerry Parker, "as many ideas as possible"[50] outside its core business demonstrated a loss of focus. Amidst the plaudits and the criticisms, Intel's financial performance suffered.

The 2001 fiscal year was Intel's worst in its 34-year history. Revenues that year plummeted 21 percent to $26.5 billion, while net income dropped 70 percent to $3.6 billion as the PC market slowed. Of the $10 billion Intel invested in new businesses since 1998, some $4 billion had achieved no growth by 2002. Intel's new businesses rang up no profits, while losses doubled each year since 1998. A former Intel executive said, "They're dabbling in everything and overwhelming nothing."[51]

In order to stem its losses, Intel exited non-processor businesses such as digital cameras, streaming media software for online audio and video transmissions, toys and networking hardware. The company announced in 2001 that its Connected Products unit, which makes many of Intel's consumer products, would be shut down in 2002. The company stopped manufacturing network servers and routers in 2001 after several of its big chip customers, including Dell and Cisco, complained that Intel was competing against them. The company spun off its interactive media-services division and phased out iCat, a web site management service for small businesses. Intel also scaled back its information-appliance business, withdrawing its web-surfing devices from every market except Spain. Intel Online Services, Intel's web hosting enterprise, failed to turn a profit by 2002, after the company spent more than $2 billion.

CEO Craig Barrett said, "I think we have cleaned up our product line. In this difficult time [these peripheral businesses] were distracting us from our core strengths."[52] Intel renewed its focus on microprocessors for PCs, servers, mobile devices and networking equipment. Together, these microprocessors generate more than 80 percent of the company's profits and sales. Intel showed its dedication to microprocessors by keeping its $4.3 billion annual research and development budget intact, and maintaining a $7.5 billion investment in new chip-making facilities. However, with microprocessors likely to make up an appreciably smaller percentage of Intel's product mix in the future, however, Intel faced numerous challenges going forward.

DISCUSSION QUESTIONS

1. Was the Intel Inside campaign worth it? What were its strengths and weaknesses?
2. Evaluate the Pentium family of processors. Did Intel make the right decision by extending the name through the Pentium 4 processor? Should the company consider changing the name of the next processor in the Pentium line?
3. Should Intel adopt its Intel Inside campaign for use with its non-PC processor products? What other marketing strategies might the company employ?
4. What do you think Intel's aggressive expansion away from its core microprocessor business? What recommendations would you make for the future?

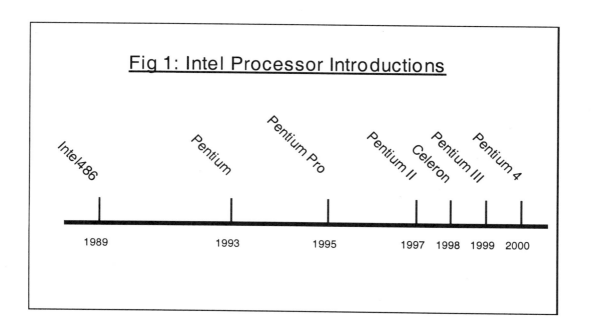

Fig 1: Intel Processor Introductions

Intel486 — 1989
Pentium — 1993
Pentium Pro — 1995
Pentium II — 1997
Celeron — 1998
Pentium III — 1999
Pentium 4 — 2000

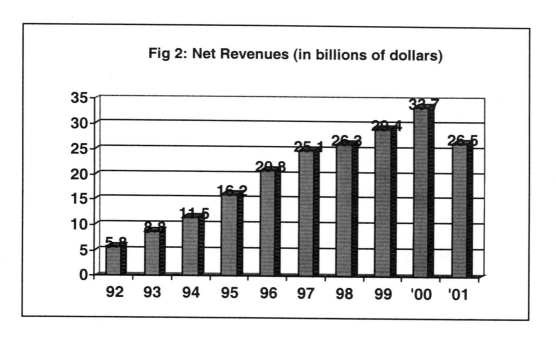

Fig 2: Net Revenues (in billions of dollars)

Year	Net Revenue
92	5.9
93	8.8
94	11.5
95	16.2
96	20.8
97	25.1
98	26.3
99	29.4
'00	33.7
'01	26.5

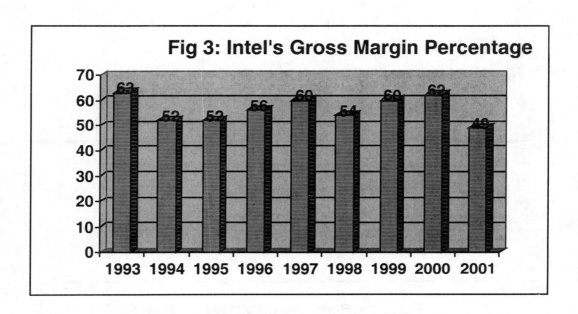

Fig 3: Intel's Gross Margin Percentage

REFERENCES

[1] This case was made possible through the cooperation of Intel and the assistance of Dennis Carter, Vice President of Marketing at Intel; Sally Fundakowski, Director of Processor Brand Marketing at Intel; and Karen Alter, Manager, Press Relations at Intel. Leslie Kimerling prepared this case with research assistance from Keith Richey under the supervision of Professor Kevin Lane Keller as the basis for class discussion.

[2] While software written for a 16-bit microprocessor would run on a 32-bit chip, the reverse was not generally true.

[3] *Wall Street Journal*, April 8, 1991. p. A1.

[4] 386 revenues are estimates found in Morgan Stanley Analyst reports dated 4/17/90 and 4/11/91.

[5] Intel chips were based on CISC (complex-instruction-set computing) technology. Microprocessor instructions are lowest level commands a processor responds to (e.g. "retrieve from memory" or "compare two numbers"). The CISC approach feeds instructions to the processor in a cluster of related operations. In contrast, RISC technology streamlines the process by using fewer instructions and imposing limits on the number of tasks contained in each instruction. The simplified instruction process ensures that tasks are performed within a split-second tick of the chips internal clock. A CISC instruction set, on the other hand, must periodically check to see that the clustered tasks are being performed in sequence. In addition, RISC processors have simpler circuits that need fewer transistors, thereby leaving extra room on the RISC chip for special, speed-enhancing circuits, such as cache memory. The speed of the RISC processor is particularly useful for computation intensive users.

[6] *Wall Street Journal*, April 8, 1991. p. A1.

[7] By 1990, Sun, Digital Equipment (DEC), Hewlett-Packard and IBM all offered RISC chips and/or RISC-based workstations.

[8] Mips Computers was acquired by Silicon Graphics in 1992.

[9] *Wall Street Journal*, April 8, 1991. p. A1.

[10] Circuit City is a retail chain selling audio and video equipment, major household appliances, and more recently, personal computer and other technology-based products. They sell primarily to the mass market.

[11] *Business Week*, April 29, 1991. In its best year with the 80286, Intel sold 4.5 million units.

[12] Circuit City is a retail chain selling audio and video equipment, major household appliances, and more recently, personal computer and other technology-based products. They sell primarily to the mass market.

[13] *Business Week*, April 29, 1991. In its best year with the 80286, Intel sold 4.5 million units.

[14] *Business Week*, September 30, 1991.

[15] *Business Week*, September 30, 1992. p. 32.

[16] *Brandweek*, October 12, 1992. p. 5.

[17] *The San Francisco Chronicle*, November 2, 1991. p. B1.

[18] *The London Sunday Times*, September 13, 1992.

[19] *San Jose Mercury News*, November 1, 1991.

[20] *Business Marketing*, February 1992, p.16.

[21] *Business Marketing*, February 1992, p. 19.

[22] *Business Marketing*, February 1992, p. 19.

[23] *Business Marketing*, October 1991, p. 48.

[24] *Marketing Computers*, May 1992, p. 43.

[25] Much of this description can be found in *Business Marketing*, January 1993, p. 36.

[26] *Business Wire*, January 13, 1993.

[27] *Advertising Age*, July 6, 1992, p. S-16.

[28] *Business Marketing*, February 1992.

[29] These are pseudonyms for the actual names chosen, but are representative of the names chosen in each of the three concept categories.

[29] Internal presentation by Intel to customer group.

[30] *San Francisco Examiner*, March, 1993.

[31] *Wall Street Journal*, October 20, 1992, p. B3.

[32] This delay represented Intel's second; Intel had announced in early 1992 that the Pentium-based computers would begin selling at the end of 1992. Subsequently, Intel had planned to introduce Pentium in conjunction with the start of sales by PC makers by the end of March 1993. In February 1993, Intel asked computer makers to delay by two months selling of Pentium-based computers to allow Intel to build up inventories of the chip to meet the expected surge in initial demand (*Wall Street Journal*, March 22, 1993).

[33] *Wall Street Journal*, March 23, 1993.

[34] *Wall Street Journal*, December 21, 1992.

[35] *Wall Street Journal*, December 21, 1992 and March 23, 1993.

[36] *Information Week*, August 23, 1993.

[37] *Advertising Age*, May 10, 1993, p.3

[38] At the name launch in October 1992, Intel had stated it expected to ship hundreds of thousands of Pentium in 1993. This number was subsequently revised downward to tens of thousands. In 1993, Intel was expected to ship 40 million 486 microprocessors. (*Information Week*, August 23, 1993).

[39] *Advertising Age*, May 10, 1993, p.3.

[40] *Wall Street Journal*, May 14 1993.

[41] *Wall Street Journal*, December 21, 1992, p. A1.

[42] *Advertising Age*, May 10, 1993.

[43] *Marketing Computers*, January 1993.

[44] *Business Wire*, November 18, 1992.

[45] Williams, Molly. "Newly Competitive AMD Challenges Intel in Corporate Chip Market." *Wall Street Journal*, December 27, 2000, p. B1.

[46] *Forbes*, "AMD Shows It's Ready for Prime Time," April 13, 2000.

[47] As quoted in *Business Week*, March 13, 2000.

[48] Williams, Molly. "Intel Is Banking on Pentium 4 Ads to Revive Sales." *Wall Street Journal*, February 15, 2001, p. B1.

[49] As quoted in *Forbes*, May 3, 1999.

[50] As quoted in *Business Week*, March 13, 2000.

[51] Edwards, Cliff. "Intel: Can CEO Craig Barrett Reverse the Slide?" *Business Week*, October 15, 2001, pp. 80-90.

[52] Boslet, Mark. "Intel's Barrett: Internet Focus of Co's Growth Strategy." Dow Jones Newswires, October 31, 2001.

THE CALIFORNIA MILK PROCESSOR BOARD: BRANDING A COMMODITY[1]

INTRODUCTION

"got milk?," one of the most popular ad campaigns of the 1990s, was borne of necessity. In February, 1993, Jeff Manning, newly appointed Executive Director of the California Milk Processor Board (CMPB), was reviewing reports on per capita U.S. consumption of milk over the last fifteen years. To anyone involved in the production and sales of milk, the numbers painted a disturbing picture. Not only had there been a steady decline in milk consumption over the previous two decades, but recently the decline was even accelerating. The CMPB's ad budget paled in comparison to big beverage marketers like Coca-Cola and Pepsi. With almost $2 billion in media spending annually in beverages as a category, Manning had to make the most of his $23 million budget to have milk's message heard among the noise.

To revitalize sales of a product in seemingly perpetual decline, Manning and ad agency Goodby, Silverstein & Partners developed the "got milk?" campaign. The campaign was based on a milk deprivation strategy that reminded consumers how inconvenient it was to be without milk with certain foods like cereal, brownies, or chocolate chip cookies. Consumers in California responded positively to the campaign, embracing the quirky ads and also consuming more milk. The campaign was licensed nationally and "got milk?" soon became a catch phrase all over America. "got milk?" was successful in California insofar as it stemmed the per capita consumption slide, but the CMPB was unable to increase consumption beyond the level of 23 gallons per person per year. Nationally, the results were similar. Critics applauded the campaign for reversing the consumption decline, but as "got milk?" entered its ninth year, some questioned whether a generic milk marketing campaign was the most effective strategy to increase consumption.

THE DAIRY INDUSTRY

The dairy industry is comprised of a relatively short list of intermediaries separating the farmer from the consumer. Basically, there are three major groups in the dairy industry: 1) the farmers who produce the milk; 2) the processors who convert raw milk into whole and lower fat milks and 3) the retailers who sell the final products. Through these channels, sales of milk reach upwards of $15 billion annually.

Farmers

As producers in the dairy industry, farmers in California are represented nationally by the National Dairy Public Relations Board (NDPRB) and the United Dairy Industry Association (UDIA), and locally by the California Milk Advisory Board (CMAB). Funding to support these groups comes directly from each farmer's profits. Hence, in order to raise money for a national advertising campaign, each farmer has to contribute some private funds which otherwise might have been used for personal or business activities. As a result, farmers are traditionally tight-fisted and scrutinize all program budgets carefully. For example, although milk sales had been declining for a number of years, the farmers did not fund a direct sales force to increase sales of milk within the channels of distribution.

Processors

The processors' primary function is to transform raw milk into the products that eventually hit the grocer's shelves (e.g., whole, 2%, 1% and skim milk). There are 40 processors of fluid milk in California. The relationship between the processors and the producers has historically been one of conflict due to incompatible goals. The producers ideally would like to produce milk for as little as possible and to sell it for as much as possible, while processors would obviously like to buy low and sell high. In contrast to the producers who are usually smaller farmers, the processors are generally big businesses that employ hundreds of people. For example, Lucerne, the processor for Safeway food stores in California, is a wholly owned subsidiary of Safeway. Processors typically either sell only fluid milk or reap the majority of their profits from the sale of fluid milk. Gravely concerned about lower sales, it was the processors who banded together in 1992 to allocate the funds that gave rise to the CMPB.

Retailers

In the early 1990s, California was dominated by two primary retailers, Safeway and Lucky food stores. Safeway obtained all of the milk sold in its stores from its Lucerne processing facility. In addition to Safeway and Lucky, there were a number of secondary grocery stores (smaller local chains) in the state. Fluid milk, in all its forms, constituted only a handful of over 50,000 products sold by most retailers. Of all these items, milk was one of the most perishable but also one of the most profitable products--commanding almost three times the profits per square foot of retail space relative to groceries. According to the Progressive Grocer's 1992 Supermarket Sales Manual, milk was the top selling supermarket product in terms of sales per shelf foot. Moreover, the dairy department racked up a total of $61.23 of sales per shelf foot, compared to $22.47 for the composite store. In fact, milk, eggs and cottage cheese were the top three products in sales per shelf foot for all supermarket products. The news was even better in terms of direct profit return on inventory dollars, an important statistic for store managers. While the average department comes in at roughly $5, milk maintained an average of a whopping $84.83 profit.

Other channels of distribution

Due in large part to the perishable nature of fluid milk, channels of distribution other than grocery stores did not account for a major portion of sales. Of the sales that did occur, school districts accounted for the majority, followed by food service establishments such as McDonald's. In California, the latest threat to milk consumption came from the school districts. Prior to 1982, all school lunches in California included milk. Since then, school children could choose from five items, including milk, for lunch. The change in school district policy certainly contributed to the 3.8 percent decline in non-commercial food service milk volume from 1986 to 1991. The trend was equally troublesome in commercial food service establishments such as McDonald's. Although the percentage of food dollars spent out of home increased to 33 percent in 1991 from 25 percent in 1971, milk did not enjoy an increase in sales to these types of establishments. In fact, commercial food service milk volume actually dropped 23 percent from 1986 to 1991.

California Milk Processor Board (CMPB).

The creation of the CMPB represented the first time that milk processors had joined together to fund advertising and public relations programs for fluid milk. The processors first became interested in the idea of a new board after consumer research revealed that per capita consumption of milk had been on a steady decline for a number of years. Sales of fluid milk was the major contributor of profits for almost all of the state's 40 milk processors. In 1993, the processors displayed their commitment to reversing the downward spiral of milk by establishing the CMPB. The idea behind the CMPB was to sufficiently fund a new board whose sole purpose was to increase the sales and consumption of fluid milk. The processors agreed to sponsor legislation requiring them to contribute three cents per gallon of milk sold in the state in the first year, with slightly smaller contributions in the remaining years of an initial three-year charter from the CMPB. In the first year, the CMPB raised about $23 million, all to promote fluid milk. Jeff Manning, previously a senior vice president with Ketchum advertising, was hired as executive director of the CMPB. Manning had previously worked with beef, potatoes, bananas and eggs in commodity marketing, and also brought a wealth of branded product marketing experience.

MARKETING A BRAND VS. MARKETING A COMMODITY

The strategies behind marketing a commodity are not the same as those for marketing a branded product. Marketing a commodity is much more similar to marketing the product category as a whole rather than marketing a single brand within the category. One obvious difference is the lack of a brand name. Not having a brand name results in many complexities, both on the supply side -- as to how the product is marketed -- and on the demand side -- as to how consumers perceive and value the product. Several differences in commodity marketing are highlighted below.

Supply side differences in commodity marketing

Perhaps the characteristic of commodity marketing most responsible for the lack of innovative programs is that each member of the industry has an input into every marketing program associated with the commodity, including the producers themselves. The fact that so many people are involved has a dramatic effect on the flexibility of the marketing programs and their ability to provide equal benefits to each group. All programs require some extra paperwork and effort from each group in the industry. As a result, adoption of new programs is difficult, and the industry members typically opt for the status quo, assuming that, perhaps mistakenly, "everyone needs the commodity." For example, something as "new" as couponing is extremely difficult in commodity markets because the redemption value would have to be paid by a broad range of processors, producers and other intermediaries.

Commodity marketers typically have significantly lower budgets available for advertising, promotion and marketing research than brand marketers. While a national brand may be able to draw on investment funds into the millions, funds for milk promotion budgets need to be raised either from the processors or directly from the farmers. If a farmer contributes three cents a gallon to a milk advertising campaign, that money comes directly out of that farmer's profits. If a farmer has sacrificed a family vacation to subsidize a "glitzy" new ad campaign, then the expectation is that the campaign will show some immediate results. Thus, once a budget is approved it is typically on a much smaller scale in commodity markets. To illustrate, the average $200 million brand will spend at least $5 million on advertising and another $5 million on promotions to the trade. In contrast, a commodity board usually spends about $5 million total--including advertising, promotion, marketing research and public relations--to increase sales of a multi-billion dollar category.

Not only are the budgets relatively smaller, but the commodity budgeting process itself is generally a slow moving, arduous system of approvals. Funding for budgets are accomplished through assessments which are contributions from each producer or processor collected on a unit basis. These assessments are usually in the form of mandatory collections put into law and administered by a government entity. Since these budgets are decided upon in advance they are fixed. In contrast to packaged goods companies, commodity marketers cannot raise short term capital by selling off assets or dipping into a emergency common fund.

Commodity marketing is also much different in the division of promotional funds allocated between "push" and "pull" strategies. Commodities generally spend almost all of the funds raised to generate some sort of pull with consumers. Advertising on television, on radio, in print, on billboards and scattered public relations spots are the most common tools used to increase sales. Pushing product through the channels of distribution is less popular. In fact, as with most major commodities, milk does not maintain a direct sales force to build relationships with retailers. With distribution penetration levels of 100 percent and equally impressive consumer penetration levels, the belief has been that there is not a pressing need to motivate retailers to carry fluid milk.

Demand side differences in commodity marketing

The demand side of commodity marketing is also quite different than the marketing of a traditional brand. The paramount challenge for commodity marketers is to attempt to change consumer attitudes and behaviors toward an entire category as opposed to trying to increase market share of a brand. Although difficult to change, category attitudes do evolve over time, and when they do change, the results can be quite dramatic. For example, a one percent increase in the consumption of milk can result in literally hundreds of millions of dollars of extra revenue to the dairy industry. Commodity marketers learned about the potentially deleterious impact of changing consumer attitudes from experiences in the beef industry. In 1950, cattlemen and meat market retailers across the country would have laughed at the notion of poultry ever coming remotely close to beef in popularity. Yet in 1990, poultry consumption passed beef in terms of per capita consumption. As the level of milk consumption has steadily declined for 15 years, Manning feared a repeat of the beef industry.

Finally, demand for commodities can be dramatically influenced by other food industries. A new product in the food service industry or the consumer packaged goods industry can increase sales exponentially. For example, when Wendy's fast food restaurants introduced hot stuffed potatoes they cleared the entire eight-twelve ounce potato market almost overnight. Similarly, when McDonald's unveiled their new salads, the iceberg lettuce market boomed. The same is true of the packaged goods industry. A new ready-to-eat raisin cereal from Kellogg's can mean millions of dollars to the raisin industry. Sometimes these new products are introduced as a result of technological advancements that make them possible. Some commodity boards are capitalizing on such opportunities by investing more funds in research and development.

THE BEVERAGE CATEGORY

When the CMPB was formed, the beverage category was characterized by intense competition and an ongoing proliferation of new products. According to a Beverage Industry survey, 1,805 new beverages were introduced in 1991 alone. All types of beverages are included in category statistics, from beer and liquor to bottled water. Media spending in the beverage category approached $2 billion, with over half of the total accounted for by beer and soft drinks. Milk spent less than 10 percent of the amount that beer spent on media. If beer and liquor sales were excluded from the totals, milk still only spent a paltry four percent of the total, even though its volume was three times that amount.

The beverage category enjoyed tremendous growth in the two decades prior to the formation of the CMPB. Between 1975 and 1993, total consumption of beverages increased by 18 percent. Although the category has increased substantially, milk was one of the few beverages to actually experience a decline in consumption over the same period. While soft drink per capita consumption increased by 80 percent from 1975 to 1991, milk consumption dropped by 10 percent and milk's market share dropped from 17 percent to 13 percent.

The winners in the non-alcoholic beverage industry were soft drinks, bottled waters and fruit drinks. All of these beverage types were perceived by consumers to be light and refreshing. In addition, they were among the most active in new product introductions, actively pursuing opportunities in diet, decaffeinated, and clear beverages. These new products capitalized on the latest industry trends -- lighter flavors, more sophisticated "adult" flavors, less sweet, more refreshing drinks with fewer calories and natural ingredients. In terms of per capita consumption and household penetration, soft drinks were the clear leader in 1993.

PREVIOUS MILK PROMOTION CAMPAIGNS

Throughout the fifteen years of declining milk consumption prior to 1993 there had been a number of advertising campaigns sponsored by one of the national or regional dairy boards. Milk advertising traditionally communicated a three-tiered message to consumers:

Adults:	Milk is good for you and should be a regular part of your diet
Teens:	Milk makes you beautiful and strong
Kids:	Milk is cool and fun

Traditional milk advertising campaigns showed a member of the target group drinking a glass of milk, followed by a brief mention of the nutrients in each glass and the benefits that would accrue to the loyal milk drinker. This relatively simple formula had been a proven winner in terms of communicating the nutritional value of milk to consumers. As a result, consumer awareness represented a major strength in terms of the positive associations consumers hold for milk. A 1992 UDIA national consumer survey revealed the following:

- 80 percent agreed that "I like the taste of cold milk."
- 89 percent agreed that "Milk is a healthful drink."
- 91 percent that "Milk is a good source of calcium."
- 83 percent agreed that "Milk is needed for growth."
- 74 percent agreed that "Adults should drink milk."
- 52 percent agreed that "I should drink more milk than I do."

In the early 1990's there were two dominant campaigns. The "Milk does a body good" campaign focused on the benefits of milk as part of a well balanced diet. In addition, the "Good fast food" campaign promoted milk, cheese and other dairy products. Both campaigns were of national scope.

In recent years, conflicting reports from consumer advocates and the milk industry created some confusion surrounding the health content of milk. First, even though prior campaigns had stressed the benefits of drinking milk, consumers remained confused about the relative nutritional value of whole milk, low fat milk, and even skim milk. In addition to the confusion about fat content, there was also widespread confusion about the effects of hormones used on dairy cows, the inability of some people to absorb calcium, whether milk causes childhood diabetes and a new report from Dr. Spock which advised mothers not to feed their children under the age of one any milk at all. The milk industry had responded to these issues through press reports, but did not respond with a national advertising campaign.

CONSUMER PREFERENCES FOR MILK IN CALIFORNIA

The per capita consumption of milk had been declining for over 15 years before the commodity board decided to take some sort of action. Perhaps of greater concern to milk producers and processors was the trend of *accelerating* decline over the past few years. In 1987, per capita consumption of milk was 26.4 gallons per person in the state of California. By 1992, per capita consumption was down to 24.8 gallons per person. Aggregated over the state population, the decline represented a $50 million loss per year in the fluid milk industry. As a result, the charter of the CMPB was clear: Increase the sales and consumption of milk in California. In particular, the CMPB focused on getting people within the population of milk drinkers to consume the equivalent of one additional eight ounce glass of milk, in any form, per week. This seemingly modest goal was hardly an easily attainable objective. Not only was the CMPB charged with reversing the decline, but also the processors wanted to actually increase consumption. If the goal of increasing consumption by one glass per week were achieved, the end result would be 3.25 incremental gallons per person, or an increase of over $100 million in profit per year.

As described above, previous advertising campaigns had been extremely effective in communicating the health benefits of milk to consumers which was good news in an age of health consciousness. Yet, this trend of health consciousness also represented a point of concern. Rather than increase overall consumption of milk by virtue of its health benefits, the last 10 years had marked a period of substantial cannibalization of milk sales. The gains in sales of low fat and skim milk had come at the expense of sales in whole milk.

Almost all consumers were aware of milk and its major types: whole, low fat (2% and 1%), and skim. Total fluid milk sales in California had actually increased by 10.9 percent in the decade of the 1980s. However, that figure was misleading because the population increased by 26 percent over the same period. In 1992, California's population was 31.3 million people. Accounting for those people who could not drink milk for various reasons such as lactose intolerance, the number of potential consumers in the state was 21.3 million people. Of those consumers, the heaviest users were under age 17.

Another positive trend for the CMPB was the changing ethnic composition of California. California traditionally attracted an extremely diverse population. In fact, by 2040 the white population was projected to be a minority in the state. Latinos were one of the fastest growing ethnic groups in the state. The good news for the CMPB was that Latinos also represented an important segment of heavy users. As a group, Latinos drank almost one-third more milk than the average individual. Latinos also drank significantly more whole milk than the rest of the population and usually bought larger sizes of milk.

Finally, research indicated that the family unit and home life was closely linked with milk. Of all milk volume consumed in the United States, 89 percent was consumed at home. Of the remaining milk consumption occasions, five percent occurred at schools, and the remainder was scattered at various establishments. Both nostalgia and ritual helped to account for this strong link between milk and the home. "Nostalgia" refers to the long-standing heritage of milk consumption in the U.S. The milkman making weekly deliveries is mentioned by consumers as one of the more vivid memories of experiences with milk. "Ritual" refers to the tendency for milk habits to be passed on from generation to generation. Many families drank milk on a regular basis at specified times -- at breakfast in cereal, at lunch with a sandwich, and at dinner with the family meal. In fact, 83 percent of all milk consumption occasions were at mealtime. In addition, many mothers regularly encouraged their children to drink milk. Research had shown that heavy adult users tended to have children that were also heavy users.

Nostalgia and ritual are grounded in history, however, and times were changing. The U.S. Census Bureau statistics revealed that the modern family size was shrinking. In 1970, the average family included 2.5 kids; by 1990, the average was 2.1 kids per family. In addition, there were now many more mothers in the workplace. In 1970, 49 percent of mothers with school age children kept a job as well. In 1990, the number of working mothers had increased to 74 percent. An outgrowth of the trend of working mothers was the surge in meals eaten outside of the home. According to the S&MM survey of buying power, Californians were spending substantially more money eating outside of the home. In 1982, per capita out of home consumption was $560, but by 1987 that number had risen to $760, a 36 percent increase. These trends did not bode well for milk consumption, a beverage consumed primarily by families inside their homes.

THE UDIA CONSUMER STUDY

In 1992, the United Dairy Industry Association (UDIA) commissioned a marketing research study to investigate the reasons behind the perpetual decline of per capita milk consumption. The study attempted to gauge consumer preferences by taking a qualitative approach through conducting 1,252 personal interviews with consumers of all age groups to talk about milk and other beverages.

The UDIA study revealed several input factors that may have been playing a role in the decline of milk consumption. These input factors included the following:

Proliferation of other beverages. As evidence to the abundance of beverages, the average American family had fifteen different beverages in the refrigerator at any given moment in time.

Lack of portability. Ninety percent of the consumption occasions for milk were inside the home, but over half of all of the meal occasions were outside of the home. While the heavy users drank 10 times the number of glasses of milk than light users inside the home, they only drank three times as much milk outside of the home.

Lack of flavor variety. To many, milk essentially came in one flavor. The lack of variety of milk flavors was especially relevant in 1993 since other beverages were flooding the market with a myriad of flavored drinks.

Not thirst quenching. A significant amount of those interviewed mentioned that one big problem with milk is lack of refreshment. Consumers noted the lack of overall refreshment, the inability to "gulp" when thirsty and the lack of a clean, crisp taste as significant barriers to milk as a thirst quenching beverage.

Lack of consumer mind share. Milk had always been a fairly "forgettable" beverage. At specific times during the day or with specific foods, milk was irreplaceable. However, beyond these particular consumption occasions, foods or outside of the house, milk was usually forgotten.

Competitive spending level. In comparison with other beverages, milk lagged well behind its competitors in terms of spending on advertising and promotion. The total media spending for milk was $70 million for milk nationwide in 1992, compared with beer media spending of $760 million and soft drink spending of $498 million.

Shared nature of consumption. As mentioned previously, milk became a part of most families through ritual and nostalgia. With such high penetration levels, virtually all people drank milk at some time during the day. This shared feature of milk often led members of a family to pace themselves and "ration" milk. If there was not enough milk for their cereal in the morning, people tended not to eat the Oreos with milk the night before. This restrained behavior could have restricted the overall consumption of milk per household.

Relationship of milk with other foods
The research included a host of transcripts from individual customer interviews and focus groups. In these interviews consumers related their consumption experiences with milk. Below are some of the typical quotes from consumers, listed by sex and age:

"With things like Oreos or any other kind of cookies or cake, none of these would be good without a big glass of milk."

- female, mid-30s

"At night with cereal, or for dunking Oreos."

- female, mid-20s

"It's a pain in the a-- because you usually find out (that you're out of milk) just after you pour the cereal."

- male, late-30s

"Of course you get P-O'd because there's not enough (milk). You can barely dampen your cereal."

- female, mid-30s

"Even Cream-o-Wheat is a drag without milk"

- female, mid-20s

"What are Cheerios? They're nothing. But you add milk and it's everything."

- male, late teens

These responses highlighted the close-knit relationship between milk and other types of food including cereal, cookies, etc. Time and time again, consumers told detailed tales of milk and its close ties with other foods. These experiences emphasized the versatility of fluid milk. Milk is used as a beverage ingredient in coffee and milk shakes; as an accompaniment to sweets such as Oreos and brownies; as a staple with cereal and sandwiches and in cooking recipes such as soups and mashed potatoes.

Indeed, beverages as a food complement were identified as one of the highly motivating forces to encourage consumers to drink beverages in general, and milk in particular. Surprisingly, nutritional requirements were only moderately motivating in beverages as a whole. Hence, the end user benefits of milk -- good for you, look and feel healthier -- moderately motivated consumers to drink milk at any point in time. Some consumers felt that if a beverage must be cold to taste good or if the drink has a strong taste, they were less motivated to drink it. For teenagers, "done something good for myself," "goes well with sweets," "satisfyingly rich" and "complements a hearty meal" were the most effective motivators.

DEVELOPING A BRANDING STRATEGY FOR MILK

Typical of most commodity markets, the milk industry had been reactive instead of proactive when it came to marketing. For years, the problems of the milk producers in terms of declining per capita consumption had been obscured by the more dominant trend of increasing population. With population growth slowing in California, the industry players could no longer afford to overlook the decline in consumption. To meet CMPB's objectives of reversing the declining trend in per capita milk consumption, Manning was considering several strategic options:

1. Invest in R&D to expand the number of flavors available
2. Expand the potential usage occasions
3. Cooperate with consumer packaged goods companies for joint promotions
4. Develop an advertising campaign to clear up confusion about the health benefits of milk
5. Generate a new image for milk through advertising
6. Target Latinos and aging Californians

Upon reviewing each option, Manning recalled the objective of increasing consumer consumption of milk by one glass per week. Given that the CMPB was created especially for this task with only a two-year charter, Manning felt a sense of urgency to act quickly.

STRATEGY IMPLEMENTATION

After carefully considering all the options, Manning and representatives from the CMPB's advertising agency, Goodby, Silverstein & Partners in San Francisco, decided that the best strategy to increase the per capita consumption of milk was to embark on a new, innovative advertising campaign. Nobody doubted that previous milk campaigns successfully achieved positive shifts in consumer attitudes towards milk. What was missing, however, was a corresponding change in consumer behavior. Consumers knew milk was good and thought they should drink more of it, but they never thought enough about milk to be motivated to change their consumption habits. The typical milk campaign -- emphasizing calcium and other vitamins --caused consumers to tune out. The recommended campaign had to break the mold for milk advertising, grab attention and shake consumers out of their "milk malaise." Manning knew that other beverages had successfully built up strong brand images over the last decade, and he believed that milk could do the same by taking a more light-hearted approach which talked directly to consumers. Manning reflected back on the decision:

> The dairy industry has taken itself too seriously. Eating is a form of entertainment...the most popular form of entertainment in California, the USA and the world. Get people smiling at your advertising and they will look, listen and, we believe, consume more milk.

Given the limited resources of the CMPB, the new campaign had to address the behavior issue directly and quickly.

Campaign objectives

Although the new advertising campaign was not like anything ever tried before in commodity marketing, the campaign was being funded by the commodity board and had to satisfy their objectives, as follows:

1. <u>Change consumer behavior</u>. The CMPB's foremost priority was to increase milk consumption by one occasion per week. Positive attitudes towards milk failed to reverse the decline in consumption. It was felt that the new campaign should change the way consumers think about milk, which would hopefully increase the potential number of milk occasions.

2. <u>Make consumers think about milk</u>. Although so many people drink milk everyday, milk suffered from a complete lack of consumer mind share. People just did not think about milk often enough at home, and they almost never thought about milk outside of the home. In order for any campaign to be successful, this lack of mind share had to change. One way to implement the change was to get consumers to stop taking milk for granted, to take them by surprise by creating a new and different image for milk.

3. <u>Halt sales decline</u>. Obviously, sales represented the bottom line for the CMPB. The advertising campaign needed to motivate people to buy more milk and subsequently get people to drink more milk. A high awareness campaign that did not result in subsequent changes in milk consumption would not be acceptable.

Target market

In order to generate quick results, it was decided to target "regular" users of milk who used the product several times a week or more. Regular users – 70 percent of the California market -- already had favorable attitudes toward drinking milk and presumably could potentially be influenced in the short-term. In contrast, non-users or light users typically restrained from milk for actual or perceived health reasons, which probably could not be changed very quickly. Manning explained:

> If the 21 million people in the state that we regard as our "marketing universe" -- those people who regularly consume milk in any form, be it a glass of milk, a bowl of cereal, instant pudding or whatever -- increased consumption by just one serving a week in any form, consumption of milk would increase in California by 9-13 percent.

Since milk was a popular beverage across a wide range of demographic and psychographic groups, past segmentation strategies were of little use. Instead, regular users were segmented according to behavior. Marketing research revealed that many consumers had specific times where milk was clearly the beverage of choice. These occasions typically identified milk as the perfect complement to certain foods. For example, marketing research revealed that cereal, cookies and peanut butter and jelly sandwiches all *needed* milk or the foods were seen as simply not the same. Regular users recognized this intimate relationship of milk with food, and they openly discussed the complementary foods in focus groups.

The behavior segmentation strategy focused attention on *when* and *where* consumers drank milk. First and foremost, almost all milk is consumed at home. The UDIA study had shown that consumers rarely drink milk outside of the home, and even when they drink milk at home it is generally during the same usage occasions. Second, as discussed above, milk is considered an essential complement to certain types of foods. The focus groups revealed that consumers talked about milk with other foods, not as a drink by itself. This was particularly revealing because although the questions typically began with a general statement about milk, the discussions almost always gravitated to milk with food. Third, consumers tended to discuss milk and these foods as though they were the same food (Oreos and milk, peanut butter and jelly sandwiches and milk, etc.). It became evident that not only were these foods highly associated with milk, but that these foods were the driving force behind milk consumption and the potential key to any future increase.

"got milk?" Campaign Creative Development

Based on the market research, Manning and the Goodby, Silverstein and Partners advertising agency decided to reach out to the regular users with a "deprivation strategy." The most effective way to capitalize on milk's relationship with food was to create an advertising campaign that paired the two together. Each ad in the campaign highlighted one of milk's perfect complements: cereal, chocolate chip cookies, peanut butter and jelly sandwiches, etc. The clever, creative twist, however, was to deprive the main character of milk. The end result was delicious food *without milk* -- the deprivation strategy. Certain foods without milk represented "cruel and unusual punishment" to most people, and the advertising campaign would set out to drive this message home. In each of the ads, a meal or snack is essentially ruined because of the absence of milk. Manning expressed his thoughts:

> Sell milk with food. The idea is almost frighteningly simple and obvious. And yet, as we reviewed milk advertising from around the country (and from around the world), we found that food was almost totally absent. We don't know why. Perhaps in an attempt to compete against soft drinks, the dairy industry lost contact with its roots. Consumers haven't. They will tell you time and time again that food -- certain foods -- drive their milk decision.

The television ads gradually built the tension that was so critical to the deprivation strategy. Each television ad began with a close-up of one of the food complements such as the peanut butter and jelly sandwich. Once the desire for the food is established, the protagonist takes a big bite. While joyfully chewing the food, the protagonist casually reaches for a glass of milk. Unfortunately, there is no more milk left in the container. A desperate search for even a single drop ensues, but all efforts are in vain. At the height of anguish, the voice-over pronounces, "got milk?".

58

One memorable ad showed an obnoxious businessperson on a busy city sidewalk talking on a cellphone. After loudly informing the person on the other end of the conversation that they are fired, the business person gets run over by a truck. The next scene takes place in "heaven" – an all-white room while soothing music plays. On a table sits a plate of Frisbee-sized chocolate chip cookies, which the businessperson greedily devours. Searching for milk to wash down the cookies, he opens the refrigerator and sees row upon row of milk cartons. He reaches for one, but finds it to be empty. Grabbing another, he discovers that it too is empty. Finally it dawns on him: "Wait a minute, where am I?" The "got milk?" logo appears with a flame effect as the man screams.

The "got milk?" tagline urged consumers to quickly run to the refrigerator to make sure the answer was "yes." It was felt that this deprivation strategy would bring back the consumer mind share for milk and begin to recreate a positive image for milk as a beverage. The ads were humorous and well received by focus groups. The campaign broke away from previous milk advertisements in two important ways. First, there was never any mention of how milk could benefit a healthy diet. Consumers presumably already knew about the benefits, so the new campaign instead urged them to change their behavior. Second, milk was never actually shown in the ads. Whereas in the past, milk was shown without food, in the new campaign, food was shown without milk. The CMPB felt that the deprivation strategy would increase mind share for milk precisely because the ads hit consumers where milk (or lack thereof) hurt them the most.

Additional Communications Programs

The creative strategy lent itself to using complementary foods as promotional tools for milk. If consumers purchased more of the foods that naturally went with milk, they should also buy more milk. Joint promotions were run with many major brands including each of the types of foods featured in the advertising campaign. One of the more bold joint promotions was a Wheaties cereal box with the "got milk?" logo in place of the brand name. Other promotions included milk coupons on many recognizable brands of complementary foods located throughout the supermarket, point of purchase displays, shelf talkers at the complementary food locations, and "got milk?" check-out dividers. Billboards were also used extensively to reinforce the television campaign. The billboards featured the same foods as the television ads with one bite taken out. Of course, each billboard prominently displayed the key question' "got milk?".

The additional communication programs complemented the television advertising by focusing on the relationship between milk and food. Breaking with the past milk campaigns, Manning and his team decided to leverage milk's relationship with food by partnering with those foods instead of relying on pulling consumers over to the dairy case. The complementary television, radio, print and billboard campaigns all leveraged this relationship and capitalized on the advertising budgets of several major brands of cereals and cookies.

Media Strategy

In order to maximize the impact on consumer behavior, the media strategy focused on consumers in the place where they typically used milk -- in the home -- and where they typically bought milk -- in the supermarket. According to Manning there were three ideal times to communicate the milk message: on the way to the store, in the store and at home where milk could be immediately consumed. The media strategy complemented the overall communications strategy to reach this goal. The advertising creative strategy motivated consumers to crave the featured food and/or check their refrigerators for availability of milk. The media strategy therefore focused primarily on television as the medium, thereby catching consumers in their homes where 90 percent of total milk is consumed. Furthermore, the media buy for the ads typically concentrated on those times of day when consumers drank the most milk, i.e. mornings during breakfast, late evening snacks, etc. It was thought that timing ads in this manner -- given the "call to action" nature of the campaign -- could potentially lead to more impulse uses of milk. Each usage occasion was further broken down into the type of user in order to purchase television advertising time. Children were targeted in the early morning hours as well as late afternoons, while adults were targeted at prime time and late night snack times.

In order to capitalize on the remaining communications expenditures within the store, the "got milk?" billboards were located near supermarkets as a reminder to consumers before they entered the store. The heavy dose of outdoor advertising included a variety of billboards and signs at bus shelters. The intention was to get consumers thinking about milk before they entered the store in order to motivate them to buy milk once they were inside.

Finally, a key objective of the media strategy was to advertise at a level competitive with other beverages. The annual budget of $23 million more than doubled the previous year's spending and placed milk among the top ten advertising spenders in all of California, on par with Coca Cola and Budweiser. Hence the campaign possessed the muscle to compete with other beverages for the first time in milk advertising history. Only one question remained: Would the deprivation strategy work?

"GOT MILK?" SUCCESS

Immediate Results

The "got milk?" campaign was launched in November 1993. Although focus groups indicated that consumers liked the ads, the actual launch exceeded all expectations. The campaign zoomed to a 60 percent aided recall level in only three months, enjoyed 70 percent awareness within six months, and surpassed the long-running "It Does a Body Good" campaign in top-of-mind awareness in less than a year. The "got milk?" campaign quickly became a consumer favorite, prompting a L.A. Times reporter to comment, "Since the ad campaign began, it has reached a near-cult following."

Not only did the campaign get consumers talking, it also exceeded initial expectations of merely stemming the sales decline by increasing actual milk consumption. The number of consumers who reported consuming milk at least "several times a week" jumped from 72 percent at the start of the campaign to 78 percent a year later. California household consumption of milk increased every month in the first year after the launch except for the first two months that the campaign began. This performance was in sharp contrast to the rest of the country where consumption actually declined over the same period. In the year prior to the campaign's launch, California milk processors experienced a decline in sales volume of 1.67 percent or $18 million. A year after the launch, sales volume increased 1.07 percent or $13 million, for a total turnaround of $31 million. On a month-to-month comparison, sales volume had increased every month to rise 6.8 percent by the end of the first year.

"got milk?" Goes National

The "got milk?" advertising campaign met with critical acclaim, as well as financial success. In 1995, the ads won an Effie Award, as well as top honors from several other major advertising award committees. In September of that same year, "got milk?" joined the familiar "milk mustache" program as a national campaign, and the Goodby Silverstein ads began receiving national exposure in television, print and outdoor media. Though the only commonly shared element of the two commercial series was the prominence of milk, consumers assumed that the two series originated from the same source. In fact, the dairy farmers' group Dairy Management Inc. (DMI) controlled the national "got milk?" campaign while the National Milk Processors' Education Program (MilkPEP) funded the milk moustache campaign. DMI had approached the CMPB to purchase the licensing rights to "got milk?" to replace their own campaign. In California, the CMPB continued to govern the "got milk?" campaign, employing Goodby Silverstein & Partners to develop the ads. Leo Burnett USA handled the national "got milk?" creative after Goodby Silverstein licensed their work, while Bozell Worldwide did the milk moustache ad work. Perhaps in an effort to consolidate the equity achieved by the separate campaigns, MilkPEP obtained licensing rights to the slogan in 1998 and replaced the milk mustache ads' tagline "Milk. What a Surprise" with Dairy Management's "got milk?" That same year, the two milk groups forged a partnership that combined their considerable advertising budgets, pooling Dairy Management's $70 million TV and outdoor budget and MilkPEP's $110 million milk mustache budget.

Products and Partnerships

In addition to buying more milk, consumers also responded positively to the advertising, and further fueled its cult status, by buying "got milk?" licensed products. Such products included t-shirts, baby bottles, mugs bearing the "got milk?" logo and even a "got milk?"themed Barbie doll. Jeff Manning, director of the CMPB, wrote a book about the "got milk?" campaign. Beginning in 1995, "got milk?" pursued major national food corporations to establish joint partnerships. Jeff Manning approached these companies with the simple proposal: "We have $22 million dollars to spend in the state of California, and we'd like to sell more of your product. Would you like to work with us?"[2] Companies such as General Mills, Nestle, Quaker, Keebler and even the Girl Scouts of America agreed to work with the CMPB. These partnerships led to numerous creative advertisements and promotions.

For example, Goodby Silverstein created an ad that featured General Mills' Trix cereal "spokesperson," the Trix Rabbit. The ad, which first ran in California in April 1995 opened with a shot of a unkempt young male prowling the aisles of a convenience store late at night. After grabbing three cereal boxes, one of which is a box of Trix, he heads for the checkout line. The cashier, upon noticing that his purchases include Trix, delivers the line "Trix are for kids" with an eerie laugh. The young man races home, locks himself inside his house with several deadbolts, and pours nearly the whole box of Trix into a bowl. Then, the commercial takes a bizarre, and humorous, twist. With the help of animation, the man unzips his body to reveal the Trix Rabbit beneath the disguise. Of course, when the Rabbit attempts to pour milk from a carton onto his ill-gotten bounty, he finds the carton empty.

The national campaign also consisted of print and outdoor advertising, as the California campaign had. A popular billboard featured the characters Snap, Crackle and Pop gathered glumly around a milk-less bowl of Rice Krispies. Some other notable characters that appeared in print and outdoor ads were Cookie Monster, the California Raisins and the Girl Scouts. The CMPB first approached the Girl Scouts about the possibility of a partnership in 1996, but the organization initially balked because they felt a "got milk?" tie-in would be too commercial. But the CMPB contacted the Girl Scouts again the following year and pointed out that "got milk?" did not represent a corporate dairy interest. The Girl Scouts agreed to participate. Goodby Silverstein designed a billboard that showed a group of Girl Scouts looking directly at the viewer, with scores of boxes tucked under their arms and lying about behind them. As usual, the words "got milk?" were placed prominently at the center of the ad. The Girl Scouts also agreed to endorse milk by supplying local troops with "got milk?" pins for girls to wear during door-to-door sales of their cookies.

Other promotions included a partnership with Dole that place "got milk?" stickers on 100 million clusters of bananas throughout the country and a venture with Mattel that developed a "got milk?" Hot Wheels milk truck. In October 1998, the CMPB established the www.gotmilk.com web site to enable consumers to learn more about milk and the "got milk?" campaign, and purchase a full line of "got milk?" products directly.

"GOT MILK?" RECONSIDERED

Revising the Deprivation Strategy

The "got milk?" campaign took a step away from its deprivation formula in October 1997. Earlier in the year, deprivation "got milk?" ads garnered less-than-the-usual enthusiasm when shown in focus groups. The consumers involved liked the new ads, but many gave responses that indicated they found the ads somewhat familiar or predictable. Concerned that consumers might soon tire of the ads altogether, the CPMB sought alternatives to the deprivation strategy. The task of redesigning the "got milk?" campaign fell to Goodby Silverstein. The advertising firm came to the CMPB with two ideas for a new ad series, one starring British comic Rowan Atkinson in his role as Mr. Bean, another built around a fictional milk-deprived town called Drysville. Soon after the ideas were pitched to the CMPB, Atkinson informed the agency that his schedule did not permit him to star in the "got milk?" spots. The Drysville scripts therefore earned the responsibility of redefining the "got milk?" campaign.

The idea for the ads took the deprivation principle and expanded it throughout an entire town. The first script, called "Ballad," gave viewers a drive-through look at the Town

Without Milk, as Drysville came to be known. During the ad, the camera passes by daily scenes that one would expect to occur in any town, the difference being that in Drysville the absence of milk made these scenes depressing rather than enjoyable. The viewer sees a police officer forlornly eyeing a box of donuts, a mother pouring tap water on her child's bowl of cereal, and a teenager paying cash to steal a glance at a photograph of a glass of milk. Another ad employed a "COPS"-style car chase as Drysville police pursue and apprehend a carload of teenagers who drove to the next town to purchase milk and are in the process of greedily consuming it when they get pulled over. The effectiveness and appropriateness of the "got milk?" tagline, which had achieved 90 percent awareness in four years, was never in question; it appeared at the end of each Drysville spot. The Drysville campaign worked as far as re-engaging the consumer with the "got milk?" campaign, but research revealed that the deprived town did not affect consumers' immediate consumption or purchase decisions to the same degree that the traditional ads did. In his book, Jeff Manning explained the difference:

> Drysville's advertising was working more on people's heads than their mouths and stomachs. People felt the deprivation only intellectually, almost abstractly. Deprivation was only happening to "them," the people of Drysville, not to me, [the consumer].[3]

Following a year in Drysville, the CMPB returned to isolated cases of deprivation for its "got milk?" scripts. According to Manning, the Drysville campaign was instructive because the agency realized that not every "got milk?" ad needed to pair food and milk. Several subsequent spots cast the dangers of deprivation in a different light. The "Paws" ad featured a grandmotherly type who attempts to feed her dozens of pet cats nondairy creamer when she runs out of milk. An ad called "Y2Kud" spoofed millennium paranoia by showcasing a "Y2K-compatible" cow that continues to graze after a power outage occurs the first minute of 2000. The CMPB kept with the "got milk?" approach, and announced in 1998 its decision to support of the campaign through 2002 at a cost of roughly $25 million per year. Pointing to a 1.6 percent rise in milk sales in the state for 1997, as compared with zero growth in national sales, as proof that the marketing program was still working.

Limited Growth

The "got milk?" and milk mustache campaigns helped fuel a one percent growth in milk sales during 1997. The dual campaigns did not enjoy similar success, however, the following year. MilkPEP spent $84.5 million in 1998 and Dairy Management spent $70 million, but national fluid milk sales dropped 0.4 percent for that year. In the three years since both campaigns began targeting national audiences, milk sales had risen by 1.1 percent, but the growth failed to offset the cost in the minds of many in the milk industry. The stalled growth in national milk sales sent many industry executives searching for alternatives to the expensive milk marketing campaigns. MilkPEP executives contended that national price increases between 10 and 15 percent in 1998 accounted for the dragging sales. In California, the price of milk rose even more sharply. A gallon of 1% lowfat milk cost as much as $3.48 in San Diego during 1998, compared with a national average of $2.69 per gallon of lowfat milk for the same year. By 1999, the cost of a gallon of milk in California had risen to over four dollars in some cities. Perhaps fearing that the rising cost of milk would once again yield a disheartening sales decline, the CMPB allocated $23 million dollars to the "got milk?" campaign in 1999. Between the start of the campaign in 1993 and 2001, milk sales in California remained flat. "We basically stopped the hemorrhaging,"[4] said Jeff Manning.

Milk Adds Flavor

In spite of MilkPEP's claim that high prices were responsible for the 1998 sales decline, some individual dairies grew impatient with MilkPep and Dairy Management. In the interest of stimulating milk sales by appealing to young milk drinkers, some dairies began manufacturing portable and flavored milk products. Many of these dairies developed extensive marketing programs in support of their new product launches. One of the biggest dairies in the nation, Dean Foods, invested $40 million to upgrade its plants for the production of Chugs, a portable and flavored milk product packaged in plastic containers made to look like old-fashioned glass bottles. The company spent an additional $12 million on an integrated marketing campaign to support the new products with television, print and outdoor advertising. Ads with the theme "Milk where you want it" showed kids and teenagers with Chugs bottles in their pockets. Jim Page, Dean's Vice President of Marketing, offered the following explanation for his company's independent marketing:

> I feel very good about what 'milk mustache' and 'got milk?' has done. It increased awareness but not consumption. Our job is to take it to the next level.[5]

The results of Dean's new initiative were favorable. Within a year after the company had introduced Chugs in 1997 to its first target market, Florida, overall sales of milk pints had risen 77 percent and sales of chocolate pints had risen 96 percent. In November of that same year, Dean introduced Chugs to Chicago and witnessed a 60 percent increase in milk sales within three months. By 1999, Chugs contributed more than $100 million in sales to the company. Overall sales of flavored milk, which rose 20 percent in 1999, contributed to 40 percent of the total growth in milk sales that year, despite only comprising six percent of total milk sales. Believing flavored milk could stimulate further growth in the following year, the CMPB approved an ad with the extended tagline "got chocolate milk?" The ad showed a teenaged boy looking in the fridge for chocolate milk to drink. Finding none, the boy takes a box of chocolate flavored cereal from the cabinet and pours regular milk into the box. When he finishes drinking the concoction, he puts the milk-sodden cereal box back on the shelf.

Health Issues

In 1998, the CMPB voted to maintain the "got milk?" campaign through 2002, but eventually incorporated a "milk is healthy" message into some of the advertisements. National research uncovered the fact that children whose mothers drink milk would consume twice the milk as children of non-milk drinkers. Additionally, the research revealed that a vast majority of women aged 25 to 49 only drank milk in order to prevent bone disease as they aged. Part of the success of the original "got milk?" strategy was attributed by the CMPB to the fact that the ads focused on milk deprivation and not health benefits, which consumers were already aware of. The 25-49 year-old female market segment's health concerns, and the link between mothers and children's milk consumption, prompted the CMPB to develop an ad highlighting a health benefit of milk. Goodby Silverstein created an ad that graphically reinforced milk's contribution to building strong bones. The ad, which debuted in the spring of 1999, opened with a shot of a mother urging her two children to drink milk at a meal. The children protest that their neighbor, a Mr. Miller, told them he doesn't need milk to stay healthy. At which point the children look out the window to wave at Mr. Miller, who is gardening next door. Mr. Miller waves back, then stoops to pick up a wheelbarrow. When he lifts, his arms break off at the shoulders. The ad closes with a shot of the two children rapidly gulping down their glasses of milk.

The "got milk?" campaign added a spot in 2000 that emphasized milk's role in preventing osteoporosis. In the ad, a group of elderly men sauntered into a roadhouse and each ordered milk. This act draws ridicule from several tough-looking characters, so the older men gulp their glasses of milk and invite the toughs to "step outside." The ad closes with shots of the older generation pummeling the younger crowd. A voice-over discusses the preventative health benefits of the beverage as "got milk?" flashes onto the screen. Another ad features a trash-talking milk carton informing playground basketball players that their game is off because they drink soda and not milk. An additional milk promotion effort that bore a health message began in July 2000, with the aid of the consolidated advertising budgets of MilkPEP and Dairy Management. That month, "Milk" became an official sponsor of Major League Soccer. In addition to grassroots MLS programs that promote the nutritional value in milk, the joint promotional plan involved the appearance of prominent MLS players in "got milk?" advertising at the beginning of 2001.

Got Next?

The "got milk?" campaign obviously resonated with consumers. Not only did it halt a two-decade decline in milk sales and stimulate additional sales, but it touched off a market for licensed merchandise and "got milk?" knockoffs. By the end of the decade, other advertisers had co-opted the slogan for such marketing projects as "Got Wine?," "Got Jesus?," "Got Porn?," "Got Stickers?" and "Got Books?" Jeff Manning contended that the success of the "got milk?" campaign demonstrated both the value and power of advertising. In his opinion, "got
milk?" accomplished more than stopping the disastrous slide of milk sales:

> "got milk?" changed the world of advertising. It proved, perhaps more convincingly than any other campaign . . . that products, even ancient products like milk, can be resurrected with smart, creative advertising.[6]

Clearly, the "got milk?" campaign stopped the decline in the milk industry, not just in California, but around the country. It accomplished this revitalization solely with effective marketing, since the product itself and consumer attitudes about its health benefits remained constant throughout. But as the "got milk?" ads became more familiar to the consumer, their effectiveness decreased. When the sole attempt by the CMPB to break with the deprivation formula with Drysville failed to entice consumers in the same manner as the original ads, the CMPB returned to the original recipe. The question of greatest priority was therefore, How long will milk-deprivation work? Beyond that, how long will the "got milk?" catchphrase last? Will fresh and creative advertising mark the next cycle in milk growth, or will product innovations like flavored and portable milk make a bigger difference, as they have in some markets already? Jeff Manning believed that the latter case would prove to be the key to future growth. He indicated that sales of milk will not increase dramatically "until the milk processors come out with a wider variety of new packages, products and flavors."[7]

DISCUSSION QUESTIONS

1. What associations do consumers have for milk? What are the implications of these associations in terms of building brand equity for and increasing the consumption of milk?
2. Evaluate the CMPB marketing program. What do you see as its strengths and weaknesses? What changes would you make?
3. What are the problems or challenges faced by the CMPB now that milk consumption has reached a plateau?

REFERENCES

[1] This case was made possible through the cooperation of the California Milk Processor Board and the assistance of Executive Director Jeff Manning. Sanjay Sood prepared this case with research assistance from Keith Richey under the supervision of Professor Kevin Lane Keller as the basis for class discussion.

[2] Jeff Manning, personal interview, September 1997.

[3] Manning, Got Milk? : The Book. p 182.

[4] Rebecca Flass. "California Processors Vote to Continue 'Got Milk?'" *Adweek*, March 26, 2001, p. 5.

[5] As quoted in *Advertising Age*, January 1998.

[6] Manning, Got Milk? : The Book. p 185.

[7] Rebecca Flass. "California Processors Vote to Continue 'Got Milk?'" *Adweek*, March 26, 2001, p. 5.

RED BULL:
BUILDING BRAND EQUITY IN NEW WAYS[1]

INTRODUCTION

Red Bull GmbH was founded in 1985 by Dietrich Mateschitz, an Austrian who was the former marketing manager for Procter & Gamble's Blendax. Mateschitz hit upon the idea of Red Bull during one of his many business trips to Asia, where an energy drink called "Krating Daeng" ("Red Bull" in Thai) was very popular. After working for two years to create a carbonated version in a colorful can, Mateschitz launched Red Bull Energy Drink in Austria in 1987 using the slogan "Red Bull verleiht Flüüügel" ("Red Bull gives you wiiings"). Red Bull was available exclusively in Austria for five years, and gradually rolled out in other European nations. Part of the growth strategy was to enter new markets slowly and methodically, in order to maximize buzz and build anticipation.

Red Bull achieved remarkable growth considering the product was available in only one stock-keeping unit (SKU), the silver 250 ml (8.3 oz.) can, and received little traditional advertising support. Red Bull's above-the-line marketing activities were limited to television commercials that adhered to the same format: using animated shorts to reinforce the "Red Bull gives you wiiings" message. By 1997, a decade after it was launched in Austria, Red Bull was available in 25 markets globally, including Western and Eastern Europe, New Zealand and South Africa. During that same period, Red Bull sales volume grew from 1.1 million units to over 200 million units. Red Bull continued its exponential growth into the 2000s by adding new markets and implementing its proven formula for success.

Several major beverage companies, including Coca-Cola, Anheuser-Busch and PepsiCo, began introducing similar products in the year 2000. Despite the additional competition, Red Bull maintained its energy drink market share lead in every mature market. Its meteoric rise and continued dominance of its category made Red Bull was one of the most successful new beverages in history. The challenge for the brand would be to continue its stellar growth as current competitors became more aggressive and additional competitors entered the market.

DESIGNING THE PRODUCT

After witnessing firsthand the potential of energy drinks in the Asian market, Dietrich Mateschitz negotiated with a Thai beverage manufacturer called TC Pharmaceuticals for the rights to license its energy drink recipe. In exchange for a 51 percent stake in Red Bull, TC Pharmaceuticals sold the foreign licensing rights in 1984. Mateschitz adapted the product to Western tastes by diluting it, lowering the caffeine content, and adding carbonation. Red Bull essentially invented the "functional energy" beverage category, named thus because the beverages were meant to be consumed for energy, not enjoyment, purposes.

Both the Thai version and Mateschitz's version of Red Bull contained the following energy-enhancing ingredients: caffeine, taurine and glucuronolactone. One 250 ml can of Red Bull had 80 mg of caffeine, about as much as a weak cup of coffee (a small coffee at Starbucks may contain more than 200 mg of caffeine). Both taurine and glucuronolactone are chemicals which occur naturally in the human body. Taurine is a conditionally-essential amino acid, a detoxifying agent, and a metabolism transmitter. Glucuronolactone is a metabolism transmitter and a detoxifying agent. These three ingredients, along with a variety of sugars and vitamins, contributed to the following properties claimed by Red Bull:

- Improves physical endurance
- Stimulates metabolism and helps eliminates waste substances
- Improves overall feeling of well-being
- Improves reaction speed and concentration
- Increases mental alertness

Between 1984 and 1986, Dietrich Mateschitz led a team of professional marketers developing the product and packaging concept for Red Bull. The process was extensive: the team conducted large amounts of market research and tested more than 200 packaging proposals.

Flavor
Red Bull's flavor was intended to communicate the product's value as a functional energy drink. It was sweet and carbonated like a cola, but also had what some consumers described as a "medicinal" taste. The strong taste indicated to consumers that the product was more than mere refreshment. "We never cared about the taste a lot because we are more concerned about the function of the product,"[2] said Norbert Kraihamer, Red Bull's Group Marketing and Sales Director. Still, directions printed on the Red Bull can recommended that the drink be served "well-chilled," since most consumers found the taste more pleasant when they drank it cold.

Package
Red Bull came in a single package, a slender silver-and-blue 250 mL can. The small can, which originated in Japan, signaled to consumers that the contents were different from and stronger than traditional soft drinks. The Red Bull logo -- an Oriental-themed depiction of two (red) bulls about to collide head-on in front of yellow sun -- appeared prominently on the front of the can. Under the logo, the words "Energy Drink" succinctly communicated the product's benefits. Consumers could only buy the cans singly; they were not offered in six-packs or cases. Some retailers sold Red Bull in these larger denominations for convenience purposes, but still charged the same amount per can (i.e., a case of Red Bull cans would cost the same as 24 cans bought separately). Red Bull also developed a brown glass bottle for use in locations where it could not list the can, but the bottle design was less preferable to consumers than the can. When Red Bull launched in Germany, demand quickly outpaced supply and the company was forced to sell bottles when it ran out of cans. Sales of the product fell off the torrid pace as soon as the bottles were introduced. Red Bull used this example to show retailers the revenue they could lose if they only allowed the glass bottles.

Positioning
Mateschitz also devised the brand positioning, "Revitalizes body and mind." This phrase conveyed the tangible benefit of the product in an easy-to-grasp manner. It also covered a broad set of appropriate consumption occasions. Mateschitz intended Red Bull to be drank

whenever consumers needed a lift, whether it was morning, noon or night. This way, Red Bull consumption would not be limited to certain occasions or activities, the way other energy-related beverages had been positioned (see Fig. 1). This broad positioning was designed to enable growth into a variety of market segments. Red Bull's advertising did not specify any consumption occasions, which further facilitated an elastic positioning.

The early adopters of Red Bull in Austria and surrounding markets were dancers, clubbers and ravers who used the drink to stay fresh at late-night parties. This party association was key for Red Bull as it expanded into other markets, because hip nightspots generated significant buzz. In these venues, Red Bull was used primarily as a mixer. Red Bull appreciated the business that mixing brought, but the company emphasized a variety of usages in its marketing. "We are not against mixing," said Norbert Kraihamer. "We even appreciate it to a degree. But, over time we must make sure that the product is regarded as much more than a mixer. This is not a drink for a restaurant, this is a nutritional item."[3] Other early adopters of Red Bull included truck drivers who used the drink to stay awake on long drives and students who drank it to help them concentrate during their studies. Though most of the original Red Bull customers were young, the company intended the brand to appeal to consumers of all ages.

Price

From the start, Red Bull pursued a premium pricing strategy. Mateschitz reasoned that consumers would be less likely to believe in Red Bull's energy-enhancing properties if it was priced the same as a cola beverage. By charging a premium price, Red Bull could reinforce the energy positioning and also stake out a unique territory in the beverage market. In every market, Red Bull set a price at least 10 percent greater than the most-expensive competitor in order to maintain a "best of class" positioning. Norbert Kraihamer explained the rationale:

> We are much more expensive than [cola]. This is OK because ours is an efficiency product, so we can charge this price premium, which is the secret of its success. . . . Due to the respect for a price premium brand . . . we can charge what is fair for the benefit.[4]

Priced between $1.99 and $3.00 in convenience stores, the 250 mL can of Red Bull cost up to 300 percent more per ounce than traditional soft drinks.

LAUNCH IN AUSTRIA

Red Bull encountered difficulty getting approved for sale in Austria. The Austrian government at the time had three categories for food and drug: 1) traditional food; 2) dietary food and 3) pharmaceutical. Red Bull sought categorization as a traditional food, but this category restricted its ability to make claims about performance benefits. Therefore, Red Bull lobbied to create an entirely new category: functional food. Functional foods had some medicinal benefits beyond a dietary product, but also contained food properties that made them different from a pharmaceutical. The functional food category combined regulations from the three other categories and required almost as much documentation as a pharmaceutical product. For example, any health benefit claim had to be supported by scientific evidence.

In order to support its claims about performance benefits, the company commissioned various studies from scientists. Red Bull's product documentation totaled more than 3,000 pages, almost as much evidentiary support as required for a pharmaceutical product. The heavily regulated functional foods category in Austria created a barrier for entry that competitors were initially unwilling to overcome. The cost of commissioning the required scientific studies was simply too high. This economic barrier, combined with the fact that the energy drink category was still unproven, led to a lack of competitors in Austria for over five years after its 1987 introduction.

While Red Bull needed reams of scientific evidence to enter a market, it did not oversell consumers on the science behind the product. Norbert Kraihamer explained, "We do not force volumes of scientific evidence down the consumer's throat. Our principle is to make the product available in the right places at the right times with the right message. Consumers then try it and make up their own mind if it works."[5] Encouraging product trial was the keystone of Red Bull's marketing strategy. Red Bull's above-the-line marketing was minimal, and for the first five years in Austria (1987-1991) the company's marketing expenditure ranged between only $700,000 and $1.4 million annually. During that time, net sales grew from $700,000 to $10 million.

MARKETING RED BULL

Dietrich Mateschitz reasoned that the best method to get consumers to try the product was testimonials from peers who bought into Red Bull. Therefore, word-of-mouth -- which Norbert Kraihamer called "the oldest and best media in the world"[6] -- was the central component in all Red Bull marketing activities. Word-of-mouth drove awareness of the brand in the early stages of entering a market. As knowledge of the product spread, a buzz would build around the brand. Red Bull supplemented its word-of-mouth strategy with event sponsorships, athlete endorsers, sampling programs, point-of-purchase marketing and select electronic media buys. Eventually, consumers everywhere would be talking about (and purchasing) Red Bull.

Developing the Red Bull Mystique

From the start, Red Bull was a source of intrigue for consumers. The functional energy category was brand new for Austrians, so curious and adventurous customers tried the brand and spread the word. Not content to let the word-of-mouth evolve naturally, shortly after the product launched in Austria the company would place empty Red Bull cans in clubs and bars to create the illusion of popularity. Between 1987 and 1992, when Red Bull was available only in Austria, consumers in adjacent countries, like Germany and Hungary, who had not been to Austria heard about the product from word-of-mouth testimonials. In this way, consumers outside Austria were made aware of product benefits, the unusual ingredients like "taurine," and the state regulations. Since the product could not be exported, it was bootlegged across the border by enterprising individuals. These factors contributed to the buzz surrounding the product, and led to what Norbert Kraihaimer referred to as the "over-mystification" of Red Bull. Most consumers outside Austria had not seen any official Red Bull marketing, and if they had not tried the product themselves they would not know what to make of it. Some thought it was a beer, others a liquor product. Rumors about the product's special ingredients (one inaccurate rumor was that Red Bull contained bull testicles) and energy benefits fueled gray markets in several countries, most notably Germany. The mystification of Red Bull, however, fueled negative rumors as well. Since Red Bull was popular in the European rave scene, rumors linked it with drug overdoses and even deaths. Though the beverage was never responsible for the overdoses or deaths, that did not prevent rumors from persisting. As a result, Red Bull garnered press coverage, which added to the buzz surrounding the product.

Market Entry Strategy

When it entered a new market, Red Bull strove to build buzz about the product through its "seeding program," where the company micro-targeted the "in" shops, clubs, bars and stores. This enabled the cultural elite to access the product first and hopefully influence consumers further down the scale through word-of-mouth. Red Bull also targeted "opinion leaders" who were likely to influence consumer purchases. These included action sports athletes, entertainment celebrities, and hip urbanites. The company attempted to reach these individuals by making Red Bull available at sports competitions, in limos before award shows and at exclusive after-parties.

Red Bull's limited availability in the early stages of development contributed to the brand's cachet, as evidenced by the presence of gray markets in Austrian border country. After six-months of seeding, the company gradually expanded its presence to locations surrounding these "in" spots. These locations were typically less price-sensitive than the seeding locations and served to widen the access point to the brand. Availability was still limited and word-of-mouth was still a main driver of awareness, but any consumer who wanted to purchase the product could do so if they sought it out. Finally, Red Bull reached the mass-market via supermarkets. As Norbert Kraihamer explained, "We are very focused on consumer base building and not just heading for maximum weighted distribution."[7]

Red Bull engaged in "pre-marketing" to establish awareness in markets where its product was not yet sold. Pre-marketing involved sponsoring events that took place in a country where Red Bull was not available, such as the Red Bull Snowthrill of Chamonix ski contest in France. The international ski contest exposed French consumers to the product and the athletes it sponsored. Red Bull also exported its television productions to countries it had yet to enter. The television programs, which featured Red Bull sponsored events and athlete endorsers, acted as ambassadors for the brand in the absence of any market presence. For example, if a Colombian athlete sponsored by Red Bull was competing in a televised Red Bull event, Colombian television stations would have interest in broadcasting the event. Colombian television viewers would then gain knowledge of the brand's involvement with their countryman or countrywoman and would associate Red Bull with that person and his or her event. Of the pre-marketing strategy, Norbert Kraihamer said, "We want to be recognized as the pre-eminent brand, even if we are not there."

Red Bull Target Market

Red Bull did not define a specific demographic or psychographic segment as its target market. Rather, the company sought to reach a broad range of consumers based on their need for a stimulating drink. Norbert Kraihamer said, "We only have two dimensions: people who are mentally fatigued and people who are physically fatigued or both."[8] These consumers fell into five broadly-defined categories: "students, drivers, clubbers, business people and sports people."[9] By not defining a narrow consumer target, Red Bull ensured that it could grow into numerous market segments. In mature markets, Red Bull achieved its highest penetration in the 14-19 age range, followed by the 20-29 range (see Fig. 7). As its consumers aged, Red Bull hoped they would continue to use the product, increasing the older end of the age distribution. As Kraihamer explained:

> The kids that are 18 or 19 years old and drink Red Bull in a nightclub have years of use ahead of them. These same people will use it in the future as a sporting drink, or for driving, or as a conference drink because business meetings are always tiring.[10]

MARKETING ACTIVITY

Red Bull engaged in a variety of marketing programs, including traditional television, print and radio advertising, event marketing in sports and entertainment, sampling and point-of-purchase promotion. The bulk of Red Bull's marketing activity was directed toward encouraging product trial. This was accomplished primarily through sampling, word-of-mouth and point-of-purchase. According to Kraihamer, "We do not market the product to the consumer, we let the consumer discover the product first and then the brand with all its image components."[11]

Advertising

Dietrich Mateschitz created the familiar Red Bull "adult cartoon" advertisement with the aid of Johannes Kastner, a colleague who owned an advertising agency. All ads featured an intelligent dialogue about product benefits using one character with an energy deficiency and others who proposed the solution: Red Bull. Unlike most beverage marketers, Red Bull did not reinforce the taste of the drink, the direct benefit of the drink or the image associations of the drink.

In one ad, a dentist informs Dracula that his teeth will have to be removed. Dracula complains that without his teeth, he will not be able to drink blood. Dracula laments, "But without fresh blood my body will wither and my mind will fade." The dentist tells Dracula "one revitalizing Red Bull and you'll be prince of the night again." A shot of the product appears on the screen, with the copy "Red Bull energy drink. Vitalizes Body & Mind." The dentist samples a Red Bull himself and tells Dracula, "You know, Red Bull gives you wings" before sprouting wings and flying away. Other famous characters to appear in Red Bull ads include Leonardo da Vinci, Adam and Eve, Frankenstein, William Tell, Rapunzel, Sisyphus and the Devil. The tagline "Red Bull gives you wiiings" grew directly out of the positioning statement "Red Bull vitalizes body and mind."

The ads were effective because they clearly communicated product benefits without promising specific physiological results. The literal message of "Red Bull gives you wiiings" was obviously an exaggeration, but taken figuratively it was clever and believable. The animated television spots also refrained from defining a specific target group; anyone with a sense of humor, no matter how old, would be able to appreciate the ads. This enabled the company to establish as wide a consumer base as possible.

The Red Bull animated ads were adopted uniformly across the company's global markets. Not only did the colorful images travel well, but also the simple execution and universal concepts of the ads ensured that they would cross cultural boundaries easily. Said

Norbert Kraihamer, "Even in a country where they speak a different language, we send the same message using the cartoon. . . . We more or less translate it word for word -- the power of our marketing mix works."[12]

Sampling

Product trial was an essential part of the Red Bull marketing program. Whereas traditional beverage marketers attempt to reach the maximum number of consumers with a sampling, Red Bull sought to reach consumers only in ideal usage occasions, namely when the consumer needs or wants a boost. For this reason, Red Bull sampling campaigns took place at concerts, parties, festivals, sporting events, at the beach, at highway rest areas (for tired drivers) and at campus libraries. Norbert Kraihamer explained the importance of getting the consumer to try the product at the proper time:

> We have to make sure that people experience the product the right way at the right moment and in the right situation when they have met with particular fatigue or are in need of food.[13]

Red Bull sent sampling teams to the ideal locations equipped with Red Bull branded vehicles and plenty of cans of cold Red Bull. In the U.K., Red Bull branded the quirky and cool Mini Cooper automobile. The sampling team's job was to explain the product benefits and encourage the consumer to drink a full can for maximum benefit. For its sampling teams, Red Bull employed individuals who could energetically and believably endorse the brand. The sampling teams were typically comprised of college students called Red Bull Student Brand Managers. Aside from sampling, student managers researched drinking trends, designed on-campus marketing initiatives and wrote stories for student newspapers. According to Henry Drnec, Red Bull's managing director in the U.K., "Sampling [is a] key element of our marketing strategy. The customer feedback we get is invaluable and the conversion rates are huge."[14] Norbert Kraihamer elaborated:

> It is our people that give us real power in the field. This is one of the reasons we are not at all afraid of the big companies, the Coca-Colas and the PepsiCos and the Cadbury Schweppes of this world. They'll find it difficult to put the same kind of focus and dedication into one product, one item, because they are spreading their marketing across a whole range.[15]

Event Marketing

Red Bull had an extensive network of events that it was involved with. Red Bull either invented the event from the ground up, or brought the product to an existing event. When Red Bull created the event, it controlled all aspects of the event, including the name, logo, promotion and media production. Classic Red Bull events included the Red Bull Soapbox Race and the Red Bull Flügtag ("Flying Day"). The Red Bull Flügtag was a comical event in which participants constructed a flying object and attempted to launch it off a ramp into a lake or ocean. The event was a perfect fit for Red Bull because it required use of both the body (in the design of the flying object) and mind (in the power to get it off the ground). The winner of the event received free lessons for a pilot's license.

Sporting events developed by Red Bull include the Red Bull Snowthrill extreme skiing competitions in France and Alaska, and Red Bull Cliff Diving World Tour Finals event in Hawaii. These events enhanced Red Bull visibility and also reinforced the brand's positioning as an independent, stimulating beverage. "People who attend one of our events have the indelible awareness that it was sponsored by Red Bull because of the unusual amount of control we can exert over our own events,"[16] said Red Bull corporate communication manager, Emmy Cortes. The more unique an event, the more likely television stations would want to broadcast it, or newspapers would want to cover it. Kraihamer explained, "We want to have the most creative ideas and do the best things so that they get automatically into the media."[17]

Sports Marketing

In addition to sponsoring sporting events, Red Bull also sponsored individual athletes. Red Bull engaged in sports marketing first and foremost to establish credibility among opinion leaders who participated in action sports such as surfing, snowboarding, skydiving, skateboarding, rock climbing, mountain biking and many other non-mainstream athletic endeavors. The athletes who played these sports exhibited many of the qualities Red Bull wanted to project in its brand personality: innovative, individual, non-conformist, unpredictable and humorous. The company started its sports marketing by simply making the product available to athletes at competitions, allowing interested athletes to seek out Red Bull and become authentic users. Following these low-key introductions, Red Bull would then work out sponsorship deals that put the logo on the athletes' equipment. Red Bull sponsored a number of athletes, but was very selective about which athletes it chose. First, the sport had to fit with the Red Bull image. According to Norbert Kraihamer, "Generally, these are extreme sports, but if there is an energetic golfer, no problem."[18] As athletes began to use Red Bull for its stimulating effect, they subsequently drove awareness among their audiences.

Once Red Bull became an international brand, it was able to sign influential and leading athletes such as Robby Naish (windsurfing), Eddie Irvine (Formula 1) and Shane McConkey (skiing). Red Bull also inked a blockbuster sponsorship deal with the Sauber-Petronas Formula One team, which gave Red Bull a globally recognizable symbol -- the racing car -- competing at the highest level.

At the other end of the competitive spectrum, Red Bull sponsored athletes who engaged in sports that had no official competitions. One example was kite-surfing, an aquatic sport where participants strapped to a sort of wakeboard use a kite sail to skim across the water. Red Bull sponsored two dedicated kiteboarders from Florida by giving them gas money and a cooler full of Red Bull. The two kiteboarders drove around to different beaches and wherever they went, they attracted a crowd with their cutting-edge kiteboarding. After their sessions, the assembled crowds would witness the pair refueling with Red Bull. If the sport were to become official, Red Bull would already be sponsoring the best competitors. Norbert Kraihamer described the kiteboarding case as a "great example of synthetic involvement in sport."

Point-of-Purchase Marketing

Red Bull's primary point-of-purchase tool was the branded refrigerated sales units. Red Bull placed these miniature glass refrigerators, which prominently displayed the Red Bull logo, in convenience stores, bars, clubs, sports shops, office buildings, cafeterias and commissaries.

These refrigerators set the brand apart from other beverages and ensured Red Bull a prominent location in the retail environment. If a location would not accept the Red Bull mini-fridge, the company would rent space in the large in-store refrigerators. To ensure consistency and quality in its point-of-purchase displays, Red Bull hired teams of delivery van drivers whose sole responsibility was stocking Red Bull. Red Bull also used a highly visible aluminum window sticker to indicate availability, rather than the traditional clear plastic. Believing the can itself to be the best promotional tool, Red Bull limited the use of posters, shelf talkers and ceiling hangers in the store.

EUROPEAN EXPANSION

In the mid 1990s, Austria was not yet part of the European Community (now called the European Union, or EU), and the company was concerned that a competitor would enter the energy drink category ahead of Red Bull. The EU's policy for approved food products dictated that if a food was approved in one EU country, it could be sold in all EU countries. The problem for Red Bull, however, was that most EU countries had a list of allowable food ingredients, and taurine was not on any of the lists. Lobbying to get taurine added to the list would be too costly and time-consuming. Fortunately, Scotland -- an EU country -- had a "negative list" of food ingredients, in other words all ingredients not on the list were allowed. So Red Bull set up its first EU test market in the U.K., and rapidly entered the rest of the EU markets. Red Bull was unable to enter the French market, however, because the product was banned until it could be proven "100 percent safe." The French government was especially conservative about new food products because of recent health scares involving foot-and-mouth disease and mad cow disease (bovine spongiform encephalopathy, or BSE). The ban in France did have the benefit of adding to the mystification effect for French consumers.

Marketing Steps in the U.K.

Red Bull varied its market entry strategy only in the U.K., which it entered in 1995. Believing the British market to be too different from Austria, the management team in the U.K. altered the Red Bull marketing formula in three significant ways: 1) they marketed Red Bull as a sports drink, not a stimulation drink; 2) they did not pursue a word-of-mouth strategy, choosing instead to sell via the largest beverage channels and 3) they created new advertising and focused on billboards rather than electronic media. As a result, Red Bull was considered a failure in the U.K. after losing more than $10 million during the first 18 months in that market. The first alteration was significant because the U.K. had an established sports drink brand, Lucozade, which had been on the market for decades. Consumers were very familiar with the sports drink category, but Red Bull did not meet their expectations of what a sports drink should be. Usually Red Bull sought to create its own new category when it entered new markets, so when U.K. managing director Harry Drnec took over in 1996, he repositioned Red Bull as a stimulation drink, by changing the word "energy" on the can to "stimulation," and established the new category.

The second strategic mistake was a departure from the word-of-mouth strategy that had fuelled Red Bull's popularity in other markets. The original U.K. management skipped all the preliminary steps and started with selling Red Bull in the largest supermarkets and convenience outlets. This move essentially precluded any buzz from building, because it did not allow a discovery phase or an opinion leader program to establish the brand as cutting edge. Said Norbert Kraihamer, "The U.K. team started from the wrong end, in the big chains, hoping the consumer would pick it off the shelf. But they were wrong, they totally misunderstood how to create a consumer base."[19] In response, Drnec and his new management team pursued the traditional word-of-mouth strategy.

Finally, the original U.K. managers overhauled the Red Bull advertising concept to suit the needs of the market as they saw them. They used the slogan, "Never underestimate what Red Bull can do for you," which did not clarify Red Bull's positioning at all and was too long to be catchy. By contrast, the "gives you wiiings" slogan communicated Red Bull's positioning as a stimulation drink and translated effectively into any market. The original U.K. team also focused the ad spending on billboards, which were not as effective in communicating Red Bull's benefits as electronic media. "We go for electronic media, because energy needs movement and dialogue," said Norbert Kraihamer. "You can hardly get smart drinks across on a billboard -- it doesn't talk."[20]

After new management made the necessary changes, Red Bull took off in the U.K. Between 1997 and 2001, Red Bull's share of the sports and energy drink market rose from under two percent to 48 percent. This share exceeded that of Lucozade, the entrenched leader for the previous 74 years. Red Bull went from selling 3.2 million cans per year in 1995 to more than 290 million in 2000. The brand claimed an 86 percent share of the "functional energy" drinks market in 2001. That same year, Red Bull was the third biggest product by value in the soft drinks market, behind Coca-Cola and Pepsi. The U.K. was Red Bull's second-largest market by volume and sales in 2001, behind the U.S.

Red Bull in the United States

For Red Bull's 1997 entry into the U.S., the company used a "cell" approach to divide key markets in the country into targeted geographic segments, rather than attempt a nationwide launch. "Our intention was never to go to the States and say 'We are launching Red Bull,'" said Norbert Kraihamer. "We chose small market cells."[21] The brand's first test market was Santa Cruz, California, a beachside town known for its active lifestyle built around surfing and skateboarding and for the University of California -- Santa Cruz. The population of Santa Cruz represented a good target audience for the brand because it contained a large number of sports enthusiasts and university students. From Santa Cruz, Red Bull moved into the nearby urban market of San Francisco, and then into Venice Beach, a trendy beachside city near in Los Angeles. Following success in Venice Beach, Red Bull established a presence in adjacent Santa Monica and then Hollywood. Norbert explained the development of the cell approach:

> When one small cell became a success story, we moved onto the next cell. Of course, after three years, these cells are becoming bigger and bigger. But initially it was towns or part of towns.[22]

To manage the cells, Red Bull established eight separate business units in the U.S. The regional office in New York, for example, was responsible for the brand in Maryland, New Jersey, New York, Pennsylvania and Virginia.

When Red Bull entered a cell, it initially targeted high-end nightclubs and bars, plus exclusive health clubs and gyms in order to reach the trendy and active consumers. Like it had done in Europe, Red Bull gradually increased distribution to include downmarket bars and clubs, restaurants, convenience stores and grocery chains. On college campuses, Red Bull recruited student brand managers to organize on-campus promotions such as renting out study rooms during finals week and stocking them with free cans of Red Bull and school supplies. Since the drinking age in the U.S. is much higher than in most other European countries, the college marketing events in the states never had an alcohol link. Red Bull also implemented its sampling program, using Red Bull branded trucks and cars and teams of "consumer educators" that worked on a street level to promote the brand.

Red Bull gradually expanded its distribution eastward in 1999, moving first into Texas and then to mountain resorts in the Rockies. After establishing seeding programs in the Midwest and Chicago area, Red Bull moved to the East coast and Florida in 2000. Red Bull's growth in the American market outpaced the company's expectations. In 2000, the company achieved sales of 108 million cans, well above the 80 million can target. That year, the company's U.S. market share stood at 65 percent.

Only when a cell was considered mature did Red Bull begin a media program in that area. "Media is not a tool we use to establish the market," said vice president of marketing David Rohdy. "It's a critical part. It's just later in the development."[23] Of the $100 million marketing budget for the U.S. in 2000, Red Bull spent less than $20 million on measured media. The company's most visible media efforts were the two new animated cartoon commercials it developed each year, and the company also used radio spots.

Red Bull also kept up its aggressive event marketing efforts in the U.S. In addition to the Red Bull Cliff Diving World Finals in Hawaii and the Snowthrill of Alaska winter sports event, Red Bull held the Red Bull Wings Over Aspen hang-gliding event and a street luge competition in San Francisco. In 2000, Red Bull introduced the Red Bull Rock 'n' Air festival, a day of extreme sports demonstrations and progressive live music. Another unique Red Bull invent was the Red Bull Music Academy. This event brought a number of DJs together in New York City in 2001 for a week of collaboration, learning and performance.

Red Bull's initial results in the U.S. mirrored the brand's success in Europe. In 2001, Red Bull was the number one seller in Store24 convenience store, bigger than any single beer, milk, water or soda brand. "It's the number one beverage and the gap is widening," said Andy Steele, a beverage buyer for Store24. "I've never seen anything like it." One new age beverage executive said, "Red Bull seems to have a cooler in every bar in every city."[24]

By mid-2001, Ohio, Tennessee and the Dakotas were among the few states that did not have Red Bull. The company's U.S. case volume more than quadrupled that of its nearest competitor and its market share hovered near 70 percent.

Competition

As Red Bull began to exhibit exponential sales growth internationally, beverage companies that had previously dismissed the drink as a fad or fashion started moving into the energy drink segment. In the U.K., Red Bull faced competition from Virgin, which developed Virgin dt; Anheuser-Busch, which entered the market with 180; Coca-Cola, which debuted a drink called Burn; Pepsi-Cola with SoBe Adrenaline Rush and Mountain Dew Amp and a host of other brands with names like Indigo, Hype, Bawls, XTC and Magic. Speaking about the emergence of major brands in the market, Red Bull U.K. managing director Harry Drnec said, "It's a lucrative market, and the many players who have been jumping in are finding it's not a game. You can't market a functional drink like you do a soft drink. But we're excited about Coke's entry -- it could push the category even further forward."[25] Between 1995 and 2000 in the U.K., the beverage consultancy Zenith International reported that more than 40 product launches occurred in the functional energy category. Many of these competitors used packaging that resembled Red Bull: small, thin metal cans, metallic hues, and animal imagery. Red Bull dominated all other competitors in the U.K. functional energy drinks market with a 72 percent share in 1999. None of its competitors had more than a six percent share of the market.

Some of the major beverage companies attempted to use word-of-mouth marketing to their advantage when launching their products. Coca-Cola entered the U.K. in 2000 with Burn essentially by keeping the product a secret, withholding details about the product's logo and ingredients. Coca-Cola also ensured very limited distribution for Burn by stocking only five select bars in London. The company hoped that the mystery launch would engender buzz among consumers. "Why use a television ad campaign if you don't have to?" said a Coca-Cola spokesperson. Coca-Cola used a similarly secretive launch strategy when it entered the Australian market in 2000. Coca-Cola used different brand names for the same product depending on the market. Norbert Kraihamer scoffed at this strategy, saying, "They don't even know what name to call it -- Plus, Play, KMX, Burn . . . Does that give you any confidence that they know what they are doing?"[26] In 1999, single cans of Red Bull outsold single cans of Coca-Cola in British supermarkets, according to Zenith research.

The competitors often employed marketing tactics similar to Red Bull's. PepsiCo's Mountain Dew Amp used a sponsorship and sampling strategy that resembled the Red Bull approach. To reach its target 18 to 24 year-old demographic, Pepsi hired young sales representatives to promote Amp on college campuses by giving away samples of the drink. Pepsi also sponsored emerging music acts with the Amp name. PepsiCo's SoBe Adrenaline Rush also pursued a grass-roots strategy involving sampling teams, point-of-purchase materials, sponsored SoBe Team Lizard athletes and distribution concentrated on bars, convenience stores and restaurants. In Britain, Red Devil sponsored the Asprilla motorbike team and Virgin dt sponsored the Radio One Love Parade dance festival.

Other brands used sex appeal to try and take market share from Red Bull. The Red Devil brand claimed that its product would "ma[ke] you horny," while the Go-Go Passion brand marketed itself as "Viagra for girls." The tagline for SoBe Adrenaline Rush was "Get it up. Keep it up. Any Questions?" While most competitors used below-the-line marketing activities in attempts to develop a viral marketing effect, some brands, like Virgin dt and Red Devil in the U.K., created radio and television advertisements. Red Devil used celebrity spokesperson Vinnie Jones, a former soccer tough and actor, to star in ads with the tagline "You can always repent."

Lots of smaller competitors attempted to capitalize on the energy drink trend as well. In 2001, Red Bull had more than 140 competitors in Germany. These competitors combined for less than five percent market share, and typically had lifecycles of around 6 months. The number of competitors diluted the category because few were seriously committed to the market and most pitched consumers with a limited usage message that focused on one dimension of stimulation. In 2001, Red Bull got an injunction imposed on a Swiss mineral water company that was marketing a knockoff product called "Red Bat." In the ruling, the judge noted that since Red Bull was a very recognizable brand, it had a greater need for copyright protection. The judge also stated that competitors were able to choose brand names that were sufficiently different from Red Bull. Still, knockoff products such as Red Devil and Red Rooster continued to saturate the market.

Red Bull had the advantage of originating the energy drink category in most markets it entered, and could therefore establish the brand's prominence on its own terms (e.g., by gradually building awareness through seeding and relying on word-of-mouth to build buzz around the brand). In markets where it was not the first mover, Red Bull often had to overcome image perceptions for the energy drinks category that competitors had engendered with their marketing. For example, Red Bull was not the first energy drink to be sold in Brazil; other European competitors had moved in first. For the most part, the competition set prohibitively high price points and marketed their beverages strictly for nightlife usage occasions. In Brazil, Red Bull set its standard 10 percent price premium and worked to reinforce its message using its proven marketing formula, eventually overtaking the competition in terms of volume. Once it established volume leadership, Red Bull pressured the competitors to lower prices while maintaining the premium.

Evolution of Red Bull Usage

Red Bull marketed its product to appeal to a broad range of consumers and to be appropriate in a variety of usage occasions. Still, the vast majority of Red Bull's business came from the youth market (see Fig. 7). In many markets Red Bull was used predominantly as a mixer. In the U.K. during 2001, half of all Red Bull consumption was in nightclubs and bars. Other European markets had similar figures. In mature markets like Austria, however, the product remained relevant even as consumers aged. Since usage was not limited to one or even a few occasions, Red Bull users could continue to use the product even as their priorities shifted. For example, a Red Bull consumer first attracted to the product as a nightlife enhancer in his or her early twenties might later use the drink as a morning pick-me-up or a revitalizer during a long day of meetings. Norbert Kraihamer said, "The reasons for consumption change, but the basics is always there: the real benefit." The benefit "keeps the consumer loyal through the years."[27] Evidence in Red Bull's debut market, Austria, where it has been sold since 1987, suggested the product was not a fad. Kraihamer continued, "We are continuing to expand our consumer base in the initial Austrian market and are growing there at a rate of 20 percent"[28] (see Fig. 5).

Red Bull in the Future

After achieving exponential growth during the 1990s and beyond, Red Bull continued seeking new markets to enable further growth. By 2002, a number of countries in South America, Latin America, the Middle East and Africa remained untapped markets. The United States was another potential area for intensive growth, since per capita consumption there was still less than one can per year. The company expected to succeed in these new markets using its proven market entry strategy while it continued to increase per capita consumption in established markets, as it had done for 15 years in Austria. As the functional energy category became increasingly competitive, and as major beverage industry players like

Coca-Cola and PepsiCo grew more serious in their efforts to establish a foothold in the category, Red Bull's dual challenge would be to maintain growth in established markets and succeed in growing into new markets. The brand would also have to ensure that it retained the interest of consumers in existing markets or risk experiencing slowed growth. The highly competitive beverage industry would require Red Bull to work hard to replicate its success in Europe as it expanded into new markets.

DISCUSSION QUESTIONS:

1. Describe Red Bull's sources of brand equity. Do these sources change depending on the market or country?
2. Analyze Red Bull's marketing program in terms of how it contributes to the brand's equity. Discuss its strengths and weaknesses.
3. How can Red Bull maintain their marketing momentum? Would you recommend that Red Bull develop any brand extensions? If so, what would they be? Would you use the same marketing strategy?

Fig. 1: Comparison of Red Bull Benefits Related to Consumption Occasions					
Occasion	Red Bull	Isotonics	Beer/Wine	Cola	Juice
Competition	✓	✓			
Sports	✓	✓			
Leisure Activity	✓	✓		✓	✓
Coffee Substitute	✓			✓	
Hangover Cure	✓				✓
Stay Awake	✓			✓	
Meetings	✓			✓	✓
Physical Labor	✓	✓		✓	
Driving	✓			✓	
Studying	✓			✓	
Cocktail	✓		✓		
Dancing/Partying	✓		✓		

(Source: Red Bull College)

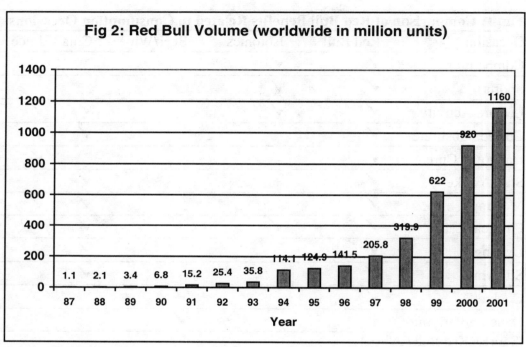

Fig 2: Red Bull Volume (worldwide in million units)

(Source: Red Bull College)

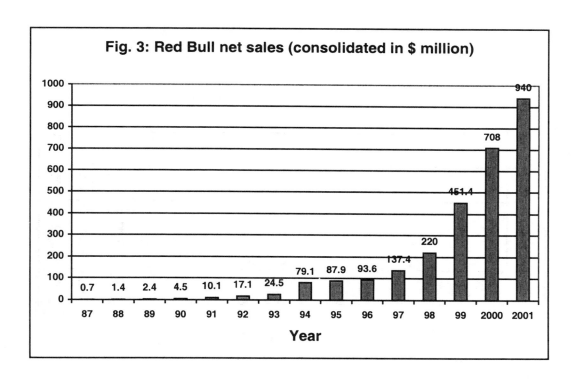

Fig. 3: Red Bull net sales (consolidated in $ million)

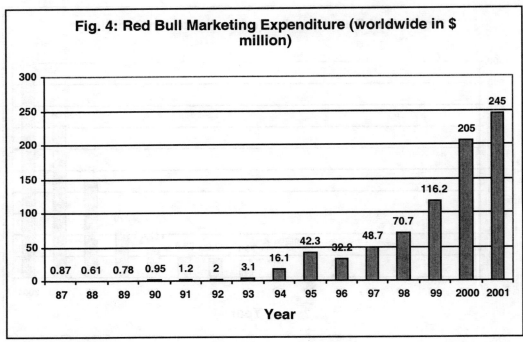

Fig. 4: Red Bull Marketing Expenditure (worldwide in $ million)

(Source: Red Bull College)

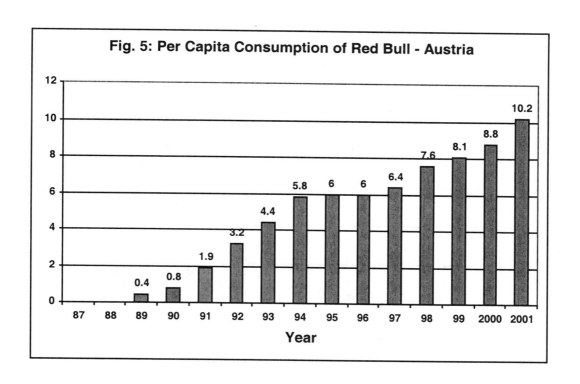

Fig. 5: Per Capita Consumption of Red Bull - Austria

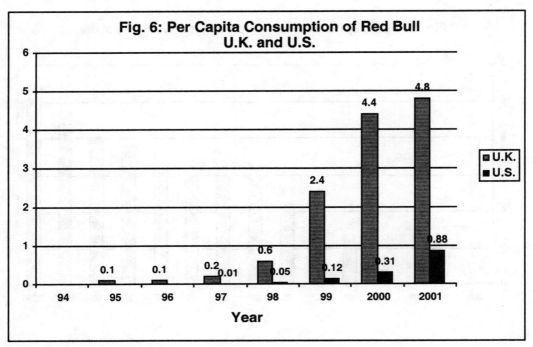

Fig. 6: Per Capita Consumption of Red Bull U.K. and U.S.

(Source: Red Bull University)

Note: Red Bull 4.5 million cases in 2000, 10.5 million cases in 2001 in U.S.

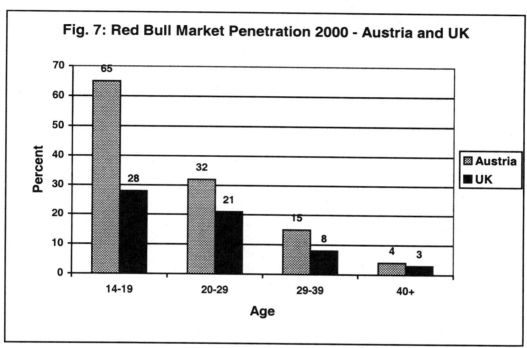

Fig. 7: Red Bull Market Penetration 2000 - Austria and UK

(Source: Red Bull College)

Fig. 8: Red Bull Market Development

1987 – Austria	1997 – South Africa
1992 – Hungary	Ireland
1993 – Scotland	United States
1994 – Germany	1998 – Italy
Slovenia	Brazil
1995 – Baltic States	Finland
Czech Republic	1999 – Australia
Netherlands	Kenya
Poland	Tanzania
Russia	Botswana
Slovakia	2000 – Israel
Switzerland	Oman
United Kingdom	Yemen
Croatia	2001 – Kuwait
Yugoslavia	Lebanon
1996 – Portugal	Puerto Rico
Sweden	Bahamas
Belgium	Dominican Republic
Spain	
Greece	
New Zealand	
Romania	

(Source: Red Bull College)

REFERENCES

[1] This case was made possible through the cooperation of Red Bull and the assistance of Norbert Kraihamer, Markus Pichler, and Eric Weinrib. Keith Richey prepared this case under the supervision of Professor Kevin Lane Keller as the basis for class discussion.

[2] Claire Phoenix. "Red Bull: Fact and Function." Interview with Norbert Kraihamer. *Softdrinksworld*, February 2001, pp. 26-35.

[3] Claire Phoenix. "Red Bull: Fact and Function." Interview with Norbert Kraihamer. *Softdrinksworld*, February 2001, pp. 26-35.

[4] Claire Phoenix. "Red Bull: Fact and Function." Interview with Norbert Kraihamer. *Softdrinksworld*, February 2001, pp. 26-35.

[5] Claire Phoenix. "Red Bull: Fact and Function." Interview with Norbert Kraihamer. *Softdrinksworld*, February 2001, pp. 26-35.

[6] Norbert Kraihamer. Personal Interview, August 2001.

[7] Claire Phoenix. "Red Bull: Fact and Function." Interview with Norbert Kraihamer. *Softdrinksworld*, February 2001, pp. 26-35.

[8] Claire Phoenix. "Red Bull: Fact and Function." Interview with Norbert Kraihamer. *Softdrinksworld*, February 2001, pp. 26-35.

[9] Claire Phoenix. "Red Bull: Fact and Function." Interview with Norbert Kraihamer. *Softdrinksworld*, February 2001, pp. 26-35.

[10] Claire Phoenix. "Red Bull: Fact and Function." Interview with Norbert Kraihamer. *Softdrinksworld*, February 2001, pp. 26-35.

[11] Norbert Kraihamer. Personal Interview, August 2001.

[12] Claire Phoenix. "Red Bull: Fact and Function." Interview with Norbert Kraihamer. *Softdrinksworld*, February 2001, pp. 26-35.

[13] Claire Phoenix. "Red Bull: Fact and Function." Interview with Norbert Kraihamer. *Softdrinksworld*, February 2001, pp. 26-35.

[14] John Cassy. "Enragingly Ubiquitous: Aged Only 22 but Already Branded." *The Guardian*, June 26, 2001.

[15] Claire Phoenix. "Red Bull: Fact and Function." Interview with Norbert Kraihamer. *Softdrinksworld*, February 2001, pp. 26-35.

[16] Kate Fitzgerald. "Red Bull Charged Up." *Advertising Age*, August 21, 2000, p. 26.

[17] Norbert Kraihamer. Personal Interview, August 2001.

[18] Claire Phoenix. "Red Bull: Fact and Function." Interview with Norbert Kraihamer. *Softdrinksworld*, February 2001, pp. 26-35.

[19] Claire Phoenix. "Red Bull: Fact and Function." Interview with Norbert Kraihamer. *Softdrinksworld*, February 2001, pp. 26-35.

[20] Claire Phoenix. "Red Bull: Fact and Function." Interview with Norbert Kraihamer. *Softdrinksworld*, February 2001, pp. 26-35.

[21] Claire Phoenix. "Red Bull: Fact and Function." Interview with Norbert Kraihamer. *Softdrinksworld*, February 2001, pp. 26-35.

[22] Claire Phoenix. "Red Bull: Fact and Function." Interview with Norbert Kraihamer. *Softdrinksworld*, February 2001, pp. 26-35.

[23] Kenneth Hein. "Brand Builders: A Bull's Market." *Brandweek*, May 28, 2001, p. 21.

[24] Kenneth Hein. "Brand Builders: A Bull's Market." *Brandweek*, May 28, 2001, p. 21.

[25] Cordelia Brabbs. "Can Coke Break Into Clubland?" *Marketing*, October 26, 2000, p. 25.

[26] Claire Phoenix. "Red Bull: Fact and Function." Interview with Norbert Kraihamer. *Softdrinksworld*, February 2001, pp. 26-35.
[27] Norbert Kraihamer. Personal Interview, August 2001.
[28] Claire Phoenix. "Red Bull: Fact and Function." Interview with Norbert Kraihamer. *Softdrinksworld*, February 2001, pp. 26-35.

MTV:
BUILDING BRAND RESONANCE[1]

INTRODUCTION

Over the course of more than 20 years, MTV built a powerful youth-oriented brand that spanned the globe. When the all-music channel -- the first of its kind -- debuted in 1981, few dreamed that it would attain such a prominent place in the pop culture media. Few imagined, either, that MTV would attract as many international viewers -- over 342 million households in 140 countries by 2001 -- as it did. Domestically and abroad, MTV was able to develop programming and content that consistently resonated with viewers over many years. As it did in America during the early 1980s, MTV attracted loyal followers in large numbers in the early 2000s in each of its broadcasting regions. The channel built more than just its own brand equity. Throughout the years, MTV served as a star-making vehicle for pop-artists and on-air talent. Experts credited the channel with changing the course of music and television and, in some cases, even having an impact upon socio-political events, such as the collapse of the Eastern Bloc communist regime. MTV's rise to cultural prominence was not achieved without difficulty. MTV endured a lengthy stretch of flat U.S. ratings in the mid-1990s as music tastes shifted and the channel lost touch with its core audience. As before, however, MTV managed to successfully reinvent itself and establish a following from a new core audience by embracing "long-form" programming and reducing the number of music videos shown by 36.5 percent from 1995-2001 while ratings increased 50 percent. This reinvention illustrated MTV's central challenge. In the fickle world of popular culture, MTV's main obstacle in its quest to remain the leading source of relevant "musically-infused" content was ever-changing audience tastes. Moreover, how should MTV be best positioned within the context of its broader sister stations such as VH1 and its direct brand extension, MTV2? Despite its enormous success, MTV seemed to have to prove itself over and over again.

MTV HISTORY

Channel Origins

MTV originated as an unlikely offshoot of a cable broadcasting joint venture between Warner Communications and American Express called Warner Amex Satellite Entertainment Company (WASEC). A number of future MTV executives worked at WASEC and germinated the idea for a music video cable channel. Jack Schneider, president of WASEC, recognized the opportunity inherent in a music channel. He reasoned, "If you have a disc jockey with a microphone, a transmitter, and 40 records, you've got yourself a radio station. So why don't we put a disc jockey on TV?"[2] Steve Casey, original director of music programming, came up with the name for the channel:

> We were under pressure to do something, so we were writing out different possibilities. Finally I came up with "MTV." I didn't like the way it sounded so much as the way it looked. It really seemed cool. No one said "Great," but no one had a better idea, and that ended the meeting.[3]

An independent designer named Patti Rogoff came up with the MTV logo, a blocky three-dimensional "M" with a graffiti-scrawled "TV" on top. The channel's creative team came up with the idea of using a picture from the first moon landing -- of Neil Armstrong in his spacesuit holding the American flag -- as its television signature. Tom Freston, current CEO and chairman of MTV Networks, explained the development of the design:

> We knew we needed a real signature piece that would look different from everything else on TV. We also knew that we had no money. So we went to NASA and got the man-on-the-moon footage, which is public domain. We put our logo on the flag and some music under it. We thought it was sort of a rock 'n' roll attitude: "Let's take man's greatest moment technologically, and rip it off."[4]

Instead of disc jockeys (DJs), MTV employed video jockeys, called VJs. Sue Steinberg, MTV executive producer, explained the VJ concept:

> We wanted VJs who would be part of our audience, who wouldn't say, "I'm the host of your show today," but "I'm so-and-so and I will be with you for the next couple of hours." The important words were "with you." We wanted you to come on this ride with us.[5]

The original VJs were a diverse group including Alan Hunter, an actor; Mark Goodman, a DJ and Martha Quinn, a radio station intern. The VJ segments were filmed in a studio that resembled a cross between "a SoHo loft . . . and a rec room"[6] and was designed to seem welcoming, interesting and avant-garde to the viewers. The VJs' personalities added value to the channel beyond the videos, and the viewership conferred celebrity status on them alongside the pop stars whose videos they introduced and who they interviewed. MTV's mediated approach to showing videos, which included packaging them with VJ introductions and station promos, helped the brand establish a unique brand identity. Co-founder Bob Pittman had an eye on brand building from an early stage:

> The concept I had was to have a clear image, to build an attitude. In other words, to build a brand, a channel that happened to use video clips as a building block, as opposed to being a delivery system for videos. The star wouldn't be the videos, the star would be the channel.[7]

Music Videos Hit the Air

MTV's business plan mirrored that of a radio station. The channel got its content -- in this case videos or "clips" instead of audio tracks -- from record companies for free and earned revenues by selling advertising. Warner Amex approved the plan and gave the channel $25 million in financial backing. Record companies were reluctant at first to give away videos, which they had to pay to produce in addition to the original recording. When MTV first launched, its video library contained a scant 250 videos. Jack Schneider spoke of the record labels' initial reluctance to produce "clips" and allow MTV to use them free of charge:

> The record companies hated [the idea]. They said, "We made this mistake in radio – you ain't gonna catch us making it again. You are going to have to pay for the rights to this video."[8]

MTV's success was contingent on receiving free videos, and the record companies eventually relented. The record companies primarily gave MTV clips from their second- and third-tier artists, however. (MTV would eventually pay licensing fees to receive videos from major record labels). MTV's first-ever aired video was a minor record titled, appropriately enough, "Video Killed the Radio Star" by an English band called The Buggles. The video aired at midnight August 2, 1981, when MTV hit the airwaves for the first time. The opening broadcast was simple, with a voice-over intoning "Ladies and gentlemen, rock 'n' roll" over footage of a space launch, followed by the Buggles video. The success of the channel, which was practically overnight, was evidenced by the fact that the channel created stars from the lower-tier acts. Artists such as Adam Ant and Billy Idol, who received little if any radio play, emerged as genuine talents after their videos aired on MTV. Billy Idol spoke of MTV (and himself) as a burgeoning cultural phenomenon:

> Radio guys would take one look at my picture with the spiky hair and say, "Punk-rocker. Not playing him." Then MTV airs my videos, and kids start calling up radio stations saying, "I want to hear Billy Idol!" It really broke the thing wide open. We'd never touched the charts, and the next minute we had a Top 10 album. It was amazing. Nobody'd ever noticed me before. Now I'm walking down the streets, and people are yelling: "Billy!"[9]

In addition to creating fame, MTV broadcasts also created record sales. The executive vice president of Warner Bros. Records, Stan Cornyn, said at the time, "It was reported back to us that records were selling in certain cities without radio airplay. We asked, 'Why?' and it turned out that there were music videos playing on MTV. An act like Devo is dancing around in their funny masks and stuff like that -- and they take off in a market where nothing else is happening."[10] John Sykes, originally the director of promotions for the channel, added further testimony:

> We finally hit pay dirt when we went into a record store and asked if there was any reaction to the songs we were playing that weren't being played on the local radio stations. The manager said, 'Yeah, we sold a box of Buggles albums.' . . . Within two weeks we had trade ads in Billboard, with quotes from all the store managers in Tulsa, claiming that MTV was having this profound impact on record sales.[11]

Soon record companies began producing more videos from bigger artists, in part because of the sales figures and also because artists were demanding to have their own videos played on MTV. The channel was soon able to play clips from the major artists of the day.

MTV Raises Awareness

Financially, the first year was difficult for MTV, since advertisers were reluctant to embrace an unproven cable upstart. Adding to MTV's trouble was the fact that many cable operators refused to carry the channel, keeping its audience well below the targeted 2.5 million for the inaugural year. In 1982, MTV devised an advertising campaign designed to spike demand in unserviced markets. The concept was simple: have famous rock stars endorse the brand by uttering the phrase "I want my MTV," then air these commercials in areas where cable providers were not showing MTV. The first star to sign on was Mick Jagger, at the time the biggest rock star in the world. Other stars to cut promos included Pete Townshend, David Bowie, John Cougar, and Pat Benatar. The results of the $2 million ad campaign were dramatic. According to Tom Freston:

> We'd go in and attack a town and we'd run like three or four weeks of this advertising and the phones would ring off the hook and every cable operator in the market would add the service.[12]

Prior to launching the campaign, MTV conducted an awareness study and found that the percentage of people who had heard of MTV or seen the channel was just below 20 percent. Four weeks after the campaign, awareness had risen to 89 percent. Still, the financial picture for MTV remained bleak. In two years, the channel had recorded $33.9 million in losses and was projecting losses of $20 million in 1983. Advertisers had not responded to the channel with the same enthusiasm young viewers had. MTV sold $6 million in advertising in 1982.

MTV developed a number of contests and promotions in order to build viewership. These were starkly different from traditional promotional campaigns. For one contest, the prize was a "lost weekend" with Van Halen. In another early contest, MTV bought a somewhat dilapidated house and gave it away to a lucky viewer. One of the most coveted items was a T-shirt with an MTV logo on it, because MTV neither sold nor gave its T-shirts away. MTV would eventually develop a lucrative licensing operation.

Music Videos Take Off

The era of modern music videos started with the Michael Jackson video for his song "Billie Jean" from the landmark album *Thriller*. The video featured Jackson's energetic dance moves and applied advanced production values to achieve a sleek look. The video helped propel sales of *Thriller* to more than 800,000 a week. The follow-up to "Billie Jean" -- "Beat It" -- added a street fight narrative that involved complex choreography. The title video from Thriller took the music video to an entirely different level. Running an unprecedented 14 minutes, "Thriller" cost $1.1 million to make, a figure more than 20 times the cost of the most expensive video on record to that point. The video, which was modeled on the horror classic *Night of the Living Dead*, featured Jackson as the star of a miniaturized feature film in which he and his date are attacked by zombies. MTV paid $250,000 for the right to air the video first and played the video three times every day. The channel also pre-promoted the video before each playing and noticed a rating spike each time. *Thriller* went on to be the biggest-selling album of all time, and Michael Jackson vaulted to mega-stardom.

Hot on the heels of Jackson's breakout success, MTV broke another new star in Madonna. Madonna's videos, though not as elaborate as Jackson's, were still more expensive than the average video. Other artists began demanding more money for videos. Budgets rose from low five digit figures to over six digit figures, which raised the aesthetic further. Accordingly, artists became more concerned about their image and appearance. They were not competing primarily on the basis of sound anymore, but the look of an artist was an important component.

Early Competition

Several networks attempted to replicate MTV's success with weekly video programs. NBC developed "Friday Night Videos" and USA's "Night Flight." The syndicated "FM-TV" contained two hours of videos and interviews (see Exhibit 1). MTV created VH1 as a "flanker brand" designed to counter Ted Turner's 1984 launch of Cable Music Channel, itself an answer to MTV's popularity. VH1 stood for "video hits" and was positioned to be distinctly different from MTV by airing adult-oriented videos. Kevin Metheny, director of programming, described the VH1 format:

> We picked three musical genres that wouldn't cannibalize MTV: R&B, country, and adult contemporary. We'd have Tony Bennett, followed by Kool and the Gang, followed by Willie Nelson; the Judds, followed by Latoya Jackson, followed by Air Supply. It was very odd . . . but the point with VH1 was to monopolize shelf space, rather than create a successful entity.[13]

The flanking strategy had the desired effect, since after a month on the air, Turner shut down the Cable Music Channel and sold its assets to MTV for $1 million.

Success Leads to New Ownership

In 1984, MTV had the highest Nielsen ratings over the average 24-hour period of any advertiser-supported cable network. At that time, the channel reached more than 21 million households. As ad revenues in the first quarter of 1984 rose 223 percent from the previous year, MTV turned its first quarterly profit of $3.4 million. Not only was MTV making strides financially, it was being recognized for its impact on American music culture. In 1984, the National Association of Record Manufacturers honored MTV with its Presidential Award in recognition of the channel's role in reviving the record industry.

Soon after, MTV became involved in negotiations that eventually led to its purchase by media giant Viacom. In June 1985, American Express decided to sell its share of WASEC to Warner Communications, which in turn looked for a buyer in Viacom. MTV's senior management attempted a leveraged buyout in order to keep the company from being purchased by a media conglomerate, but the financing fell through when Viacom upped its bid to $525 million. MTV was now part of a vast media empire.

MTV GROWS UP

Changing the Format

After four years of growth, MTV suffered a ratings decline in 1985 and 1986. From a high of 1.2 in 1983, MTV ratings dropped from 0.9 in the third quarter of 1985 to 0.6 in the fourth quarter. By the second quarter of 1986, ratings had risen again, but only by a tenth of a point. MTV addressed the ratings slide by developing programming that would keep viewers tuned in for longer periods of time. This involved a significantly larger number of long-form programming. "I think they finally realized that in order for them to be around for the long term, they're going to have to act a bit more like a 24-hour TV station," said one industry analyst. "You just can't get by showing clips for 24 hours a day, seven days a week."[14]

MTV worked to change its all-videos, all-the-time format. Between 1986 and 1989, MTV introduced a number of long-form programs that were successful for many years. Most of these programs focused on music videos or live performances:

- "120 Minutes" – introduced in 1986, a weekly two-hour showcase of progressive and underground music.
- "Headbanger's Ball" – introduced in 1987, a weekly hour-long show dedicated to hard rock and heavy metal. Often featured studio guest appearances by famous bands such as Megadeth, Anthrax and Metallica.
- "Yo! MTV Raps" –introduced in 1988, a weekly hour-long program featuring the latest rap videos as well as studio guests.
- "Unplugged" – introduced in 1989, featured artists playing songs from their catalogue acoustically and in an intimate small theatre setting. Artists that performed on the show in the first two seasons included Paul McCartney, Elvis Costello and R.E.M. Other legendary performers to appear on "Unplugged" included Eric Clapton, Nirvana, Neil Young, Lauryn Hill and Jay-Z.

Not all the long-form programs revolved around music. In 1989 MTV introduced a fashion program called "House of Style," hosted by model Cindy Crawford, that took a weekly look at the world of fashion. Also that year the channel debuted a comedy show starring VJ Julie Brown called "Just Say Julie."

The years 1992 and 1993 marked the introduction of two of MTV's most popular programs ever, "The Real World" and "Beavis and Butthead," respectively. "Beavis and Butthead" was a half-hour animated cartoon series about two low-IQ teenaged title characters with an MTV obsession. When they were not watching videos -- making fun of the ones they thought "sucked" and worshipping the ones they thought "ruled" -- Beavis and Butthead were causing trouble in their neighborhood or at school. In one early episode called "Frog Baseball," which was later pulled from the air following a healthy public outcry, Beavis and Butthead hold a batting practice using live frogs. The show resonated with different types of viewers, such as young adults who recognized the show as a social satire, and pre-teens who recognized the show as pure slapstick. Even *Time* magazine's pop-culture critic called the show "the bravest show ever run on national television."[15]

Critics of the show called it "inappropriate" and "vacuous," and cited incidents where children copied stunts, such as mooning their teacher or sniffing paint thinner, as examples of the show's corrupting influence on children. To appease concerned viewers, MTV moved the show from its primetime 7 p.m. slot to a late night 10:30 p.m. slot. Amidst the controversy, "Beavis and Butthead" routinely doubled MTV's ratings whenever it was shown during the week. The show's popularity led to lucrative licensing agreements with clothing and toy manufacturers, and even a feature-length film called *Beavis and Butthead Do America.* "Beavis and Butthead" spawned another popular long-form animated series called "Daria," about a smart and witty female classmate.

The "Real World," introduced in 1992, was one of the first television programs to fit into the now-familiar "reality TV" genre. Conceived by a documentary producer and a soap-opera producer, the show recorded the lives of seven people between the ages of 19 and 25 cast to share a loft in New York City's SoHo district. The producers selected the seven occupants to precipitate some racial, gender and sexual tension. Co-producer Jon

Murray stated, "We set up the situation purposefully so there would be conflict and sexual tension."[16] In exchange for a $2,600 payment, plus free rent and food, the initial seven stars of "The Real World" gave MTV unlimited access to videotape their personal lives and also story rights for a three-month period. The crew shot 30 to 50 hours of videotape each week that would then get edited to fit into a half-hour show. The first 13-week season captured lots of videotaped real-life drama, and also captured a large viewing audience that averaged approximately 700,000 people. The show was continued in 1993 -- this time in Los Angeles -- and every season after that through 2002 in Chicago, in the process becoming MTV's longest running show. "The Real World" had typically received more than 5,000 applications from prospective stars, while the average episode in 2002 drew more than 2 million viewers. The show also paved the way for other "reality TV" programs, most notably "Survivor."

The popularity of these new non-music-video shows indicated a new direction of growth for MTV. Tom Freston acknowledged MTV's expansion beyond music in 1993 when he said, "We're not just about music. We're about all issues associated with pop culture."[17]

MTV's Image Crisis

In 1994, Tom Freston spoke of the difficulty of staying relevant to young viewers:

> MTV is in rather a vulnerable position because it's sort of out there on the leading edge of what's going on in the popular culture. It has, for 13 years, managed to reinvent itself, stay interesting, keep its audience levels up, and I think that's quite an accomplishment.[18]

By 1996, this difficulty had manifested itself as MTV's ratings stayed low through that year. Despite the success of its long-form programming, the channel's ratings continued to hover near 0.5. The grunge genre that MTV and its viewers had embraced in the early 1990s -- typified by Nirvana, Pearl Jam, and Soundgarden -- was falling out of favor. So too was the gansta rap genre popular with young viewers especially. The channel had yet to find any suitable musical replacement that resonated with its core audience. While MTV was struggling to connect with its audience, however, the channel was achieving unprecedented growth in its international markets.

MTV GOES GLOBAL

MTV launched MTV in Europe in 1987. At first, MTV had a single satellite feed that broadcast primarily American programming and used English-speaking VJs. The music and entertainment tastes of the people varied widely among European nations, and soon competitors took advantage of MTV's undifferentiated broadcast by establishing locally-produced music channels. MTV watched much of its viewership, and consequently, its advertiser base, abandon the channel in favor of local competition. Tom Freston acknowledged the error, saying, "We were going for the most shallow layer of what united viewers and brought them together. It didn't go over well."[19] MTV established regional feeds in 1995 and by 2000 had five different regional channels for the U.K. and Ireland; Germany, Austria and Switzerland; Scandinavia; Italy and one for 28 countries including

France, Israel and Greece. By 1999, MTV had 22 different satellite feeds globally. In 1999, Viacom estimated that two million people watched MTV at any given moment and that 1.2 million of these viewers were overseas. Still, MTV had enormous opportunity for growth abroad. Of MTV Network's $1 billion operating profit in 1999, only $50 million came from outside the U.S.

MTV Latin America was launched in 1993 using a single feed that originated in Miami. About 70 percent of MTV Latin America's viewership was Argentine and Mexican, with the rest in other Latin American countries, the Caribbean and some U.S. markets. The channel was criticized early on for the prominence of English-language videos, which outnumbered Spanish-language videos by a four to one margin. MTV increased the Spanish-language content and split the feed into three parts -- North, South and Central -- that enabled customized programming in accordance with regional tastes. The number of subscribers rose from 3.2 million in 16 countries in 1993 to 11.5 million subscribers in 21 countries by 2002.

Another successful international operation was MTV's channel in Italy, called MTV Italia. MTV Italia offered local music content such as MTV Supersonic, a weekly live-music show featuring two well-known acts and one unsigned band, and an Italian version of Total Request Live. Italian-produced lifestyle shows included Stylissimo, a fashion program; Sexy Dolls, a show where audience members got intimate with celebrity look-alikes; and MTV Kitchen, which featured pop artists cooking and discussing music. In 2002, MTV Italia earned the highest ad revenues of any of MTV Networks International channel, as its 12 million weekly viewers spurred an ad revenue increase of 352 percent since 1997.

Another area targeted by MTV's global expansion was Asia. In 1995, MTV launched MTV Mandarin, which broadcast to China, Hong Kong, Taiwan and Singapore. MTV Mandarin played Mandarin-language music videos as well as international videos. That same year, MTV debuted MTV Southeast Asia, which broadcast to nine countries in the region, including Hong Kong, Indonesia, Vietnam and the Philippines. The music mix contained videos in Bahasa Indonesia, Bahasa Malaysia, Thai and Tagalog languages, and popular international hits. In 1996, MTV split MTV Southeast Asia to create a new channel, MTV India, which broadcast to India, Bangladesh, the Middle East, Nepal, Pakistan and Sri Lanka. In 2000, MTV launched MTV Japan, which featured Japanese programming targeted to 16 to 34 year olds. MTV Korea, a Korean-language channel, debuted in 2001. MTV was aware of the enormous potential for growth in the Asian market, where cable and satellite coverage was still minimal in the 2000s, but was rapidly expanding.

One of the keys to MTV's international success was its willingness to offer local content to local audiences. Though as much as 60 percent of the programming originated in the U.S., in most of MTV's global markets 70 percent of the videos featured local artists. Said Bill Roedy, president of MTV Networks International, "We've had very little resistance once we explain that we're not in the business of exporting American culture."[20] MTV India was an example of a channel with both local programming and videos. Most of the music on MTV India came from Hindi-language movies produced in Bollywood, India's film industry. The Indian channel also produced 21 shows locally, including *MTV Cricket in Control* all about the sport of cricket, *MTV Housefull* featuring Hindi film stars, and *MTV Bakra* modeled after *Candid Camera*. MTV India's VJs speak "Hinglish," a hip mix of Hindi and English popular in the countries urban areas. Between 1996 and 2000, ratings for MTV

India increased 700 percent. The channel reached 13.3 million Indian homes in 2000 and claimed a 50 percent share of the music channel market.

As digital broadcasts become more prevalent in Europe in the early 2000s, MTV planned to roll out more channels, as it did in the U.K. when it created seven different versions of MTV that focused on specific genres, such as R&B or dance. MTV also used Internet technology to bolster its presence in international markets. In Scandinavia, the company introduced MTV Live for consumers with broadband Internet access. On MTV Live, viewers played virtual games such as Trash Your Hotel Room, where they pretended to be rock stars and caused as much damage to a hotel as possible. MTV created a wireless Internet service for Japan where users could download news, music and other entertainment. In 2000, MTV Asia launched LiLi, a virtual animated VJ that appeared online and on air in five different languages. The character became so popular that Ericsson developed a line of LiLi mobile phones.

COMEBACK IN THE U.S.

MTV Addresses Ratings Slump

As ratings remained essentially flat in the U.S. between 1992 and 1996, viewers and analysts alike criticized the channel for the level of non-music video content of its programming mix. In December 1996, MTV addressed these concerns by adding six additional hours of music video programming each week. The channel continued to develop long-form programming. Though the long-form programming was the subject of some consumer backlash -- particularly from older viewers who remembered MTV in its early period as an almost exclusively video channel -- long-form programming was a boom for ratings. In 1996, MTV's two highest-rated programs were "Road Rules," a reality-TV road trip, and "Singled Out," a dating show. The long-form programming kept viewers tuned in on a regularly basis, whereas the video-only mix encouraged "grazing" behavior where viewers looked for videos they liked and tuned out during ones they did not care for. Tom Freston commented on the positive effects of long-form programming:

> [Long-form programming] works. The consumers like it. We think it's a way to sort of stretch ourselves out and make MTV a bigger, more interesting, more vital place for its audience. . . . Long-form programming serves sort of as a punctuation mark, if you will, and as a way to bring attention to the network. . . . I think the diversification of MTV from a pure music network to a network that's not only about the music but about the things the music is about has worked well for us.[21]

The company also changed the genres of music it played, shelving the grunge, alternative rock and gangsta rap that had been its hallmark from the early 1990s. MTV briefly programmed an eclectic mix of styles, ranging from electronic dance music to traditional pop tunes. This was usurped by the teen pop phenomenon. As Tabitha Soren, a news anchor for MTV from 1991 to 1998, recalled:

> I remember going to a meeting [in 1996] where they told us we were going after cutting-edge, free thinking, revolutionary minds. But six months later we were told "Forget all that.

101

Thirteen-year-olds are buying records. Britney Spears is gonna be the hottest thing since sliced bread. That's gonna be our base." It was just this total flip.[22]

MTV responded to its static ratings by revamping its programming schedule. It repackaged its music video offerings into discrete shows, such as "Total Request Live." MTV also sought to establish stronger connections with its viewers by holding more contests and promotions, encouraging live interactions via call-ins and web-votes and building a flagship studio in New York's revitalized Times Square

MTV also launched an all-music channel called MTV2 to cater to an older audience, namely 18 to 28 year olds, for whom music video viewing was important. In surveys conducted by the channel, viewers from this segment revealed that they did not appreciate the move away from music-video programming that MTV had made in recent years. MTV2 satisfied this older segment's need for a greater percentage of video content, and enabled MTV to continue to build its ratings with long-form programming.

"Total Request Live," or TRL for short, was a call-in video request program started in September 1998. The show was molded from two previous show concepts, the unsuccessful talk show MTV Live and a tape-delayed countdown show called Total Request that debuted during the summer of 1998. Host Carson Daly would count down the top 10 videos of the day, as chosen by viewers voting on the net and via telephone. The teen pop genre received the bulk of the attention on the program, since that was what TRL's core audience of teenage girls wanted to hear. On TRL and in MTV's playlist overall, teen pop was the most-played genre (see Fig. 6). The show also featured live interviews in the studio with famous artists and movie stars, as well as celebrity guest-hosts and videotaped interviews. With its live interactive element, its "A-list" guest list and video playlist and its "hottie" host, TRL was an unqualified success, particularly among viewers aged 12-17. The Times Square studio where TRL was taped became something of a touchstone for viewers, who lined up outside daily in the hopes of getting on camera. The crowd outside eventually became so large that police were required to provide crowd control to keep the throng from spilling out onto the street. Fans lucky enough to make it into the studio audience would get to see and hear the action up close. The truly lucky fans got the opportunity to plug their favorite video on camera, usually spoken fast and breathlessly, signing off with the exuberant "WHOOOOOO!" that became standard on the show.

In response to this surge of support, TRL expanded to a 90-minute show from an hour in the summer of 1999. At that time, the show attracted more than one million viewers every afternoon. MTV news chief Dave Sirulnick referred to the show as "the franchise of the channel."[23] Many of the bands featured on the TRL countdown became big stars. Britney Spears, Backstreet Boys, Limp Bizkit and *NSYNC all achieved mega-stardom after their videos received heavy rotation on the show. Carson Daly became a celebrity of the same magnitude as many of the artists and actors featured on the program. The show continued to draw daily viewers into the millions in its sixth season in 2002.

The channel also developed more non-video long-form programming to complement "The Real World" and "Road Rules." In 1998, MTV created a claymation animated series called "Celebrity Death Match" that pitted two similar celebrities against each other in a graphic boxing match. One match featured Little Richard fighting Lil' Kim because he claimed she stole the "Lil'" from him. Other animated bouts included Howard

Stern vs. Kathie Lee Gifford, Hillary Rodham Clinton vs. Monica Lewinsky, and Michael Jackson vs. Madonna. One of MTV most successful shows was the "Tom Green Show," which featured oddball Canadian host Tom Green performing madcap sketches and stunts. The show, which premiered in 1999, consisted of a studio talk show hosted by Tom Green and videotaped clips of Green's bizarre stunts. For example, in its premier episode, Green drank milk directly from a cow's udder. In another stunt, Green found a dead moose on the side of the rode and proceeded to sit on it while yelling "My bum is on the moose!" Both "Celebrity Deathmatch" and "The Tom Green Show" aired late at night.

The revamping of the channel led to dramatically higher ratings (see Fig. 2). MTV's ratings reflected its development of more programming devoted to the teenage female demographic. Between 1997 and 2000, the channel's largest rating surge came from the female 12 to 17 grouping (see Fig. 3). The male 12 to 17 grouping also experienced ratings growth, but at a reduced rate. The other age grouping to show growth of more than .15 percent between 1997 and 2000 was the female 18 to 24 grouping. Both the male and female 25 to 34 grouping grew by only .05 percent during that period. The increased ratings helped build advertising rates to between $10,000 to $20,000 for a 30-second commercial in 2001. Since MTV had become a daily destination for male and female viewers between the ages of 12 to 17, and was the most recognizable network among young adults age 12 to 17, advertisers coveted space on the channel. According to one ad buyer, "If you're targeting young people, MTV has to be part of your strategy."[24]

Teen Pop Backlash

While the focus on the teenage girls demographic helped MTV ratings to climb, the emphasis of teen pop programming was alienating some viewers. Males and older viewers were experiencing disconnect with the channel because they saw the teen pop programming as "not for me." While teen pop remained very popular, MTV executives new it was just the latest in a series of trends. The channel could not afford to exclude large numbers of its audience on the basis of a temporary trend, so MTV altered its programming to reduce the boy-band perception. In particular, the channel created a number of shows aimed at an older audience. A racy nighttime soap-opera called "Undressed" centered on the sex lives of high school and college students. One episode involved a stepbrother and stepsister trying to conceal a sexual relationship from their parents.

In October 2000, MTV debuted a show called "Jackass," in which a pseudo-stuntman and his friends performed absurd and sometimes dangerous stunts. The show's star was featured in stunts where he lit himself on fire, rode a bull, sat in a working portable toilet while it was turned upside down and allowed himself to be shot at close range with a paintball gun. The actors often performed their stunts in public and filmed the reaction of passersby. One such stunt involved driving around with a baby carrier -- which unwitting members of the public assumed to be full -- on the roof of an SUV. In another stunt, two actors driving a hearse stopped on a hill, allowed the back door to swing open, and watched in mock-horror as a coffin containing another actor playing dead slid out of the hearse onto the street. "Jackass" was MTV's highest rated show in 2000.

Another show popular with a broad range of viewers, called "MTV's Cribs," debuted in 2000 and gave viewers an insider's look at stars homes. "MTV's Cribs" -- which was sort of a "Lifestyles of the Rich and Famous" for Generation X -- featured the homes of such stars as Nelly, Destiny's Child, Mariah Carey, Tommy Lee, and Jason Kidd. In 2001, MTV launched a sketch-comedy show similar to "The Tom Green Show." Called "The Andy Dick Show," the half-hour comedy show featured comedian Andy Dick in sketches, short films and music video parodies. A dating show called "Dismissed" also debuted in 2001. On "Dismissed," one dater chose between two potential suitors who had to fight to win his or her affection. The show had a reality TV angle, since a camera followed the trio on their date and recorded the action.

The results of MTV's new programming approach was a more balanced audience across the 12 to 17 year old and 18 to 24 year old demographic. Between 1996 and 2001, the 18-24 age group grew 33 percent over last 5 years, compared with 17 percent for ages 12 to 17. Advertisers took note of this trend, and ad sales in 2000 rose 20 percent. In 2001, MTV was the number one cable network for the 12 to 24 year old demographic.

MTV's numerous programming shifts in the last half of the 1990s and the early 2000s demonstrated one of the channel's key properties: dynamic programming. MTV was able to represent itself as a leading source of entertainment for each of the major music trends that have swept the nation since the early 1980s: new wave, hair metal, grunge, gangsta rap, teen pop and hip-hop. President of programming Brian Graden discussed MTV's ability to constantly reinvent itself:

> Music television is a term that has to be redefined for each generation. You have to find new ways to package it, celebrate it, reinvent it, or somebody else would create tomorrow's music television.[25]

Kurt Loder, MTV's news anchor for 13 years, took a similar view:

> MTV serves the purpose that American Bandstand did. It reflects whatever's going on in pop culture at the moment. And if you like the moment, you're gonna like MTV. And if you don't, well, this too shall pass. . . . As soon as the public gets tired of this stuff, MTV will move on to something else. There is no loyalty in television.[26]

MTV continued to make changes to its programming in 2001 and 2002.

A NEW ERA FOR MTV

MTV Educates Its Viewers

On September 11, MTV and VH1 broadcast the CBS News feed all day. In the immediate aftermath of the September 11 attacks, MTV pulled all its long-form programming and broadcast only videos and news updates. *The New York Times* reported that in the week following the attacks, 31 million 12 to 34 year olds watched MTV in order to get information. Only on the Monday following the Tuesday attacks did the channel return to its regular programming schedule. MTV continued to add to its information content in the weeks following, quadrupling its daily news coverage in order to air special programming covering the issues ranging from the life of Afghani teens to domestic anti-Arab sentiment, from Islam to military activity. Similar coverage was offered on the MTV.com web site. "MTV has provided more in-depth coverage and explanation as to why the Taliban is the way it is than I have seen on any other channel," said Aasma Khan, spokeswoman for Muslims Against Terrorism, a youth group organized by young Muslim professionals since September 11. "They're reaching out to people of Muslim and Arab descent and bridging that gap."[27] MTV received positive feedback from many corners of the world for its coverage of the war on terror.

Scoring a Huge Hit

In 2002, MTV scored a major hit with a long-form program, a "reality sitcom" called "The Osbournes" that chronicled the domestic life of heavy metal legend Ozzy Osbourne and his family. Cameras followed Ozzy, his wife Sharon and his teenaged children Jack and Kelly as they went through their daily routines in their Beverly Hills mansion. With the Osbournes, even the most mundane household tasks were charged with comic potential. Viewers watched plotlines such as Ozzy, Sharon and Kelli ineffectually attempting to use a vacuum cleaner, the family feuding with noisy neighbors and the family attempting to housebreak several pets. Other episodes depicted life on tour with Ozzy and his family. The show built a buzz almost immediately, attracting 6 million weekly viewers by the end of its first season. This audience enabled "The Osbournes" to surpass studio wrestling as the highest-rated cable show at the time and to achieve the distinction of being MTV's all-time ratings leader. MTV capitalized on this success by airing various episodes of the show 15 times a week.

Some considered the success of the show unlikely, because they did not predict Ozzy, who had been rocking since the late 1960s, would be able to pull the teenage audience. Viewers across many age groups, however, enjoyed the show. The younger viewers could identify with the teenagers in the house, while older viewers could enjoy watching Ozzy and Sharon's parenting style. One analyst, commenting on the show's broad appeal, said, "You have people in their 40s talking about MTV, which hasn't happened in a while."[28] Others expressed opinions that the program was more compatible with VH1's brand identity -- which had been built on classic music and "Behind the Music" historical bios -- than with MTV's contemporary focus. The show was consistent with past MTV long-form hits such as "The Real World" and "Road Rules" though.

Other Channel Developments

At the time of MTV's success with "The Osbournes," VH1 debuted a nightly talk show called "Late World With Zack" that barely registered with viewers. Two weeks after its debut, the show had a 0.2 rating, 50 percent below the rating for the same time slot the previous year. The show was symptomatic of VH1's general problems attracting viewers. VH1's primetime Nielsen ratings dropped 35 percent in 2001, and its overall ratings with the core 18 to 49 year old demographic fell 7 percent on the year. One analyst had the following to say about VH1: "It's in a rut. They might have gotten lost in the shuffle, since there's a lot out there for people age 25 to 54 to watch. I think they lost their way in their branding effort."[29]

MTV and VH1 introduced several sister channels in the early 2000s that targeted more specific viewer groups. The channels -- MTVX, MTVS, VH1 Classic, VH1 Soul, and VH1 Country -- all offered commercial-free music video-only programming to digital cable and satellite subscribers:

- MTVX – Played hard rock, active rock and heavy metal videos.
- MTVS – Played Spanish-language music videos.
- VH1 Classic – Played rock videos from the 1960s, 1970s and 1980s.
- VH1 Soul – Played classic R&B and adult urban music.
- VH1 Country – Played current and classic country music.

VH1 Classic was included as part of the increasingly popular Directv package. MTV2 also made some adjustments during the early 2000s. In a major break from tradition, the channel added commercials to its broadcasts in January 2001. Some long-form programming started to appear on MTV2, such as the second version of the classic MTV program "Unplugged," which was called "Unplugged 2.0." The sound on the channel was diverse, ranging from hip-hop to electronica, from nu-metal to folk rock. MTV2 was available primarily on digital cable and satellite feeds, and therefore had more limited viewership than its parent network. By 2001, MTV2 was seen available to more than 30 million households, up from 10 million in 1996, its first year.

MTV Online

The MTV brand made its debut online in 1991 with an unofficial newsgroup hosted by an employee. In 1993, MTV sued former VJ Adam Curry for copyright infringement. Curry had built a web site called MTV.com on which he posted music reviews, industry gossip, concert dates and occasionally held t-shirt giveaways. The parties settled in 1995, with Curry relinquishing the name. In 1994, MTV partnered with America Online to produce MTV Online, its first official Internet site. By 1999, MTV.com attracted more than two million visitors each month. That year, MTV formed a separate business unit called MTVi (for MTV Interactive) that oversaw the brand's music sites. In November of that year, MTV redesigned its web site by adding content designed to turn surfers into viewers. One such feature was a game show called "Webriot" that users could play online, but also was broadcast on MTV.

The development of an audio-compression format, called mp3, led music fans to download and upload music files efficiently over a network. As file-sharing software such as Napster enabled free mp3 swapping over the Internet, music fans were able to search for music and download it at no cost. Downloading mp3s became very popular among computer users, particularly those with broadband Internet connections, as a means of acquiring a library of music without paying for it. Record companies filed numerous lawsuits against file-sharing software manufacturers and Internet sites devoted to mp3s for copyright infringement. The record industry began to develop ways to prevent copying of CDs. At the same time, the industry recognized the Internet as an excellent medium for music, and several companies started services that enabled consumers to download mp3s legally and for a fee via subscription services. In 2001, MTV contracted with a music download service called RioPort to offer downloadable music on the MTV.com web site for as little as 99 cents per song. MTV.com also offered entire album downloads for as much as $18.98 per album.

MTV also established a web site for MTV2, and created a special, all-girls web site called MTVgirl.com. MTV2.com contained information about programming on the channel, downloadable video and music clips, plus news and feature content designed especially for the site. MTVgirl.com offered content specifically designed for teenage girls, such as information on shows typically watched by that demographic, profiles of current male and female pop stars, and games such as "Rock Star Match" where girls entered personal information to find out what rock stars they are compatible with. The site also contained health and beauty tips offered in paid advertisements by corporate partners such as Neutrogena and Johnson & Johnson.

MTV also developed web sites for each of its international channels. These sites resembled the MTV.com site, but with content designed specifically for the local market. For example, MTV France's web site (www.mtv.fr) offered live footage from the annual Printemps de Bourges music festival. Both MTV Japan's website (www.mtvjapan.com) and MTV Brazil's (www.mtv.com.br) website contained content relating to each country's Video Music Awards. The international sites featured local artists and information on local concert events. Some local content was just for fun, such as a game featured on MTV's Russian website (www.mtv.ru) called "Kill 'Em With a Pillow" in which players walked through a virtual MTV studio and hit Russian and international celebrities with a pillow to earn points.

In 2001, MTV launched a campaign called "MTV 360" designed to lure MTV viewers to MTV.com and MTV2. The campaign, which involved spending of $100 million over 12 months, involved integrated programming on all three channels. For example, during a live performance by the Dave Matthews Band on MTV's TRL, MTV2 played a block of older videos by the band, and MTV.com offered visitors the opportunity to download a live performance of a song from the band's upcoming album. In April 2002, traffic to MTV.com approached 2.5 million visitors for the month.

CONCLUSION

From its roots as a start-up cable network, MTV grew into a dominant youth brand in the music and television industry. Within a decade of its first broadcast, MTV established itself as one of the premier media properties in American cable television. Over the next decade, MTV expanded and strengthened its brand both domestically and abroad. In 2000, *Forbes* magazine estimated that MTV properties (including Nickelodeon/Nick at Nite, TNN, TV Land, TNN, CMT and Showtime Networks) were worth $24 billion. MTV Networks revenues increased 19 percent in 2001, to $600 million. MTV was available to more than 380 million households worldwide, and more than 79 million households in the U.S., in 2002.

As the channel achieved unprecedented success, a number of issues remained for MTV to contend with. The biggest challenge would be to remain relevant to the core audience of young consumers. With the Internet playing an increasingly important role as a form of entertainment, this task appeared to be complicated. MTV also needed to evaluate its positioning vis-à-vis MTV2, VH1 and other sister networks (see Figure 6). To maximize viewership, MTV would need to minimize overlap with these other channels. Finally, the channel needed to stay on top of musical and cultural trends in order to ensure the continued growth of its audience. Since the network had managed to do so for more than two decades, MTV executives were confident that the channel would continue to succeed.

DISCUSSION QUESTIONS

1. What is the MTV brand image? How valuable are the MTV brand associations? What should its core values be?
2. Describe the current sources of MTV's brand equity. How have they changed over time?
3. What is the role of music with MTV? Do they need to put the "M" back in MTV?
4. Discuss the role of the Internet in MTV's programming. How should MTV best integrate the Internet into its brand? How might technology impact MTV's future?
5. How have MTV's sister networks affected the parent channel's brand equity? What changes, if any, would you make in the positioning of the sister networks in order to create the optimal brand portfolio?

Exhibit 1:
MTV's Competition

Throughout its history, MTV did not encounter a powerful competitor that challenged its category leadership in a significant way. The first-mover advantage was a powerful brand-building tool in the case of MTV, since it established early on a connection with the youth audience and worked to maintain this connection. The fact that MTV remained the leader after two decades of broadcasting did not guarantee its future leadership, however.

What follows is a historical overview of MTV's major competitors, both domestically and abroad:

BET
Black Entertainment Television (BET) was founded in 1980 to address the underserved African-American audience. Programming included music videos, college sports, movies, news and talk shows. In the late 1990s and early 2000s, BET developed a niche by showcasing cutting edge hip-hop and R&B videos. Audience reach doubled to 60 million households between 1991 and 2000, and BET was seen as a legitimate competitor to MTV as a source for urban music. Viacom bought BET in late 2000 for $2.3 billion and added it to the MTV Networks unit.

The Box
The Box was an innovative music video channel where viewers could tune in for free to watch videos voted on by other viewers using call-in system. The Box also functioned like a jukebox, where viewers could pay a small fee to watch a selection of their choice. MTV purchased The Box in 2000 and combined it with MTV2.

MuchMusic
MTV's acquisitions of The Box and BET left MuchMusic as the closest competitor. MuchMusic, a Canadian music channel, launched in the U.S. in 1994. The channel received limited distribution primarily on satellite and digital cable networks, and was available in only 14 million U.S. homes at the beginning of 2001. The channel initially broadcast the Canadian feed to the U.S., which by Canadian law had to include 30 percent of its videos from Canadian bands. The company created a separate entity -- MuchMusic USA -- in 2001 in order to cater to the American pop music tastes. This expansion brought the total number of households that saw MuchMusic to around 40 million. In Canada, MuchMusic was the dominant channel, with more than 6 million households to its name. It also had a number of sister networks, including MuchMoreMusic and two French-language channels, Musiqueplus and MusiMax.

International Competition
MTV's success abroad inspired competitors such as News Corp.'s Rupert Murdoch and AOL Time Warner. Channel V -- a 24-hour music channel based in Hong Kong and owned by Murdoch's Star TV satellite network -- was in 47 million households in Asia in 2002, but was not yet profitable. MTV's largest European rival, VIVA, was part-owned by AOL Time Warner, EMI and Vivendi Universal and also was not profitable as of 2001.

Fig. 1: MTV's Global Network

North America	Europe
Households: 84.6 million Channels: 6 Web Sites: 2 Languages: 2	Households: 124.1 million Channels: 15 Web Sites: 9 Languages: 7
Latin America	Asia/Pacific
Households: 28.1 million Channels: 4 Web Sites: 2 Languages: 2	Households: 137.9 million Channels: 8 Web Sites: 6 Languages: 8

(Source: Viacom Inc., from Kerry Capell, et. al. "MTV's World." *Business Week,* February 18, 2002, p. 81.)

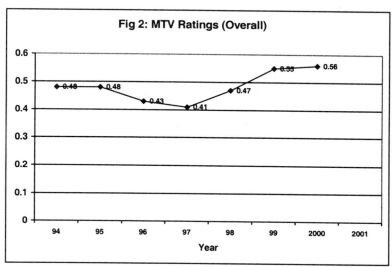

(Source: Average of Nielsen Quarterly Data)

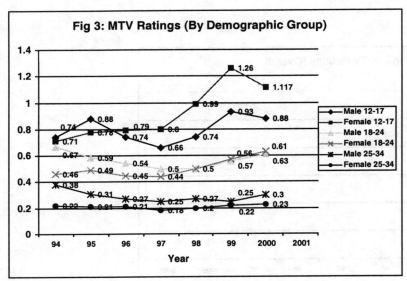

Fig 3: MTV Ratings (By Demographic Group)

(Source: Average of Nielsen Quarterly Data)

Figure 4: MTV Channels

United States
        -MTV
        -MTV2
MTV Brazil
MTV Europe
MTV Canada
MTV China
MTV France
MTV Germany
MTV Holland
MTV India
MTV Italy
MTV Japan
MTV Korea
MTV Latin America
MTV Nordic
MTV Poland
MTV Russia
MTV Southeast Asia
MTV Spain
MTV Taiwan/Hong Kong
MTV U.K.
MTV2 Europe
MTV2 Germany

(Source: www.mtv.com; Jeff Leeds. "Rocking the World In 20 Years, MTV Has Grown Into a Marketing Titan and Set Off a Dramatic Shift of Power In the Record Industry." *Los Angeles Times*, July 22, 2001, p. C1.)

Fig. 5: MTV Programming Sample, May 2002

MTV
12am-1am	WWE Tough Enough (reality TV)
1am-6am	MTV After Hours (videos)
6am-8am	MTV Video Wake-Up
8am-11:30am	Music Videos
11:30am-12pm	Making the Video
12pm-12:30pm	MTV Soul (videos)
12:30pm-1:30pm	$2 Bill Presents (live performance)
1:30pm-2:30pm	Music Videos
2:30pm-3pm	Jennifer Lopez Movie Special
3pm-3:30pm	Making the Video
3:30pm-4:30pm	TRL: Star Wars Edition
4:30pm-5pm	MTV Now What? (teen sitcom)
5pm-5:30pm	Kidnapped (game show)
5:30pm-6pm	Who Is: The New Faces of Hip-Hop
6pm-7pm	Def Jam Uncensored
7pm-8pm	MTV's Direct Effect (video requests)
8pm-10:30pm	WWE Tough Enough (reality TV)
10:30-11pm	Celebrity Deathmatch (animated)
11pm-11:30pm	Jackass (videotaped stunts)
11:30pm-12am	TRL: Star Wars Edition

MTV2
12am-1am	MTV2 Hip-Hop (videos)
1am-9am	Music Videos
9am-11am	Soul*Rhythmic*R&B (videos)
11am-3pm	Music Videos
3pm-5pm	MTV2 Rock (videos)
5pm-7pm	Music Videos
7pm-9pm	Control Freak (video requests)
9pm-10pm	Chart2Chart (videos)
10pm-11pm	Def Jam Uncensored
11pm-12am	MTV2 Hip-Hop

(Note: Sample TV Schedule for May 16, 2002. Source: MTV.com)

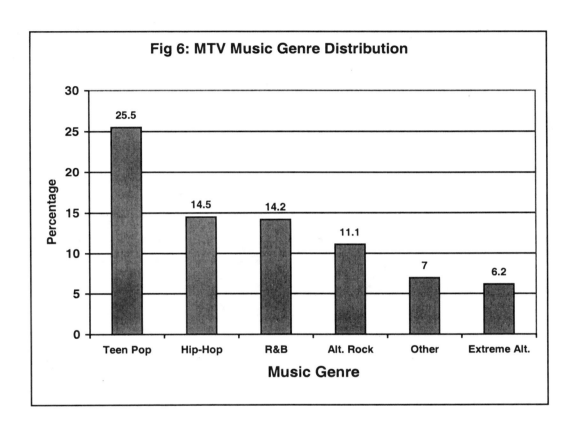

Fig 6: MTV Music Genre Distribution

Figure 7: Brand Definitions

MTV	Where young adults turn to find out what's happening and what's next in music and popular culture.
MTV2	Let's the viewer discover, control, and connect to the music they love. MTV2 is the ultimate music experience where viewers turn for an all music video experience they can't get anywhere else.
VH1	Takes audience behind the music and beyond. Our original series, concerts, and live events, music movies and new music videos consistently keep adults coonected to the music they love.
VH1 Classic	24 hours of the greatest music from the 60's, 70's and 80's.

REFERENCES

[1] Keith Richey prepared this case under the supervision of Professor Kevin Lane Keller as the basis for class discussion.

[2] Robert Sam Anson. "Birth of an MTV Nation." *Vanity Fair*, November 2000, pp. 206-248.

[3] Robert Sam Anson. "Birth of an MTV Nation." *Vanity Fair*, November 2000, pp. 206-248.

[4] Robert Sam Anson. "Birth of an MTV Nation." *Vanity Fair*, November 2000, pp. 206-248.

[5] Robert Sam Anson. "Birth of an MTV Nation." *Vanity Fair*, November 2000, pp. 206-248.

[6] Robert Sam Anson. "Birth of an MTV Nation." *Vanity Fair*, November 2000, pp. 206-248.

[7] Robert Sam Anson. "Birth of an MTV Nation." *Vanity Fair*, November 2000, pp. 206-248.

[8] Robert Sam Anson. "Birth of an MTV Nation." *Vanity Fair*, November 2000, pp. 206-248.

[9] Robert Sam Anson. "Birth of an MTV Nation." *Vanity Fair*, November 2000, pp. 206-248.

[10] Robert Sam Anson. "Birth of an MTV Nation." *Vanity Fair*, November 2000, pp. 206-248.

[11] Robert Sam Anson. "Birth of an MTV Nation." *Vanity Fair*, November 2000, pp. 206-248.

[12] Robert Sam Anson. "Birth of an MTV Nation." *Vanity Fair*, November 2000, pp. 206-248.

[13] Robert Sam Anson. "Birth of an MTV Nation." *Vanity Fair*, November 2000, pp. 206-248.

[14] Steven Rea. "Who Wants Their MTV?" Knight-Ridder News Service, June 22, 1986.

[15] Rick Marin. "Beavis and Butt-head: You Have to Ask?" *New York Times*, July 16, 1993, p. 41.

[16] Daniel Cerone. "MTV's Sort-Of Real World." *Los Angeles Times*, May 28, 1992, p. Home 1.

[17] Brenda Hermann. "How Do You Like Your MTV?" *Orange County Register*, April 2, 1993, p. 58.

[18] Rich Brown. "Tom Freston: The Pied Piper of Television." Interview. *Broadcasting & Cable*, September 19, 1994, p. 36.

[19] Brett Pulley and Andrew Tanzer. "Sumner's Gemstone." *Forbes*, February 21, 2000, pp. 107-111.

[20] Kerry Capell, et. al. "MTV's World." *Business Week*, February 18, 2002, p. 81.

[21] Rich Brown. "Tom Freston: The Pied Piper of Television." Interview. *Broadcasting & Cable*, September 19, 1994, p. 36.

[22] Lorraine Ali and Devin Gordon. "We Still Want Our MTV." *Newsweek*, July 23, 2001, p. 50.

[23] Dave Karger. "'Total Eclipse: MTV's Total Request Live Is Interactive Hitmaking at a Fever Pitch." *Entertainment Weekly*, October 22, 1999, p. 25.

[24] Lorraine Ali and Devin Gordon. "We Still Want Our MTV." *Newsweek*, July 23, 2001, p. 50.

[25] Lorraine Ali and Devin Gordon. "We Still Want Our MTV." *Newsweek*, July 23, 2001, p. 50.

[26] Lorraine Ali and Devin Gordon. "We Still Want Our MTV." *Newsweek*, July 23, 2001, p. 50.

[27] Jim Rutenberg. "MTV, Turning Serious, Helps Its Generation Cope." *New York Times*, October 2, 2001, p. E1.

[28] David Bauder. "MTV's Wizard of Ozzy." Associated Press, April 10, 2002.

[29] David Bauder. "MTV's Wizard of Ozzy." Associated Press, April 10, 2002.

NIKE:
BUILDING A GLOBAL BRAND[1]

INTRODUCTION

Nike had firmly established itself as the premier shoe company in America by the early 1990s. The company next looked to translate this domestic dominance into success internationally. In 1993, David Kottkamp, General Manager of Nike International, deliberated on how to invigorate the sluggish sales of the division. Although Nike commanded market share leadership in the U.S. athletic shoe industry -- e.g., controlling over half of the $1.2 billion basketball shoe business -- the company had experienced comparatively less success in Europe since its introduction in 1980. Despite intensive marketing activity surrounding the 1992 Summer Olympics in Barcelona, the Nike brand still had not achieved as much success in Europe as management had hoped. Additionally, the company sought to develop other global markets in the Asia Pacific region and Latin America.

The basic question was how to best approach the internationalization of Nike. Should the company attempt to duplicate their past marketing efforts in the U.S. that had made them so successful? If so, how? Essentially, the company had to decide how to best build global brand equity for the Nike brand. This task was complicated by image issues, both domestically and abroad, that threatened to have negative impact on Nike's brand equity. Nike was criticized in the U.S. and elsewhere for its labor practices and its aggressive marketing strategy. Nike's efforts to achieve dominance in the international sports equipment market would be met with numerous other challenges during the 1990s. The company's ability to meet and surpass these challenges would determine its success in the global sports market.

NIKE'S DOMESTIC HISTORY

The Early Years

The Nike story begins with its founder, sports enthusiast Phil Knight. Knight grew up in Oregon -- a haven for the running micro-culture -- with a deep passion for athletics in general and running in particular. In 1962, Knight started Blue Ribbon Sports, the precursor company to Nike. At the time, the athletic shoe industry was dominated by two German companies, Adidas and Puma. Knight recognized a neglected segment of serious athletes that had specialized needs that were not being addressed by the major players. The concept was simple: Provide high quality running shoes designed especially for athletes *by* athletes. Knight believed that "high-tech" shoes for runners could be manufactured at competitive prices if imported from abroad. After completing his degree in 1962, Knight embarked on a world tour that included a visit to Japan. During his visit, Knight contacted Onitsuka Tiger -- an athletic shoe manufacturer with a reputation for high quality products -- to convince them of his vision for the athletic shoe market. When asked who he represented, Knight made up a name -- and Blue Ribbon Sports was born.

In December 1963, Knight received his first shipment of 200 Tiger shoes, which he promptly stored in the Blue Ribbon warehouse -- his family's basement. In the 1960's, Oregon was filled with impassioned runners who possessed a hard-wired dedication to their sport. Without much cash to do any advertising for his products, Knight crafted his "grass roots" philosophy of selling athletic shoes: Speaking to athletes in their language and on their level, sharing their true passion for running and listening to their feedback about his products and the sport. Each weekend Knight would travel from track meet to track meet, high school and college, talking to athletes and selling Tiger shoes from the trunk of his green Plymouth Valiant.

In 1964, Knight asked Bill Bowerman, his track coach at the University of Oregon, to join him at Blue Ribbon Sports. Bowerman had a knack for designing running shoes for the track team and constantly experimented with new products. Knight approached Bowerman with the concept for his business plan, and, that year, the Blue Ribbon Sports partnership was formed, with Knight and Bowerman each contributing $500. In the first year of their partnership, Blue Ribbon Sports sold 1,300 Tiger running shoes totaling $8,000 in revenues.

In 1965, sales rose to $20,000 and profits rose to $3,240. Needless to say, Knight kept his job as an accountant and Bowerman kept his job as a track coach. In 1967, Bowerman developed the Marathon, the first running shoe made with a lightweight, durable, nylon upper. Sales for Blue Ribbon began to rise as word about the innovation spread in the running community. The next year Bowerman developed two new products: the Cortez -- Blue Ribbon's best seller -- and the Boston -- the first running shoe with a full-length cushioned midsole, a radical innovation in running shoe design. By 1969, sales reached $300,000, and Knight, then an Assistant Professor of Business Administration at Portland State University, resigned to dedicate himself full time to Blue Ribbon Sports which now employed 20 workers.

The Formative Years

By 1971, the company had reached $1 million in sales and Knight decided to venture out on his own. Manufacturing his own line of shoes required choosing a new, marketable brand name as the Blue Ribbon name seemed too cumbersome for consumers. Knight wanted to use the name "Dimension Six" to reflect the six dimensions of sports -- the fan, the event, the arena, the equipment, the media, and the shoes or apparel. Other Blue Ribbon executives felt the name was too long and lobbied for something else.

Just days before the product was to go out to distributors, Jeff Johnson -- the company's third employee -- suggested the name Nike, the winged Greek Goddess of victory, which had come to him in a dream the night before. Although nobody else liked the name or knew what it stood for, it seemed better than Dimension Six, and thus the Nike name was accepted. Around the same time, Knight had asked a designer friend to propose some ideas for a logo for the new product. She submitted twelve proposals, none of which were liked by anybody at Blue Ribbon. Due to time constraints -- the product was set to hit the shelves in days -- the management team finally decided to go with the least objectionable logo, "a fat check mark." Thus, the famous Nike "swoosh" was born for a total cost of $35!

The year 1973 witnessed Nike's next big marketing move. University of Oregon running star, Steve Prefontaine, became the first athlete to be paid to wear Nike shoes.

Prefontaine epitomized "the athlete against the establishment" attitude that was at the foundation of the company's irreverence and challenge the status quo. Knight explains, "Pre(fontaine) was a rebel from a working-class background, a guy full of cockiness and pride and guts. Pre's spirit is the cornerstone of this company's soul." Knight had founded the company with the attitude to do whatever it would take to defeat established running shoe companies and "the system." Just as Prefontaine did not care what other people thought, Knight was nurturing a corporate culture along the same lines. Knight explains:[2]

> We were able to get a lot of great ones under contract -- people like Steve Prefontaine and Alberto Salazar -- because we spent a lot of time at track events and had relationships with the runners, but mostly because we were doing interesting things with our shoes. Naturally, we thought the world stopped and started in the lab and everything revolved around the product.

Nike's first sponsorship of athletes was relatively inexpensive but, more importantly, very productive. Prefontaine never lost a race in four years at the University of Oregon and went on to set a number of U.S. running records. Jon Anderson, another long distance runner, won the Boston Marathon in a pair of Nike shoes. The early success of these Nike-sponsored runners led Knight to sign up athletes in other sports. The abundantly talented, mercurial Ilie Nastase became Nike's first tennis athletic endorser shortly before becoming the world's top-ranked tennis player. The budget was still tight, however, so only the most cost-effective athletes could be signed.

In 1974, Nike introduced to the general public a Bowerman prototype called the Waffle Trainer. The diffusion of the Waffle Trainer benefited from the so-called "pyramid of influence" that Nike had come to believe characterized the athletic shoe marketplace -- i.e., the fact that product and brand choices of consumers in the mass market were influenced by the preferences and behavior of a small percentage of top athletes. The reality was that the vast majority of athletic shoes were never actually used "on the court," but rather were used in other settings, e.g., for just "walking around." Nevertheless, Nike was convinced that the choices of these more casual users were affected by the choices of more serious athletes. Fueled by this "trickle-down" marketing, it quickly became the best-selling training shoe in the country.

By the end of 1974, Nike revenues had reached $4.8 million, and the company employed over 250 people. In 1978, the company officially changed its name from Blue Ribbon Sports to Nike, Inc., reflecting the growing recognition of the Nike brand name and the popularity of the Bowerman innovations. By 1980, the company had 2700 employees and sales of $270 million, surpassing Adidas as the number one athletic shoe company in the United States with almost 50 percent market share.

The Troubled Years

The popularity of running, however, was beginning to give way in the early 1980's to new categories such as fitness and aerobics. The new trends were dominated by women, a market segment that had thus far remained largely unaddressed by Nike. As a result, growth for Nike started to tail off as competitors such as Reebok were better positioned to ride the aerobics wave. Around this time, Reebok made a batch of aerobic shoes with soft, garment leather instead of the traditional "tough" athletic shoe leather. The shoes caught fire in the market place. In the process, Reebok introduced new attribute, and benefit considerations to the athletic shoe industry, namely "style," "fashion," "comfort" and "for women." Their soft leather shoes were supple, comfortable to wear and made women's feet look smaller. Suddenly, Reebok became the industry darling. Nike's reputation for performance and innovation, its dedication to serious athletes and its focus on the male consumer segment did not help them much in the more fashion-conscious aerobics market. Market share began to drop, and warehouses became overstocked with running shoes. Nike's first layoff occurred in 1984, followed by two money losing quarters in 1985. Finally, although Nike reached $1 billion in sales in 1986, they lost the market share lead to Reebok. By 1987, Reebok dominated the U.S. athletic shoe market, owning 30 percent of the market as compared to Nike's 18 percent. Phil Knight explains:[3]

> Reebok came out of nowhere to dominate the aerobics market, which we completely miscalculated. We made an aerobics shoe that was functionally superior to Reebok's, but we missed the styling. Reebok's shoe was sleek and attractive, while ours was sturdy and clunky. We also decided against using garment leather, as Reebok had done, because it wasn't durable. By the time we developed a leather shoe that was both strong and soft, Reebok had established a brand, won a huge chunk of sales and gained momentum to go right by us.

The Transition Years

Reebok's meteoric rise forced Nike to chart a new direction with a fresh approach to the market. Nike had learned some valuable lessons. Subsequently, the company would put the spotlight on the consumer -- not just the product -- and become more marketing-oriented as a result. Nike would broaden their marketing effort to embrace consumers and the brand as well as the design and manufacture of products. Rather than copy Reebok's emphasis on style, Nike decided to keep their focus on performance, but devote more attention to basketball, which had continued its recent rise in popularity. Perhaps more importantly, Nike set out to change how they marketed new products, creating a new marketing formula which linked concepts related to shoes, colors, clothes, athletes, logos and their first-ever wide-spread, mass market television advertising.

Nike had never really advertised much because they felt advertising did nothing more than possibly come between the intimate relationship that a runner had with his or her shoes. Advertising and commercialism was felt to be nothing short of heresy for the purist athlete. Nike had only advertised in peer-group running journals which they tolerated only because they were published by runners themselves. Even then, all advertising remained performance-oriented, with no models, no gimmicks, and no hype. As part of "reinventing," Nike decided to take to the airwaves for the new basketball campaign. For the task of developing the campaign, Nike turned to Dan Wieden, president of Wieden and Kennedy, a little-known advertising agency just a short drive from Nike headquarters. Wieden fondly recalls Phil Knight's first word, "Hi. I'm Phil Knight and I don't believe in advertising." Wieden and Kennedy would soon change his mind.

Nike developed an innovative new cushioning technology that was used first with the Air Max running shoes. The ad that showcased this new shoe was in its own way a bold innovation, albeit a daring and risky one. The "Revolution in Motion" spot used the there-to-fore untouched Beatles song as an anthem (at the cost of hundreds of thousands of dollars in licensing fees) in a TV ad that used novel black & white, 16mm, hand-held cinematography to depict professional athletes and "regular people" of all ages involved in sports. Close-up shots in the ads clearly depicted the heel of the shoe compressing and springing back after contact with the ground. Complimentary print ads were run in horizontal and vertical publications. The campaign debuted in March 1987. Scott Bedbury, Nike's Director of Advertising at the time, recalls:

> The Revolution ad was a powerful brand statement and a massive handshake from Nike to the consumers. The ads successfully got across, both implicitly and explicitly, the product technology. It was able to communicate to a wide range of people, but still was true to the Nike brand. It reflected Nike's "soul" and a deep, almost genetic understanding of what it meant to be "Nike" and how that could and should be expressed in advertising.

Air Max was a huge success, selling $75 million at retail in its first year. Within a year, air technology was also introduced into selected higher-end shoe models in basketball, tennis and other categories. Applying this new marketing concept to basketball required choosing a new athlete to represent the product benefits and Nike attitude. In 1985, Nike managed to sign then-rookie guard Michael Jordan to endorse Nike basketball shoes after Adidas, Jordan's first choice, refused to match Nike's offer. Although Jordan was still an "up-and-coming" basketball superstar, most basketball followers agreed that he was going to be something special. Nike bet on Jordan, and it paid off. His very first commercial began by showing a basketball rolling along an outdoor court towards the future superstar. As Jordan picked up the ball and drove toward the basket, the sound of jet engines roared in the background. As Jordan took flight, the engines screamed louder. The slow motion camera followed Jordan's body as he gracefully glided towards the basket for a full ten seconds. At the end of the thirty seconds, Michael Jordan was a household name and later became the premier superstar in basketball.

The Air Jordan line of basketball shoes literally flew off the shelves. Nike sold over $100 million of Air Jordans in the first year alone, although sales slipped when Jordan broke his foot in the following year. Considering that "successful" new product launches typically sold $20 million, Air Jordans represented one of the lone bright spots for the company as Reebok continued its surge ahead in the aerobics market in the mid-1980's. Everything about the Air Jordan line was a perfect fit. The air technology was a hit with consumers, Michael Jordan quickly became recognized as the best player in basketball, and the advertising campaign captivated Nike's target segment. Knight reflects back on the success of Air Jordans:[4]

> Basketball, unlike casual shoes, was all about performance, so it fit under the Nike umbrella. And the shoe itself was terrific. It was so colorful that the NBA banned it -- which was great.... Michael Jordan wore the shoes despite being threatened with a fine, and of course, played like no one has ever played before. It was everything you could ask for, and sales just took off.... (Air Jordan's) success showed us that slicing things up into digestible chunks was the wave of the future.

The Dominant Years

The Air Jordan line sparked a new wave of momentum for Nike. As Michael Jordan flew through the air on his way to three championships, the image-consciousness of the market gave way to a re-emphasis on performance. This time it was Reebok who got lost in the midst of a transition. Just as Nike had paid too little attention to the rise of the aerobics trend of the mid-1980's, Reebok paid too little attention to a consumer desire for performance-related products in the late 1980's. Also during this time, new competitors entered the market chasing Reebok, not Nike. Nike stayed on the forefront of performance, while competitors such as L.A. Gear vied with Reebok for control of the fashion market.

While Reebok tried to breathe life into the fashion segment, Nike continued pushing the performance of its shoes. In 1988, Nike aired its first ads in their new "Just Do It" ad campaign. The $20 million month-long blitz -- subtly urging Americans to participate more actively in sports -- featured 12 TV spots in all. The campaign marked the launch of a category -- cross-training shoes designed for athletes who played more than one sport -- which was new to Nike and the athletic shoe industry as a whole. The "Just Do It" campaign challenged a generation of athletic enthusiasts to chase their goals no matter how difficult or elusive they might seem, a natural manifestation of Nike's attitude of self-empowerment through sports. "It" could refer to anything or any sport that the consumer wanted to play, and for every sport, Nike wanted consumers to believe that they had the perfect shoe. Self-empowerment reflected an attitude relevant to both celebrity and non-celebrity athletes, and the "Just Do It" advertising used both. One non-celebrity ad featured Walt Stack, an 80 year-old long distance runner, running across the Golden Gate bridge as part of his daily morning running routine. The "Just Do It" trailer appeared on the screen as the shirtless Stack made his way past the center of the bridge on a chilly San Francisco morning. Talking to the camera as it zoomed in and while still running, Stack remarked, "People ask me how I keep my teeth from chattering when it's cold." Pausing, Stack matter-of-factly replied, "I leave them in my locker."

By 1990, sales had surpassed $2 billion, and Nike had reclaimed the market share lead from Reebok in the U.S. Nike successfully applied their new marketing formula -- blending performance and attitude through strategic product development, endorsements and advertising -- to other categories including tennis and baseball. Nike ads, reflecting the company's character, addressed controversial issues head-on. The ads ranged from Charles Barkley pronouncing that he was "Not a Role Model" to a 1995 ad showcasing a long distance runner inflicted with the AIDS virus. Finally, Nike continued to court the world's best athletes that they felt could represent some aspect of the Nike "soul" and image. Sports marketing at Nike -- the sponsorship side of the business -- was undeniably of huge importance. As Knight recalled:

> The whole thing happens on TV now. A few years back we were extremely proud of a novel, three-quarter-high shoe we'd developed. But we only sold 10,000 of them the first year. Then John McEnroe had ankle trouble and switched to the shoe. We sold 1 1/2 million pairs the following year. The final game of the NCAA basketball tournament is better than any runway in Paris for launching a shoe. Kids climb up next to the screen to see what the players are wearing.

Nike kept their "finger on the pulse" of the shoe-buying public, in part, through their use of "EKINs" (Nike spelled backwards) -- sports-loving employees whose job was to hit the streets to disseminate information about Nike and find out what was on the minds of retailers and consumers. Nike's "Brand Strength Monitor" -- created by their marketing research and insights guru, Jerome Conlan -- more formally tracked consumer perceptions three times a year to identify marketplace trends. In areas where they felt less knowledgeable, e.g., outside of track and basketball, Nike was more likely to commission customized research studies. Nike's inventory control system, called "Futures" also helped Nike to better gauge consumer response and plan production accordingly. Nike required retailers to order up to 80 percent of their purchases six to eight months in advance in return for guaranteed delivery times and a discount of up to 10 percent. Nike sweetened their relationships with retailers such as Foot Locker by also giving them early looks at new models, as well as the rights to exclusively sell certain models.

Sales soared past $3 billion in 1991 as Michael Jordan took the Chicago Bulls to their first of three championships. By 1993, Nike athletes included 265 NBA basketball players, 275 NFL football players and 290 baseball players. Half the teams that won the NCAA college basketball championships over the past 10 years had worn Nike shoes. In total, Nike had arrangements with college coaches and athletic departments that resulted in over 60 top tier "Nike schools." Many of these arrangements included apparel -- an area that had grown in importance to Nike. As part of a complete overhaul in 1993, Nike decided to re-focus their apparel business. Before, with the exception of track & field, apparel was mostly designed to just complement shoes. Nike decided to put more emphasis on top-of-line performance wear -- uniforms and apparel worn in actual competition -- through their Organized Team Sports group and F.I.T. lines. Although representing only a small percentage of apparel revenues, these new initiatives were thought to provide halo to other apparel lines and be consistent with broadening the Nike brand meaning to encompass "performance in sports" and not just shoes.

NIKE'S EUROPEAN HISTORY

The same year that Nike overtook Adidas as the number one athletic shoe company in the U.S. -- 1980 -- Phil Knight dispatched five employees to Europe to establish a presence for the U.S. shoe manufacturer there. Because of its favorable tax and business operation laws, the group set up an office in Amsterdam and began its mission to establish the Nike name and brand. Though Nike had succeeded in breaking Adidas' dominance in the U.S., taking over from the leader in its home arena would be a greater challenge.

Initial Growth

In the early 1980's, the most popular sports in Europe were soccer, track and field and tennis. If Nike wanted to have a significant presence in Europe, the company would have to establish its name in each of these sports in each of Europe's five primary markets -- Germany, France, England, Italy, and Spain -- which accounted for the bulk of the European sports shoe and apparel sales.

Nike's European marketing team knew it needed to attack one sport at a time. Given the company's track and field heritage, Nike initially focused on developing links in track and field whose sizable popularity in Europe was reflected by the fact that it was the second most televised sport (after soccer). Using track and field as its entry, the company sought ex-runners with the same devotion and intensity to the sport as Nike to help develop the brand. Finding such athletes to work with Nike, however, proved to be an elusive task. Of its key country accounts, only in England was Nike successful in recruiting an ex-runner, Brendan Foster -- Britain's premier distance runner in the 1970's and a 1976 Olympic gold medalist -- to be its local distributor. With Foster's connections and persona, Nike was able to pursue its grassroots approach to brand development there. Elsewhere in Europe, however, Nike was forced to partner with the largest local athletic shoe and apparel distributor.

Nike faced formidable competition in Europe. Adidas, the German shoe company, dominated the European sports market. Together with Puma -- a spin-off of Adidas -- the two companies controlled over 75 percent of Europe's athletic shoe and apparel market. For decades, the two companies had developed grassroots allegiances of local sports teams, particularly soccer, track and field, tennis and rugby. They both had endorsement contracts with top European athletes in each of these sports and sponsored many local teams in cities and towns across Europe. Adidas, in particular, was respected for the quality of its shoes and had earned the reputation as the European performance brand. For any company to establish a presence in Germany -- Europe's largest country market -- in the face of these two companies was considered nearly impossible.

Early Nike advertising was conducted at the country level. In 1981, Nike highlighted American tennis star, John McEnroe, in a set of print ads that were run around the time of Wimbledon. These ads played on McEnroe's "nasty boy" image, showing a Nike tennis shoe and a headline underneath that read, "McEnroe Swears by Them." In another version, the headline read "McEnroe's Favorite Four Letter Word." McEnroe's triumph at Wimbledon that year helped Nike gain some badly needed exposure, as well as credibility as an authentic athletic shoe among European consumers.

Further Expansion

For seven years, Nike struggled to build its presence in Europe. By the end of 1987, Nike's European revenues had grown to $150 million, representing 5 percent of the European athletic shoe market and a growing percentage of Nike's total revenues. Compared to its U.S. position, however, Nike's penetration of the European market was comparatively insignificant. Perhaps even more disturbing to Nike was its inability to control the growth of its brand. In most countries, the Nike distributor who controlled marketing and advertising rights was not necessarily highly motivated about selling Nike. To overcome this limitation -- but still maintain its quality image -- Nike restricted its product line to primarily high-end, higher priced shoes. In doing so, the company forfeited volume and hence market share. Though the company also sold some low-end, relatively inexpensive shoes, it had no product offerings for the expansive "middle market." Moreover, as a result of this pricing policy, many European consumers saw Nike as an aggressive, expensive American brand.

Because Nike distributors controlled advertising in their local markets, each continued to develop their own interpretation of the Nike brand and identity programs. While Nike productively embarked on the "Just Do It" umbrella campaign in the U.S., Grey

Advertising -- the agency that managed the Nike account in five countries -- was developing separate, and not necessarily reinforcing, ad campaigns in each European country. Nike also did not have the same means of displaying their shoes and retailing them to customers as in the U.S. -- athletic shoe specialty stores did not really exist in Europe.

In late 1987, Nike sent a new man to head its European operations -- David Kottkamp -- with a mission to focus on building the brand there. It became clear to Kottkamp that the only way to take control of the brand was to take greater control of the advertising and product strategies. To enable this to happen, Kottkamp focused on repurchasing licensing rights to Nike products from their licensed distributors in Europe.

While Kottkamp was initiating these negotiations with Nike distributors -- a task that would take several years -- he launched Nike's first centralized print campaign in 1988 as a means to introduce "Air" technology in that market. Despite objections from Nike's European distributors, the campaign achieved some success. As a result of its favorable response, Nike decided to develop additional pan-European advertising campaigns for both print and TV. Looking for broad appeal, Nike hoped to recreate the success of its umbrella "Revolution" ad campaign from the U.S. Instead of focusing on country *differences*, however, the campaign would attempt to highlight country *similarities*. Lacking the stable of famous athletes in Europe that Nike had back home in America, the pan-European approach seemed to make the most sense. To reach this audience, the company doubled its advertising campaign from $5 million in 1987 to $10 million in 1988. In an effort to be cost effective, Nike wanted any European campaign to be broad enough to be used in multiple countries. In 1989, Nike introduced its "Gospel" campaign. This powerful, uplifting campaign was unquestionably American in its look and Nike in its attitude. Using the tag line, "True to its [Nike] soul", the campaign ran primarily on MTV Europe and Star TV in Asia, as well as various national TV networks. The print campaign developed the theme that there was air in Nike shoes because there was none in various places where well-known athletic events took place -- such as the Chicago Stadium, Bislett Stadium, and Ku'Damm.

Regaining Control

Over the next three years -- while Kottkamp worked on repurchasing licensing rights -- Nike relied heavily on advertising to promote its brand. The direction to take with that advertising, however, was not obvious. Research revealed that a 2-minute TV spot designed to portray Nike products and attitude -- featuring Jimi Hendrix' adventurous rendition of the National Anthem at the Woodstock rock festival and the tag line, "Play Hard. Die Old." -- was seen as too aggressive and was not well received. Nike attempted to blend centralized and localized work. Thus, Nike did import some of its American heroes to promote the brand in Europe -- European marketing managers could look at Wieden & Kennedy's latest creations and chose ads they felt were relevant. For example, the "Tennis Lessons" spot that spoofed Agassi and McEnroe's rebellious image was shown in Italy, Germany and elsewhere. In 1991, the "Instant Karma" spot used John Lennon's powerful tune to introduce the "radical" new line of Air Huaraches. Interspersed with scenes of Nike's star athletic endorsers -- Michael Jordan, Scottie Pippen and Joan Benoit Samuelson -- as well as everyday people working out were, in the American and English-speaking market, a series of English phrases. Overseas, stick-figure symbols designed by a Nike art director, Michael

Prieve, were used instead. This creative solution -- literally devising a new graphics language -- allowed the ads to be run ultimately in 65 countries in all.

By the end of 1991, Kottkamp had successfully regained control of 90 percent of Nike's European distribution. In comparison, Adidas only controlled 65 percent and Reebok only controlled 40 percent of their European distribution. Getting European retailers, who were used to ordering whatever they wanted, whenever they wanted from the Adidas warehouse, to adopt Nike's Futures program, so successful in the U.S., was a harder sell. Nevertheless, now that they had greater control over their marketing, Nike could concentrate on developing their brand in the manner that they desired.

Nike in 1992

Without question, Europe in 1992 represented a tremendous growth opportunity for Nike. At that time, 400 million pairs of athletic footwear were sold in the U.S. Europe with 130 million *more* people than the States, bought 280 million *fewer* pairs of shoes. The largest buying group there, those in their teens and 20's, owned an average of just two pairs each (compared to an average of at least four pairs in the U.S.). There were several explanations for the discrepancy. First, Europeans had a different view of the role of sports and top athletes and were not as idolizing of their sports heroes as were Americans. The American workout ethic, epitomized by health and fitness clubs and a firm belief of the essential importance of exercise, was not as widely embraced in Europe. Moreover, as a general rule, Europeans were slower to embrace sneakers as off-court shoes and were more likely to wear fine leather shoes even in casual settings. Either on or off the court, Europeans just needed fewer athletic shoes.

The image of athletic shoes was changing, however, and sneakers were no longer a dead giveaway that a person was, more likely than not, an American tourist. Youth especially seemed captivated by the "American" image of Nike and Reebok. As a result, some progress had been made in Europe. By 1992, Nike's European sneaker revenues were approximately $1.1 billion -- nearly six times the 1987 figure! Revenues grew 100 percent between 1989 and 1990. Its European promotion budget had risen from $10 million to $50 million. Adidas -- with over $1.5 billion in revenues -- still had more than double the market share of Nike in Europe. Though Adidas still dominated the European market, Nike had made significant inroads in the last five years, and the German giant and its counterpart, Puma, had lost market share to Nike and Reebok. To realize its goal of being the number one sport and fitness company in the world, Nike had to dominate Europe.

Its two main competitors, Adidas and Reebok, posed very different challenges. Adidas was the established brand with a loyal consumer base, especially among the 35-and-older generation. Its strong grass-roots presence and entrenchment in amateur sports sponsorships -- particularly soccer -- had bolstered Adidas' number one market position in Europe. Reebok was a relatively new company in Europe, but its success in the U.S. women's fitness market had carried over to Europe. Reebok was the third-place brand in most European countries, behind Adidas and Nike. Determined to overtake Adidas and prevent Reebok from continuing to gain ground, Nike focused its attention on the 1992 Barcelona Olympics, raising their overall global advertising and promotion budget to $240 million, up from $150 million the previous year, committing $50 million to Europe. Tom

Clark, Nike's VP for product marketing at the time, explained: "We're looking to increase worldwide market share by 10 percent and to grind Reebok and Adidas down."[5]

With the rise in popularity of basketball as an international sport, Nike planned to lead its marketing charge with its strong stable of basketball superstars. Leading up to the Olympics, U.S. Olympic "Dream Team" members such as Charles Barkley, Michael Jordan and others were featured in European exhibition tours (where they signed autographs and participated in basketball clinics) and in a series of ad campaigns. Nike extended its superstar endorsement approach beyond just basketball and sought to play up its endorsements of other top flight world-class athletes who would spotlight Nike products in the Olympic games. Besides Michael Jordan, Nike concentrated their promotion efforts on U.S. sprinter Michael Johnson, Ukrainian pole vaulter Serge Bubka and Algerian middle-distance runner, Noureddine Morceli. Lacking its own superstar stable, Reebok responded by paying millions to outfit U.S. Olympic team members -- including the basketball Dream Team -- and NBC announcers in Barcelona with Reebok warm-ups and attire. In many ways, the 1992 Barcelona Olympics were a great success for Nike -- the publicity surrounding key members of the U.S. basketball Dream Team's objection to wearing their Reebok warm-ups at their gold medal award ceremony, combined with the medaling of scores of Nike athletes offered unprecedented exposure to the brand and the loyalty it instilled from the world's best athletes.

Many European consumers, however, still found the brand intimidating, aggressive, unreachable and unattainable. Moreover, retailers bristled at the Nike's Futures program and product mix, viewing the company as arrogant. To reach its growth goals in Europe, Nike needed to find a way to change consumers' perceptions of Nike as an expensive, aggressive American brand.

Hitting Its Stride

Despite some successes, Nike was clearly struggling to extend its U.S. reputation for performance and innovation into the European market. In hindsight, Nike had probably over-relied on advertising and American sports heroes, and had not spent enough time and money "authenticating" the brand as they had so carefully done in originally building the brand in the U.S. As a result, the Nike brand image was too fashion-oriented and not performance-oriented enough. A more grassroots approach was needed that built some credibility and relevance with the Nike brand in European sports -- especially soccer. As an important first step, Nike became more actively involved as a sponsor of soccer youth leagues, local clubs and national teams. Unlike how they had approached other categories, apparel -- not footwear -- would provide the entry point to build the consumer franchise for the Nike brand in soccer.

As had been the case in the U.S., Nike also needed to first win on the true "field of sport." Winning in the stores would then follow. Authenticity required that consumers see the product used by the right athletes in the right way -- winning. As luck would have it, Brazil, the only national soccer team for which Nike had any real sponsorships during the 1994 World Cup -- a number of the Brazilian stars had individual contracts to wear Nike shoes -- won the premiere event. Their victory provided two very different benefits for Nike: Internally, it inspired confidence and motivation; externally, it lent credibility to a soccer-crazed world. Other soccer endorsements followed, e.g., leading soccer teams

Borussia Dortmund in Germany, Paris Saint Germain, Boca Juniors in Argentina, and the Italian national team and soccer players such as Romario, Bebetto, Paolo Maldini, Andreas Moller, Ian Wright and Eric Cantona. A Nike ad created for the 1994 World Cup, dubbed "The Wall," showed many of these prominent players springing to life from billboards as they literally kicked a soccer ball around the world. Nike also out-bid Adidas and Reebok for the sponsorship rights to the men's and women's U.S. national team. Outside soccer, Nike tried to sign up the best athletes in other countries to push Nike products locally, e.g., baseball player Hideo Nomo in Japan and Formula I race car champion Michael Schumacher in Germany.

Nike's new focus was to become seen as more culturally, geographically, and personally relevant to local consumers abroad. The challenge, however, was to find the right local country managers who would have the necessary intuitive understanding and feel for the Nike brand to understand which elements of the marketing program should stay the same and which ones should be adapted and how. In August 1992, Weiden & Kennedy had opened up an Amsterdam office, headed by creative director Susan Hoffman, to better learn and understand the local market. The first campaign that was produced there -- operatic Air Max spots that ran during the 1992 Olympics -- were so successful they were even used in other markets outside Europe, including the U.S.

Building on the success of its "Just Do It" campaign in the U.S., Nike attempted to introduce the tag line into its European advertising in the Spring of 1993. Nike hoped that this campaign would successfully communicate Nike's core values of authenticity, performance and athletics, and help establish an emotional connection with European consumers through sports. The new campaign was a nice counterpart to the flashy, Barcelona-inspired Olympic spots featuring celebrity athletes. The "Just Do It" ad campaign was adapted for the European market in 1993 by going "back to basics." Designed to make the Nike brand more approachable, understandable and applicable to people's lives, the new campaign wrapped up an inspirational message in visuals showing common folk displaying a passion for sport. The four spots featured kids and adults running and playing soccer in the streets, wheelchair athletes climbing mountainous hills as part of a race, and two runners winding their way beside a picturesque lake. Overall, Nike allocated $80 million to $100 million to European advertising and promotion in 1993. Four commercials showing professional athletes engaged in competitive sports also were translated and showed in 52 local markets.

PROGRESS AND CHALLENGES

Throughout the 1990s, Nike's marketing and advertising program was able, in their own marketing terms, to "widen the access point" and make the brand relevant to an increasingly broader range of consumers. To meet their corporate goal of "enhancing people's lives through sports and fitness" and "keeping the magic of sport alive," Nike's unique approach creatively blended "footwear," "apparel," "advertising," "sports marketing" and "retail." While maintaining relatively constant retail distribution and premium pricing strategies, Nike's innovative product development -- putting out more than one shoe style, on average, *every day* -- and bold advertising demonstrated that the brand was as much about attitude and imagery as shoes and clothing. Riding the wave of increased sports participation and consumption of sports entertainment, Nike's marketing formula was characterized as, "integrating the swoosh into the cultural fabric of sports and harnessing its emotional power." In 1996, Knight publicly set a corporate goal of growing the $6.5 billion company to $12 billion by decade's end.

Nike Marketing Evolves

By 1993, Nike's marketing strategy had evolved to a two-tiered approach where individual markets were targeted with ads featuring local heroes and local settings, while ads featuring sports popular across Europe (e.g., soccer, tennis, track and fitness) were marketed throughout the continent. This approach enabled Nike to earn further credibility at the local level and reach a broad consumer base at the same time. The company increased its marketing intensity, allocating as much as $100 million to European advertising in 1993 alone. As a result of its reworked advertising strategy, Nike's European revenues climbed from $920 million in 1994 to $1.3 billion in 1996, and its lofty goal of European market leadership seemed attainable.

By the end of fiscal 1996, Nike was poised to pursue aggressive growth in its European markets. The company had bolstered its image as a top-flight global sportswear manufacturer with a successful advertising campaign coinciding with the 1994 World Cup. Sports marketing efforts were improved by the signing of the Brazilian and Italian national teams in soccer in 1996 to long-term deals. Observing the success of Nike's soccer campaigns and anticipating the global marketing opportunities to come with the 1996 Atlanta Olympics, Nike's CEO Phil Knight set ambitious growth goals in the company's 1995 annual report. Knight expressed goals of growing into "an 11-digit company" and ultimately "transcend[ing] the industry."

As Nike set its sights on lofty targets in Europe, it also began rapid expansion into Asian markets. Much of Nike's manufacturing and production was based in Asian factories, but Nike had yet to place particular importance on Asian consumers. Asian-Pacific countries contributed less than 10 percent of Nike's total sales, yet over half of the world's population resided there. The potential for growth in this market was enormous.

Soon after Nike's ambitious market expansion into Asia, the company experienced several setbacks domestically. First, as fashions inevitably changed, Nike found itself behind the curve, much like their experience with the aerobic fitness wave in the 1980s. Generally, many consumers viewed trainers or running shoes as out of style, useful only for exercise. Second, Nike's corporate image suffered, due in part to controversial marketing projects (such as contributing $25,000 to the legal defense fund for Tonya Harding – the figure skater accused of conspiring to injure a competitor before the 1994 Winter Olympic Trials) and accusations of unethical labor practices in its Asian factories. Perhaps worst of all, Nike was losing its appeal in the eyes of its core consumers, youths between 12 and 18 years of age. According to one research firm,[6] 40 percent of kids surveyed considered Nike to be one of the "coolest" brands in 1998, a 12 percent drop from the previous year. As Nike pursued global business, the company faced the dual challenges of increasing its international market share while ensuring that its image did not tarnish in the process.

NIKE'S GLOBAL GROWTH

International Advertising Efforts

Nike's first truly global advertising campaign consisted of sponsorships and advertisements during the 1994 World Cup. The campaign helped Nike to earn credibility as a sportswear provider for the world's most popular sport. Recognizing that soccer represented one of the best entry points into new markets, Nike embarked on a mission to become the world's leading soccer equipment provider by 2002. To gain visibility in the sport, the company began adding national teams to its sponsorship roster. It spent an unprecedented $200 million in 1997 to sponsor Brazil's national team for 10 years, and added several other countries to its list, including Italy and Nigeria. Domestically, Nike began sponsoring the U.S. national teams in 1994, and shortly thereafter signed on with Major League Soccer to sponsor five of the 10 teams in the league. Nike also supported their high-profile campaigns by sponsoring youth soccer leagues in Europe and forming a tournament called the Nike International Premier Cup that featured the best youth teams from throughout the continent. Nike's goal in sponsoring both world champion teams and local clubs was to become a household name in all levels of soccer competition, as market leader Adidas had been for decades.

After the '94 World Cup, Nike's next global marketing opportunity came from the 1996 Summer Olympics. Nike was not an official sponsor of the Games, but along with its stable of sponsored athletes providing guaranteed global exposure, the company targeted audiences worldwide with 32 separate print and television ads. Among the most notable advertisement from the $35 million campaign was a controversial series featuring athletes pushing themselves to physically and visually agonizing limits. The television version of this ad used a boisterous Iggy Pop song called "Search and Destroy" as its soundtrack, and showed graphic footage of a boxer losing his mouthpiece after a punch, as well as a clip of American marathoner Bob Kempainen vomiting on his shoes after winning the U.S. marathon trials in 1996. The latter image appeared in a print campaign with the caption "If you can't stand the heat, get out of Atlanta" attached. In addition to TV and print advertising, Nike developed a web site to promote its involvement with athletes in the Games. The web site, titled "@LANTA," featured daily updates from Atlanta showing event results and photos, as well as descriptions of shoes and apparel that Nike-sponsored athletes wore. Though available to anyone with web access, the site was intended primarily for members of the press. Nevertheless, the site provided an opportunity for global advertising since it contained product information and showcased Nike endorsed athletes. Additionally, the site contained still photos from the controversial television spots mentioned above that provided browsers with further connections to Nike's commercial endeavors.

A Kinder, Gentler Marketing Approach

Throughout its campaigns in the years between 1994 and 1997, much of Nike's advertising kept in the tradition of its irreverent, rebellious spirit. This irreverence did not sit well with many European consumers, however. An ad that ran during the 1996 European Soccer Championships pitted a team of international soccer stars against a satanic figure and assorted demons on the pitch of a rather hellish stadium. Called "Nike vs. Evil," the controversial ad received a strongly ambivalent response, meeting with success in some markets but drawing considerable ire from the media in others. Some television stations even refused to run the ad during prime time, for fear of upsetting children viewers.

Another soccer advertisement profiled the flamboyant French star Eric Cantona, who proudly recounted how his history of rude behavior, such as spitting on his manager and calling him a "bag of s---," earned him a Nike contract. Again, the media responded with strong indictments of the ad, including a biting editorial in the newsletter of FIFA, international soccer's governing body. Similar reactions resulted from a billboard ad displayed in America during the 1996 Summer Olympics that proclaimed, "You don't win silver, you lose gold." While this aggressive marketing approach had helped to propel Nike to the top of the American market, the European public responded less favorably to this strategy. Despite all the work Nike was doing to establish its brand on the grass-roots level, the brand image still suffered from negative public perceptions as a result of these aggressive ad campaigns.

Compounding this image problem was the company's extravagant spending as it burst onto the soccer scene. Nike's deep pockets enabled it to have an impact immediately, in terms of marketing and sponsorships, but some consumers resented what they saw as a powerful corporation muscling in on smaller heritage brands like Umbro, Diadora and Puma. Even market leader Adidas, which was several times larger than Nike in European soccer sales for most of the 1990s, met with success when it marketed itself as an underdog to Nike. Phil Knight, responding to these image problems, said, "Now that we've reached a certain size, there's a fine line between being a rebel and being a bully."[7] For Nike, casting itself as anti-establishment fit poorly with consumers who perceived the company as *the* establishment. The local marketing strategies lent authenticity to the brand and nurtured a positive brand image, but the expensive sponsorship deals, and the elaborate, aggressive advertising contributed to public perception of Nike as overly aggressive and worked against the positive image the company strove to cultivate.

So, starting in 1997, Nike adjusted its global advertising strategy. In soccer, the local and national team sponsorships were kept because they were seen to provide links to soccer's heritage. The violence in the advertising was toned down considerably, and new ads featured famous American Nike pitchmen like Michael Jordan and Charles Barkley, playing soccer with Euro stars. Nike spent considerable R&D funds sending a research team on a global expedition to study foot morphology for application to better soccer shoe. Nike applied the results of this research to the design of their flagship soccer shoe, the Mercurial, which debuted in 1998. To tune their general global advertising so it resonated with regional tastes, the company sought cultural input from experts residing in major national markets like Japan, Germany and Brazil. Nike used two of its best-recognized athletes, Tiger Woods and Brazilian soccer star Ronaldo, in global ads to project a more international image.

Growth in Asia

After Nike had safely established itself as a contender in the European market, with sales exceeding $1 billion in 1996, and growing another 38 percent in 1997, the company sought global growth in Asia, Latin America, South America, Africa and the Middle East. Of these other regions, Asia harbored the most potential in terms of customers. Nike had long operated manufacturing plants in Asian countries such as Japan, Taiwan and South Korea, but before the 1990s the company had not focused on Asia as a target market. Japan was the first country to embrace Nike products. As early as 1992, Japan was importing $100 million worth of Nike products, and by 1997 Nike had surpassed Japanese brands Asics and Mizuno to occupy the market leader position. In the last few years of the decade, Nike began marketing projects in an effort to capitalize on the large number of potential customers in other Asian countries. China received much of the advertising attention, primarily since its population of over 2 billion spent over $2 billion annually on sneakers. Learning from the example of its mixed reception in Europe, Nike abandoned the brash attitude for its first marketing offerings designed specifically for China. The ads, from which the corps of elite American athletes usually deployed by Nike as global ambassadors of their product was primarily absent, celebrated local athletes as heroes. With these concerted efforts to demonstrate a softer side, Nike hoped to improve global perception of its brand. Nike also began courting consumers in many other countries, such as India, Thailand and Malaysia. In fiscal 1997, Nike's sales grew a stellar 76 percent in the region from the previous year. To meet this rising demand, Nike looked to expand its production and distribution operations in Asia by opening new facilities in Vietnam and upgrading existing ones in Japan, Korea and Australia.

Sales figures soared and production in the region increased into late 1997. Rapid international growth drove Nike's stock price above $70 a share for the first time in the company's history. Japan, where sales had grown fivefold over the previous seven years, now constituted Nike's second-largest market. In Asian markets, demand often exceeded supply, even with Nike shoes selling at high premiums. The company expected revenues to double in 1998. Then, the bottom fell out of the Asian economy, and suddenly Nike's booming business there stalled. The collapsing economy withered sales figures and left Nike facing canceled orders from retailers everywhere. In Japan, where shoes had sold for as much as $200 dollars a pair in recent years, sales dropped precipitously and distributors were left with excess Nike products exceeding 2 million units. The results were disastrous for Nike's overall business. In 1998, stock prices fell sharply to less than half the 1997 high of $75, worldwide orders dropped 34 percent in the fourth quarter, domestic market share dropped from 43 percent to 41 percent and the company reported its first earnings decrease in thirteen years. Nike's employee base had expanded from 9,500 to almost 22,000 in the three years between 1994 and 1997, but in early 1998 the company announced plans to trim this figure by seven percent. This measure came as part of Nike's attempt to cut net expenses by $200 million that year. Nike also reduced costs by shaving $100 million from its advertising budget, dropping many lower profile endorsers and sponsorships. In spite of the prolonged Asian recession, Nike executives remained optimistic about growth in the region. They anticipated a turnaround in the Asian economy by spring of 1999, and stood by their prediction that by 2002, Japan would constitute a billion-dollar market.

Rather than simply waiting for the Asian economic recovery to occur, Nike undertook a major marketing initiative in 1999 to boost the brand image in the region. Nike developed its first line of shoes intended for consumption solely in Asian markets. In the spring of 1999, Nike launched the Play Series 100, an entry-level offering intended to combine technology and affordability. In many Asian countries, fewer than 10 percent of the population could afford traditionally high-priced Nikes. The Play Series, priced between $15 and $40, targeted customers who did not yet own a pair of Nike shoes. With the intention of communicating to Asian consumers their region's importance in the company's growth, Nike introduced a new slogan: "It's my turn." In the Philippines, Singapore, Thailand, Indonesia, Malaysia and India, Nike constructed playgrounds, called Play Zones, for use by area youth. In addition to widening their marketing strategy, Nike expanded their retail operations in several countries. The company constructed multiple Nike-only stores in Malaysia, and the company expected to open more in other major Asian cities such as Bangkok, Singapore and Jakarta by June 2000.

This proactive approach to the Asian market yielded results as early as mid-1999. In the fourth quarter of that year, despite a continuing sales decline, orders were up 19 percent in the region while canceled orders dropped from 40 to 15 percent. This followed a third-quarter earnings increase of 70 percent. This "rebound in slow motion,"[8] as Phil Knight called it, drove the stock above $50 in the spring of that year. Growth in Asia had returned, though not to pre-recession levels. With the 2000 Olympics in Sydney, the 2002 World Cup in Japan and Korea providing excellent opportunities for Nike to reach Asian consumers live and direct, company officials expected the region to be a "great growth engine" for the future.

NIKE'S IMAGE CRISIS

The Asian economic collapse was not the only factor contributing to Nike's global sales woes during fiscal 1998. Domestically, and to some extent abroad, Nike's corporate image suffered from negative public perceptions and increasing public outcry. Two issues that brought Nike under fire from consumers were the company's labor practices in Asia and the ubiquity of its corporate logo, the swoosh.

In 1997, a labor watchdog agency published the results of Ernst & Young's 1996 audit of a Nike factory in Vietnam that found unsafe working conditions there. The audit included findings that workers were forced to work 65-hour weeks and were improperly compensated for overtime labor, they worked in areas with poor ventilation while being exposed to dangerous levels of carcinogens, and they earned little more than $10 a week. As the media reported further findings of low wages, teenage laborers and poor treatment of employees, human rights and workers' rights groups lined up to attack Nike. Among these groups were the Interfaith Center for Corporate Responsibility and Global Exchange and the United Students Against Sweatshops (USAS). Organized opposition to Nike's global practices ranged from boycotts of the company's products to letters-of-protest from congresspersons to a lawsuit against the company charging that "lies" about the company's labor practices constituted false advertising.

Nike's Counter-Measures

In response to the allegations and condemnations pouring in, Nike implemented comprehensive changes in its corporate labor policy. Perhaps sensing the rising tide of global labor concerns from the public would become a prominent media issue by the end of the decade, Nike sought to be an industry leader in employee relations. With respect to the audit, the company first stated that the unsafe conditions reported in the 1996 had already been improved, via the installation of new ventilation systems, and the enforcement of its pre-existing limit of 60-hour work weeks. Furthermore, Nike asserted that though wages for its Vietnam factory workers were extremely low by Western standards, Nike workers enjoyed a salary well above the national average. The company pointed to a 1997 assessment of its factories -- conducted by former Atlanta mayor and UN ambassador Andrew Young and his company Goodworks International -- that "found no evidence of widespread or systematic abuse."[9] In 1998, the company formally announced the implementation of new global labor standards. These new standards included age requirements for footwear workers of 18 years, the use of water-based solvents and adhesives in manufacturing, compliance with OSHA indoor air quality levels and the monitoring of labor practices by independent agencies. The same year, Nike created a Corporate Responsibility Division that consolidated the labor, environmental and community action groups already a part of the company. The stated mission of this new division was "to lead in corporate citizenship through programs that reflect caring for the world family of Nike, our teammates, our consumers and those who provide services to Nike." Additionally, Nike became a charter member of the Fair Labor Association, a White House initiative that establishes a code of conduct for global manufacturers and accredits monitoring processes in the industry. Nike enlisted FLA-approved PriceWaterhouseCoopers to conduct annual audits of each of their 500 global factories.

In 1999, Nike continued efforts to improve its labor relations and its public relations. The company instituted a 40 percent wage raise for factory workers in Indonesia. It joined the Global Alliance for Workers and Communities, a cooperative effort between private, public and non-profit companies designed to provide young adults involved in global manufacturing with the means to improve their lives and their communities. Global Alliance seeks to identify the needs of workers and their surrounding community, and then uses investments from companies such as Nike to develop programs that help meet these needs. Independently, Nike engaged in this type of local investment with their microloan program. The program, which began in Indonesia during 1999, provided small business loans to Nike factory employees and others in the surrounding community. By the end of 2000, the company expected to provide 5,000 microloans to women from communities near factories in Vietnam, Indonesia, Thailand and Pakistan in order to help them create small businesses.

Nike's measures to improve and monitor its global manufacturing conditions met with decidedly mixed responses. While some commended Nike for its community involvement, its environmental consciousness and its comparatively high wages and clean factories, others continued to condemn the company. Some activists claimed that annual audits paint an inaccurate portrait of actual conditions, since in some cases the factory management knew the date of the audit in advance and modified conditions so they appeared more favorable. Others complained that Nike employees' yearly pay did not constitute a "living wage" and continued to accuse Nike of using "sweatshop labor." To respond to the continued accusations, Nike initiated measures to provide the public with access to information about its labor practices and the results of audits. The company referred to this project as "Transparency 101," and the first step was an agreement to disclose the results of all factory audits to the public by posting them on Nike's web site starting in May of 2000. Another facet of "Transparency 101" occurred during college Spring Break the same year, when the company sent 16 undergraduates, each of whom had applied for the opportunity to tour several of Nike's global factories firsthand, to a total of

32 factories worldwide. The company then made full-text copies of every report available on the Internet.

Swoosh Ubiquity

As Nike's labor crisis in Asia seeped into the American public's consciousness, so did an increasing awareness of the company's corporate ubiquity. Nike's shorthand symbol -- the swoosh -- appeared on shoes, jerseys, hats, billboards and soccer balls across the globe with remarkable and, to some consumers, alarming frequency. One shoe model in particular boasted swooshes in nine different locations. Writers sometimes referred to newspaper sports sections as the "Nike Pages" because of the abundance of swooshes on pictured athletes. One author wrote a piece for Sports Illustrated entitled "The Swooshification of the World" that imagined a future in which the swoosh transcended sports to become a letter of the alphabet and the new presidential seal, among other things. As of 2000, 97 percent of American citizens recognized the brand logo, which perhaps explains why the average American spent $20 a year on Nike products. But many consumers felt that the overabundance of swooshes was symptomatic of Nike's aggressive corporate philosophy, which had fallen out of favor with consumers in recent years. In the eyes of many members of the American public, the swoosh represented one or both of two modern societal ills — the commercialization of sports and the globalization of capitalism. Additionally, research revealed that products emblazoned with the swoosh were no longer as widely accepted by the coveted teenage segment of the market. In 1997, Young & Rubicam removed Nike from their annual list of preferred labels among teens for the first time in a decade, and as of 2000 Nike had yet to be reinstated.

Since the swoosh was rapidly accumulating negative connotations, Nike executives began searching for ways to downplay the logo's visibility. Nike spokesman Lee Weinstein explained that "having the swoosh be the ID for everything we do is probably too much pressure on that symbol."[10] Phil Knight later joined in the criticism of the swoosh's ubiquity by saying, "If you blast [the swoosh] on every T shirt, every sign in the soccer match, you dilute it."[11] Mark Parker, Nike's vice president for global footwear, put it more succinctly when he stated "clearly, we had the swoosh on everything and it was just ridiculous."[12]

Beginning in 1998, Nike often removed the swoosh from its corporate advertising and letterhead and replaced it with the script lowercase word "nike." Around the same time, the company developed separate business units for its proprietary Jordan, All Conditions Gear (ACG) and NikeGolf brands. Each brand claimed its own logo, and management was empowered to develop a unique marketing strategy using the advertising firm of their choice. Nike intended for these proprietary brands to ease the pressure on the swoosh. A sub-brand of shoes and apparel, called the Nike Alpha Project emerged as a strategy to diversify the brand's appearance and subdue the swoosh. Though products in the Alpha Project line bore the Nike name, a new logo made up of five small dots arranged in a horizontal line usually replaced the swoosh. Nike positioned the Alpha Project products as the company's most technologically advanced products, and company president Tom Clarke referred to them as "the modern-day version of what Nike's mission has always been, creating breakthrough products for people who compete and recreate." Nike anticipated that Alpha Project merchandise, which comprised 20 percent of the company's product mix in 1999, would attract consumers who otherwise might be turned off by conventional swoosh-bearing goods. Hence, Alpha Project designs included a watch aimed at surfers that contained 50 years of tide charts stored in its memory, a specially treated shirt that provided its wearer with SPF 30 UV protection and a basketball sneaker modeled after a snug-fitting mountain bike shoe. Despite all the efforts to de-emphasize the swoosh, Nike officials recognized that the logo aided the company's rise significantly and stressed that the swoosh would not be abandoned.

NIKE IN THE NEW MILLENNIUM

Room For Improvement

By the year 2000, Nike had recovered from the Asian economic meltdown and addressed many of the problems related to its global labor practices. The company expanded its presence on the web, expecting Internet sales to exceed $10 million in 2000, a 700 percent increase from 1999. It continued to develop innovative products, such as the new golf ball Tiger Woods used to decimate the field at the 2000 U.S. Open, the Air Presto shoe designed to fit four foot sizes with one shoe and created a new division dedicated to high-tech electronic fitness accessories. Yet, on February 8, 2000, Nike announced that earnings for 2000 and 2001 would fall short of estimates, causing Nike stock to plunge 18 percent to $37 per share almost overnight. The company officially blamed the shortfall on contracting channels caused when big retail chains absorbed competitors closing stores in the process, and poor currency exchange rates as a result of a strong dollar. But, while European and Asian markets recovered and experienced nearly double-digit growth, Nike expected the domestic market to grow a paltry three to four percent. Channel contraction and residual negative image perceptions shared some of the blame for these domestic market woes, but additional problems stemmed from lukewarm consumer receptions of new product categories.

In the past decade, the company was caught behind the curve in the "action-sports" (formerly called "extreme sports") arena and the fashion trend toward "brown shoes" -- casual shoes and hiking boots such as those made by the Vans and Timberland brands. Action-sports like mountain biking, skateboarding, and snowboarding had gained enormous popularity in the 1990s. Celebrated in Mountain Dew commercials and with ESPN's "X-Games" competitions, this relatively new breed of sports attracted large followings in the youth market, the segment that had been Nike's main target for years. Nike was late getting into the action-sports game, and when the company finally started introducing apparel, shoes and gear targeting participants in these sports, the products were either largely ignored or even disdained. Young consumers criticized Nike's skateboarding shoe, first launched in 1995, for wearing down easily and for lack of comfort. Others referred to it as simply "not relevant."[13] In the world of fashion, Nike chose not to respond to the surge in popularity of "brown shoes" until recently because the company had already experimented with the style in the early 1980s and failed. Competition from "brown shoe" manufacturers making stylish shoes and selling them at nearly half the price of the average Nike sneaker forced Nike to reconsider, and the company offered hiking boots and low-cut casuals bearing the ACG logo as of 1999. But, when Nike unveiled these new products, consumer response was chilly. The reason identified by the company was that by falling behind in fashion, and overextending the swoosh, the company wasn't perceived as being as cool as it once was.

As a result, it now had to work harder to convince young consumers that Nike had any cachet.

To remedy this problem, Nike focused on revitalizing All Conditions Gear, the division responsible for most of these products. In 1998, Nike granted ACG its own business unit. The company hired top executives from other apparel firms, such as outdoor-apparel manufacturer Helly-Hansen and shoe manufacturer Fila. ACG management then set up a design studio in Southern California, from where most of the skateboarding and surfing culture takes its cues, in order to develop more relevant products. Accompanying these measures was a large marketing campaign debuting in Summer 2000 and an initiative to open dozens of ACG stores at outdoor resorts. As a result of these dramatic changes, the company expected sales of ACG products to grow 20 percent annually, as compared to the 8 percent annual growth prior to the establishment of the separate unit. Another contributor to Nike's woes in the action-sports and brown shoe categories was the size of the company, which restricted its maneuverability into new markets. To better equip the company for continued growth, Nike began hiring veterans from big companies, such as PepsiCo, Microsoft and Disney. With this restructuring, Nike aimed to stimulate growth in previously lackluster markets.

Positive Indicators

In spite of financial and market setbacks that occurred in the late 1990s, Nike had reason to think positively about its global corporate position in coming years. In the fourth quarter of 1999, Nike overcame low earnings projections and reported a net income increase of 34 percent. Net profits for the entire year rose 32 percent as revenues exceeded $9 billion. Though revenue for the fourth quarter fell one percent domestically, revenue rose between eight and 17 percent in Asia, Europe and the Americas. Additionally, future orders in those regions increased between 13 and 21 percent while domestic orders fell 5 percent, further proof that Nike's best hopes for long-term lie in international markets. Despite falling domestic revenues in 1998 and 1999, Nike's total revenues rose on the strength of growth in international markets, especially Europe (see Fig. 1). In 1999, a year in which every other regional market experienced tapered revenues, the company's European revenues rose, albeit slightly. Two significant contributors to continuing annual revenue growth in Europe were Nike's success in soccer and apparel. Nike's global market share in soccer products increased more than sevenfold between 1994 and 2000, and sales exceeded $375 million in fiscal 1999. Additionally, in 1999 the company's soccer orders from Europe grew over 100 percent from the previous year. Nike's total apparel sales rose against declining footwear sales in 1997 and 1998 (see Fig. 2). Though global apparel sales flattened in 1999, apparel revenue in Europe rose 26 percent, on top of 34 percent the previous year.

Though soccer was Nike's most important global game in 2000, a Nike athlete from a different sport garnered international attention. Tiger Woods provided the new sub-brand NikeGolf with a marketing boost as he dominated the PGA tour in 2000 using Nike's specially designed Tour Accuracy ball. With victories at the U.S. Open, British Open and PGA championships, Tiger became only the second player in the history of modern golf to win three major tournaments in one year. After his record 15-stroke victory at the U.S. Open in June, Nike estimated that sales of their golf balls rose between 50 and 75 percent within one month. Nike also stood to gain additional advertising power in international markets from Tiger's exceptional play, since Nike has successfully employed the international superstar in worldwide advertising campaigns before. According to Mike Kelly, vice president of marketing for Nike Golf, in 2000 Tiger enjoyed even greater popularity in Asia than he did in the U.S. and compared the golfer to Michael Jordan in terms of "transcend[ing] his sport."[14]

Whatever the dawn of a new century brought for Nike, the company planned to maintain their competitive edge. In his letter to shareholders from Nike's 2000 annual report, Phil Knight spoke of the company's need to "recommit [itself]" after several years of stagnant revenue growth. Though the company had become a household name throughout the world and, more importantly, achieved the position of global sportswear leader, Nike was still $3 billion shy of reaching the goal of $12 billion that Knight initially intended the company to reach by 2000. In the letter, Knight addressed the issue of how to jumpstart his company's slowed growth and offered the following formula: "We need to expand our connection to new categories and toward new consumers." What Nike learned from the last four years of the 20th century might be summarized with a slogan from one of its early eighties running shoe advertisements that now serves as a unofficial brand mantra prominently placed around company headquarters and on company documents. The phrase "There is no finish line" emphasizes the need for Nike to consistently explore opportunities to grow its business whether or not times are prosperous.

DISCUSSION QUESTIONS

1. How would you characterize Nike's Brand Image and sources of brand equity in the U.S.?
2. How might Nike's effort to become a global corporation affect its sources of brand equity abd brand image in the U.S., Europe and Asia?
3. Are sponsorships and endorsements vital to Nike's business? For instance, what effect would Nike becoming an official sponsor for the Olympics have on the company's relationship with consumers?
4. Why did Nike become a target for critics of globalization? Do you think Nike's response to allegations of unfair global labor practices was appropriate and/or effective?

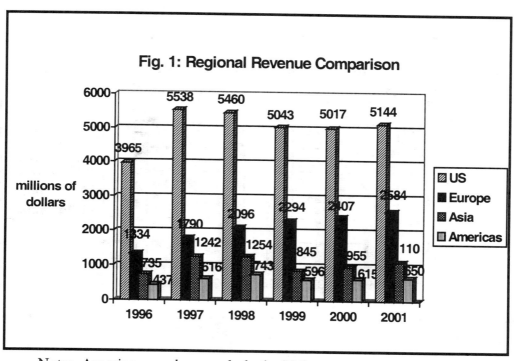

Fig. 1: Regional Revenue Comparison

Note: Americas numbers exclude the U.S.
        Europe numbers include the Middle East and Africa.
(Source: Nike annual report, 2001)

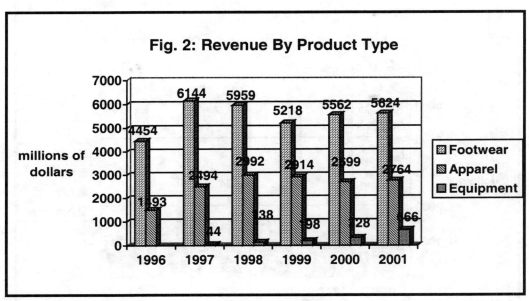

Fig. 2: Revenue By Product Type

(Sources: Nike annual report, 2000, 2001.)

REFERENCES

[1] This case was made possible through the cooperation of Nike and the assistance of David Kottkamp, General Manager of Nike International; Liz Dolan, VP of Marketing; Bill Zeitz, Director, International Advertising; Steve Miller, Director, Sports Marketing and Nelson Farris, Director, Corporate Education. Leslie Kimerling, Sanjay Sood and Keith Richey assisted in the preparation and writing of the case under the supervision of Professor Kevin Lane Keller as the basis for class discussion.

[2] Geraldine E. Willigan, "High Performance Marketing: An Interview with Nike's Phil Knight," Harvard Business Review, July-August 1992, pp. 91-101.

[3] Geraldine E. Willigan, "High Performance Marketing: An Interview with Nike's Phil Knight," Harvard Business Review, July-August 1992, pp. 91-101.

[4] Geraldine E. Willigan, "High Performance Marketing: An Interview with Nike's Phil Knight," Harvard Business Review, July-August 1992, pp. 91-101.

[5] ADWeek, April 20, 1992, p. 19.

[6] Teenage Research Unlimited.

[7] Time, March 30, 1998.

[8] Forbes, May 3, 1999.

[9] The Atlanta Journal and Constitution, May 13, 1998.

[10] CNNSI.com, September 16, 1998.

[11] Business Week, February 21, 2000.

[12] The New York Times Magazine, September 13, 1998.

[13] Business Week, February 21, 2000.

[14] The Chicago Tribune, July 5, 2000.

DUPONT:
MANAGING A CORPORATE BRAND[1]

INTRODUCTION

Over the 19th and 20th centuries, E.I. du Pont de Nemours transformed from a small, Delaware-based gunpowder manufacturer into a Fortune 500 powerhouse with a diverse array of science-based products serving many markets including agriculture, transportation, construction, healthcare, safety, apparel and electronics. Since 1802, DuPont used its superior scientific research strengths to make discoveries that have made the lives of millions easier and the operations of businesses around the world safer and more efficient. DuPont has risen to become the world's premier science company and continues to show impressive growth in the high-performance materials and life sciences sectors. As of 2002, the company maintained a portfolio of more than 2,000 trademarks and brands, many of which had attained the highest levels of recognition among consumers for ingredient brands.

DuPont has long been revered for its success with corporate branding. Since the 1930s, the "Better Things for Better Living" slogan helped win brand recognition among DuPont's business customers and consumers alike. In 1999, DuPont decided to drop the "Better Things for Better Living" slogan and launched a new corporate image with the introduction of its The miracles of science campaign. The new strategy raised some important questions. How would DuPont's broader focus on biotechnology affect its traditional materials business? Would the corporate brand remain an asset in marketing and supporting DuPont's sub-brands? The company addressed these and other questions as it developed its strategy for the new century.

COMPANY BACKGROUND

Early History

The DuPont of the early 19th century was much different from the mammoth enterprise that exists today. Founded near Wilmington, Delaware in 1802 by E.I. du Pont de Nemours, DuPont's first century of operations was devoted to the production of a variety of gunpowder product lines. DuPont's early research with sodium nitrate led to a replacement for traditionally-used explosives in 1857, a revolutionary development in the warfare technology of the time. Three decades later, DuPont established itself as a leader in polymer chemistry research by inventing a process to manufacture smokeless gunpowder. Throughout the rest of the nineteenth century, the growing company continued to dominate the explosives market as the primary manufacturer of dynamite, nitroglycerin, guncotton and smokeless powder for the United States government. While DuPont's production of explosives technologies decreased dramatically in the 20th century, the company continued to serve as the United States Armed Forces' primary supplier of explosives during World War I.

In 1902, DuPont began to pursue new business opportunities as its competitive advantages in the explosives business started to sour. Pivotal to the reorganization of the company from an explosives manufacturer into a diversified chemical company was DuPont's investment in one of the first American industrial research laboratories, the Eastern Laboratory, located in New Jersey. Another research facility, DuPont's

Experimental Station in Delaware, was built soon after. In addition, during the 1910s, DuPont began acquiring a diverse group of smaller companies within the nitrocellulose, fabrics, heavy chemicals, dyes and finishes industries. A major restructuring in 1920 further facilitated DuPont's growth into a multi-billion dollar enterprise. That year, DuPont reorganized its various business units into autonomous operating departments whose production activities were organized by a central corporate headquarters. This modern form of corporate organization allowed the company's business units to pursue growth independently, and thus free from the inefficiencies associated with more centralized organizational structures of other industrial giants of the time. The 1920s also saw DuPont's first expansion of production activities abroad with the establishment of subsidiaries in Mexico and Brazil.

The efforts of DuPont's major research facilities in combination with R&D support from its acquired businesses, led to DuPont's early developments in cellulose-based products including fibers, plastics, finishes and films. Realizing that the company's future success hinged on continued commitment to scientific research, DuPont created an internal department in 1927 charged with "establishing or discovering new scientific facts." This department advanced DuPont's understanding of various processes in polymer chemistry, leading to an explosion of both consumer and industrial products in the decades that followed.

Research and Development: Supporting Two Centuries of Growth

The driving force behind DuPont's history of consistent growth in the specialty chemicals, high-performance materials, pharmaceuticals and biotechnology sectors has been the company's aggressive investment in scientific research. As the corporate slogan adopted in 1999 -- The miracles of science -- suggested, the company dedicated itself to developing breakthrough products. DuPont's discoveries and technological improvements led to what company executives described as "dramatic leaps forward," making significant differences in the lives of consumers throughout the world. Current DuPont CEO, Chad Holliday, explained that the company has never been interested "in serving transitory needs. The kinds of products that DuPont manufactures help to feed, cure, clothe and shelter humanity."[2] DuPont avoided developing products that meet short-term consumer demands resulting from ephemeral trends, but rather, the company invested in research that met the long-term needs of businesses and consumers alike.

Annual DuPont research and development expenditures, which topped $1 billion annually in the 1990s, supported research activities aimed at the creation of new or improved product lines across six major areas: chemicals, fibers, polymers, petroleum, biotechnology and diversified businesses. DuPont's extensive R&D budget supported more than 3,700 scientists and engineers working at 24 major industrial research laboratories in 11 countries. In addition to the $1 billion spent on pure scientific research, DuPont additionally invested close to another $1 billion on manufacturing, technical, marketing and engineering technologies, all of which have been instrumental in its growth.

In the 1990s, an increasing percentage of DuPont's research funds were dedicated to improving the environmental soundness of the company's products. For example, DuPont engineers developed processes in which bio-hazardous waste generated in the production of certain plastics could be broken down to simple molecular forms so they could be reused later in the manufacture of other products. Moreover, DuPont researchers initiated studies on how to refine the production processes of its plants so that zero hazardous waste is generated. DuPont also formalized its decades long safety consulting business into a new strategic business unit -- DuPont Safety Resources -- dedicated to helping other companies manage "hazards" resulting from industrial activities throughout the world. DuPont also continued to invest heavily in the development of improved replacements for its current product lines. In 1998, for example, DuPont introduced two new carpet fibers -- the Antron Stainmaster and Antron Teflon SuperProtection brands -- which had improved easy-care properties, durability and aesthetic capabilities over the original Stainmaster carpet brands. Another example is DuPont's 1993 introduction of Suva, a chemical refrigerant replacement for Freon, which was invented by DuPont in 1931. R&D funding for Suva development spawned from increasing scientific evidence that chlorofluorocarbons contributed to ozone depletion.

DUPONT RESEARCH

DuPont's advanced research in chemicals and polymers led to some of the company's initial breakthroughs as a diversified chemical company. Through a joint venture with General Motors, DuPont embarked on the development of its new-generation "wonder chemicals" with the invention of Freon in 1931, a fluorocarbon refrigerant that began being used in refrigerators and cooling systems by the 1940s. Other significant DuPont chemical products include Ti-Pure titanium dioxide white pigments, Vertel cleaning agents and Dymelaerosol propellants. DuPont's progress in deriving chemicals with myriad industrial applications throughout the twentieth century earned it the number one position in the chemicals industry in terms of profit share. In 1999, DuPont forged a partnership with Ciba Specialty Chemicals to develop a repellent finish for cotton fabrics. In 2000, sales in DuPont's Pigments & Chemicals division rose five percent to $3.9 billion.

Research in polymers has led to a myriad of industrial applications in construction, chemical processing, textiles and transportation. For example, the automotive industry alone uses more than 100 DuPont products in the manufacture of a single automobile. Polymer research has led to the creation of well-known consumer products such as Teflon and Silverstone non-stick cookware finishes and Corian surfaces. In the late 1990s, DuPont placed the bulk of polymer research efforts on developing new innovations that would replace common metals used in commercial applications. For example, in the 1990s DuPont introduced an enhanced version of Zytel, a nylon composite with a new blend of tougheners and additives that reduced the weight of a comparable metal part by 50-60 percent. Other advancements in DuPont's polymer business unit included an antimicrobial version of Corian surfaces, Butacite interlayer for safety glass, Tynex toothbrush filament and a variety of fluropolymer finishes, resins, and films. Moreover, a joint venture between DuPont and Dow -- DuPont Dow Elastomers -- made progress on developing hydrocarbon rubber by combining the polymer chemistry strengths and resources of both companies. In the late 1990s, DuPont developed Zenite liquid crystal polymers (LCP) for use in electronics -- such as computers and mobile devices. Revenues for the Performance Coatings & Polymers division reached $6.5 billion in 2000, while the Specialty Polymers division boasted sales of $4.5 billion.

One of DuPont's first consumer breakthrough products in the fiber category was nylon, which hit the market in 1938 and launched what DuPont labeled "the modern materials revolution." While all production of nylon was devoted to military applications during World War II, popular nylon consumer products rebounded dramatically after the war. Nylon stockings, in particular, reached record sales by the 1950s as they became common staple products in the ladies' fashions departments of clothing stores throughout the world. The invention of nylon marked the beginning of DuPont's extensive product line growth of fiber applications for the apparel industry. Later fiber-related research would lead to the creation of other well-known consumer products such as Lycra and Dacron polyester, as well as Stainmaster and Antron carpet fibers. More recent inventions contributing to DuPont's healthy sales of fiber products for apparel and other applications included products such as Coolmax and Thermolite performance fibers used primarily in sportswear -- as well as Micromattique, which was used in the high-fashion apparel sector as an alternative to silk.

In 1999, DuPont introduced 3GT, a new form of polyester whose physical properties surpassed previous polyester variations in terms of improved resiliency, stretch recovery and easy dye capability. 3GT was unique because its chemical structure was not based on petroleum-based hydrocarbons like older polyesters, but rather was produced using corn sugars generated with help of bioengineered microbes. DuPont research teams thus developed a method for producing high-quality fibers from low-cost, renewable resources --an achievement that is indicative of DuPont's new focus on increasing the efficiency and environmental-soundness of its products and production activities.

In addition to introducing new materials products, DuPont invested in research that led to breakthroughs in process technologies used to produce the company's polyester and nylon product lines. For example, in 1998, DuPont developed a new process technology called NG-3, which allowed the company to make higher quality polyester PET resins. DuPont also sunk millions of research dollars into the development of polymerization processes that could easily replace existing process technology in current factory locations, leading to more efficiently produced, higher-quality polyesters produced at significantly reduced costs. Revenues for DuPont's Specialty Fibers division reached $3.5 billion in 2000.

DuPont began in the late 1990s to refocus itself away from chemicals and placed greater emphasis on the life sciences as an avenue for future growth. According to DuPont CEO Chad Holliday in 1999, life sciences was to become "the centerpiece of DuPont in the future."[3] According to DuPont brand managers, "the challenge [was] to move away from the 'chemicals' image to one that better aligns with our ability to apply science to human needs and contribute to an improved quality of life for people around the world."[4]

In the 1990s, DuPont carved a strong presence in the life sciences sector with the introduction of environmentally-friendly herbicides and processes that incorporated biotechnology in agricultural production. Furthermore, in 1997 in an effort to facilitate greater involvement in biotech agriculture. DuPont invested $1.3 billion to acquire Ralston Purina's soy protein division Protein Technologies International and paid $1.7 billion for a 20 percent interest in Pioneer Hi-Bred International, the world's largest seed company. In 1999, DuPont purchased the remaining 80 percent interest in Pioneer with a cash and stock deal valued at $7.7 billion. Seeds from Pioneer will enable DuPont to deliver bio-engineered traits to the agriculture and nutrition markets.   They may also be able to to grow corn capable of producing bio-engineered chemicals to make the various chemicals, polymers and fibers produced by the company.   Instead of relying on nonrenewable petroleum sources as the base for chemicals vital to DuPont's product lines, the company could eventually use renewable crop resources to satisfy some raw material needs.

DuPont's R&D efforts in the life sciences business unit were directed at a number of specific projects which could potentially result in a number of additional breakthrough commercial applications for the company.   In the late 1990s, DuPont completed construction of a state-of-the-art research facility dedicated to understanding corn and soybean genomes so that these organic materials could be better integrated as raw materials in DuPont products. DuPont also introduced the Qualicon system, a technology able to recognize the DNA of various toxic microorganisms found in food, allowing for greater safety in food processing. In 2000, DuPont's Agriculture & Nutrition division had revenues of $2.5 billion.

DuPont's increasing interest in pursuing pharmaceutical applications led to the channeling of more R&D funds towards drug development and medical imaging chemical agents. DuPont investigated possible partnerships with various pharmaceutical companies, but the pace of these potential deals was criticized by industry analysts for proceeding too slowly. DuPont bought Merck's share of the joint venture in 1998. The two companies had developed a number of blockbuster drugs while partners, including Sinemet -- a Parkinson's drug -- and Sustiva -- a promising drug for the treatment of HIV/AIDS with sales of $386 million in 2000.

Total prescription drug sales for DuPont fell six percent, however, in 2000, to $1.5 billion. At the time, DuPont had a number of experimental drugs in development, including cancer, blood clot and depression treatments, but these would not be market-ready for years. In 2001, DuPont sought a buyer for its pharmaceuticals unit. Bristol-Myers Squibb, the world's fifth-largest drug maker, agreed to purchase DuPont Pharmaceuticals for $7.8 billion.

TRENDS IN DUPONT BRANDING

While DuPont's scientific research strengths engendered top-quality products, many marketing professionals argued that the company's expertise in corporate branding had been the cornerstone of DuPont's success. Marketing experts praised DuPont for integrating its corporate branding campaigns with ingredient branding efforts geared at promoting the company's various sub-brands.   The experts credited DuPont's creation of a strong corporate identity with enhancing the company's bargaining power with other players in the value chain and creating consumer loyalty. In essence, efforts to build a strong corporate brand identity paved the way for the healthy growth of DuPont product sales in a variety of categories—many argue that sales of popular DuPont products such as Teflon, Lycra, and Stainmaster would never have been as impressive without the support of the DuPont name.

DuPont Corporate Marketing Program

DuPont's first advertisement appeared in a newspaper in 1804 and read:

> The subscriber offers for sale, American manufactured Gun-Powder, from the Brandywine Mills, of a quality which is warranted equal and believed to be superior, to any imported from Europe, and at prices much under those of the imported Powder.[5]

Throughout the 19th century, DuPont advertising appeared primarily on handbills and lithographs that depicted hunting scenes. The company was largely content to meet existing demand, and therefore the products were not advertised aggressively. By the 19th century, DuPont looked to expand into new markets and induce demand for its products. The familiar oval DuPont logo was conceived in 1907, and in 1909 the company officially established the corporate umbrella brand when it dictated that the DuPont name would be attached to each product. That same year, the company established an Advertising Division. One of the first series of advertisements developed by the Advertising Division was titled "DuPont American Industries." One ad indicated that products originally thought of as luxury items were in fact necessities. Another ad connected DuPont with the revolutionary automobile by highlighting the company's Rayntite car tops, Fabrikoid artificial leather upholstery and Duco exterior finish.

DuPont's experience with corporate branding extended back to the 1930s, when market research revealed that consumers still associated the diversified chemical company with its involvement in the explosives industry. DuPont's heritage as an explosives manufacturer became a liability during the 1930s, when a Senate committee investigating the munitions industry grouped DuPont with other so-called "Merchants of Death." To promote a new socially-conscious image that conveyed DuPont's emphasis on scientific discovery as a means for the creation of products that made the lives of American's easier, DuPont hired Batton, Barton, Durstine & Osborn (BBDO) to lead its direct consumer advertising efforts. BBDO's branding efforts led to a tag line that became associated with the DuPont brand for the next five decades --"Better Things for Better Living Through Chemistry." In addition, the red DuPont oval became the company's primary marketing symbol and was used to build brand identity in marketing campaigns geared both toward promoting specific sub-brands as well as those tailored specifically to promoting the corporation as a leader in industrial sciences.

DuPont's largest advertising investment in the 1940s was a weekly radio show called Cavalcade of America. The Cavalcade of America moved to television in 1952, and after a few years the company sponsored the DuPont Show of the Month and Show of the Week. For each episode, DuPont ran a commercial that showcased "the other 99 percent" of the company's products, or its non-munitions offerings. By 1957, consumer polls showed that nearly 80 percent of the public had a favorable impression of DuPont.

DuPont continued to expand its marketing program through the years. By 1980, the company employed six major advertising agencies and worked with more than 60 others globally. In 1981, following the purchase of Conoco, an oil and gas company, DuPont dropped the "Through Chemistry" from the slogan to change popular consumer perceptions that DuPont was solely a chemical company. DuPont was, after all, developing

"Better Things for Better Living" that included energy products and well as a growing number of brands related to the biological sciences.

Domestically, DuPont continued to use a product-oriented strategy to convey its "better living" message to consumers. One memorable television ad featured real-life amputee Bill Demby who was able to play basketball with the help of prosthetic legs made from DuPont plastic. The ad showed Demby on a playground basketball court removing his warm-up pants to reveal the prosthetic limbs. Demby competed one-on-one with another man while a voiceover intoned "When Bill Demby was in Vietman, he dreamed of coming home and playing a little basketball -- a dream that died when he lost both legs to a Viet Cong rocket." The ad emphasized DuPont's role in Demby's ability to play with a line about the "remarkable DuPont plastic that could help make artificial limbs more resilient, more flexible, more like life itself." DuPont also used corporate advertising to convey its environmental achievements. One television spot highlighted DuPont's double-hulled oil tanker design. In the spot, assembled sea creatures applauded and cheered DuPont while the "Ode to Joy" played in the background.

DuPont augmented its corporate advertising with other marketing activities, including sponsorships and public relations. DuPont sponsored numerous scientific events and programs, which fit naturally with the company's core competency of science research. Science projects funded by DuPont included the world's first human-powered airplane, which flew from England to France, and the first solar-powered airplane. As a DuPont spokesperson explained, DuPont seeks events "that involve innovative uses of our products, events that have contests or prizes that have an engineering orientation."[6]

The company also engaged in several high-profile sponsorships. Between 1991 and 1996, DuPont sponsored the American cycle race formerly called the Tour de Trump and renamed it the Tour DuPont. One of DuPont's most visible marketing programs was its lead sponsorship of NASCAR driver Jeff Gordon, started in 1993. The sponsorship was logical considering Gordon raced with the help of numerous DuPont products, including a driver's suit made of Nomex heat-resistant fiber, a helmet with Kevlar body protection fibers and a car painted with DuPont automotive finishes. Gordon went on to become one of the most successful drivers in Winston Cup. The brightly painted car that prominently displayed the DuPont logo inspired the nickname for Gordon's pit crew, "The Rainbow Warriors." In 2001, DuPont signed a contract to sponsor Gordon's team, Hendrick Motorsports Car 24, through 2005, and updated the paint scheme to a "Fire and Flames" design. In 2002, DuPont included Gordon's car in its 200th anniversary celebration designing a special paint scheme for selected races that used the DuPont 200 Years logo (a flask with confetti streaming from the top) as the primary logo on the car.

INGREDIENT BRANDING

One of DuPont's most successful and long-standing marketing strategies was ingredient branding. When DuPont found consumer applications for its scientific discoveries, as was the case with Teflon, Stainmaster, and Lycra, the company licensed its technology to consumer products companies. A variety of manufacturers, therefore, made goods containing trademarked DuPont products. The DuPont technology was an ingredient in the finished product, and the company sought to build consumer awareness in the ingredient name, so that, for example, consumers would look for cookware made with Teflon or clothes made with Lycra. DuPont advertised its ingredients as early as the 1950s, when it developed campaigns to raise consumer awareness for brands such as Cordura and Orlon fibers. The ingredient brand strategy had several advantages compared with finished product branding. For one, it transformed what consumers considered to be fiber and chemical commodity products into sought-after branded merchandise. As a result, rather than buying a carpet for its color and weave, for example, consumers sought out Stainmaster carpets. Additionally, an ingredient with multiple uses could be marketed as a component in more than one product. Teflon, initially used in products for the military, is an example of an ingredient with various industrial and consumer product applications. Difficulty can arise when the ingredient brand appears in products representing diverse markets. As one DuPont executive noted about the Kevlar ingredient brand, "It's always a challenge to make sure that the message that we're using for the overall Kevlar brand is still consistent for a police officer, for a canoe owner, versus [an] aircraft company."[7]

DuPont also leveraged its corporate name with ingredient brands, particularly in business-to-business applications. For example, the company's automotive finishes business, which produced ingredients for the auto industry, did not have a coined ingredient brand name, but was called simply DuPont Automotive Finishes. Other ingredient brand products to also carry the DuPont corporate name included: DuPont Flooring Systems, DuPont Polyglide and DuPont XTI Nylon. This strategy enabled DuPont to establish awareness for its ingredient brands by leveraging the well-known DuPont name.

The benefits of ingredients branding also translated to manufacturers and retailers. Manufacturers who made products containing DuPont ingredients enjoyed the positive associations consumers had with the ingredient name and/or the DuPont name. DuPont also shared some of the production, development, and promotion costs with its manufacturers. Retailers attained larger operating margins because of the price premiums commanded by products containing DuPont ingredients. Retailers also received additional promotional support from DuPont.

What follows is the history of three of DuPont's well-known ingredient brands (Teflon, Stainmaster, and Lycra), plus a fourth ingredient brand, Solae that the company is just beginning to attempt to make well known:

Teflon

Discovered in 1938, Teflon fluoropolymer initially found its way into military applications and remained outside the consumer product realm for the first 12 years after it was introduced. After World War II, DuPont scientists and product development teams realized that consumers would find Teflon as useful as the military because of its non-stick properties and stability at extreme high and low temperatures. Specifically, DuPont pegged Teflon as a perfect candidate for the cookware market since consumers had long expressed a desire for cookware that prevented heated food from sticking to its surface. Adapting Teflon coatings for consumer use was a challenge because of the fact that they were non-stick on both sides, making it difficult to apply Teflon coatings to surfaces of standard pots and pans. But by the early 1960s, DuPont had perfected a method for adhering the non-stick surfaces to cookware and began preparing to market the product to cookware manufacturers and consumers.

As with many other DuPont products, the Teflon brand name was selected from a list of possible product names generated by a computer program that randomly combined words and sounds. Teflon was chosen because it sounded scientific enough to convey the wonders of non-stick surfaces yet it was simple enough for the average consumer to remember. Early Teflon branding efforts centered around television advertisements that stressed the "easy clean" properties of Teflon cookware. DuPont brand managers felt that television was the only advertising medium that could successfully convey the benefits of Teflon because consumers in the 1960s were unfamiliar with the concept of non-stick surfaces and needed to be shown how they worked and how they could be of use in their daily lives. By pursuing a mostly direct-to-consumer campaign, DuPont depended on a pull strategy in which Teflon sales would be supported by demands for non-stick cookware as consumers realized its advantages.

In the 1990s, DuPont developed improved versions of Teflon, as well as a new type of non-stick coating branded by DuPont as Silverstone. At the same time, DuPont scaled back its marketing of Teflon and Silverstone cookware applications, most likely because both brands have achieved 95 percent recognition among consumers according to DuPont branding research. While consumer advertising of Teflon had waned during the 1990s, DuPont continued to market its non-stick surfaces for industrial uses. The stable heating and cooling properties of these surfaces facilitated its use in a myriad of industrial applications from rocket engines to cryogenics. In 2001, DuPont started a consumer campaign for its Teflon brand that highlighted its use as a stain- and wrinkle-repellant in fabrics. Said Teresa Kleinhans, global textiles manager for Teflon, "We are progressively increasing our presence and refining our strategy in ready-to-wear, which represents a significant opportunity."[8]

Stainmaster

Stainmaster is unique to DuPont's portfolio of trademarks because it was designed in response to a specific consumer preference or need. Most other DuPont products are discovered through years of scientific research and then must be marketed to appeal to specific end-users who could potentially find the product useful. While DuPont had generated healthy sales with its Antron nylon carpet line, consumers in the 1980s voiced a preference for a carpet that could resist stains better than the current Antron brand fibers. As fourth generation nylon fibers, Antron carpets represented a vast improvement over previous generations of nylon fibers in terms of look, feel and durability. However, the fluorocarbon treatment applied to Antron carpets could only resist dry soils; wet stains still had the potential of seeping through the nylon fibers, destroying the carpet. In response to the heightened consumer preference for stain resistance, DuPont began experimenting with chemicals that could be added to its Antron brand fibers in the early 1980s and successfully produced dye-resistant agents by 1985. These agents would later be integrated into a new carpet type branded as Stainmaster, which DuPont launched in 1986. Carpet mills were allowed to market their products under the DuPont Stainmaster name if their carpets stood up to the rigorous weight, density and pile height specifications demanded by DuPont and if Stainmaster chemical additives were applied.

Branding of Stainmaste consisted of a two-part strategy. First, DuPont used a push strategy by giving mills incentives to use the new Stainmaster nylons in their carpets. For example, DuPont supplied mills with Stainmaster chemical agents for free as long as they continued purchasing DuPont's premium nylon fibers. Offering incentives like free use of stain resistant chemical agents was important because competitors like Monsanto began entering the market with similar, low-cost stain resistant agents that employed the same chemical formula as DuPont's products. In addition, DuPont targeted retailers with extensive trade promotions, including supplying merchandisers with marketing tools such as posters, banners, labels, tags and retail display units which could be used in stores to attract customers to buy the Stainmaster brand. This encouraged carpet retailers to demand more Stainmaster products because they could rely on DuPont to fund the marketing program while the retailers directly benefited from the dramatic increases in carpet sales that resulted from the branding efforts. Furthermore, DuPont spent more than $35 million on training and support for exclusive Stainmaster distributors. With the launch of Stainmaster, DuPont sent 50 field representatives to train more than 1,500 retailers to best employ the marketing tools provided by DuPont to boost sales.

While marketing to mills and retailers was important, DuPont's consumer advertising of Stainmaster -- the pull aspect of the campaign -- was the more critical aspect of the branding program. The Stainmaster promotional campaign was the biggest marketing endeavor ever pursued by DuPont, totaling $65 million alone for the initial branding campaign, an amount unheard of in the floor covering market. The initial advertising program featured two television spots that creatively -- and humorously -- captured the stain resistance, comfortably and durability qualities associated with Stainmaster carpets. DuPont's "Landing" commercial, which featured an infant tossing his airplane shaped plate full of messy food onto Stainmaster carpet, even won the Clio Award for Best Commercial of 1987. While DuPont's branding efforts for Stainmaster remained strong throughout the 1980s at over $20 million annually, by 1994, annual marketing expenditures for the brand declined to $2 million. Later ads depicted house pets conspiring to trip their owner while he is carrying a plate of food. The pets ate the food while the owner returned to the kitchen to get cleaning implements; the owner then returned to find his Stainmaster carpet completely clean.

Lycra

Lycra stretch fiber was originally developed by DuPont in the 1950s to replace rubber used in women's girdles, but by the 1990s it was found in a wide variety of garment types including exercise apparel, skiwear, swimwear, golf and tennis knit shirts, compression shorts, cross-training apparel and leisure wear. The use of Lycra in a myriad of apparel-related applications stemmed from its superior physical properties; it can stretch up to six times its original length. Fabrics blended with Lycra offer improvement in fit, shape retention, drape and wrinkle resistance over 100 percent natural materials such as cotton and silk, which have traditionally been used in these types of apparel. DuPont branded Lycra in order to gain competitive advantage over companies in the U.S., Europe and Asia that began marketing spandex-like products that had similar attributes to Lycra. Lycra marketing efforts first focused on generating brand awareness among apparel textile manufacturers. DuPont calculated that manufacturers would be more likely to choose Lycra over other ingredient brands if they were made aware of the high-quality and the useful physical attributes Lycra could bring to their products. DuPont's various trade publication advertisements stressed to manufacturers the potential of leveraging the strong DuPont brand identity through its association with Lycra which would appeal to consumers who associated DuPont with quality.

Lyrca brand managers also targeted consumers directly. The necessity of direct-to-consumer advertising stemmed from the fact that while natural fibers such as cotton, wool and silk were familiar to consumers, DuPont fibers like Lyrca were not. DuPont first began marketing Lyrca using a series of retail promotions and by using "hang-tags" on Lycra apparel bearing the fiber's name along with the familiar DuPont oval. Later, DuPont launched an advertising campaign centered around the simple tag line "Lycra Sensations." However, Lycra brand managers soon realized that the tag line spoke nothing of the benefits of buying Lycra over other materials. Therefore, a new advertising campaign based on the "Nothing Moves Like Lycra" concept was pursued, emphasizing the ease, comfort and maneuverability of apparel containing Lycra. The accompanying logo embodied motion with its creative use of wavy lines. Magazine advertisements captured active women in athletic wear, as well as new creations by fashion leaders such as Donna Karan and Gianni Versace that contained Lycra. Later Lyrca marketing efforts included the development of an independent DuPont Lyrca web site which addressed consumer questions about the product as well as DuPont's introduction of its own line of sportswear and other types of clothing which solely used Lycra. The Lycra marketing campaigns were successful: the fabric commanded two-thirds of the world's spandex market share in 2000. In 2001, DuPont launched an estimated $12 million advertising campaign for Lyrca that linked the fabric with Levi Strauss, Liz Claiborne, Diesel, Armani, J. Crew, DKNY and others. The campaign, themed "What do you look for in a great pair of jeans?" advertised Lycra's freedom of movement, stretch and comfort. In 2002, Lycra was one of the world's top ten apparel brands with roughly a two-thirds share of the global spandex market.

Solae

In 2001, the DuPont Protein Technologies division branded its soy protein products with the name Solae. The Solae logo consisted of a border resembling a leaf and the word Solae inside. DuPont referred to this logo as a "trust mark" that would enable consumers to connect with the brand, and likened it to the red swirl that became associated with the aspartame sweetener NutraSweet in the 1980s. The company chose to de-emphasize its role in the product, and thus the Solae ingredient brand was not strongly tied to the DuPont corporate brand. The first product to bear the Solae brand was 8th Continent soymilk, which resulted from a joint venture between DuPont and General Mills. On 8th Continent bottles, the Solae logo appeared along with the phrase "made with Solae brand soy protein." The label also contained information about potential health benefits, stating, "Helps lower cholesterol: 25 grams of soy protein a day, as part of a diet low in saturated fat and cholesterol, may reduce the risk of heart disease." 8th Continent milk came in original, vanilla, and chocolate flavors and was sold in 8-oz. and 32-oz. bottles. The 8th Continent brand also set up a web site (www.8thcontinent.com) that contained information about health benefits and recipes.

All DuPont's marketing efforts, at the time of the launch, were developed with the partner companies. For example, ads for 8th Continent milk targeted women, using ads to emphasize the health benefits of soymilk. Preliminary research identified soy protein may

155

protect against heart disease, osteoporosis, hormone-related cancer and menopausal symptoms. Stephan Tanda, the president of DuPont Protein Technologies, said, "Women shoppers . . . have told us that they are looking for a symbol that helps them sort through the clutter of health messages in the supermarket. The Solae brand offers a good health seal that is unique in the food industry."[9]

DuPont also intended for Solae to capitalize on the trend toward healthy eating among the entire population. J. Erik Fyrwald, nutrition and health vice president and general manager, said, "We know that more than 70 percent of consumers polled want nutritious foods. When they see the Solae mark on packages, they will be assured that their families are getting great tasting, nutritionally advanced products."[10] At the time of the Solae launch, DuPont negotiated with a variety of food companies to use the soy protein in products ranging from cereals to baked goods to and meat.

Other Ingredient Branding Activities

In 2000, the DuPont Nylon subsidiary launched an unorthodox Internet advertising campaign that targeted chemists, a group typically wary of web ads. Chemists did, however, use the web as a means of researching new chemical properties. So, said Caroline Riby, DuPont's account representative at Saatchi & Saatchi Rowland in Rochester, N.Y., "We had to make sure the ads wouldn't offend [the target], but would complement them and their need to discover. . . . If we smelled like an ad, we'd scare them off."[11] The agency created targeted "microsites" that contained a wealth of product information. When users of the Lycos search engine input a designated word, a pop-up would appear asking them if they wanted more information and then linked them to the microsite. Between April 2000 and November 2000, DuPont Nylon's web response rate rose 286 percent. DuPont's ingredient branding strategy had proven successful for decades, and the company saw no reason to alter it significantly.

DUPONT'S BRANDING EFFORTS INTO THE FUTURE

By the mid-1990s, DuPont had embarked on a massive reinvention of its business plan that dramatically transformed the focus of the company. DuPont would no longer simply remain a chemical and energy products corporation. Instead, the company would pursue a strategy that placed greater emphasis on developing products related to the biological sciences while retaining healthy business units that were connected to the company's traditional chemistry research. In 1998, DuPont's corporate branding team began developing a marketing strategy that captured the dynamics of the company's new dual chemistry/biotechnology focus. Branding executives at DuPont felt that "Better Things for Better Living," which the company had used since 1935, needed to be replaced by a more contemporary campaign that captured DuPont's focus on using pure scientific research to develop products that added convenience and safety to the lives of consumers. "Better Things for Better Living" was viewed as too product oriented. It conveyed an image that DuPont was solely concerned with using science to improve its current products while, in reality, the company had placed a great deal of emphasis on pure scientific research aimed at "breakthrough" products never conceived of before.

Research showed that consumers viewed DuPont as a leader in "smoke-stack science" -- the materials and industrial sciences -- because its research often led to products that had purely industrial applications. But consumers had not yet become aware of the company's competencies in biological research and their ability to integrate strengths from a variety of scientific disciplines to develop revolutionary products. One DuPont marketing executive admitted that DuPont traditionally had difficulties relating its scientific endeavors to the lives of average consumers. DuPont needed a new image showing that the company "is not simply providing a playpen for scientists to cook up inventions, we want to help people." The "Better Things for Better Living" campaign also confused consumers because of its similarity to other companies' corporate branding efforts such as BASF's "We don't make a lot of the products you buy, we make a lot of the products you buy better," Phillips Electronics' "We Make Good Things Better" and General Electric's "We Bring Good Things to Life."

Finding a New Tagline

In the fall of 1998, DuPont CEO Charles Holliday informed the advertising agencies bidding for DuPont's global account that the company needed to reinvent itself. In particular, Holliday felt the company needed to express to consumers how its chemicals and biotechnology businesses collaborated to create innovative products. Speaking on the need for a new name, Kathleen Forte, vice president of global corporate affairs said, "Clearly, we don't want to be seen as a chemical company. It's really limiting, and it doesn't describe who we are."[12] One ad executive saw a similar need for change, saying, "How many taglines can last for seven decades? It was time to move on to something new."[13] In developing their winning pitch, McCann-Erickson sought insights by analyzing DuPont's research and conducting its own research. McCann interviewed DuPont employees, who revealed that they viewed DuPont as a science company that applied discoveries to improve the quality of life for consumers. Nat Puccio, McCann's executive vice president-director of strategic planning, detailed how this insight reconciled DuPont's biotech and chemicals businesses:

> If you think of DuPont as a science company, suddenly the material sciences and life sciences really become two flavors, if you will, of the larger mission.[14]

The task of summarizing this insight with a concise tagline, however, proved challenging. The day before the final pitch, a McCann creative director came up with the succinct four-word phrase "The Miracles of Science." When the new concept was embraced by a committee of DuPont executives, as well as focus groups made of consumers and employees, the company went ahead with the change. The buy-in among employees was something DuPont was monitoring closely, and the The Miracles of Science slogan immediately earned employee praise. Said one North American employee, "[the slogan] did a good job of tying together all of DuPont's businesses and . . . can last forever."[15]

In April 1999, DuPont introduced the The Miracles of Science campaign with a 12 page advertisement supplement in the *Wall Street Journal* which emphasized DuPont's ability to "make miracles happen in every field from fashion to pharmaceuticals to agriculture to aerospace." The ad indicated that DuPont scientists developed some of the major breakthroughs that influenced life in the 20th Century. These breakthrough products included Mylar polyester film, which aided the space program's quest to put a man on the moon and Teflon fluoropolymer, which helped make the computer chip possible. The campaign, which cost an estimated $30 million, appeared in popular magazines, newspapers, trade publications and television. According to one DuPont marketing executive, The Miracles of Science campaign "[set] the record straight on what kind of company we are and what we are becoming"[16] -- that is, it emphasized DuPont's use of pure scientific research to develop new-age products that had wider applications than the company's previous product portfolio. Accordingly, CEO Charles Holliday commented, "Over two centuries, we have delivered big miracles and small miracles...Going forward, our common focus will be to leverage our collective scientific knowledge and competencies to innovate, originate and realize many more miracles."[17]

By changing the marketing campaign focus from "Better Things for Better Living" to the "The Miracles of Science," DuPont attempted to show consumers that it was essentially a new company with a new look and feel. The "miracles" came from the company's new ability to take the best research from a wide variety of scientific disciplines and generate innovations that make a difference in people's lives. The marketing campaign helped clarify consumer and investor confusion concerning the direction of DuPont, making clear that DuPont was neither solely a chemical nor biotechnology company, but rather was dedicated to science in general. DuPont's branding team also viewed the The miracles of science tagline as a way to change consumer perceptions of DuPont as stodgy and old-fashioned. The campaign captured a more humane image for DuPont and showed consumers that the company is concerned with developing innovations that "improve the quality of human life."

In September 1999, DuPont launched its first-ever global advertising campaign. The campaign, themed "To Do List for the Planet," launched simultaneously with regional and national television and print ads in North America, South America, Europe and Asia. On the "to do list" featured in the ads was a number of health and safety issues including: Find food that helps prevent osteoporosis; Turn ocean water into drinking water; Invent fabric that knows to either cool or warm you; Develop medicines that fight HIV and humorously, Add Lycra to Leather. These ads supported CEO Holliday's overall objective of "sustainable growth" which DuPont defined as creating value for society and shareholders while reducing the company's environmental "footprint".

DUPONT BUSINESS DEVELOPMENTS

Fine-Tuning DuPont's Positioning

As activists began boycotting genetically modified foods, DuPont adjusted its biotechnology focus somewhat. By 2000, less than three percent of DuPont's revenues came from genetically modified seeds. CEO Charles Holliday revealed that the company would wait to gauge consumer opinion before releasing a number of genetically modified products that were otherwise ready for the market. While DuPont continued to develop biotechnology products, or "biosolutions," the company aimed to use these products in polymers, rather than in foods. Additionally, DuPont placed added emphasis on developing materials and chemicals useful in electronic devices and the information industry. The company renamed its Electronic & Communication unit, calling it DuPont *i*Technologies, and established itself as a leader in lightweight and energy-efficient polymer displays. These displays were designed for use in electronic devices such as cell phones, personal digital assistants, notebooks and high definition television. In 2000, DuPont acquired UNIAX Corporation, a California company that produced the first polymer-based plastic display. UNIAX's co-founder, Alan J. Heeger, was one of three scientists who received the 2000 Nobel Prize in Chemistry for research on conductive polymers.

Also in 2000, DuPont unveiled another innovation called Sorona, the first product from the company to come from the integration of biology and chemical research. Sorona was a bio-based material with applications in the textile fiber business. Sorona bore properties similar to polyester: stretch, softness, dye-ability and ease-of-care. The product also illustrated DuPont's focus on "sustainable growth," since Sorona was made from renewable biological resources.

Sorona was only a small part of DuPont's sustainable growth mission. In 2001, DuPont set a target to get 10 percent of its energy and 25 percent of its revenue from renewable -- or "non-depletable" -- resources by 2010. DuPont's efforts to improve its environmental record since the 1990s were largely successful. Across its global operations, DuPont reduced greenhouse gas emissions 60 percent, air toxins dropped 70 percent and air carcinogens fell 90 percent between 1992 and 2000. Dr. Paul Tebo, vice-president for health, safety, and the environment at DuPont, spoke in 2001 of sustainability as DuPont's "next step:"

> If you effect the environment the right way, you can grow your business. It then becomes fundamental not having waste in your corporation and so the whole concept of sustainability begins to make sense to business people.[18]

In 2001, CEO Charles Holliday stated that DuPont was still striving toward a goal of "zero waste and zero emissions."[19]

Focusing on the Core Business

In 2002, DuPont announced that it would spin off or sell its core fibers businesses by the end of 2003. Due to challenging conditions in the textile and apparel markets, DuPont's fiber brands had suffered financially over the last several years. In the fourth quarter of 2001, earnings from nylon products dropped 73 percent compared with the same quarter a year earlier, and the company's polyester business lost $29 million in the quarter. The company's first move was to establish a new Textiles & Interiors unit that combined its polyester, nylon, Stainmaster, and Lycra brands. The move was designed to let the company focus on developing higher-growth products. DuPont also announced that it would reorganize the rest of the company into five new units: 1) Electronic & Communication Technologies; 2) Performance Materials; 3) Coatings & Color Technologies; 4) Safety & Protection and 5) Agriculture & Nutrition.

DuPont sought to build awareness for its Textiles & Interiors brands by bolstering its ingredient branding program. To do so, the company used a two-part initiative that 1) developed new uses for core brands and 2) fostered relationships with partners who use DuPont ingredients. For example, DuPont partnered with Ciba Specialty Chemical to jointly create a new brand called Easy Care that marketed Teflon as a wrinkle- and odor-repellant. Carol Gee, global brand director of DuPont Textiles & Interiors said, "Teflon will come to mean more than nonsticking and stain-resistance." As part of the total $300 million marketing program, DuPont established a fashion-services unit that provided trend analysis for partners. The program also included a fabric library, retail activities and point-of-purchase displays. A small percentage of the total was devoted to traditional advertising. "We can't live with just media buys," said Carol Gee.

Another example of DuPont expanding the market for a particular ingredient brand was its high-end kitchen countertop Corian. Originally developed as more cosmetic alternative to plastic laminated countertops, the new uses DuPont created for Corian included sculpture and furniture. DuPont sponsored a private exhibition of sculpture made of Corian called "Exercises in Another Material" at Chicago's Museum of Contemporary Art in 2000 and donated a number of armchairs made of the material to Grand Central Terminal in New York. Whereas Corian had previously been available only through DuPont-selected kitchen and bath boutiques, the company also began selling Corian in mass market retailers such as Home Depot, in order to attract more customers. DuPont partnered with Dennis Miller Associates New York in 2000 to produce custom-made Corian chairs that sold for more than $2,000. Since the late 1990s, sales of Corian grew 15 percent annually, to more than $500 million in 2000.

In 2002, CEO Charles Holliday said that new products would contribute a third of DuPont's revenue by 2007, up from 20 percent at the time. This statement indicated that DuPont would continue to dedicated itself to discovering new innovations that had consumer applications.

CONCLUSION

In 2002, DuPont celebrated its 200th anniversary. Among the marketing activities chosen to commemorate the occasion was a web site (www.heritage.dupont.com) that gave a retrospective of DuPont's achievements over the two centuries. As the site depicted, DuPont successfully reinvented itself many times throughout its history. Its most recent reinvention as a company combining chemical expertise with biotechnology or "biosolutions" knowledge, however, proved to be problematic due to the initially slow development of commercial applications for sustainable growth biotechnologies. DuPont had already decided, however, that its traditional focus on chemicals would limit its growth. The company faced the challenge of finding new ways to reinvent itself while remaining relevant to modern consumers. DuPont felt confident that its tradition of innovation and scientific discovery would enable the company to successfully transition to a new era of growth.

DISCUSSION QUESTIONS

1. How would you characterize DuPont's brand equity? What factors contribute to the company's equity? How can DuPont best preserve that equity?

2. Compare the benefits and drawbacks of a corporate brand strategy with that of an ingredient brand strategy. Do you think DuPont should emphasize one strategy more in the future?

3. Evaluate the "Miracles of Science" tagline. Do you think this effectively communicates DuPont's positioning as the world's premier science company? Does it support DuPont's ingredient branding strategy? Do you think it has the potential to last as long as the "Better Things for Better Living" tagline?

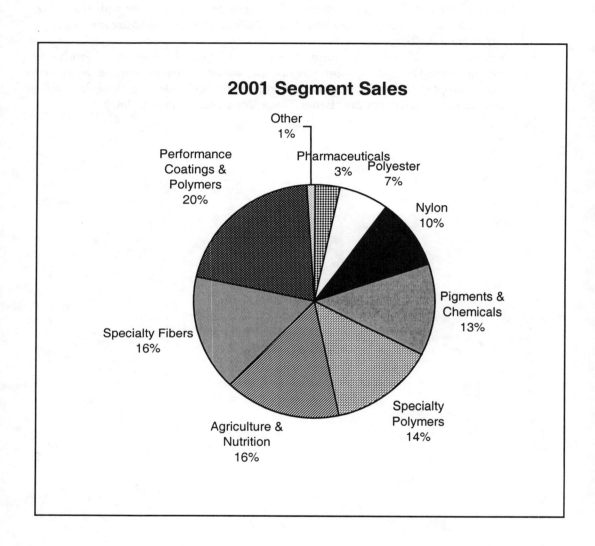

2001 Segment Sales

Other 1%

Performance Coatings & Polymers 20%

Pharmaceuticals 3%

Polyester 7%

Nylon 10%

Pigments & Chemicals 13%

Specialty Polymers 14%

Specialty Fibers 16%

Agriculture & Nutrition 16%

Total sales $27.7 billion

(source: Susan Warren. "DuPont Cajoles Independent Units to Talk to One Another." *Wall Street Journal*, February 5, 2002, p. B4.)

REFERENCES

[1] This case was made possible through the cooperation of DuPont and the assistance of Barbara Pandos, Scott Nelson, Jamie Murray, and Cheryl Gee. Keith Richey prepared this case under the supervision of Professor Kevin Lane Keller as the basis for class discussion.

[2] www.dupont.com

[3] Fortune 4/26/99

[4] DuPont Relaunch Brief

[5] www.dupont.com

[6] Gail S. Bower. "How Corporations Pay Their Dues." *Focus*, September 30, 1987, p. 23.

[7] DuPont video, April 13, 1998.

[8] Sandra Dolbow. "Teflon: We 'Let Life Happen.'" *Brandweek*, January 29, 2001, p. 5.

[9] "Ingredients Makers Seek Food's 'Intel's Inside.'" *Dairy Industries International*, December 1, 2001, p. 8.

[10] Coeli Carr. "The Wholesome Outlook: Consumer Research Gives Marketers Good Reason To Focus on the Nutritionally Aware Baby Boom Population." *Supermarket News*, December 10, 2001, p. 19S.

[11] "Best & Brightest: Caroline Riby." *B to B*, September 3, 2001, p. 20.

[12] Sean Callahan. "Marketing Miracles: DuPont Replaces 1935 Tagline To Reflect Corporate Change." *Business Marketing*, June 1, 1999, p. 1.

[13] Sean Callahan. "Marketing Miracles: DuPont Replaces 1935 Tagline To Reflect Corporate Change." *Business Marketing*, June 1, 1999, p. 1.

[14] Sean Callahan. "Marketing Miracles: DuPont Replaces 1935 Tagline To Reflect Corporate Change." *Business Marketing*, June 1, 1999, p. 1.

[15] Sean Callahan. "Marketing Miracles: DuPont Replaces 1935 Tagline To Reflect Corporate Change." *Business Marketing*, June 1, 1999, p. 1.

[16] Sean Callahan. "Marketing Miracles: DuPont Replaces 1935 Tagline To Reflect Corporate Change." *Business Marketing*, June 1, 1999, p. 1.

[17] DuPont Magazine No. 2, 1999.

[18] Jennifer Hewet. "DuPont Turns Into a Green Crusader." *Sydney Morning Herald*, June 4, 2001, p. 33.

[19] "Chemicals: DuPont's Punt." *The Economist*, October 2, 1999, p. 75.

NIVEA:
MANAGING A BRAND HIERARCHY[1]

INTRODUCTION

As 2001 drew to a close, executives at Beiersdorf's (BDF) cosmed division could reflect on the growth of their NIVEA brand during the last 11 years. NIVEA, the largest skin and face care brand in the world, had successfully defended its position during a decade of intense competition in its major European markets. Additionally, the company had expanded to many new markets in South and Latin America, Eastern Europe and Asia. By the end of the 1990s, NIVEA was known on a global basis. In addition to entering new markets, NIVEA created a number of new sub-brands that broadened the company's product offerings. The biggest new product developments were the 1996 launch of NIVEA Hair Care Styling and the 1997 launch of a decorative cosmetics line, called NIVEA Beauté. NIVEA also introduced a major scientific breakthrough -- an anti-aging coenzyme called Q10 -- that became an unqualified success and was included in a number of products representing many of the sub-brands. NIVEA's growth during the 1990s was reflected by its sales. Between 1990 and 2001, net sales grew from $660 million to $2.2 billion.

As NIVEA's brand portfolio expanded, the company faced a new challenge: maintaining growth while preserving the established brand equity. During the 1970s and 1980s, BDF's cosmed division had successfully extended the NIVEA brand from a limited range of products -- NIVEA Creme, Milk, Soap, and Sun -- to a full range of skin care and personal care products. Over time, these different product lines had established their own identities as "sub-brands," independent of and yet still connected to, the NIVEA Creme core brand. Given the breadth of products sold under the NIVEA name, however, there had been debates in the 1990s as to how to achieve the proper synergy between the NIVEA Creme core brand and the sub-brands from other product classes. In planning new product developments, cosmed management sought to ensure that the NIVEA brand met the market needs of the 1990s while also remaining true to the heritage of NIVEA, as exemplified by NIVEA Creme.

NIVEA's marketing program in the 1990s followed a "sub-brand strategy" where individual sub-brands received budget allocations for independent marketing communications activities, rather than an umbrella brand strategy where the NIVEA corporate brand was promoted first and foremost. Still, the individual sub-brands retained significant links to the parent brand, since the first word in the name of each sub-brand was always "NIVEA." The brand also continued to invest in image advertising for its flagship brand, NIVEA Creme. Internally, however, executives debated whether the NIVEA Creme brand should continue to receive significant marketing dollars. Some felt that NIVEA Creme was the core brand in the NIVEA brand franchise and therefore played the most valuable role. Others worried about how the traditional NIVEA Creme image could be maintained if the company also needed to innovate and modernize it. Now that the company had a broad spectrum of successful sub-brands, the big question going forward was: How could the company best manage its brand hierarchy?

DEVELOPMENT OF THE NIVEA BRAND: 1912-1970

NIVEA Creme was first introduced into the German market in 1912. In the early 1900s, industrialization led to the emergence of mass markets and branded articles. Society -- women in particular -- began to appreciate to a greater degree physical appearance and look for products to both care for and beautify the skin. Prior to the introduction of NIVEA Creme, fat and oily skin cremes were all that were available, sold primarily to upper class women. NIVEA Creme's unique water in oil emulsion was the first creme to offer both skin care and protection at a reasonable price. The NIVEA name came from the Latin word, nives, meaning "snow" -- reflecting the snow white color of NIVEA Creme. As the world's first multi-purpose, "universal" skin creme, NIVEA Creme took skin care "out of the boudoir and onto the boulevards. . . . democratizing a piece of luxury." NIVEA Creme was quickly adopted for use by the entire family. NIVEA Creme was introduced throughout Europe in 1912, in the U.S. in 1922 and in South America and other parts of the world in 1926.

Recognizing the value of NIVEA Creme and the need for other reasonably priced skin care products, Beiersdorf introduced over 48 other skin care products under the NIVEA brand name between 1911 - 1970. As BDF expanded its range of product offerings, it maintained a "mono-product" philosophy -- typically offering one multi-purpose product in each skin care market segment and category it entered.

Throughout this period, NIVEA Creme remained the company's primary product and the carrier of the NIVEA brand name. The famous NIVEA Creme blue tin with white lettering, standardized in 1925, was a familiar sight in millions of households worldwide. In addition to NIVEA Creme, the brand's other primary products during this period were body soap and powder and two sun care products -- tanning lotion and oil.[2]

NIVEA Creme Brand Identity and Values

Over the years, NIVEA -- primarily through NIVEA Creme --had acquired a unique, widely-understood brand identitity as a "caretaker" of skin. Used by the entire family, NIVEA Creme had a universal, uni-sex brand image. Throughout Europe, most users were first introduced to NIVEA Creme during their childhood, learning that it was a product that could be used by the entire family to satisfy all kinds of needs. Because of consumers' own personal history and brand advertising, NIVEA had become strongly associated with shared family experiences -- e.g., mother and child relationships, family vacations at the beach, etc. The childhood and family associations of NIVEA users facilitated the development of a rich set of other brand associations such as "care", "mildness", "reliability", "gentleness", "protection", "high quality", "feeling good", and "reasonably priced." Over time, the NIVEA name became synonymous with protection and caring for the skin and attained a special, almost mythical, status among users. By the 1960s, NIVEA Creme could be found in almost every German household, in the majority of households across Europe and was the dominant multi-purpose skin creme worldwide.

Early NIVEA Advertising

BDF first began advertising NIVEA products -- primarily NIVEA Creme -- in 1912. The company viewed advertising as a means of strengthening consumer perceptions after a NIVEA product had established a quality reputation for itself. For over 60 years, NIVEA advertising promoted the basic themes of skin care and protection. Ads were always simple, plain and informative. In the 1910s and 1920s, BDF advertised three main NIVEA products -- creme, soap, and powder. Early ads established the image of the NIVEA woman as clean, fresh and natural.

Over time, NIVEA ads were altered to reflect changes in self-images and lifestyles. For example, in the 1920s, when German women were becoming more active athletically, NIVEA ads began to show women in more outdoor and active settings. In the 1930s, when tanning came into fashion, BDF responded by highlighting the skin protective qualities of NIVEA creme and introducing a new product -- NIVEA oil -- against sunburn. In the 1950s, following the end of World War II, NIVEA ads reflected the German population's desire to enjoy life by showing NIVEA products used in relaxed and happy settings, primarily outdoors in the fresh air and sunshine.

While the settings of the ads changed, the clean, fresh and natural image of the NIVEA woman remained essentially unchanged. Though she was modernized to reflect the styles of the time, she was always a face with whom the average woman could identify. Over time, NIVEA ads sought to link the clean, fresh and natural image of the NIVEA user to related elements of nature -- fresh air, light and sunshine. The development of these associations was particularly strong in NIVEA's sun care ads. In these ads, BDF additionally introduced special objects and symbols to strengthen the linkage of these associations. For example, in its 1932 sun care campaign, BDF introduced the NIVEA weather calendar -- a graph that showed the "weatherman's" predictions for the summer months -- to help Germans plan their summer holidays. This weather calendar became very popular in Germany and was used for decades to come. Later, in 1964, NIVEA offered a blue beach ball with the NIVEA logo as part of a holiday season pack that contained a variety of skin care products. The NIVEA ball was a tremendous success and could be found on beaches all over Europe, and was a recognizable symbol in NIVEA sun care ads. The NIVEA ball was used throughout the 1980s and 1990s.

NIVEA'S FIRST COMPETITIVE CHALLENGE: THE 1970s

During NIVEA Creme's first fifty years, the market for multi-purpose creme grew steadily. By 1970, NIVEA held over 35 percent of the multi-purpose creme market in Germany and majority market share in Europe. In the late 1960s and early 1970s, the multi-purpose creme market changed substantially as BDF faced its first strong competition in 60 years. Henkel-Khasana, a small German toiletries company and subsidiary of Henkel, launched its own multi-purpose creme -- Creme 21 -- in 1972. A direct copy of NIVEA Creme, this product was backed by extensive advertising and a distribution strategy designed to take advantage of a broader, fundamental shift in consumer purchase habits for cosmetics from specialized outlets to mass market, self-service outlets such as food stores. Also at this time, a number of manufacturers -- including Ponds, Unilever, and Lingner-Fisher (now part of Procter & Gamble) -- introduced a variety of specialized cremes into the market, particularly moisturizing cremes, designed for specific skin care uses.

Concerned with this new competition and its effect on consumer perceptions of the NIVEA brand, BDF commissioned a German university marketing professor, Reinhold Bergler, to perform a study of the NIVEA brand image in the German market. Bergler's study found that, among both consumers and the trade, the NIVEA brand enjoyed a high degree of goodwill and confidence, representing reliability, quality and honesty. Yet, the brand had an "older" image and was not viewed as young, dynamic and modern, as was the case with many of the recently introduced competitive brands.

In recognition of these new competitive challenges and current consumer perceptions of the NIVEA brand, BDF developed a "two-prong" strategy. First, BDF sought to stabilize the strong historical market position of NIVEA Creme. Second, the company sought to exploit the strength of NIVEA Creme by transferring the goodwill it had created for the NIVEA brand to other product classes.

Revitalizing NIVEA Creme

To address the first objective, BDF evaluated its current NIVEA Creme marketing program. Because research showed that consumers liked NIVEA Creme's current product formulation and logo, no changes were made there. The company did, however, introduce larger sized units, alter its distribution strategy by shifting from special-line outlets to food outlets and increase its level of promotional activities with the trade and within stores. Nevertheless, the primary means to revitalize NIVEA Creme's brand image was the introduction of a very aggressive ad campaign aimed directly at the competition.

The initial campaign, launched in Spring 1971, used the tag line -- "NIVEA, the Creme de la creme" -- for which a series of ads was developed. One of seven distinct slogans was used as a headline for each ad – for example, "There is none better," "No creme is better for your skin," "For 60 years, we have produced skin-care Creme" and "If there was a better one, we would make it." These ads ran in magazines across Europe, though primarily in Germany[3]. After two years of the "Creme de la creme" campaign, cosmed developed a new series of ads directly aimed at updating the "old" brand image. The "Only Me" campaign ran internationally and made a new brand promise: NIVEA Creme meets all skin care needs. With this campaign, cosmed wanted to preserve NIVEA's reputation for skin care competence and safeguard NIVEA Creme's unique historical market position while also differentiating it from the competition.

Prior to Henkel's Creme 21 introduction, the name NIVEA had been synonymous for the skin creme product category. This new competition now forced BDF to more directly tell consumers about NIVEA Creme's actual product benefits. Previous ads had always shown NIVEA Creme used in a variety of settings but had never emphasized *specific* product benefits. Each ad in this new campaign highlighted a single, but different aspect of product performance. The objective was to negate competitors' claims for special cremes by positioning NIVEA Creme as the best creme for every kind of special need. Taken together, these ads reinforced caring and mildness as key consumer benefit and presented NIVEA as the universal skin creme that embodied all the needs of consumers in one product.

The initial set of "Only Me" ads were introduced in 1973 in both print and television form. In Germany, the campaign made an emotional appeal to the hearts of the consumer by using folk art-like cartoon drawings. Each ad showed the blue and white NIVEA tin being embraced by an element of nature -- day, night, wind, snow, winter, summer, spring, at holiday time, at home, etc. -- and highlighted a specific purpose for the use of NIVEA Creme. At the bottom of each ad was the slogan, "There is no better creme." The cartoon campaign ran in Germany from 1973-1988.

Extending the NIVEA Brand

In addition to strengthening the brand image of NIVEA Creme, BDF's second objective was to use the recognition and reputation of the NIVEA brand name to introduce new products -- both in categories where NIVEA products were currently sold, as well as in related categories where NIVEA did not have a product. While BDF had been selling a variety of different products under the NIVEA name for years, NIVEA Creme -- dominating company sales -- was the primary image maker for the NIVEA brand. Bergler's study clearly demonstrated that the NIVEA brand had a strong, positive reputation in the marketplace with a great deal of consumer loyalty. Since the market for multi-purpose creme was stagnating, BDF actively targeted new and growing market segments in which to extend the NIVEA brand. The company's long term objective was to evolve NIVEA from a *skin creme* brand into a *skin care* and *personal care* brand by providing a range of new products that would both complement NIVEA Creme and broaden the meaning of the NIVEA brand name.

At this time, the NIVEA family of products included: NIVEA Creme, NIVEA Milk, NIVEA Baby (oil and powder), NIVEA Sun oil and milk and regular soap (sold only in Germany). To establish NIVEA as a skin care brand, the company decided to create a family of products that symbolically could be represented as the "NIVEA universe." At the center of the NIVEA universe was the NIVEA Creme core brand. NIVEA products -- some already existing, some new -- would function as satellite sub-brands around this center.

Cosmed established a set of guidelines for NIVEA brand extensions. All new products had to be compatible with the NIVEA brand and be targeted to market segments with attractive current and potential size. While the company wanted to expand the NIVEA brand to include new product classes, their "mono-product" philosophy meant that there would be only one primary product promising consumers universal application in each product category. A second version or variety of a particular product could only be introduced if it satisfied a unique need not met by the current product(s) in its product category. The company further established a set of guidelines that any possible new products had to satisfy:

1. Meet a basic need: clean and/or protect
2. Offer the special care/mildness benefit of NIVEA creme
3. Be simple and uncomplicated
4. Not offer to solve only a specific problem
5. Maintain a leading position in terms of quality (at a minimum, be as good as the leading product)
6. Offer the product at a reasonable price such that the consumer perceived a balanced cost-benefit relationship
7. Offer the broadest possible distribution

These criteria were established to ensure that all products reflected the desired NIVEA brand image and were consistent with the philosophy of providing high quality skin care products at a reasonable price. All new products were to offer "continuity plus innovation" -- that is, maintaining the essential NIVEA core while offering something new through the product itself. In addition, existing products were expected to be continuously modified and improved, reflecting cosmed's product philosophy to follow market trends and to innovate through research and development. As one long-time cosmed executive explained:

> It was like taking a teaspoon of NIVEA Creme and putting it into every new NIVEA product as a special benefit -- as an additional amount of care. In this way the new product was really a two-in-one product: satisfying a basic need plus offering the care of NIVEA Creme as a symbol. For example, NIVEA sun care products protect the skin, but in a mild and caring way.

RATIONALIZING THE NIVEA BRAND

By the early 1990s, it was clear that BDF had succeeded in extending the NIVEA brand from skin creme to a skin care and personal care brand. In 1992, NIVEA Creme accounted for only 22 percent of total NIVEA brand sales. While NIVEA Creme remained the largest single contributor to total revenues, the newer product lines each made significant contributions of their own. NIVEA products held strong market positions throughout Europe, especially in smaller volume markets where advertising costs were lower, as BDF was a small company relative to its competition (e.g. Unilever, Proctor & Gamble and L'Oreal) and its advertising budget was substantially lower as a result. NIVEA's highest percentage market penetration was in Belgium, Switzerland and Austria. Germany -- the largest skin and personal care market in Europe -- however, remained its largest volume market.

Though marketed independently, all NIVEA sub-brands carried some of the brand associations established by NIVEA Creme while also expanding the set of associations that consumers linked to the NIVEA brand name. BDF's success in establishing NIVEA as a broad skin care and personal care brand now presented the company with a new set of issues and challenges.

In the process of establishing sub-brands, everyone worried about the management and development of the NIVEA brand itself. There was concern that the NIVEA brand image -- in particular, the NIVEA Creme image -- had been weakened through all of the product introductions. Moreover, there was fear that continuing to develop the sub-brands independently of one another -- given the breadth of the NIVEA product lines -- would be complicated, risky, and could send a confusing set of messages to consumers about what NIVEA represented. Currently, ad campaigns were developed independently by three different ad agencies. While there were similarities in the various campaigns, there was no consistent message strategy or standardized presentation. Because of these concerns, cosmed management decided it was necessary to bring more consistency to the marketing of the NIVEA sub-brands.

At the same time, the cosmed Division came under new leadership. Dr. Rolf Kunisch, head of Proctor & Gamble's European Division, joined BDF to head the cosmed Division after 22 years with one of BDF's major competitors. In an effort to educate himself about the company's understanding of the NIVEA brand, Kunisch -- who became CEO and president of BDF board in 1994 -- joined a task force to define the NIVEA brand philosophy. Years of discussions about the NIVEA brand had resulted in an informal brand philosophy shared and respected by management. However, Kunisch believed that in preparation for the development of a new NIVEA communications strategy, adaptation of a formalized brand philosophy would be an invaluable tool. Kunisch explained :

> NIVEA is the most fascinating brand in the world, second only to Coca-Cola. The company had done a tremendous job over the last 50 years to keep the NIVEA brand focused yet diversified in a very reasonable way. But, at the same time there was a lack of conscientiousness of what it meant to be a brand. In the good old days, BDF had a brand relationship that was very personalized. Only three people knew how it had all been done -- one retired, one left the company and one died. When these people had gone, BDF, working with consultants, had created 12 SBUs - strategic business units - and put a chief on top of each one. In addition, there were three advertising agencies who did not talk with one another. In preparation for our first communication strategy meeting, I asked, why we did not have a logo on the wall? Someone finally came to me three days before the meeting and said NIVEA did not have one clearly defined logo. I began with the basics and asked: What is NIVEA? The data was all there, the feeling was there, but no one had put it on a piece of paper.

While working internally on rationalizing the NIVEA brand philosophy, the company also undertook a set of market research studies. The "Inner Visuals" imagery study focused on consumer perceptions of, and associations with, the NIVEA brand, whereas a semiological analysis of socio-cultural values sought to identify general consumer trends and values for the 1990s.

Linking the NIVEA brand to consumer values in the 1990s

The "Inner Visuals" imagery study, conducted by HTP research firm in Germany, showed consumers a variety of pictures and sequences and asked them to indicate which skin care brand the particular scene best represented. The pictures had been designed based on results from two earlier phases of the study.[4] The images with which NIVEA was most often identified by consumers were those scenes that depicted the following: the traditional family ideal; communities (e.g. groups doing something together); symbols which crossed boundaries (e.g. the earth, the blue planet, symbols which evoke a feeling of community) and single properties and qualities associated with the product (e.g. scenes depicting moisture, freshness, relaxation, a classic).

The second study was a semiological analysis of consumers' socio-cultural values in the 1990s, conducted by the RISC Group, that evaluated the socio-cultural positioning of NIVEA Creme and other major NIVEA sub-brands (NIVEA Body, NIVEA Visage, NIVEA Sun and NIVEA Bath and Shower). As part of the analysis, the study also examined the brand "territory" for each sub-brand, relative to main competitors, as conveyed by product packaging, and TV and print ads. The research was primarily restricted to socio-cultural attitudes in France and Germany, NIVEA's two largest volume markets in Europe.

The results of these two studies showed that NIVEA's brand associations fit well into the values of the 1990s consumer: The return to a more simplistic, holistic approach to life; the desire for fairness, authenticity, openness and belonging and an integration of the past with the present were all values that were also associated with the NIVEA brand and particularly NIVEA Creme. NIVEA's core brand associations -- mildness and caring -- were key needs of the 1990s consumers. The results of this research clearly suggested that the 1990s presented an opportunity to grow and expand the NIVEA brand.

Developing cosmed's corporate strategy

Combining the results of the external research with their own internal research and discussions, the cosmed task force developed a common brand philosophy for NIVEA to be adopted by the entire company and become the basis for developing a corporate strategy that the cosmed Division could implement at the product level.

The brand philosophy centered on maintaining the association of "universality" for NIVEA products. Now that the NIVEA brand represented comprehensive skin care and personal care, the company wanted to develop a marketing strategy that would continue to nurture core NIVEA associations while widening their applicability and enhancing their meaning via sub-brands. Kunisch explained, "We want to build on the image of the blue tin where we are number one almost everywhere in Europe." NIVEA Creme continued to represent the heart of the NIVEA image, evoking the most trust and sympathy of the consumer. Even as NIVEA's lines of products continued to be expanded in the 1990s, NIVEA Creme was to remain the primary representative of the brand's history and myth. Though its sales share had declined some over the years, NIVEA Creme was still considered the company's most important product for its role in establishing and renewing basic trust in the NIVEA brand.

The role of the other sub-brands was to continue to cater to the specific skin care and personal care needs of their target market segments and contribute back their particular product class associations to reinforce and elaborate on the image of NIVEA as a skin care specialist. Since facial skin care represented 75 percent of the European skin care market and was very closely related to NIVEA's strong association of "general skin care" from NIVEA Creme, NIVEA Visage was considered the primary sub-brand to upgrade NIVEA's image into the 1990s. NIVEA Visage, the company's face care brand, had the most sophisticated, contemporary and specialist brand image of all NIVEA sub-brands. At the same time, it benefited from the "halo" of the NIVEA name that represented trust, care, mildness and fair price. The primary challenge facing NIVEA Visage was how to effectively upgrade the NIVEA image as a skin care specialist while continuing to represent the universality and accessibility of the NIVEA brand. As with Visage, other sub-brands were expected to offer something back to the NIVEA brand. Through this combination, BDF sought to maintain NIVEA's leading position in the mass-market segment of the European skin care market.

While the NIVEA brand was BDF's leading skin and personal care brand, the company also derived considerable revenue from other skin and personal care products sold under different brand names. The most important of these other brands were: 8x4 deodorant and bath products, Labello lip balm and Atrix HandCreams and Lotions.[5] In total, these other brands represented nearly 40 percent of cosmed's sales in 1991. These brands had been developed out of the company's historical desire not to rely exclusively on one brand. While these brands would continue to be part of BDF's skin care and personal care product offerings, the company decided -- with much cajoling by Dr. Kunisch -- that the company's primary focus in the future would be on the further development of the

NIVEA brand through the introduction of new products. Only "extra" efforts and investments would be devoted to the development of these other brands.

EXECUTING THE NIVEA BRAND PHILOSOPHY IN THE 1990s

Having established corporate objectives, cosmed now needed to design a communications strategy. cosmed worked with its advertising agency, TBWA, to develop a set of guidelines that would communicate a certain "NIVEAness" to ads and promotions for all NIVEA products while also allowing the individual products to speak effectively to their specific target markets. This "NIVEAness" was to be represented not only in the layout of the ads, but also in their message and image. The core brand, NIVEA Creme, represented a set of desirable brand values: timeless and ageless; motherhood and a happy family; honesty and trustworthiness and the product benefits of mildness and quality. Any campaign for NIVEA Creme would have to incorporate these values; any campaign for a sub-brand would have to reflect elements of these values, although not necessarily only those values.

This process of creating a "NIVEAness" to all products and ads had begun in 1990 when the company decided to internationalize its sub-brands by creating a universal name for each product category and common packaging on a worldwide basis. With the brand philosophy now in place, the company was able to establish additional guidelines for the ad agency to follow. These guidelines included: evoking common emotion in all ads; use of a uniform and unchangeable NIVEA logo for all packaging; consistent use of lettering and typeface for all headlines using the NIVEA bold font from the Creme; incorporation of real, aspirational people in ad and dialogue about the product in an understandable way.

POSITIONING STRATEGIES FOR NIVEA SUB-BRANDS

Over the decade of the 1980s, the NIVEA category extensions grew into distinct sub-brands. To effectively establish the individual sub-brand images, the company historically had adopted separate ad campaigns for each sub-brand. Consequently, each sub-brand had built its own personality and developed its own set of brand associations that were consistent with, but independent of, the NIVEA Creme core brand image. Through their own ads, each sub-brand promoted the product attributes and benefits that best satisfied the needs of their target market, although a common "NIVEA" message of quality and care existed in all ads. To reinforce this continuity, the word "care" (or a word with a similar connotation) was found in all ad headlines. In addition, all ads utilized the NIVEA logo color code of blue background with white letters. Except for these two requirements, however, each product group was allowed to develop ads as it chose.

Until 1990, each of these new product classes carried their own set of descriptive category names to easily identify what the particular NIVEA products were used for. Since products had historically been launched in the national language of the country -- in an effort to give the brand a local character -- the same product often had different names in different countries. Given the breadth of products and the increased integration of Europe, cosmed management redefined the products names such that each product fell into one of the following product class groupings:

NIVEA Body
NIVEA Visage
NIVEA Sun
NIVEA for Men
NIVEA Shower & Bath Care
NIVEA Hair Care

By 1998, the NIVEA brand portfolio was considerably larger than in 1993, as reflected by the following product class groupings:

SkinCare
NIVEA Creme
NIVEA Body
NIVEA Soft
NIVEA Hand
NIVEA Sun
NIVEA Baby
Face Care/Cosmetics
NIVEA Visage
NIVEA Vital
NIVEA Beauté
NIVEA Lipcare
NIVEA for Men
Personal Care
NIVEA Deo
NIVEA Bath Care
NIVEA Hair Care

SKIN CARE
NIVEA Creme

NIVEA Creme, NIVEA's first product, was introduced in 1911. It was the first stable water-in-oil emulsion available in the world, and its white appearance led to the name "NIVEA," after the Latin for snow. The initial NIVEA Creme advertisements were stylish interpretations of popular notions of beauty and fashion. Original NIVEA Creme tins were pale yellow with "NIVEA Creme" in blue print in the center and a red and blue Art Nouveau border, but were changed in 1926 to the now-familiar blue and white design. The tin design and advertising style evolved over the years, but both always reflected the simplicity and caring embodied by the brand.

Historically, most NIVEA ad campaigns had been developed from a predominantly German perspective, largely because BDF had built the NIVEA brand around the local needs of the German market. With the increasing internationalization of the cosmetics and toiletries market and the international strength of its main competitors, BDF felt that it was very important in going forward to build the NIVEA brand through a strong European base. Consequently, in the 1990s, the company sought to develop a true international ad campaign. Because NIVEA Creme was still the company's most important image carrier, but was plagued by stagnating sales, cosmed decided first to develop a worldwide ad campaign that presented a common brand image for NIVEA Creme. As one executive explained:

> Throughout Europe, the NIVEA image is really well established and is more or less the same for everyone -- and this image was built by NIVEA Creme. The main reason to have a more brand identity weighted campaign for NIVEA Creme was to keep this heritage alive.

The "Blue Harmony" campaign, initially introduced in January 1992, included a series of television and print ads highlighting NIVEA Creme. With "Blue Harmony", BDF believed it had captured the essence of the spirit of NIVEA through NIVEA Creme in a way that spoke directly to the 1990s consumer. A video introducing the "Blue Harmony" campaign described the message behind the new campaign as follows:

> "The year is 1992. A new generation of consumers has grown up. A new consciousness had gripped the consumer of the '90s. The young generation -- our new target group -- is discovering family life, discovering what is really important in life, what people really need . . . less glamour, more substance, less "chic-chic," more product, less show, more impact. What the new consumer is looking for is equilibrium and harmony. Again, less is more.
>
> This trend toward simplicity opens new opportunities for the NIVEA brand – a new era for NIVEA Creme. 1992 sees the start of a new campaign that once again shows the brand with an idea that reveals the secret of the brand and brings its fascination to life. The idea is as simple as it is brilliant and derived from the product itself . . . or to be more precise from one of the world's greatest logos – the NIVEA Creme lettering."

The campaign included five 20 second television spots and seven print ads. All television ads were shot with a blue tinted background. The first ad showed a group of seagulls flying together through the air as circus music played in the background. The headline read: "Harmony in Blue." "Harmony" was written in the NIVEA logo lettering while "in Blue" was written in white cursive letters. At the end of the ad a picture of a tin of NIVEA Creme flashed on the screen with the tagline " All that skin needs to live." But, as this ad did not show any people as being part of the mandatory elements for NIVEA Creme, the ad never went on air. The four other ads were identical in tone, style and look. For example, one television ad showed a couple kissing while the song, "I've Got You Babe" played in the background. The headline of this ad read, "All you Need." NIVEA also ran a print version of this ad. Another television spot showed a family with the headline, "Take Care." Once again "Take" was in NIVEA logo lettering and "Care" was written in cursive letters. The print version of the ad was identical. The final television ad showed a couple first looking at each other and then moving towards one another. The headline on this ad read, "Touch Me." Again, the combination block and cursive lettering was used. In the additional print ads, the same style -- the blue tint, the NIVEA lettering, the same tagline and a picture of NIVEA Creme at bottom -- was employed but with different faces and headlines.

As the flagship brand, NIVEA Creme continued to receive considerable marketing support with the "Blue Harmony" campaign begun in 1992. Funding for the campaign was eventually scaled back in the second half of the 1990s as the introduction of NIVEA Visage worldwide and the launch of NIVEA Beauté was given first priority. The company sought to revitalize the brand and attract new consumers by targeting a younger audience. NIVEA updated the ad campaign by creating ads with unexpected themes and youthful models. One print ad depicted two young boys (obviously cross with one another) sitting with their backs to each other and glowering at the camera. Because the two boys sat so close together, the ad implied that they remained friends and whatever differences they currently had would be overcome. The title of the ad, which used the familiar NIVEA font, read "True Friends." In 2001, for the 90th anniversary of NIVEA Creme, NIVEA released collectible tins representing each decade in NIVEA Creme's history. These collectors' items signified NIVEA Creme's long history as a premier skin care brand.

NIVEA Soft

NIVEA Soft, a lighter skin cream distinct from NIVEA Creme, was introduced in 1994. The NIVEA Soft formula was designed to be lighter because some consumers did not enjoy the heavier, greasier feeling of NIVEA Creme's Oil and Water formulation. However, the company was careful to not to position NIVEA Soft as simply a "young NIVEA Creme." The company wanted to establish a separate identity for NIVEA Soft and not cannibalize sales from NIVEA Creme. The product was positioned in all markets as a cream for general, all-purpose use on the skin, except in Latin America, where it was repositioned as a face cream after a disappointing launch.

NIVEA Soft was launched initially in the U.K., with an innovative marketing strategy called "fast marketing" internally. The fast marketing strategy involved collapsing the annual marketing budget into a single week of intensive television and print advertising, sampling and promotion. After the fast marketing was deemed successful in the U.K., NIVEA employed the strategy for NIVEA Soft introductions in other markets. The launch commercial showed a young woman in a sunlit apartment. She compared the sensation of NIVEA Soft on her skin to a warm summer rain. Images of her applying the cream are juxtaposed with shots of her enjoying an outdoor rain shower. The ad closed with a sequence showing the woman with a male companion. NIVEA retained the summer rain theme for subsequent ads, including a new execution from 2000 that used a younger model.

Awareness for NIVEA Soft was low initially, but sales continued to climb. By 2001, NIVEA Soft was the number two product in its category throughout most of Europe. Despite the fact that NIVEA Soft and NIVEA Creme were similarly positioned as all-purpose creams, there was no cannibalization of sales. NIVEA Creme sales held steady while NIVEA Soft grew, because many consumers were purchasing both products. These dual purchases were attributed to the fact that the company set out to establish a distinct positioning for NIVEA Soft. The sole product in the NIVEA Soft range was an intensive moisturizing cream, which was offered in both a jar and a tube.

NIVEA Visage

In 1982, cosmed introduced in Europe its first set of face care products for women, called NIVEA Visage after a line of products sold in France since 1960. Early Visage ads stressed the mildness of NIVEA products in caring for the face. The initial ad campaign used the tagline, "The mildest way to cleanse your face." Within one year, Visage became a leading face cleanser in many European countries.

For the next five years, NIVEA Visage's message focused on mildness. Realizing that that they would have to enter the moisturizing segment of this market to establish themselves as a specialist in the face care market, BDF introduced a beauty fluid (liquid moisturizer) in 1987. The product performed poorly and BDF learned that the benefit of "mildness" which had been such a successful point of difference in the cleansing segment of the market was not as unique in the moisturizing segment of the market. Rather, consumers in this market segment were looking for proof of a product's effectiveness. Franziska Schmiedebach, Marketing Director Corporate Vice President responsible for NIVEA Visage explained at the time:

> The moisturizing segment is much more sophisticated than the cleansing segment for face care. You have to talk about anti-age benefits, specific ingredients, etc. The added value of the product in terms of packaging and claims and advertisement is much more sophisticated than what you have in the cleansing segment. The benefit of mildness in cleansing was strong enough but the benefit of mildness in moisturizing is really a standard in that category and everyone will say "so what." In our packaging, we were much too close to our cleansing product.

To effectively sell in this largest segment of the face care market, cosmed upgraded NIVEA Visage's image through a series of actions. First, cosmed changed the packaging of its products from plastic to glass. Second, the company altered the logo for NIVEA Visage. Third, the company improved its product offerings, including the introduction of a moisturizing day creme and night creme in 1989. Finally, cosmed introduced a new series of ads that focused on highlighting specific benefits of NIVEA Visage products. In this second campaign, the ads moved away from NIVEA's traditional codes of simplicity and universality to develop a more sophisticated specialty image. A 1989 Italian TV commercial exemplified their approach. Showing a woman preparing to go out for the day, the voice-over says: "Discover the beauty of your face. NIVEA Viso the new moisturizing cream rich of precious components (like jojoba oil.) NIVEA Viso gives your skin all the elasticity and smoothness it needs to be beautiful. NIVEA Viso reveals your natural beauty." In 1990, NIVEA Visage ranked second behind L'Oreal Plentitude in European market share and generated over $44 million in revenue. NIVEA Visage had been extended to include over a dozen products and had evolved from offering simple cleansing products to providing sophisticated, technology-based problem solving products for face care. With the addition of its first "anti-age" products in 1991, BDF introduced a third ad campaign, "Science in all confidence" that sought to blend the image of the best in face care science with the trust historically attached to the NIVEA brand name. This new campaign was launched in 1991 both in print and television form. The TV commercial showed a young woman by herself as she prepared to go out for the day. The camera moved around the apartment with her as she dressed. The only skin product that she used before leaving was NIVEA Visage Liposome Creme. The voice-over said: "We have just created the first NIVEA Visage rejuvenating liposome range. Of course, we could tell you how fast our liposomes carry active anti-aging agents directly into your skin. We could even show you what they look like. But instead, we decided to show you the result of their efficacy. Because a woman is much prettier than a liposome. NIVEA Visage. Science in all confidence." This ad ran throughout Europe.

By 1996, NIVEA had passed L'Oreal to become the number one face care brand in Europe, with an 18 percent market share compared to 13 percent for L'Oreal. In 1998, NIVEA introduced a scientific breakthrough called Q10 that would soon become one of the company's best-selling products. Q10 is a coenzyme produced naturally by the skin that helps reduce wrinkles. In scientific tests conducted by the company, usage of Q10 visibly reduced wrinkles after six weeks. Q10 was first used in the NIVEA Visage line, in a product named NIVEA Visage Anti-Wrinkle Q10 Day Cream. The Q10 coenzyme was used in other products, including products in the NIVEA Body, NIVEA Vital and NIVEA Beauté sub-brands. Between 1998 and 2001, Q10 products achieved 20 percent growth, making the product, according to NIVEA's current Vice President of International Brand Management Franziska Schmiedebach, "the biggest success story in the last 20 years."[6] In the three top-selling markets, Q10 products represented one quarter of all NIVEA Visage sales. The success of Q10 enabled the NIVEA Visage sub-brand to become the number one face care brand in the world, with a 13 percent global market share in 2000.

The introductory print ads for the U.S. in 2000 centered around conveying product benefits showed a smooth-skinned model on one page with the question, "What is the world's #1 anti-wrinkle treatment." The next page prominently featured the silver logo "Q10" on a dark blue background. An open jar of NIVEA Visage Anti-Wrinkle Q10 Day Cream was displayed under the copy "NIVEA Visage Q10 Wrinkle Control. #1 in the world." Since Q10 was a scientific breakthough that deserved explanation, the bottom quarter of the page contained product information.

In 2000, NIVEA introduced an innovative new product, NIVEA Visage Cleansing Wipes. These facial wipes borrowed the wipe technology developed by the NIVEA Baby division. Print ads in the U.K. read "One cleansing wipe. Three benefits. No hassle." Text explained that the wipe removed makeup and impurities in a single step, prevented skin from drying out and worked on all skin types. Another innovation was the 1999 introduction of NIVEA Visage Beauty Flash. This product provided thorough facial cleansing and moisturizing in a form similar to the Clear-UP Strip, but intended for use under the eyes. Australian print ads read "Intensive care in a flash."

NIVEA Body

The NIVEA Body sub-brand was one of BDF's smallest product groups, consisting of NIVEA Milk, a moisturizing milk introduced in 1963, and NIVEA Lotion, a moisturizing lotion introduced in 1986. NIVEA Milk, like NIVEA Creme, was a water-in-oil emulsion, but in liquid form to provide long-term storage of moisture for dry skin. NIVEA Lotion was an oil-in-water emulsion designed for daily care of normal skin. By offering liquid skin care for dry and normal skin in addition to the classic NIVEA Creme, BDF sought to provide a comprehensive range of products that met the specialized skin care needs of different skin types.[7]

NIVEA Milk and Lotion were advertised together in the late 1980s. A 1989 print ad headline read: "A first choice twice." The copy continued: "NIVEA milk for the dry skin. Cares creamy and intensively, penetrates gently into the skin and the skin becomes soft and supple again. NIVEA lotion for normal skin. Cares with a fresh perfume and is light as a lotion, penetrates quickly into the skin and gives the skin natural moisture." The tagline read: "What your skin needs to be beautiful".

In 1996, NIVEA developed the first special care product for the NIVEA Body line. Called the Skin-Firming Complex, it produced "noticeably firmer skin and increased elasticity."[8] Other innovative products introduced by NIVEA Body included NIVEA Whitening Cream, which targeted the Asia-Pacific region where white skin is considered fashionable. The company also produced a Body Spray (called Sheer Moisturizing Spray in the U.S.) and a Shimmer Lotion with reflective properties that made skin appear to shine. Print ads for the Sheer Moisturizing spray pictured models using the product and used two different taglines: "Spray yourself soft," and "Moisturizing will never be the same." In television commercials, a model applies the product while a narrator asks "What does the new NIVEA Body Spray feel like?" The answer: "NIVEA Body Spray cares like a lotion, feels like a spray."

In 2000, the company introduced NIVEA Body Firming Lotion with Q10. European print ads depicted a model reaching up with both hands over her head, while the tagline read "After some stretching, do some firming." Ads in the U.S. used a different tagline that spelled out the product benefits more explicitly: "Firmness. Texture. Elasticity. NIVEA Body Skin Firming Lotion improves all three." Television ads showed a woman exercising while a voiceover informed viewers of the benefits of exercise and of the lotion:

> This firms the belly. This firms the legs. But what firms the skin? New NIVEA Body Firming Lotion. Now with skin's own coenzyme Q10. Proven to make skin firmer in just three weeks.

NIVEA for Men

In 1980, NIVEA introduced its first product specifically designed for the men's skin care market -- an after-shave balsam. This product was also the first NIVEA product marketed on a European-wide basis that focused exclusively on care of the face. The product, an emulsion with moisturizing qualities, embodied the NIVEA brand extension requirements of product innovation with brand continuity. It was the first after-shave product to provide both alcoholic water -- common to other after-shave products -- and a moisturizer to care for the face. From the beginning, the NIVEA for Men ads emphasized the mildness and caring of NIVEA as their distinguishing customer benefits. The first print ad for the after-shave balm carried the tag line, "Less alcohol, more care."

From the initial introduction of the after-shave balsam in 1980, the NIVEA for Men sub-brand had grown into a full line of men's skin care products by the end of the decade, including shaving creme, gel and foam and after-shave lotion and creme, among others. Even as cosmed expanded the men's product line, the caring and mildness themes remained constant as ads continued to emphasize the protective and moisturizing qualities of NIVEA.   In the late 1980s, cosmed ran a European television campaign called "The Couple." In this ad, a man's girlfriend brings him NIVEA After-Shave Balsam to put on his face as he get ready for work. The voiceover said: "NIVEA for Men After Shave Balsam refreshes, relaxes and cares for the skin in a fascinating way. The After Shave with the care of NIVEA -- NIVEA for Men."

In 1998, Philips and NIVEA engaged in a partnership that led to the Philishave Cool Skin electric razor with NIVEA for Men shaving emulsion. The razor emits a branded NIVEA for Men lotion that "smoothes, cares for, and refreshes the skin" during shaving, thus combining elements of a wet and dry shave. Recently, NIVEA also developed a number of products previously unavailable in the men's skin care category, including a face scrub, face mask and a revitalizing cream with Q10. NIVEA for Men has three lines -- Normal, Sensitive, and Refreshing -- and offers foams, creams and balms in each line.

The 1999 introduction of the NIVEA for Men Clear-up Strip for nose pores occasioned a need to educate male consumers about the product. A print ad for the U.K. featured a hand-drawn product tutorial that demonstrated proper use. The ad also showed a model wearing a Clear-up Strip with the product benefit "Peel away dirt and blackheads" printed on it. The copy read, "Yes, they look daft. But they get the job done."

In 2001, the NIVEA for Men line was introduced in the U.S. The launch was supported by an advertising campaign from TBWA/Chiat/Day titled "For men who dare to care." The introductory television ad for NIVEA for Men Sensitive After Shave Balm depicted men attempting to relieve the post-shave discomfort in humorous ways, as one man does when he sprays his face with a hose. The tagline for the television spot was, "Finally there's a better way to soothe your skin." A shot of a model applying the Sensitive After Shave Balm followed.   NIVEA also developed a web site (http://www.NIVEAusa.com/nfm/) that featured product updates, face care tips and guidelines for a four-step face-care program.

In 2001, NIVEA for Men had a relatively small segment of the global men's skin care market, at 11 percent. In Europe, NIVEA for Men claimed only a 10 percent share of the men's shaving product market, compared with 38 percent for Gillette. The company did, however, have 15 percent share of the European aftershave market in 2000, compared with only 6 percent for Gillette.

NIVEA Sun

After NIVEA Creme, NIVEA Sun is one of the oldest NIVEA products. In the 1980s, it had the most extensive product range of any NIVEA sub-brand, having expanded its oil and creme products to include lotions in a variety of SPF factors and after-sun products, among others. NIVEA sun care products had a long advertising history dating back to the 1930s. Only in the early 1970s, however, did BDF consciously begin to develop NIVEA Sun as an independent sub-brand. A unique logo and design was developed and a conscious decision was made to create a unique NIVEA Sun "world" in its advertising where people were happy -- enjoying the sun and one another -- under the care and protection of NIVEA Sun products.

In the late 1980s and early 1990s, BDF extended the NIVEA Sun line to include more specialized sun care products, including a line of sensitive skin and after-sun products, further demonstrating the innovativeness of the NIVEA Sun brand and its ability to fulfill specialized needs.

NIVEA introduced a line of co-branded products in 1997 with moisturizing sun creams called NIVEA Sun Visage. These products offered "active cell protection and vitamin E-plus to prevent sun wrinkles" as well as high UVA and UVB protection levels. In 1999, NIVEA launched the successful NIVEA Sun Spray line. These sprays contained advanced sun protection, were waterproof, non-greasy and applied easily. A series of humorous and award-winning television commercials reinforced the product benefits. In one TV ad, a woman at the beach is flying a kite in a strong wind. She is distracted by the sound "Psst, Psst," and momentarily looks behind her to see what is creating the sound. By doing so, she loses control of her kite and is carried up in the sky. The camera pans to reveal the source of the sound: a young man applying NIVEA Sun Spray with squirts of the pump.

Another innovative product was a NIVEA Sun Kids Sun Spray that showed up in color when applied to the skin. In order to let parents know if their children were adequately protected, the spray appeared green when first applied to the skin. The color disappeared after a few minutes. An ad showed a young child with the product on his face, arms, and chest in a manner resembling warrior paint, while the copy read, "Where it's green, it won't be red."

In 2000, NIVEA Sun developed a product containing Q10, called NIVEA Sun After Sun Cream with Q10. The product was designed to prevent the wrinkles and lines that result from repeated sun exposure. One U.K. print ad showed a smiling, tanned model against a backdrop reminiscent of a sunset and used the tagline "Protection from wrinkles after sunset."

NIVEA Vital

NIVEA Vital was introduced in 1994 in order to address the different values and needs of women consumers over the age of 50 with mature skin. Because older women tend to be more educated and critical consumers, NIVEA chose to advertise using models the target audience would be able to identify with. By using a 52-year old German model in the introductory campaign showing grey hair, NIVEA broke the unwritten rule of the cosmetics category that mature women should not be depicted in advertising. A television spot developed for European countries depicted the model and detailed the product benefits. The voiceover informed the viewer "Mature skin needs daily care with Vitamin A. It activates cell renewal and improves the elasticity of the skin noticeably." The tagline went, "Activating day cream from NIVEA Vital. For more elasticity . . . that you can even feel!"

NIVEA redesigned the packaging and logo for NIVEA Vital in 1999. The new design, which incorporated the color red and curved gold bands, was intended to suggest energy and femininity. In 2000, the NIVEA Vital range included cleansing, day and night creams, body lotion and intensive special products that support the cell renewal process.

OTHER SKIN CARE SUB-BRANDS
NIVEA Baby

The NIVEA Baby line was introduced in Central Europe in the 1970s, but the products failed to meet sales targets in Austria, Germany and Holland and were pulled back within a few years. The line was reintroduced in the 1980s in some countries, but did not contribute much to the bottom line. In 1996, NIVEA relaunched the entire NIVEA Baby line. In 2000, NIVEA Baby had a total market share of 13 percent in Western Europe. Of the major baby care brands in this region, only Pampers had a higher market share at 17 percent. As of 2001, NIVEA Baby remained a significant competitor in 20 countries. Research for baby wipes was translated by other NIVEA sub-brands into successful products. Both NIVEA Deo and NIVEA Visage developed innovative new products using wipe technology. Wipes products contributed more than $100 million in sales during 2000.

NIVEA Hand
NIVEA Hand was launched in 1998 with a hand cream named NIVEA Hand Age Control Lotion designed to counteract skin aging. A introductory print ad showed a close-up of a smooth set of hands, and the copy read "Apparently, you can tell a woman's age by her hands . . . Now you can lie a little." The ad indicated that women could essentially "cheat time" with the new NIVEA Hand lotion. The five products in the NIVEA Hand assortment provided one or more of the following benefits: moisturizing, anti-ageing, and nourishing.

NIVEA Lip
NIVEA Lip is available in a limited number of new markets, including China, Korea, Turkey, England and Poland. In older markets, Beiersdorf lip care products are marketed under the Labello brand. NIVEA Lip Care Repair and NIVEA Lip Care Medicated provide dry lips with renewed moisture and added protection. NIVEA Lip Care UV protects against UV rays and NIVEA Lip Care Essential is designed for daily use.

PERSONAL CARE
NIVEA Deo
In 1991, BDF extended NIVEA's presence in the personal care area with the introduction of a line of deodorant products called NIVEA Deo. Though cosmed had discussed introducing a deodorant product under the NIVEA brand name since 1983, management was not convinced the time was right until 1991. Uwe Wolfer, Director of cosmed Germany explained:

> In the deodorant field, there is demand today for mildness and caring that wasn't there before. Ten years ago, people wanted freshness, fragrance, efficacy and they wanted the product to be transparent. Today, even in the deodorant field, people want assurance of mildness. So we introduced a product with this caring and mildness image. If we had done the same operation ten years ago, we would not have succeeded. It is a question of timing when to enter [product] categories.

The initial Deo line included aerosol, roll-on, pump-spray and creme products. Deo Creme was considered an innovative product and hence was the lead product used in most advertising. In the advertising, NIVEA Deo went beyond the traditional "efficacy" appeals to emphasize the additional dimension of "caring" through the introduction of a feather as a symbol of mildness and caring. The initial TV spot showed a woman placing NIVEA Deo on her underarm as the voice-over said: "Now there is a deodorant that guarantees you not only secure efficacy, but also extra mildness. Because it is from NIVEA. New NIVEA Deodorant. The harmony of mildness and efficacy."

The company introduced a sensitive-skin version of NIVEA Deo in 1995 products with NIVEA Deodorant Sensitive Balsam. Ads for the products retained the feather symbol, which reinforced NIVEA's long-standing reputation for gentleness. A 2000 print ad for NIVEA Deo Roll-on showed the product with a feather resting next to it accompanied by the tagline "No perfume. No alcohol. Just kind to your skin."

Two innovative products developed for the Japanese market in the two years the company was in that market -- NIVEA Deo Wipes and NIVEA Deo Compact -- became key products in other markets. In 2000, NIVEA launched NIVEA Deo Wipes, a convenient and effective underarm cleanser in a wipe form. The launch commercial focused on the product's ease-of-use by depicting a woman at work getting an unexpected call from her boyfriend informing her that he is ready to pick her up outside. She reaches for a NIVEA Deo Wipe, uses it, and heads out for a night on the town. The NIVEA Deo Compact, introduced in 2001, is a portable spray deodorant – small, but efficient and long lasting as an aerosol -- that can fit easily in a purse or pocket, allowing for quick and convenient application anywhere. In 2000, NIVEA relaunched the NIVEA Deo range using the new concept "Mild Care and Natural Freshness." That year, NIVEA Deodorant was NIVEA's third-largest sub-brand.

NIVEA Beauté

NIVEA Beauté was the company's second-biggest brand extension, after Q10. In 1997, NIVEA made its first appearance in the color cosmetics category with test markets in France and Belgium. The brand was positioned with primary focus on the skin-care attributes of the products by using the slogan "Colors that Care." For every new product introduction, NIVEA conducts a suitability study to test whether the product fits with consumers' perceptions of NIVEA. With respect to the "Colors that Care" positioning, consumers felt that NIVEA Beauté products were consistent with NIVEA's core competency of caring, and the new line scored well in terms of suitability. The products were packaged in stylish containers made in deep-blue hues that resonated with the NIVEA Creme packaging. NIVEA Beauté set price points at the top of the mass market in order to compete with entrenched competitors Maybelline and L'Oreal. NIVEA Beauté consisted of a full line of color cosmetics with more than 100 different SKUs. After successful launches in the test markets, NIVEA Beauté moved into Germany, Switzerland and Austria in 1998, and Greece, Turkey, Portugal, Finland, Norway, Sweden and Denmark in 1999. After successful launches in the test markets, Nivea Beauté moved into Germany, Switzerland, Denmark, Turkey and Austria in 1998, and Greece, Portugal, Finland and Sweden in 1999, followed by introductions in Norway and Brazil in the year 2000.

The first year for the NIVEA Beauté sub-brand was not without difficulty. First, Beauté encountered intense competition from established color cosmetics companies like L'Oreal, which increased its ad spending and aggressively launched new products in order to stay a step ahead of NIVEA Beauté. NIVEA also had problems with the product line at first. The company had not planned to develop seasonal colors for its decorative cosmetics, but soon found that seasonal colors were an imperative in the marketplace. So, NIVEA

Beauté created seasonal product lines that emphasized its color competence. By 2000, NIVEA was developing products coordinated with seasonal color themes, such as Sahara Gold lipstick, foundation, nail polish, and eyeliner.

NIVEA spent lavishly marketing NIVEA Beauté. Ads emphasized the caring aspects of the products, as well as their high-fashion design. A 1998 television spot for NIVEA Beauté Stay-On Lipstick featured a young woman who is granted three wishes, but only for her lips. She answers that she wants long-lasting color and no dryness. The NIVEA Beauté Stay-On Lipstick fulfills here two wishes. As for the third, she demurs by whispering, "That's my secret!" Early print ads for the sub-brand were primarily informational, with lots of copy text detailing product ingredients and benefits. A 1998 ad for NIVEA Beauté Teint Nature Compact featured a full-page picture of a female model, with a single product shot in the lower left-hand corner and the NIVEA Beauté logo in the upper right-hand corner. A full ten lines of text accompanied the pictures. Later ads contained more of the fashion and glamour of traditional decorative cosmetics advertising. A 2000 print ad for the Sahara Gold line featured a model and backdrop chosen to emphasize the color, a shot of the product line and the NIVEA Beauté logo. The only text in the ad was "Sahara Gold. Spring Collection."

In 1999, the company combined its Q10 innovation with the NIVEA Beauté line and developed NIVEA Beauté Time Balance Q10 make-up. Its closest competitor, Oil of Olay, launched a color cosmetics line at the same time as NIVEA, yet had less than two percent of the European market. NIVEA considers the NIVEA Beauté line to have a halo effect on the overall brand. Not only does having a product in the high-image cosmetics category give the brand more cachet, but the Beauté line attracts younger consumers new to the brand that, are then more likely to try other NIVEA products.

NIVEA developed elaborate in-store display cases for the NIVEA Beauté line. Each case, which cost $500, contained the full range of NIVEA Beauté products. Since the packaging for most NIVEA Beauté products is the deep blue of the familiar NIVEA Creme jar, the display case forms a "blue wall" of NIVEA products. In Germany in 2000, NIVEA sold 131 million units of NIVEA Beauté products, which were available in grocery and discount stores, drugstores and department stores. Eye makeup was the largest seller, with 41 million units, followed by lip, nail and face products, all of which sold around 30 million units. By 2000, NIVEA Beauté had a 10 percent share of the European color cosmetics market, making it the fourth-largest brand.

NIVEA Bath Care

NIVEA Shower and Bath (now called NIVEA Bath Care) was NIVEA's first sub-brand developed primarily for personal care, extending the NIVEA brand into important skin-related personal care categories. Since their initial introduction, ads for NIVEA shower and bath products promoted the high-quality, mild, caring benefits of the NIVEA brand while also emphasizing the added emotional benefit of pleasure. The bath ads stressed relaxation and well-being and typically showed a woman relaxing alone, confident she was in care of NIVEA bath products. The shower ads highlighted the feeling of revitalization and care experienced when showering with NIVEA shower products.

In 1993, NIVEA introduced a line of co-branded bath care products that combined the NIVEA Body Milk lotion with NIVEA Bath Care products. NIVEA Shower Milk was a pH-neutral formulation of liquid soap that moisturized and cleaned. In 1995, NIVEA Milk Bar, a bar soap form of Shower Milk, was introduced. NIVEA Aroma Bath Care was introduced in 1997 to capitalize on the aromatherapy trend. Two products for children, NIVEA Bath Care Shampoo and Shower for Kids and NIVEA Bath Care Foam Bath for Kids, were developed in 1998. NIVEA Bath Care Shower Gel debuted in 2000.

In 2000, the company relaunched its NIVEA Bath Care brand by changing the packaging, price and formulas for the entire line. Whereas the company had marketed unisex Bath Care products in the past, with the relaunch it sought to project a more feminine image. NIVEA introduced the Aquasoft Formula, which were designed "to offer a better skin feeling with every shower," for its Shower Gels and Bath Gels. When rinsed, the Aquasoft ingredients wash away from the skin entirely, leaving the skin's own moisture levels undisturbed. Ads for the Aquasoft products emphasized the gentle, caring and refreshing sensations that came with using the product. In 2001, NIVEA Bath Care was the company's fourth-largest brand in terms of sales, and overall market share reached 10 percent. NIVEA Bath Care was the market leader in several markets, including Germany, Austria and Russia.

NIVEA Hair Care

In 1983, NIVEA introduced its first hair care product, a multi-purpose shampoo, followed by the introduction of a conditioner a year later. The introduction of hair care products extended NIVEA's presence even further in the personal care market. Unlike NIVEA Bath and Shower, however, hair care was not viewed as a skin-related product line and hence was not to be closely aligned with NIVEA's key association as a skin care provider. To maintain a strong link to other aspects of NIVEA's core brand image, though, the two products were named (in German) "Pflege-Shampoo" and "Pflege-Spülung". By adding the word "Pflege" (Care) to the product names, it was clear that these products continued in the NIVEA tradition of caring. The initial print ad headline read: "The entire care for frequently washed hair." Over the next few years, ads for NIVEA Shampoo and Conditioner remained essentially unchanged. Primarily in print, they continued to emphasize the mildness and care qualities of NIVEA shampoo for daily hair care.

The biggest development in the NIVEA Hair Care sub-brand was the launch of the all-new NIVEA Hair Care Styling line in 1996. NIVEA Hair Care Styling began with three different hair sprays and three different hair foams that catered to individual hair styles. In keeping with the NIVEA tradition of manufacturing caring products, the styling products were gentle and effective, providing hold and promoting healthy hair. They were called the "first caring Styling range". Sales for the first year of availability topped $11 million. In 1997, NIVEA unveiled Ultra Strong Hair Laquer and also a Gel, which was launched with an ad depicting a woman with a stylish hairstyle riding a wild roller coaster. When the ride is over, the hairstyle remains intact. NIVEA Hair Care Styling products sold $18 million in 1997.

While the brand extension was achieving growth, market research revealed that consumers perceived that NIVEA Hair Care Styling did not provide long-lasting hold because of its positioning as a mild styling product that did not damage hair. NIVEA therefore decided to relaunch the entire product line in order to better focus on the message of "hold." In 1998, the company developed new formulations for its range of hairsprays and mousses, designed new packaging and introduced a line extension with Ultra Strong Mousse. A new advertisement, titled "Powershopping," was developed in order to emphasize the new concept. The ad depicted a model in a shop busily trying on clothes. Though she pulls several tops on and off, her hairstyle never loses its form. The voiceover describes the product: "Ultra-strong hold for hairstyles that have to put up with a lot. Try on -- yes! Redo your styling -- no! NIVEA Hair Care has the mousse that holds." The tagline, "100 percent styling, 100 percent you" followed.

In 1999, the company launched NIVEA Hair Care Shampoo for Men designed for frequent use. NIVEA Hair Care Liquid Gel and NIVEA Hair Care Aqua Gel were introduced in 2000 as the "wet look" became popular. The company also introduced Hold and Protection for dyed hair that included a UV filter to protect hair from harmful UV rays. The Styling sub-brand continued to prosper financially. In 2000, sales exceeded $33 million, and market share climbed above six percent, up from two percent during the introductory year in 1996. As of 2001, NIVEA Hair Care products were found in over 15 countries, but the company was looking to further expand the brand. In 2001, NIVEA Hair Care was launched in Italy. The brand achieved immediate success, doubling the forecasted sales in the first year in Italy. The Hair Care Styling range was also launched in Greece, Slovakia and Czech Republic, increasing the distribution of that product range to 12 countries.

NIVEA'S BRANDING STRATEGY
Marketing Guidelines
In the mid-1990s, NIVEA began standardizing its advertising formats to establish a consistent look among its sub-brands. While the "Blue Harmony" campaign was designed specifically for NIVEA Creme, ads for other NIVEA sub-brands adopted some of the design elements of the NIVEA Creme ads, particularly in the use of the NIVEA logo lettering -- e.g., the block and cursive combination. The block letters were always used to identify the product and the cursive lettering was used to highlight specific product attributes. Though no other ads used the blue tinted background, most did use blue in the background of their print ads.

NIVEA's International Brand Management cosmed (IBC) worked with agencies FCB and TBWA to develop the marketing concepts and ad executions. In each market, local agency affiliates changed the copy of the ads according to the best local adaptation, but did not alter the execution. Dr. Rolf Kunisch, CEO of the company, stated, "Pictures travel, words don't."[9] In some Latin American, South American and Asian Pacific markets, the ads used different models to reflect the local culture, but in almost all cases the advertising formats remained constant. NIVEA distributed booklets with every product that detailed packaging and advertising guidelines. The company also printed a booklet for internal use detailing its brand philosophy called the "Blue Bible." The Blue Bible contained basic information about NIVEA's brand identity, vision, mission, success factors and the role of its sub-brands. Part Two of the Blue Bible gave guidelines for products, packaging, communication, promotion, public relations, direct marketing and pricing. Norbert Krapp, NIVEA's vice president of skin care, referred to the Blue Bible as "the best [branding step] we did in recent years," calling it the "key anchor" for all brand decisions.[10]

Direct Marketing

NIVEA initiated a number of direct marketing programs around 1995, primarily for its NIVEA Vital and NIVEA Visage brands. NIVEA's largest national direct marketing campaign, in France, involvd a database with more than one million consumers. Consumers in France received periodic mailings that contained product samples and information, coupons and a survey. Another large effort was the development of NIVEA magazines, which started in Germany. NIVEA published two proprietary magazines, one for adults called "More Time For Myself" and another for younger consumers called "About You." A total of more than 10 million of these magazines appear as inserts in other periodicals two times a year. In addition to the latest NIVEA advertising, they contained information about a wealth of NIVEA products, beauty advice, decorating tips, feature articles related to beauty and other content commonly found in fashion magazines. In 2000, NIVEA magazines were published in several European nations, including Germany, Spain, the Netherlands, Austria, Poland, Greece and Italy.

Non-Traditional Marketing

In addition to its print and television advertising, NIVEA engaged in numerous non-traditional advertising methods. One of NIVEA's most enduring promotional tools was the blue NIVEA beach balls that the company distributed at European beaches each summer. These balls had been standard issue for more than 30 years, and helped to reinforce NIVEA's image as a caretaker of the skin in a fun way. Other unique promotional devices included a Blue Santa Claus giving away NIVEA Creme in Germany during the holidays, a double-decker NIVEA-branded blue promotional bus in Russia and a "mega-poster" advertisement covering the outside of the Kremlin.

Another non-traditional marketing tactic was the development of NIVEA Clubs. The first NIVEA Club was founded in Austria in 1995. For an annual membership fee of about $10, members received a quarterly magazine, between four and six new product samplings and a birthday gift. Also in Austria, NIVEA arranged for home parties, similar to Tupperware parties. Customers planned to host the party in their homes, and NIVEA paid for a beautician to visit the party with an assortment of NIVEA products. NIVEA ran "workshops for body & soul" in Germany, where up to 30 women attend a three-day conference at resort locations. The workshops, which werr-e advertised in the NIVEA magazines, had different themes, such as "beauty feng-shui," "astro-beauty" and "total beauty." Consumers who attended receive beauty advice through a professional consultation in addition to other activities. Total cost to the consumer was around $200.

In partnership with hospitals, NIVEA sponsored young mothers in maternity wards by sending "care packages" of NIVEA products. The company then provided care in the form of free product samples and informational brochures for the mothers for one year after the birth of the child. Through the first three years following birth, NIVEA provided important baby care information to mothers at regularly-scheduled intervals that corresponded with stages in infant and toddler development.

Event Marketing

NIVEA devoted a portion of its marketing budget to event marketing activities. As Inken Hollmann-Peters, Corporate Vice President of Personal Care noted, "Classic advertising receives a large share of the focus, but more attention should be paid to new marketing methods."[11] Each country had an event manager that coordinated sub-brand marketing activities and was responsible for developing special events, such as sponsorship. NIVEA sponsored various organizations in Europe, including beach lifesavers (lifeguards), children's sailing programs and a beach volleyball tour. NIVEA also sponsored school education programs for safe sunbathing in several countries under the auspices of its NIVEA Sun brand. NIVEA sponsored beauty contests in diverse markets such as Poland, the U.K. and Thailand.

NIVEA created a branded double-decker bus that traveled to concerts and other youth-oriented events. The bus promoted such youthful products as NIVEA Hair Care Styling and NIVEA Beauté. Consumers could get a total hair and face makeover at the bus. Another vehicular promotion occurred when NIVEA painted a car on the high-speed French TGV train and held a product trial and beauty consultation for travelers.

During 2000, NIVEA developed a promotion for its NIVEA Hand products in the Netherlands. Free with each tube of NIVEA Hand Anti-Age Creme Q10 was a pair of metal relaxation balls. The balls, which are designed to stimulate circulation in the hands and calm the nervous system, came with instructions on use.

In 2000, NIVEA developed an in-store display concept called the Beauty Center. The Beauty Center was a large point-of-sale display that integrates NIVEA's Visage, Vital, Beauté and Hair Care sub-brands. At each Beauty Center, NIVEA hired beauty advisors to help customers. The Beauty Center concept was in retail stores. As with the in-store displays for NIVEA Beauté, the Beauty Center comprised a "Blue Wall" of blue-colored NIVEA products. The Beauty Center enables the company to introduce customers from one sub-brand to the other sub-brands.

NIVEA.com
NIVEA.com was a global web site with information about the company, its history, its products, its markets, as well as a beauty advice page and e-cards with the popular Blue Harmony theme. National NIVEA web sites, such as Turkey, U.K., Belgium, Germany, Brazil, Australia, Kuwait and the U.S. were linked with NIVEA.com. Each sub-brand also has a web site, with information about individual products and specialized beauty and skin care tips.

New Market Rollout Guidelines
NIVEA entered new markets first with its flagship product, NIVEA Creme. As the company's most basic and all-purpose cosmetic product, NIVEA Creme sold well in developing markets. Once the company established NIVEA Creme as a market leader, it introduced NIVEA Body, the sub-brand that shares the most common elements with NIVEA Creme. Next, the company rolled out NIVEA Visage, followed by NIVEA Soft, then NIVEA Deo. Once these sub-brands were established in a market, NIVEA introduced what it considered its most sophisticated sub-brand, NIVEA Beauté. NIVEA Visage had to be a market leader before the company could launch NIVEA Beauté in that market. Since the color cosmetics category wass highly competitive and heavily developed, this hierarchical rollout strategy sought to ensure that a national subsidiary had the expertise and experience necessary to give proper support to NIVEA Beauté.

OVERALL BRAND HEALTH

At the beginning of the 1990s, NIVEA was already a global brand with a wide assortment of products catering to the full spectrum of consumer segments. The company had a widely recognized and respected brand, which it leveraged across a range of sub-brands. Throughout the decade, NIVEA nurtured its existing sub-brands and moved into additional market segments by adding new sub-brands. The company's sub-brand strategy yielded remarkable results; between 1990 and 2000, every NIVEA sub-brand experienced sales growth and gained market share. In 2000, NIVEA ranked as the number one cosmetics brand in many markets in Europe, and elsewhere was often in the top three. NIVEA management decided that the sub-brand strategy was effective, and therefore did not develop an umbrella image advertising campaign. The company did, however, continue the "Blue Harmony" campaign for its flagship product, NIVEA Creme. The Blue Harmony ads were the company's most image-oriented.

Many in the company felt that NIVEA Creme, though it was not the company's most dynamic or high-growth brand, was nevertheless the most vital sub-brand in terms of its contribution to NIVEA brand equity. Historically, the value in the NIVEA brand was created by NIVEA Creme, and as the flagship brand, it maintained the highest visibility in the most number of markets. NIVEA CEO Dr. Rolf Kunisch identified NIVEA Creme as the essence of the brand:

> If I wake you up in the middle of the night and say 'Describe NIVEA,' people would say 'It's blue, it's white, it's round' . . . they are describing NIVEA Creme.[12]

Others at the company were less than enamored with the sub-brand strategy NIVEA had followed during the 1990s. "We tried for 10 years to give the sub-brands a life of their own, and I think we more or less failed,"[13] said corporate vice president of skin care Norbert Krapp. According to Krapp, rather than thinking of a particular NIVEA sub-brand when they are making a purchase, consumers are saying "I'd like to buy the blue bottle of NIVEA" (meaning NIVEA Body Milk) or "I'd like to buy the white cream" (meaning NIVEA Soft). The problem with sub-brands, in Krapp's view, is that "Nobody is able to cope with 13 brand groups."[14] Krapp did not believe a corporate image campaign would improve the state of the brand because "whenever you talk about NIVEA, people think of NIVEA Creme first . . . then they start thinking about their personal favorites."[15] Since NIVEA Creme enjoyed such high awareness already -- as much as 99 percent in many mature markets -- an umbrella image campaign would essentially be an attempt "to increase the 99 percent, which is useless." Instead, Krapp wanted to see more marketing dollars devoted to the flagship product, NIVEA Creme. Because he believed NIVEA Creme to be central to the equity of the overall brand, Krapp maintained that "the image [of NIVEA Creme] needs to be polished otherwise the core of the brand is losing strength."[16]

As the number one skin and face care company in the world, NIVEA maintained an enviable position in the early 2000s. Going forward, the challenge for NIVEA would be continuing to find new markets and developing new products without spreading the NIVEA brand too thin. Additionally, the company would need to ensure that the NIVEA image was protected and enhanced by these new developments. NIVEA also had to determine where to invest the brand equity it had worked so hard to achieve. The company had to consider whether to follow a sub-brand strategy, or to leverage its recognizable name in other ways.

DISCUSSION QUESTIONS

1. What is the brand image and sources of equity for the NIVEA brand? Does it vary across product classes? How would you characterize their brand hierarchy?

2. What are the pros and cons of the sub-brand strategy? Should NIVEA run a corporate brand or umbrella ad for all of their products? What is the role of the NIVEA Creme advertising? Should it be changed?

3. What would you do now? What recommendations would you make to NIVEA concerning next steps in their marketing program?

Fig 1: NIVFA Market Share Rank

Category	Europe 1999	World
Hand & Body	No. 1	No. 1
Face Care	No. 1	No. 1
Sun Care	No. 1	No. 1
Baby Care	No. 1	
After-Shaves	No. 1	
Bath & Shower	No. 1	
Deodorants	No. 1	
Haircare	No. 5	
Color Cosmetics	No. 4	

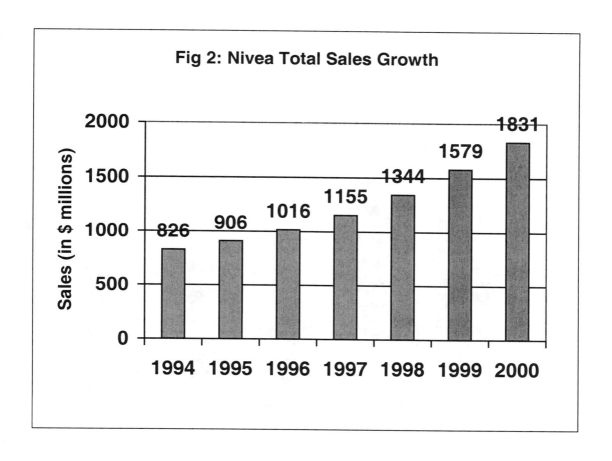

Fig 2: Nivea Total Sales Growth

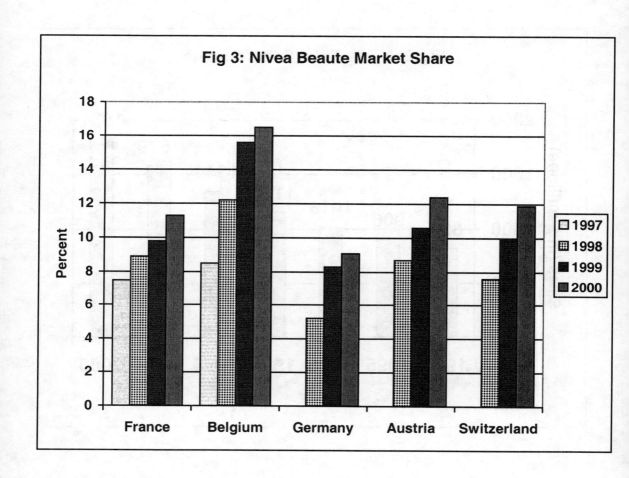

REFERENCES

[1] This case was made possible through the cooperation of Dr. Rolf Kunisch and Cosmed Division management, including Norbert Krapp, Franziska Schmiedebach, and Inken Hollmann-Peters for Beiersdorf AG in Hamburg, Germany. Leslie Kimerling and Keith Richey prepared this case under the supervision of Professor Kevin Lane Keller as the basis for class discussion.

[2] Nivea oil was introduced in the 1930s. In the 1910s and 1920s, Nivea body powder was a popular product.

[3] Some of BDF's competitors challenged these ads in the German courts, arguing that the ads violated German fair competition laws severely restricting comparative advertising, and in fact, "decrees" were issued against BDF to stop publication of certain motifs.

[4] In Phase 1, HTP had developed a set of words that provoked mental images of the Nivea brand. In Phase 2, the research group had developed a series of images associated with the sight, smell and touch of Nivea Creme. Using the output from these two research phases, the firm created a set of 42 storyboards to show consumers and to analyze their reactions.

[5] Other principal brands included Basis pH, Limara and Doppeldusch, Guhl, Azea and Solea.

[6] Franziska Schmiedebach. Personal Interview, August 2001.

[7] BDF also offered a line of problem solving products called Nivea Body Specifics sold only in France, Belgium, and Italy.

[8] Nivea Book, 2001

[9] Norbert Krapp. Personal Interview, August 2001.

[10] Norbert Krapp. Personal Interview, August 2001.

[11] Inken Hollmann-Peters. Personal Interview, August 2001.

[12] As quoted by Norbert Krapp. Personal Interview, August 2001.

[13] Norbert Krapp. Personal Interview, August 2001.

[14] Norbert Krapp. Personal Interview, August 2001.

[15] Norbert Krapp. Personal Interview, August 2001.

[16] Norbert Krapp. Personal Interview, August 2001.

STARBUCKS CORPORATION:
MANAGING A HIGH GROWTH BRAND[1]

INTRODUCTION

In less than a decade, Starbucks was transformed from a fledgling whole-bean coffee retail chain into a globally recognized brand. In 2002, Starbucks was comprised of more than 5,400 stores located throughout North America, Latin America, the Pacific Rim, Europe and the Middle East. Growth of the corporation's coffee retail business continued at a steady pace of one store opening a day on average, and annual revenue for 2001 topped $2.7 billion. Moreover, joint ventures with some of the nation's strongest corporations, including Pepsi, Kraft, Dryer's and Capitol Records, allowed Starbucks to launch a lucrative consumer products division to complement its cafe business. Licensing partnerships with other companies such as United Airlines, ITT Sheraton and Host Marriott further added to the growth of the Starbucks brand. Indeed, Starbucks rose to become one of the most impressive high growth brands in the 1990s. Despite this remarkable growth, some questioned whether Starbucks began to lose focus as the company strove to constantly reinvent itself. Critics wondered if perhaps the brand grew too quickly rapidly to remain focused on its core values and business objectives.

LAUNCHING THE BRAND

Company Background

American coffee consumption had been on the decline for more than a decade when Seattle entrepreneurs Jerry Baldwin, Gordon Bowker and Zev Siegl opened the first Starbucks in Seattle's Pike Place Market in 1971. By the 1970s, the country's major coffee brands were engaged in a bitter price war that forced them to use cheaper beans in their blends to reduce costs, resulting in a dramatic decline in the quality of America's most popular coffees. Accompanying this decline in quality, was a decline in coffee consumption, which had peaked at 3.1 cups per day in 1961. As Americans gradually became disenchanted with the store brands, java enthusiasts, concentrated primarily on the West Coast, began experimenting with the finer coffees of Europe that offered richer, fuller flavors. To harness the potential of the gourmet coffee trend in the Seattle area, the founders of Starbucks experimented with the new concept of a store dedicated to selling only the finest coffee beans and coffee brewing equipment. This emphasis on quality whole-bean coffee retail was fairly unique; only a handful of American cities had stores like Starbucks up to that point. Such a store would satisfy the demand of Seattle's gourmet coffee enthusiasts for high-quality coffee products that could previously only be obtained through catalogs from companies in Europe. Starbucks also sought to convert Seattlelites who had never experienced gourmet coffee to break away from traditional brands and integrate the finer European coffee blends into their daily lives.

From the start, Starbucks placed quality as its top priority. The Starbucks founders recognized that if they wanted to enhance Seattle's appreciation for fine coffee, they had to provide the best ingredients and brewing equipment to ensure that customers had the most enjoyable coffee experiences possible. The Starbucks management dedicated a great deal of their time and financial resources to establishing strong relationships with coffee growers from around the world. To distinguish their coffee from the bland and tasteless store brands, Starbucks only purchased arabica beans from a carefully selected network of suppliers across the globe, from places like Sumatra, Kenya, Ethiopia and Costa Rica. Arabica beans were selected because the bean's chemistry is such that it can withstand high roasting temperatures, resulting in a richer flavor. Starbucks also sought vendors who sold products that would protect, and even enhance, the arabica's flavor. This required the formation of partnerships across the globe with coffee brewing equipment suppliers who provided products that captured the essence of the coffee brewing tradition. Simplicity was valued over advanced technology because the machines Europeans and others had been using to brew coffee for centuries often proved the most effective in delivering the richest flavors.

STARBUCKS REINVENTED

It was not until Howard Schultz, current CEO of Starbucks, came to the company in 1982 that a vision for expanding the scope and reach of the Starbucks brand came under serious consideration. Schultz realized the powerful business opportunities that lay ahead of the company if he could preserve Starbucks' core values while exposing a wider range of people to the brand. The fledgling company had seen great success in converting its small group of loyal Seattle customers into coffee enthusiasts, but Schultz recognized that the conservative business plans of early Starbucks management hindered the company from reaching other potential coffee lovers. Schultz saw that the next logical step for Starbucks was to begin serving freshly brewed coffee by the cup in every store.

Transforming Starbucks from a coffee retailer into a cafe business resulted in several important benefits for the company. First, coffee prepared by knowledgeable Starbucks employees allowed for greater quality control; Starbucks stores would brew coffee the way it was intended to be brewed, giving customers the best coffee experience possible. Second, serving brewed coffee in the stores would allow the company to capture the business of Seattle's business community who loved high quality coffee, but whose hectic schedules did not leave time for them to pursue their passion. Starbucks would make enjoying good coffee convenient, thereby enabling the entire community to enjoy the brand had to offer. Lastly, incorporating a coffee service aspect into the business differentiated Starbucks from its coffee retail competitors, who were quickly growing in Seattle and in other major American cities.

With the coffeehouse model as the primary focus of the company's retailored business plan, Schultz began to concentrate on reshaping Starbucks' brand identity. As the company entered a period of explosive growth through market expansion it needed a reinvented image that captured the elegance of European coffeehouse culture, but was familiar enough to appeal to a broad range of Americans. Although Schultz's Il Giornale had acquired Starbucks in 1987, Schultz recognized that keeping the Starbucks name was pivotal to the brand's success since it was already familiar to Seattleites and patrons of the nationwide mail order business and was more recognizable and memorable than the obscure Il Giornale name. The Starbucks name captured all the aspects of Schultz's innovative coffeehouse concept; it was bold yet not overwhelming, mysterious yet not foreign, and romantic yet not impractical.

Creating A Look

The Starbucks name alone could not yet evoke the tradition, luxury and romance that Schultz had hoped to make synonymous with his brand. Starbucks needed to shape the look and feel of the environment of its stores to reflect the synergy of Italian elegance and American informality that Schultz envisioned for his unique coffeehouse model. First, the original Starbucks logo was updated to appear more contemporary and the color was changed from the original earthen brown to the green used by Il Giornale. Next, each of the original Starbucks stores was redesigned so that they echoed the romantic atmosphere of Italian coffee bars.

Rich browns in the wooden fixtures and vibrant green logos on the detailing and packaging formed the primary color scheme of Starbucks store design. This palate was selected to represent the company's emphasis on European romance and elegance coupled with casual American warmth. In addition to selling only "best-of-class" coffee, Starbucks worked to fill its stores with only the highest quality of everything, from the coffee-making equipment to the fixtures and furnishings to the music and artwork. In Schultz's words, each Starbucks store "is carefully designed to enhance the quality of everything the customers see, touch, hear, smell or taste."[2] Schultz envisioned that the Starbucks store would become a "personal treat" for its customers, whether they saw it as a convenient stop on the way to work, a refreshing break in their day or a place to relax at night. Starbucks was to be, for its clientele, a "Third Place," a comfortable, sociable gathering spot bridging the workplace and the home. Designing a warm, inviting environment was essential to Schultz's objective of making Starbucks symbolize not just a coffeehouse, but a pleasurable coffee-centered experience.

Investing Ahead of the Growth Curve

This focus on developing creative solutions for solidifying a rich brand identity complemented the Starbucks executive team's philosophy of "investing ahead of the growth curve."[3] Constant reinvention -- critical to developing a healthy Starbucks brand -- could only be accomplished by making fundamental changes to the structure of Starbucks management and by investing in innovation. As Schultz assumed the role of CEO of the new Starbucks, he recognized that although he possessed keen entrepreneurial skills and had the drive, motivation and vision to lead Starbucks in this period of immense growth and brand redevelopment, he would also need the support of experienced professionals to assist him in setting his vision into motion. Schultz needed a dynamic management team that would facilitate Starbucks' needs beyond the current development plans so that innovation could continue at an aggressive pace indefinitely. To professionalize Starbucks, Schultz offered competitive compensation and benefits packages to target individuals at some of the country's most successful and innovative corporations such as Nike, Deloitte & Touche and Macy's. Each executive joining the Starbucks team brought years of experience and fresh creative perspectives on how to maximize the company's profit growth during the implementation phase of Schultz's expansionary vision.

Investments in Starbucks infrastructure and process efficiency were equally as crucial to building the brand. Schultz's team of executives identified the need for state-of-the-art facilities (namely roasting and packaging plants) that would allow Starbucks to continue producing the highest quality products on a nationwide, and eventually global, scale. Therefore in 1989, Starbucks invested in high-speed coffee roaster and packaging equipment that would meet the needs of the growing business for at least 10 years. The company later implemented an advanced computer information system to keep track of sales across the hundreds of stores that would be opening within the first decade of expansion. Between 1990 and 1991 alone, Starbucks raised $18.5 million in venture capital to fund this expensive internal development. Although it was difficult at first to convince investors of the need for infrastructure improvements far in advance of the company's need for them, the fact that Starbucks revenues were rising at more than 80 percent per year in the early 1990s and that expansion into new markets such as Chicago, Los Angeles and New York had been successful, soon attracted vital venture capital to the company.

Innovation to Support Growth of the Brand

As Starbucks began focusing on a nationwide growth strategy, the problem of how to protect the freshness and flavor of coffee during shipments to distant Starbucks locations became a pressing issue. In the time it took to ship fresh roasted beans thousands of miles across the country to store locations in Atlanta or New York, for example, the quality of the coffee would decline dramatically. Therefore, significant time and resources were invested to develop a vacuum packaging system that prevented harmful air and moisture from seeping into the coffee. After the roasting process, coffee would be sealed in "FlavorLock" bags that would remain unopened until ready for use in stores. Such an investment allowed Starbucks to preserve its commitment to quality, while saving the company from the much more significant costs entailed in building roasting plants in every new Starbucks market. Innovations such as the FlavorLock bags highlight the flexibility that Starbucks was able to successfully leverage to reinvent business processes to adapt to new business climates.

Starbucks Core Values

In reinventing Starbucks by integrating the coffeehouse concept, Schultz also needed to reassert core values that would guide his management team in designing the company's new high-growth oriented business plan. The new Starbucks management strengthened many of the same core values that the company founders had established in the early years and reinvented others to meet the unique challenges it faced as a high growth brand. To articulate these core values, a diverse group of employees contributed to the development of the Starbucks Mission Statement. In drafting the mission statement, the Starbucks executive team sought to hear the views of employees at all levels and to incorporate their beliefs into company policies; consensus on company values among the diverse group of Starbucks employees was imperative for Schultz's vision of a unified team. "People growth" committees comprised of non-executive partners from stores, plants and offices were given a crucial role in determining the objectives of the statement. Moreover, "mission review committees" were formed so that employees at all levels could evaluate Starbucks' adherence to its guiding principles as it expanded and explored new business opportunities.

Pivotal to the values asserted in the mission statement was a continued commitment to investing in both Starbucks employees and customers. Schultz and his colleagues observed that the company had become too product oriented; Starbucks had to focus on people to achieve healthy organic growth. The key to the company's success and widespread appeal among loyal customers had always been the employees, whose knowledge and dedication attracted customers to continue returning to the store. But Schultz recognized that he could only achieve effective word-of-mouth publicity as the company expanded if he continued to recruit and retain talented individuals to lead the company in new markets and communicate Starbucks' strong values to communities who knew little about the brand. Attracting these talented individuals to the company required nothing less than a serious investment of company resources to establish relationships built on trust and confidence.

Schultz firmly believed that his business could not grow without the strongest team possible at all levels of the organization. Starbucks could only attract loyal customers if employees were skilled in delivering the highest quality service possible. The Starbucks work force deserved a disproportionate amount of company resources because they were essentially the key component in the revenue generating functions of the company. Therefore, under Schultz's leadership, Starbucks management adopted several policies that focused on recruiting and retaining a strong team of "partners" -- the company's term for employees.

The first and most important policies concerning the development of a strong team of partners regarded the company's commitment to training. More money was spent at Starbucks on training than on marketing, a fact that highlights the crucial role Schultz assigns to his employees -- that of fostering positive customer relations so as to engender widespread word-of-mouth publicity. Starbucks also assembled several policies regarding partner compensation and benefit packages to attract and retain a competent work force. These benefit packages included full health insurance coverage for all employees and the Bean Stock program, which awarded every partner between 12 percent and 14 percent of his or her annual base pay in Starbucks stock options. In extending equity to employees, Starbucks hoped to communicate that every employee would benefit as the company grew and performed well, providing an incentive for partners to work as a unified team toward achieving business objectives.

New philosophies were also adopted regarding Starbucks commitment to customers. Whereas the original company had always valued its patrons, the Starbucks founders maintained that customer service objectives must focus on educating the customer to appreciate coffee the way Starbucks liked it. But Starbucks President Howard Behar and other top executives argued that the company needed to become more customer service oriented by listening to their needs in an effort to serve coffee the way customers like it. Behar proposed another model that called for Starbucks to "do whatever it takes to please the customer as long as it is moral, legal and ethical."[4] While the "customer is always right" philosophy made sense to Schultz, he also recognized that it posed a threat to the integrity of Starbucks products. How could the company uphold its commitment to preserving certain coffee brewing traditions and keeping Starbucks products authentic if it encouraged customer input that could potentially jeopardize this authenticity? Schultz wondered how much flexibility should be given to customer demands when they compromised the traditions that the company's products were based on.

When health conscious customers began to request skim milk as an option in place of the cream used in various coffees, Schultz was forced to tackle this issue of flexibility head on. While at first he remained steadfastly committed to preserving the authenticity of his coffees by forbidding the use of skim milk in recipes, Schultz finally conceded, recognizing that "a lost customer is the most powerful argument you can make to a retailer."[5] If Starbucks wanted to maintain its loyal following, it had to listen to customer feedback. Compromise had to be integrated into Schultz's decisions regarding product development. As long as Starbucks could continue to deliver the highest quality products possible, flexibility would be favored over dogmatic adherence to tradition.

GROWING THE BRAND

Geographical Market Expansion

Pivotal to Starbucks' high-growth strategy was the carefully planned expansion of its specialty coffee stores to new markets throughout North America and eventually worldwide. The first phase of the Starbucks expansion strategy focused on securing a major foothold in the Pacific Northwest while experimenting in other key markets that were farther away, but had a high potential for rapid growth: cities such as Chicago, Los Angeles, San Francisco, New York and Washington, D.C. Each of these new markets had its own strategic purpose for the company's market expansion program.

Expansion to Chicago in 1987, for example, allowed the company's management to test how the coffeehouse concept would be accepted by average urban Americans who had not yet been heavily exposed to the gourmet coffee trend. Market entry in Chicago also allowed Starbucks to evaluate methods of building brand awareness in a community that had never previously been exposed to the brand. In contrast, Los Angeles was selected as an experiment that would prove that coffee had a potential for trendiness and could be seen as part of a "chic" lifestyle. Schultz knew that if Hollywood adopted Starbucks as its coffee of choice, the brand would gain awareness throughout the country as the "in vogue" beverage. Later expansion to cities such as Boston and Atlanta, served as testing grounds for how Starbucks would fare in parts of the country that had distinct regional identities like New England and the South. Successful expansion throughout Florida and Hawaii later showed that fine coffee could be a hit in warmer climates as well as in the cold cities of the Northeast and Midwest. The creation of Starbucks International in 1996 with the successful launch of Japan's first store in Tokyo's Ginza business district showed that the coffeehouse concept even had cross-cultural appeal. Success with the original Starbucks in Tokyo led the company to open another 25 stores in Japan by 1998.

The Starbucks management team agreed at the beginning of the company's massive expansion program that all stores would be owned and operated by the company instead of pursuing a franchise model like so many other successful American food service companies. While franchising offered advantages for some companies -- a source of capital, an inexpensive means of rapid entry into new markets and a guaranteed commitment by franchisees to the financial success of the business -- it posed potentially negative consequences for brand development. In building a strong brand, Schultz recognized that he and his executive team needed complete control over the brand to cultivate an unparalleled image of quality. In too many other companies, franchisees did business their own way and could potentially sacrifice Starbucks' commitment to excellence in order to turn higher profits. Schultz could not risk compromising the brand's image and knew that control of the brand had to be unified under the control of the Seattle headquarters to foster healthy growth.

The success of the expansion program rested on investment in extensive word-of mouth publicity campaigns that created brand awareness even before the first Starbucks arrived to a new market. The brand's success in new communities depended on built-up anticipation among local consumers who would become excited about welcoming Starbucks to their towns because of the attraction of having a trendy cafe environment for relaxation and personal enrichment. Grand openings became community events that encouraged local consumers to experience the new cultural dimension that Starbucks brought to their communities. Once a new Starbucks opened, highly skilled "baristas" (or bartenders) and managers would further strengthen the positive brand image by delivering the highest level of service possible.

Starbucks also employed a "hub" market strategy where its coffeehouses entered a new market in a clustered group. For each new region, a large city would serve as the hub where teams of professionals trained to support new stores were located. In the large hub market, the goal would be to rapidly open 20 or more stores within the first two years. From the established hub, Starbucks stores then spread to new "spoke" markets. These spoke markets consisted of smaller cities and suburban locations with demographics similar to the typical customer mix. This deliberate saturation strategy predictably resulted in cannibalization of almost 30 percent of own store sales by virtue of the introduction of a near-by store. This drop in revenue was offset, however, by efficiencies in marketing and distribution costs, and an enhanced image of convenience.

JOINT VENTURES & PARTNERSHIPS

With Starbucks' geographical market expansion proceeding at a phenomenal rate and with much success, many companies across the country began to approach Schultz with partnership proposals. These companies undoubtedly aimed at benefiting from the profitable business opportunities that would arise from being associated with the dynamic, high-growth Starbucks brand. While partnerships with some organizations would likely strengthen the Starbucks brand by broadening its exposure and leading to new product innovations, Schultz was wary of any business opportunity that involved compromising his executive team's control of the brand. Selecting the wrong partner company or the wrong product to introduce with a partner could have devastating consequences for the brand; no partnership was worth the potential risk of destroying the brand equity that Starbucks had built on its own. Therefore, Schultz decided from the beginning that Starbucks would only enter into partnerships with companies who maintained the same commitments to quality and people that Starbucks had as the foundation of its business.

Joint venture partners had to respect the integrity of the Starbucks brand, benefit the brand by exposing it to a broader range of consumers and maintain a commitment to preserving the authenticity of Starbucks products. Ultimately, these partnerships had to present a clear benefit for the brand. If it was not clear that the brand would grow stronger from the partnership, then the deal was rejected. Moreover, partnerships had to allow Starbucks to play a hands-on role in all aspects of the joint venture, especially with the product development aspect since Schultz was concerned that potential partner companies would seek to leverage the Starbucks name, but develop a product that clashed with Starbucks' commitment to highest quality and authenticity.

Host Marriott Partnership

The first partnership arrangements with which Starbucks agreed to be involved focused specifically on increasing brand awareness. By allowing contracted vendors to sell brewed cups of Starbucks' coffee at busy airports, hotel lobbies, malls and convention centers, the brand would be discovered by a broader range of potential consumers who would then be attracted to trying Starbucks products within coffeehouses. While in theory exposing more consumers to the brand through licensing agreements with vendors seemed to be the next logical step for Starbucks, Schultz was concerned about how the quality of the coffee would be affected if it were not to be brewed by Starbucks. A high level of trust would have to be placed in the hands of Starbucks' vending partners that the coffee would be brewed in a manner that was up to Starbucks' uncompromising standards. While exposing new customers to good coffee would surely help cultivate a stronger brand image, serving poorly brewed, low quality coffee with the Starbucks name would prove detrimental to the brand's image. Schultz was also concerned that the Starbucks' emphasis on educating customers about coffee would also be compromised because concessions employees would not be as well versed in their knowledge of the coffee and customers would typically be in such a hurry at crowded airports and conference centers such that they would never take the time to explore the life-enriching qualities of the brand.

Despite Schultz's reservations about contracting with vendors, Starbucks engaged a partnership opportunity with Host Marriott in 1991 that allowed for Starbucks coffee to be brewed and served at concession stands in airports across the country. While the opportunity provided a chance to expose the Starbucks brand to a large group of potential consumers --airline travelers -- Schultz's concerns about dealing with concessions companies were realized in that consumers were not encountering the same quality of customer service at airport concessions stands as in Starbucks coffeehouses. The frenzied environment of most airports accounted for most of the customer service problems; customers were simply not willing to learn about various aspects of Starbucks coffee as they dashed from gate to gate to catch connecting flights. Moreover, Host Marriott's staff was simply not as educated about coffee as the baristas in Starbucks stores and therefore could not adequately educate customers about the coffee they were selling and often did not set the highest standards possible for how Starbucks coffee should be brewed.

Fortunately, Host Marriott and Starbucks were able to collaborate effectively to solve some of the most pressing customer service problems so that Starbucks' brand image would not be harmed in the partnership. Crucial to improving customer service was employee training. Host Marriott funded a program that gave new concessions employees the same level of training as new hires at Starbucks. Moreover, Host Marriott agreed to devise ways to improve operations at concessions stands by adding more staff and cash registers during peak travel times to ensure that customers received their Starbucks coffee in the same efficient manner as in the company's coffeehouse locations. These improvements -- which were only possible as a result of the positive relations and similar philosophies maintained between both companies -- ensured that customers did not wait in long lines, that the coffee was brewed with the highest flavor standards and that customers would be educated about the brand by knowledgeable employees.

United Airlines Partnership

The Starbucks partnership with United Airlines beginning in 1996 presented similar benefits and potential problems as the Host Marriott joint venture. With United's adoption of Starbucks as the official coffee served on all of its 2,200 daily flights, the brand stood to gain a tremendous advantage in generating awareness. The partnership clearly also benefited United. Serving high quality Starbucks coffee to passengers was yet another way that the airline could differentiate itself as a carrier dedicated to providing passengers with the best service possible. However, once again Starbucks encountered a situation in which the coffee's quality would be risked because Starbucks was allowing an outside source to brew its coffee. At issue in the United Airlines joint venture was the fact that many of the aircraft on which the coffee was to be brewed did not have appropriate brewing equipment to deliver the flavor Starbucks expected its coffee to have. Furthermore, flight attendants were usually not as concerned as Starbucks employees with the coffee's quality because of more pressing job functions like maintaining passenger safety.

Starbucks recognized that if bad tasting coffee was being served to the thousands of passengers who flew United every day, then the brand would develop a negative connotation and the partnership would hinder the goal of attracting new customers to try other Starbucks products in coffeehouses across the country. Like Host Marriott, however, United was quick to remedy coffee quality problems by working with Starbucks to install more effective filtering devices in aircraft brewing equipment, and to better educate flight crews on how to protect the quality of the coffee. The partnership with United did reap some benefits to Starbucks: 14 percent of Starbucks' loyal customers had their first cup of the brand's coffee on a United Airlines flight prompting them to try Starbucks coffees in stores.

Other Retail/Service Partnerships

Based on the success of these early deals, partnerships were later set up between Starbucks and companies such as Nordstrom, ITT/Sheraton, Westin, Holland America Cruiselines, Barnes & Nobles and Albertson's (retail food-drug chain) as a further attempt to increase brand awareness and encourage consumers to regard Starbucks as a world class brand.

Pepsi and Dryer's Joint Ventures

Starbucks partnerships with companies like Pepsi and Dryer's Grand Ice Cream not only generated increased brand awareness for the coffee company, but also facilitated innovative product development. Although Starbucks always viewed coffee as its central focus, Schultz recognized that the development of new products was essential to the company's quest for continual reinvention. As long as the newly developed products did not destroy the integrity of Starbucks coffee, then they would be viewed by Schultz and his executive team as viable means to promote the Starbucks brand to people who may have never tried coffee in Starbucks stores.

A partnership with PepsiCo, Inc. starting in 1997 led to the creation of Frappuccino, a popular bottled cold coffee beverage using extracts from Starbucks' famous arabica beans. Frappuccino put the Starbucks brand into supermarkets for the first time, an environment Schultz had never dared to bring his coffee products before for fear that the quality of the coffees could not be protected. Although Starbucks was one of the least advertised major brands in the U.S., an advertising campaign was launched to support Frappuccino that was intended to reinforce and enhance Starbucks core values of humility, humor, a "homey" feeling and rich, sensory experiences.

Over time, the Pepsi partnership could result in the bottling of a variety of other Starbucks beverages including the Tiazzi, a fruit juice and tea combination that hit Starbucks stores in the summer of 1998. Product off-shoots of Frappuccino could also likely be seen in grocery stores throughout the United States in the coming years, with Frappuccino Blended Coffee Bars having led the way with their entrance into stores in selected markets in 1997.

The Dryer's joint venture with Starbucks led to the creation of six popular Starbucks coffee ice cream flavors that are marketed under the Starbucks name, but produced and distributed by Dryer's. Sales of Starbucks ice cream surpassed even the most skeptical industry analyst's predictions, beating sales of Häagen-Dazs within the first month its introduction into supermarkets and increasing category sales 54 percent in the year that it was launched while becoming the market leader.

Kraft and Supermarket Sales

After test marketing supermarket sales of packaged whole coffee beans in the Portland and Chicago markets starting in 1996, Starbucks initiated a large-scale supermarket sales effort in 1998 with the introduction of the Starbucks brand to 3,500 stores across 12 western states. The move toward supermarket sales strengthened even further Starbucks' recent agreement with Kraft to market and distribute the Starbucks Coffee brand to more than 25,000 grocery, warehouse club and mass merchandise stores across the United States.

By partnering with Kraft, the second largest packaged-foods company in North America, Starbucks was able to benefit from Kraft's extensive distribution network as well as the company's 4,000-member sales team. Kraft marketed Starbucks coffees as a super-premium brand with a suggested retail price of $7.45 for a 12-ounce bag. By marketing Starbucks coffee as "super-premium," Kraft aimed at preventing the Starbucks line from biting into sales of its Maxwell House brand, which has traditionally been marketed as a middle-priced brand. The Kraft partnership also left the door open for Starbucks to explore the possibility of marketing food products with the help of Kraft's distribution and marketing expertise.

OTHER PARTNERSHIPS

During these same years, Starbucks formed many partnerships that did not involve major national corporations. In 1998, Starbucks inked a deal with famous NBA star Magic Johnson and his company, Johnson Development Corporation, to bring Starbucks to inner city America. The new enterprise was called Urban Coffee Opportunities. Under the agreement, Johnson's company developed the store locations and Starbucks operated them, and the two companies split the profits evenly. The stores contained visual cues, in the form of wall murals, signaling Johnson's involvement in the enterprise. Within a year, Starbucks and Johnson had opened three locations on the West Coast, and expanded to other major cities such as New York. The partnership expected to open 10 additional stores in the U.S. by the end of the year 2000.

Starbucks also developed some partnerships with environmental agencies. In 1996, Starbucks teamed with Alliance for Environmental Innovation to develop a less wasteful carryout coffee cup. The result, published in the spring of 2000, was that while a single-cup solution was not achieved, the partnership did formulate a design that reduced waste: the single cup wrapped by a cardboard sleeve. As a result of another partnership, formed between Starbucks and Conservation International in 1999, Starbucks offers Shade Grown Mexican coffee in its stores. This type of coffee is grown exclusively on farms in the El Triunfo Biosphere Reserve in Chiapas, Mexico using environmentally sound agricultural methods that help protect tropical forests in the surrounding area.

In April of 2000, Starbucks endured pressure -- in the form of a national protest organized by human-rights group Global Exchange called "Roast Starbucks!" -- to offer Fair Trade certified coffee. While most growers sell coffee for 50 cents a pound, Fair Trade certification requires coffee to be sold at $1.26 a pound through small farm cooperatives in the hopes that the farm workers will see some of the extra profit. Starbucks agreed to work with the TransFair USA nonprofit organization to obtain and sell Fair Trade coffee in its stores and on its web site. "Roast Starbucks!" campaigners had expected the protest to last as much as a month, and were caught completely by surprise when Starbucks agreed within a week to offer the certified coffee.

In addition to environmental work, Starbucks formed several partnerships that contributed to its Starbucks Foundation charity efforts. Starbucks entered into a licensing agreement with Garry Trudeau in 1998 to offer Doonesbury-themed products in its stores and online, with all net proceeds going to literacy programs across the country. Within a year, the partnership had raised over $300,000. In 1999, Starbucks embarked on an additional campaign to raise money for literacy efforts by teaming with baseball star Mark McGwire that raised $340,000 in one season. And just before the holidays in 1999, Starbucks partnered with the Salvation Army and UPS to sponsor the Starbucks Holiday Angels program. The program, which operated in about 500 Starbucks stores in the West, distributed thousands of gifts to children and families in need in local communities.

Other Products

Starbucks also developed other products. November 1999 saw the launch of the Starbucks Barista Aroma thermal coffeemaker which was positioned as a "durable, convenient and consistent" way to brew coffee. An insulated brewing process ensured that water temperature and coffee flavor were retained throughout the brewing cycle and by brewing directly into an insulated carafe, coffee could remain fresh and hot for five hours without an external heat source and be transported anywhere. Starbucks retail locations and its web site offered over 30 coffee- and tea-related products, from brewers to grinders to infusers. Starbucks decided to allow national retail chains to stock these products as well.

Cafe Starbucks

Believing that a reinvention strategy was the only way to stay on top, Starbucks introduced its first full-fledged restaurant in Seattle under the name of Cafe Starbucks in 1998. The restaurant served light entrees to complement a full menu of coffee beverages. The impetus behind opening a restaurant division to complement the coffee bar business was that almost

85 percent of all Starbucks' sales were completed by 3 p.m., with the majority of daytime purchases occurring in the morning. Cafe Starbucks was aimed at capturing customers later into the evening with its full dinner menu. The restaurant business could also serve as a testing ground for a variety of potential food products that could be sold in supermarkets in coordination with the recent partnership with Kraft. Starbucks planned to open several more Cafe Starbucks throughout the West and then expand to other major American cities within the next few years if the venture proved successful. In 1999, Starbucks opened its first cybercafe -- a coffeehouse/restaurant that provides web access along with food and beverages -- in San Francisco, called Circadia.

MAINTAINING THE GROWTH

Initial Results

Looking back, Starbucks early successes were due in larger part to a recognition that, fundamentally, what America needed was "a really good cup of coffee." Starbucks delivered a superior product via its extreme vertical integration and their personal involvement from start to finish -- from the selection and procurement of the coffee beans to their roasting and blending to their ultimate consumption. Starbucks company-owned coffeehouses became a "Third Place" -- not work and not home -- where Starbucks could reward customers with a rich sensory experience by appealing to all five senses: through the rich aroma of the beans, the premium taste of the coffee, the product displays and attractive art work adorning the walls, the contemporary music playing in the background and even the cozy, clean feel of the tables and chairs. The "Starbucks experience" created stores with an "inviting, enriching environment that is comfortable and accessible yet also stylish and elegant."

The startling success of Starbucks was evidenced by the fact that by the late 1990s, their customers averaged 18 store visits a month with an expenditure of $3.50 a visit. A one-a-day "latte plus scone" habit could add up to over $1400 a year price tab. Given that 50 percent of the American public drank at least one cup of coffee a day, there was much opportunity for Starbucks to create an enormously profitable customer franchise. Moreover, Starbucks introduced new products leveraging their coffee reputation such as Frappuccino iced coffee and premium coffee ice cream. This high level of consumer involvement and aggressive product development resulted in Starbucks realizing an annual growth rate of sales and profits exceeding 50 percent through much of the 1990s.

NEXT STEPS

Fifteen years of continuous and spectacular growth (1982-1997) built the Starbucks success story. In that time, Starbucks added about 30,000 employees, and as of 1998 the company added another 500 employees each month. In 1996, the company opened a new store every business day, and in 1997 it opened another 325. Net sales grew from just under $700 million in fiscal 1996 to over $1.3 billion in fiscal 1998. As a result of the remarkable growth rate of Starbucks' sales and profits, its market capitalization rose dramatically. Popular culture media outlets began to take note of these remarkable trends, naturally. In a 1999 episode of *The Simpsons*, Bart entered a mall that contained a Starbucks store. When he exited a brief time later, every store in the mall was a Starbucks. In the second Austin

Powers movie, the villain Dr. Evil returns to Earth to find his evil enterprise disguised by the legitimate business front of the Starbucks Corporation. Nevertheless, sales performance in 1999 confirmed a slowdown of growth first experienced in 1998 within Starbucks core business. First, the pace of the opening of new coffeehouses fell behind schedule and same-store revenue growth flattened. Additionally, the initially high growth of Starbucks ice cream tapered considerably, and the supermarket launch of Frappuccino failed to meet sales expectations. To keep the brand on track, Starbucks continued to pursue strategies launched in 1997 to push Starbucks beyond coffee shops to find alternative potentials of development. The challenge for Starbucks, however, was to manage growth and diversification while strengthening Starbucks core values and keeping customers trustful and loyal toward the brand.

Starbucks' strategy for 1999 relied on two main projects. The first directive was to sustain Starbucks core business by implementing a dynamic marketing program in coffee shops. The second initiative was to keep developing the brand outside its boundaries and included programs such as the expansion of the brand in the UK and Asia, further product portfolio extension and ambitious investments on the Internet.

Sustaining Starbucks Core Business

By 1998, the coffeehouse market in many American cities had become heavily saturated as a result of the entrance of other coffee and food service companies -- including Caribou Coffee Co., Tully' Coffee, Dunkin' Donuts and even Wal-Mart, along with dozens of other local cafe franchises -- into the gourmet coffee business. This increased competition coupled with dismal growth rates of 2 percent in store sales by the summer of 1998, forced Starbucks to reevaluate its business plan once again. To differentiate itself from its gourmet coffee competitors, Starbucks continued to aggressively develop new products as part of its reinvention process. As a first step to putting its core coffeehouse's business on track again, Starbucks implemented a wider scope of food and drink offerings in its stores. The purpose was to expand current customer's experience of Starbucks brand, as well as to chase new customers looking for an alternative to coffee.

Two new lines of proprietary products were launched in 1999, both positioned at high-end markets: chocolates and hot apple cider. Starbucks also introduced a line of coffee blends, called Milder Dimensions that aimed at capturing demand for lighter roasted coffees. Starbucks' January 1999 purchase of Tazo Tea, an Oregon tea retailer, indicated a potential new trend for Starbucks to acquire companies as a means of extending product lines. Starbucks' planned to replace its In-house Infusia brand of tea with Tazo Tea, a move that would likely attract new customers who are looking for alternatives to coffee. Tazo Tea, once expected to become the Starbucks of the tea market, produced authentic, premium tea. Tazo's quirky image -- each tea bag promotes that it contains "the mumbled chantings of a certified tea shaman" as part of its ingredients -- could likely rub off on Starbucks' marketing messages, adding another dimension to the brand's image. With the wish to reinvent the tea culture in the same way as it reinvented coffee culture, Starbucks expected this acquisition to lead the company into growth opportunities by attracting new consumers. This new line of premium product, priced at an 80 percent premium of a typical competitor's loose tea, was distributed in Starbucks coffee shops, as well as restaurants and supermarkets by year end.

Joe magazine, the result of a partnership with Time, Inc., was the second major innovation launched in Starbucks retail stores. This magazine was on the same strategic wavelength as their prior sponsorship of writers and music groups. The objective was to tighten the relationship the brand has with consumers by sharing similar values and by enhancing their life. Original, warm and conversational, this lifestyle magazine was inspired by the coffeehouse's traditional atmosphere of community, culture and conversation. It was also a means of re-asserting Starbucks core values such as a feeling of romance, relaxation and trust. The aim was clear: let customers be believers, sustain the myth. Starbucks also planned to strengthen its in-store and catalog product sales of CDs and books. Since 1995, Starbucks has sold special mix CDs in their stores custom-made for the company by Capitol Records. The CDs were released seasonally, and were available on-line, as well as inside store locations. A partnership with Oprah Winfrey to sell books recommended by the Oprah Book Club proved highly successful since its formation in 1998.

Market Expansion Into the Next Century

In 1987, Starbucks had only two coffee bars in Seattle and one in Vancouver, British Columbia. By the end of 1999, Starbucks had launched nearly 2,000 company-owned coffeehouses in virtually every major North American city, throughout the Pacific Rim and Great Britain. The current Starbucks growth strategy aimed at increasing market share in existing markets while continuing to explore new areas in which the company could become the leading coffee retailer. Starbucks' store designs were seen as flexible enough to be tailored to a variety of location types including office buildings, malls, airports and supermarkets, allowing the company to expose the brand to diverse market segments.

A minimum of a half million dollars needed to be invested in each new site to lease property and tailor buildings to meet Starbucks' uncompromising specifications for store interior design. Store location sites were typically selected based on anticipated customer traffic volume, store visibility and access to pedestrian street traffic. With so much money invested in each new market, however, Starbucks could not afford to make location selection errors. Starbucks specialty coffee retail stores were the core focus of the business, generating over 80 percent of the company's revenues. Because the coffee store business was so crucial to the success of Starbucks, precise calculations concerning the timing and location of new store openings was essential for the company to remain profitable.

Starbucks only deviated from the high-traffic, high-visibility equation for store site selection in a small number of cases such as its experimentation with drive-thru Starbucks locations. Located throughout the Southwest, the West Coast and most recently in the Chicago suburbs, these drive-thru Starbucks locations targeted commuters who want their morning jolt as they battle traffic on the way to work instead of waiting until they reach the downtowns and business centers where Starbucks have typically been located. These drive-thru locations were therefore conveniently placed on common commute routes in and around urban centers and therefore targeted drivers instead of pedestrian customers.

Starbucks's acquisition of Pasqua Coffee Company in 1998, a California-based coffee retailer that operated more than 50 locations in the San Francisco Bay Area, Los Angles and New York, indicated that a new acquisition strategy is part of Starbucks' North American expansion plan. These new stores were converted into Starbucks throughout 1999. The Pasqua acquisition gave Starbucks the opportunity to further saturate the important San Francisco and Los Angeles markets. Pasqua also operated in 8 airports in California that gave Starbucks desirable exposure to the business traveler market segment. Industry analysts predicted that acquisitions such as these would be one way that Starbucks could fuel growth in the coming years. If the competition was not being swallowed by Starbucks, then they were struggling to stay afloat, it seemed. Brothers Coffee, which got out of the retail coffee business in 1996 to focus on the wholesale market, filed for bankruptcy in 1998. New World Coffee shifted its focus to the bagel market, citing broader opportunities. The inability of other companies to compete with Starbucks prompted the CEO of a former rival to proclaim, "going up against Starbucks is just not a wise strategy. Everybody who tried it is in trouble."[6]

Starbucks also used acquisitions to expand its international network beyond its 300 plus stores. In September 1998, Starbucks acquired London-based Seattle Coffee Company for $84.5 million in equities, effectively establishing a foothold in the growing British coffee market, as well as a jumping-off point for future European expansion. Seattle Coffee Company -- started by two enterprising American coffee connoisseurs in 1990 -- had much the same feel as Starbucks with its emphasis on serving gourmet coffees and offering a Euro-American style coffeehouse atmosphere. Betting on a dynamic coffee bar culture trend, Starbucks publicly announced its wish to implement its core concept in the UK as fast as possible. In 1998, Starbucks opened 40 coffee stores, in addition to transforming all of the Seattle Coffee Company's 56 locations across Britain, as well as its two stores in South Africa and one store in Kuwait. In 2001, Starbucks made its first foray onto the Continent, opening locations in Switzerland and Austria. The following year, Starbucks expanded its European presence into Spain, Germany, and Greece. Also in 2002, the company announced ambitions plans to expand into Latin America. By 2005, Starbucks plans to have 900 locations in Argentina, Brazil, Chile, Columbia, Mexico, Peru, Puerto Rico and Venezuela.

Starbucks also achieved further international expansion to the Middle East and new markets in the Pacific Rim. By the end of fiscal year 1998, Starbucks already operated 26 stores in Japan, 11 in Singapore, six in Taiwan, five in the Philippines and one in Thailand. Late 1998 and early 1999 saw the opening of Starbucks specialty coffee stores in Malaysia, New Zealand and China. Over the next year, Starbucks continued to enjoy success in Asia. The growth in Japan exceeded expectations, with over 125 locations opening in the country by spring of 2000. These locations exceeded sales expectations as well: while the average U.S. Starbucks store's sales are $750,000 annually, the average turnover at the Japanese locales is nearly twice that. In fact, the number one selling Starbucks store for 1999 was in Tokyo. Large sales volume was the key contributor to this figure, since a cup of Starbucks coffee costs almost the same in Japan as it does in Manhattan.

Investors as well as consumers were clamoring for coffee. In June of 2000, the Hong Kong Stock Exchange added six Nasdaq stocks, of which Starbucks was the only non-tech stock. Starbucks expected that its presence in Asian stock markets will provide the company with more inroads into Asian commerce -- particularly in China, where it had only 50 shops by 2002 -- as well as bolster domestic stock prices. The company expected to grow to over 500 Asian shops by 2003 and ultimately more than 1,000 in Japan alone. Eventually, Starbucks anticipates that international expansion will outpace North American growth. Indeed, if Starbucks executives wanted to achieve their stated goal of 20,000 locations worldwide, international expansion would have to move at a more rapid rate than domestic growth.

Starbucks' longtime chairman and CEO Howard Schultz, had his sights fixed firmly on the international market. On June 1, 2000, he surrendered the title of CEO to then-president and COO Orin Smith. Schultz remained chairman of the company and assumed the new title of "chief global strategist," a role that enabled him to focus on overseas growth and brand development. Schultz, who estimates that the global market for Starbucks over 10,000 stores, is certain that Starbucks will continue enjoy success in Asia. He stated that the growth overseas "will be a mirror image of what we did here (in North America)."[7]

Starbucks Internet Developments

In 1998, Starbucks began to develop an Internet strategy as another tool to increase sales and strengthen its brand image. Starbucks had already launched a direct mail catalogue program through which consumers, located anywhere in the U.S., could order Starbucks coffee and other products. Benefiting from a large base of loyal customers, Starbucks' web site offered a glimpse into Starbucks products and marketing activities while also supporting product sales to consumers who are located far away from any store (complementing existing catalog and 1-800 sales). To enhance content and target women, in June 1999, Starbucks signed a partnership with Oxygen media, the company started by Geraldine Laybourne to develop programming for women on television and especially the Internet.

Starbucks' Internet strategy hit a bump in the road, however, in early July 1999. The company arranged a conference call with Wall Street analysts to explain that profits for the current fiscal year would be 10 percent below expectations, in part the result of an expensive internet start-up (roughly $4 million), higher labor costs and a slow-starting Frappuccino supermarket launch. Perhaps to appease the predictably disappointed analysts, CEO Howard Schultz devoted the bulk of his presentation to describe Starbucks' plans to aggressively pursue an Internet expansion by creating "the premier lifestyle portal" that would offer "a feeling of romance and relaxation"[8] and, more concretely, a place to buy products ranging from home furnishings to gourmet food.

Specifically, Schultz explained that there was a tremendous opportunity for Starbucks to capitalize on the growth of the Internet to become the leader of a $100 billion market by extending Starbucks leadership as a specialty coffee retailer to new and highly complementary products centered on the lifestyle of Starbucks core consumers. Schultz sized up this opportunity as follows: Starbucks had 8 million loyal female customers frequenting its coffeehouses every week; premium kitchen products and home furnishings, as well as gourmet coffee, appeal to this target market of women 25-49 and the home furnishing and kitchen equipment market was tremendously fragmented and under-retailed. As part of this plan, Starbucks would include high-end retailers on its web site that would be consistent with its consumers' lifestyle and satisfy their unmet needs in this area. Starbucks, by driving their loyal consumers from stores to this new "canopy" web site, could therefore win the leadership of this market. Long rumored to be buying Williams-Sonoma, Starbucks made a bid for the company in mid-June of 1999, two weeks after signing the deal with Oxygen media. The acquisition attempt made sense from Starbucks' perspective: Williams-Sonoma's customer demographics matched those of Starbucks, their product inventory would fit nicely in Starbucks' "lifestyle portal" and their customer database of 20 million names, addresses and buying histories, combined with their own web plans, would enable Starbucks to rapidly develop its target customer base. Unfortunately for Starbucks, Williams-Sonoma chose to remain independent and rejected the bid. A month later, Starbucks did announce a $20 million investment in Living.com, a start-up that planned to sell non-branded furniture via the web.

Uncertain about the practicality of these plans and still reeling from the bad news concerning sales and profits, on the day following this announcement, Wall Street hammered the Starbucks stock, resulting in a drop in share price of 28 percent in one day -- a $2 billion loss in the company's market capitalization. On July 1, Starbucks shares slid to 26 15/16 from a pre-announcement price of 37 9/16. Wall Street seemed to be condemning these plans, accusing Starbucks of losing focus and diluting earnings. Some traditional retail investors interpreted the announcement as an early signal that the company's core retail business was weakening, while investors regarded Starbucks' retail locations as excess physical overhead that would hamper its web presence. In response to the negative reaction, Starbucks revised its web strategy. The company shelved the "lifestyle portal" plans, choosing instead to make small-scale acquisitions and invest in other net companies. In addition to its investment in Living.com, Starbucks put $20 million into the Internet chat site TalkCity and bought a $10 million stake in Cooking.com. The company stuck to its plan of opening a web site for its coffee products, however, and unveiled Starbucks.com in early 2000. In February of that same year, Starbucks announced that bike delivery service Kozmo.com would pay the company $150 million over five years to advertise in its stores and install boxes to return videotapes rented from Kozmo. These scaled-back web developments assuaged the fears of investors and Starbucks stock began climbing steadily in late 1999.

Starbucks continued its strong performance in 2000. The company expected revenues to exceed $2.1 billion, an increase of nearly half a billion dollars over fiscal 1999. Same store sales grew from an average of six percent in 1999 to 10 percent in the second quarter of 2000. With 17 states currently Starbucks-less, the company intended to pursue aggressive growth plans domestically as well as internationally. According to CFO Michael Casey, Starbucks would continue to forge business alliances with food service operators such as hotels, universities, offices and restaurants. Fueled by this growth, the stock performed above expectations. In March 2000, the stock soared to a new 52-week high of 45 1/4, up from a low of 19 7/8 only seven months earlier. Starbucks expected their stock to earn 71 cents a share for fiscal 2000, up from 54 cents per share in 1999. Other stock successes followed: their entrance into Asian stock markets in the spring of that year coincided with the inclusion of SBUX stock on the S&P 500 for the first time.

The sole setbacks for Starbucks in the first half of 2000 came in the form of product extension failures -- their "lifestyle portal" plans stalled in the on-ramp, while sales of their lifestyle magazine *Joe* faltered, and the project was axed less than year after its launch. But with Starbucks successfully extending its core retail business to the far corners of the globe, rolling out new product offerings and forming new retail partnerships, these setbacks may prove to be inconsequential. Before the summer in 2000, Starbucks positioned itself in new Asian and Middle Eastern markets, opening stores in Hong Kong, China, Australia and Dubai. The company announced plans to enter markets in Qatar, Saudi Arabia, Bahrain and continental Europe by the end of the year. In the spring of 2000,

Starbucks unveiled two new Frappuccino flavors, Chocolate Brownie and Orange Mocha Chip. Additionally, Starbucks entered into a licensing agreement with Marriott to open locations in hotels and conference centers owned by the chain. The question remained, though: with rapid expansion in retail, product inventory and strategic partnerships, would Starbucks run the risk of becoming a cookie-cutter chain? In a May, 2000 interview, Howard Schultz addressed this very issue:

> We can't hide the fact that we've become a large company with almost 3,000 stores around the world. But then there's our approach to the business in terms of the quality of the coffee, the experience, how we take care of our people, and how strongly involved we are in local communities philanthropically.[9]

Starbucks' ability to grow without alienating large segments of their consumer base would hinge on the public's perception of the company.

CONCLUSION

Many view Starbucks' meteoric rise from a tiny local retailer to an international coffee powerhouse as one of the great success stories in American business in the last decade. The fact that Starbucks garnered such media and investor attention in the midst of the Information Age without an ounce of "tech" in its product made this growth all the more remarkable. Incredibly, Starbucks achieved its market leader position largely without aid from advertising campaigns. Instead, the company built the brand by relying on the quality of their products and services to induce free word-of-mouth "advertising" from customer to customer. As Starbucks continued to push for new product innovations and business opportunities as a way to differentiate itself from its competitors, the company ran the risk of straying too far from its original focus of spreading its passion for fine coffee. Schultz vowed to keep Starbucks "small" in terms of its close interactions with employees and customers, however, the ballooning size of the corporation suggested that the quality of Starbucks products and services, and the strength of the company's relationships with its most valued people, would need to be closely monitored. A larger, global Starbucks had to find the right balance in pursuing product-driven, people-driven, values-driven and sales-driven objectives.

DISCUSSION QUESTIONS

1. What were the keys for success for Starbucks in building the brand? What were their brand values? What were their sources of equity?

2. How would you evaluate Starbucks' growth strategy? Are there things you would do differently? How would you evaluate their partnerships (e.g., with United Airlines)? How do you know whether it is a "good" or "bad" thing?

3. What does it take to make a world-class global brand? Can Starbucks become one? What hurdles must they overcome? In terms of the American market, what do you see as Starbucks' biggest challenges?

REFERENCES

[1] The initial draft of this case was written by Peter Gilmore, Dartmouth '99 and Keith Richey with assistance from Emmanuelle Louis Hofer.

[2] Howard Schultz. *Pour Your Heart Into It.* Hyperion: New York, 1997.

[3] Howard Schultz. *Pour Your Heart Into It.* Hyperion: New York, 1997.

[4] Howard Schultz. *Pour Your Heart Into It.* Hyperion: New York, 1997.

[5] Howard Schultz. *Pour Your Heart Into It.* Hyperion: New York, 1997.

[6] Nelson D. Schwartz. "Still Perking After All These Years." *Fortune*, May 24, 1999, p. 203.

[7] Robert T. Nelson. "Now, Barista to the World." *Seattle Times*, April 7, 2000, p. C1.

[8] "Trouble Brewing." *Newsweek*, July 19, 1999, p. 40.

[9] "Interview: Starbucks Chairman on Asia, Expansion." Dow Jones International News, May 10, 2000.

YAHOO!:
MANAGING AN INTERNET BRAND[1]

INTRODUCTION

In the second half of the 1990s, Yahoo! grew from a tiny upstart surrounded by Silicon Valley heavyweights into a major contender in Internet media. The company expanded rapidly from its humble roots by making acquisitions, adding a vast assortment of content and services, expanding into foreign markets and attracting the biggest dot-com advertisers to pay premium prices for banners on Yahoo! sites. By 2000, what began as a mere search engine had become an Internet giant, with a meteoric rise in stock value to match its new economy renown. Soon after Yahoo! hit its peak on the stock market, however, the dot-com frenzy began to lose momentum and the economy began its slide into recession. As dot-coms either went bankrupt or were forced to cut back on spending, Yahoo!'s advertiser base began to shrink. As the economy gradually worsened in 2001, Yahoo!'s once-lofty stock lost more than 90 percent of its value, and industry analysts wondered if the company was ripe for a takeover by a large media company. Determined to remain independent, Yahoo! made a number of personnel changes, including hiring a new CEO, and redesigned its business plan to emphasize selling services in addition to advertising space. Through it all, Yahoo! remained one of the most popular destinations for web surfers and therefore was one of the premier properties on the Internet. Yahoo! needed to develop new ways to translate this strong brand equity into strong financial results.

Yahoo! History

David Filo and Jerry Yang, two computer science Ph.D. students at Stanford University, created the Yahoo! search engine in 1994. Using a homespun filing system, the pair catalogued various web sites and published the directory for free on the Internet. The original version was called Jerry and David's Guide to the World Wide Web, which was renamed Yahoo! once Filo and Yang left their studies to devote serious attention to the search engine. The name Yahoo! is an acronym standing for "Yet Another Hierarchical Officious Oracle," which is a tongue-in-cheek definition of the search engine in technology jargon. Founder Jerry Yang discussed the various meanings inherent in the Yahoo! name: "For us, it had the meaning of being kind of a bunch of Yahoo!s, and that was fine. But I think for a lot of people, it was kind of like, 'Wow, this is great. Wow, I'm getting excited. I'm really getting used to the Internet. I can really do stuff on the Internet.'"[2] The humorous name caused some confusion among consumers early on, but it worked in setting Yahoo! apart from traditional companies. Vice President of Brand Marketing Karen Edwards recalled:

> I remember when we first started doing some of this stuff, people would say, 'Oh, is that the chocolate drink?' Our goal really was just to get awareness. We knew that the name was really catchy, and we knew that people would respond just to the name. If they just knew the Yahoo! name, we had a pretty good shot at hooking them.[3]

215

Jerry Yang added, "[The name] was easy for people to remember. People could tell other people [about it] very easily, and they had an emotional attachment to it."[4]

The company's search engine was unique because in addition to the standard word search features, Yahoo! offered its users a massive searchable index. Surfers could search for sites in generic categories like Business and Economy, Arts and Humanities and Entertainment, organize the results by country or region and search within a category. Since Yahoo! was among the very first searchable guides of the Internet, the site attracted hundreds of thousands of web surfers within a year of its introduction. The dissemination of Yahoo!'s product was fueled by Netscape founder Marc Andreessen's decision in January 1995 to make Yahoo! the default search engine of his browser. Whenever Netscape users clicked on the Internet Search icon, they were brought to the Yahoo! homepage. This early attention attracted investors, and in April 1995, Filo and Yang raised $1 million in first-round venture capital. The company also hired Tim Koogle, a veteran technology industry executive who worked for Intermec, a Seattle-based telecommunications manufacturer, and Motorola, to serve as its CEO. Later that month, Japanese media conglomerate Softbank paid $106 million for a 37 percent stake in Yahoo!

Online Advertising

Yahoo! announced plans to generate revenues through advertiser support in July 1995. To test the effectiveness of this plan, five different advertisers rotated ad placements on the top five most visited pages in the Yahoo! directory. The ads were typically rectangular boxes, called "banners," placed in prominent locations at the top or bottom of a web page. These five charter sponsors were MCI Communications, MasterCard, the Internet Shopping Network, NECX (an online retailer) and Worlds (a web software developer). Yahoo! enlisted new media agency Interactive Marketing to manage ad sales. Advertisers typically paid a preset fee for every 1,000 "impressions," which occur whenever an Internet surfer loads a page with an advertisement on it. Yahoo! charged a fee of about $200 per 1,000 impressions. One of the advantages of online advertising was the ability to target consumers based on their web surfing behavior. For example, an advertiser like E*Trade could target its banner ads so that when a Internet user input a certain keyword such as "stock market" into the Yahoo! search engine, he or she was shown an E*Trade advertisement. The percentage of visitors to an ad-sponsored site who clicked on the advertisement to follow its link was called the "click-through rate." When Internet advertising first emerged, click-through rates were above 20 percent, but rapidly fell to two or three percent in 1996.

Yahoo! could deliver a large number of web surfers to its advertisers because of the nature of a search engine. Search engines were among the most heavily trafficked sites on the Internet because they offered services that could be accessed by anyone and were essential to gathering information on the web. As traffic to the Yahoo! site increased, so too did its advertiser base. Between the second quarter of 1996 and the second quarter of 1997, the average number of times people viewed Yahoo!'s homepage per day grew from 9 million to 38 million. Over that same period, the number of Yahoo! advertisers grew from 230 to 900. By the fourth quarter of 1997, the company averaged 65 million page views daily and had 1,700 advertisers buying space on its sites. As the top-rated search engine, Yahoo! was able to charge premium rates for ad space. Between the first quarter of 1996 and the first quarter of 1997, average monthly ad rates grew from $6,000 to $20,000. Total ad sales in 1996 topped $19 million.

Yahoo! Marketing Strategy

From its start, Yahoo! sought to convey an irreverent and fun attitude to Internet users and potential users. This attitude originated from the top of the corporate ladder, in the personalities of founders Filo and Yang. The two had conceived of Yahoo! while housed "in a trailer full of empty pizza boxes,"[5] and each of their business cards bore the title "Chief Yahoo!."

Yahoo! generated revenue of $1.4 million in fiscal 1995 and had net losses totalling $634,000. Yahoo! went public in April 1996, just weeks after competitors Excite and Lycos generated a mild buzz with their IPOs. Yahoo! priced its offering at $13, and saw it jump 154 percent by the end of the day to close at $34. In order to capitalize on the momentum from its successful April 1996 IPO, Yahoo! hired a small Bay Area advertising agency called Black Rocket to develop an estimated $10 million awareness-building campaign. Black Rocket, formed by former Goodby, Silverstein & Partners and Hal Riney & Partners executives, worked to position Yahoo! as a consumer brand rather than a technology company. Karen Edwards, director of marketing for Yahoo!, explained that this positioning emerged because "It's all happened so fast; search engines are no longer [just] search engines. We feel a lot more like media companies, providing information via various formats."[6]

The Black Rocket agency created the tagline "Do You Yahoo!?" Black Rocket also created the "Yahoo! yodel," the audio cue designed to reinforce customer recall of the brand. A partner with Yahoo!'s advertising firm remembered that while other tech companies were aiming above most consumers "with talk about the global, complex power of technology, putting their products on a pedestal," Yahoo!'s initial advertising "position[ed] itself as a familiar face people could trust when they got online."[7] Another partner added, "We knew the message had to be simple -- what you would tell your dad or grandpa at Thanksgiving."[8]

To introduce the "Do You Yahoo!?" slogan, Yahoo! began traditional media advertising in April 1996 with a television campaign that was followed by print and radio ads. The company's original marketing communication consisted primarily of publicity and word-of-mouth. Yahoo! was one of the first Internet portals, however, to realize that mainstream media buys were important in generating new customers that had yet to spend time on the web. Most advertising was done either online or in industry magazines such as *Wired*. Edwards pointed out that this approach "was all about talking to people who were already online."[9] For this reason, the new marketing effort targeted consumers who intended to use the Internet for the first time within a year, referred to as "near surfers." Edwards explained "Near surfers are more brand loyal. People who tend to be brand sensitive tend to be more brand loyal . . . By going after the mainstream, it was a means to brand the category and ourselves."[10]

Acclaim for Yahoo! Marketing

Yahoo!'s integrated marketing program projected a targeted image to different audiences. An article in *Fortune* had high praise for Yahoo! brand building:

217

Yahoo! is an awesome marketing machine targeting three different audiences with three distinct message: consumers who might use Yahoo! ("We're fun, wacky and easy to use"); the press and financial analysts ("We're professional and well run") and media buyers ("We're the market leader and experts in online advertising").[11]

Other sources praised the Yahoo! marketing program as well. Karen Edwards, director of brand management at Yahoo!, won *Brandweek*'s Marketer of the Year award for 1997.

The marketing program measurably increased consumer knowledge of Yahoo!. According to a report released by IntelliQuest, 82 percent of Internet users and 23 percent of prospective users recognized the Yahoo! name by the end of 1997. The previous year, 64 percent of users and 8 percent of prospective users recognized the name. When Yahoo! first began operating, America Online maintained significantly higher public awareness than any other Internet company. Among Internet users, AOL held 60 percent awareness, followed by Netscape, which had 45 percent, and Yahoo!, which had 40 percent awareness. Yahoo! had only two percent awareness among non-Internet users, compared with 12 percent for Microsoft and 17 percent for AOL. This changed by 2000, when Yahoo! had aided awareness levels of 90 percent, compared with AOL and MSN levels of 81 percent and 51 percent, respectively (see Fig. 1).

Many felt that a key to Yahoo!'s success was the consistency of its advertising program. Karen Edwards said "In this industry, where others are always changing their names, their taglines and their positioning, we've stood out from the chaos by sticking to the same brand image."[12]

Transformation to a Destination

Yahoo! executives realized early on that the key to long-term success in the cutthroat portal market was to transform the site from a portal to a destination site where web surfers lingered and perhaps stayed. The key to retaining an audience was developing a "sticky" site with appealing content that kept consumer "eyeballs" glued to the site's page. Yahoo! offered content besides the original searchable directory, but these satellite sites were not visited often. At the time, Jerry Yang said, "Most of our users today approach Yahoo! and type in a keyword and go from there. They do not stop at our other sites."[13] This behavior, while consistent with the function that portals originally performed, did not appeal to advertisers on Yahoo!, who naturally wanted their advertising to be seen often. As the need to expand beyond a search engine portal increased, Yahoo! executives looked to boost the time spent at the site per user in a variety of ways. This required the addition of homegrown content and vastly expanded onsite offerings, such as Yahoo! Finance, Yahoo! Trave, or the Yahoo!ligans kids directory, which would attract new users and keep them on Yahoo! pages. Jerry Yang professed the following vision for Yahoo!'s future with its users:

> As we continue to make Yahoo! a bigger part of our users' lives, our goal is to build the Yahoo! brand to be something that makes users feel empowered on the Internet and, ultimately, form a long-lasting relationship that our users trust.[14]

To bolster its content offerings, Yahoo! began acquiring companies with expertise in other Internet services aside from web searches. One of Yahoo!'s first acquisitions was its purchase of free e-mail provider and directory service Four 11 Corp in October 1997. This acquisition enabled the company to offer its users Yahoo! Mail, a free e-mail service. The company's June 1998 acquisition of Viaweb, a provider of software and services for hosting online stores, enabled Yahoo! to develop more e-commerce capabilities. By acquiring online direct marketing firm Yoyodyne in October 1998, Yahoo! improved its marketing services for ad buyers.

Early Financial Success

After two years in a tightly contested portal market, Yahoo! eventually achieved separation from its competitors. Yahoo! attracted a much larger audience than competitor portals, as much as 8 million more than second ranked Web Crawler per day in 1997. As Yahoo! became one of the leading Internet portals, ad dollars began pouring in. Between the second quarter of 1996 and the fourth quarter of 1997, traffic at Yahoo! sites increased four-fold while ad sales generated $34 million in revenue. By mid-1997, the company was selling ad space to over 900 advertisers. These ad sales contributed about $13 million to revenues, more than four times the previous year's sales. Karen Edwards credited Yahoo!'s success partly to its early entry into the search engine category:

> When there's a lot of clutter and noise, it bodes well for the brands that people trust and know. Unestablished brands will have a very difficult time stealing loyal users away from services that have critical mass.[15]

Among the most abundant Yahoo! advertisers were burgeoning dot-coms. As one analyst said, "Yahoo! brings eyeballs and that's what matters. Because of Yahoo!'s powerful brand position, they've become the first choice for other companies that want to get into the Internet."[16]

The most remarkable story about Yahoo! may have been its stock, which skyrocketed after the IPO. In fiscal 1997, the company's revenues grew by 242 percent to $125 million, while its stock rose 517 percent during the same period. By Spring 1998, the stock had risen 745 percent from its original price. Its price/earnings ratio in May was a lofty 1,062, compared with Microsoft's P/E ratio of 55 that month, yet was considered a blue chip stock by many. Yahoo! garnered additional media attention when *Business Week* featured the company on the cover of its September 7, 1998 issue under the headline "Yahoo!: the Company, the Strategy, the Stock."[17] Despite earning only about $16 million per quarter that year, Yahoo! achieved a market capitalization of $50 billion by March that year.

Joining the E-Commerce World

Yahoo! made its first move into e-commerce in February 1998 with the debut of a Yahoo! branded Visa card. Cardholders could use a Yahoo! Visa site to view card balances, make purchases from an online catalogue featuring various merchants and redeem points earned on the card. This initiative was followed by a full-blown online shopping mall, called Yahoo! Shopping site. In keeping with its roots as a web directory, the Yahoo! Shopping area enabled users to search for items from a variety of retailers that the site catalogued. Karen Edwards explained, "We think the brand needs to stand for commerce."[18]

For merchants, Yahoo! developed its Yahoo! Store site where merchants could pay to have their products listed in the Yahoo! Shopping directory. Yahoo! Store also offered merchants the opportunity to create and manage their own secure online stores. Additionally, Yahoo! Store included a service where merchants could apply online to set up payment accounts and credit card processing with third-party providers. The Yahoo! Store site appealed to small business that lacked the means to sustain an independent web site, but still wanted an e-commerce presence.

To support its new e-commerce venture, Yahoo! developed an estimated $10 million national advertising campaign that debuted on television during the 1999 World Series, in time to reach consumers as they began their holiday shopping. One commercial, developed by Black Rocket, depicts a family living in a desolate and frigid wasteland. As the family huddles around their frozen computer, from which icicles hang, the father purchases a hot tub from the Yahoo! Shopping site. The next sequence shows the family sitting happily in their warm tub, and the ad closes as the father dashes to an outdoor grill to cook some hotdogs. In another ad, a man protects his trailer in Australia's Outback from an oncoming meteor by purchasing pillows on Yahoo! Shopping. The campaign was part of a $64 million marketing effort in the fourth quarter of 1999, up from $42 million in ad spending the same quarter of the previous year.

Another effort aimed at retaining an audience for more than a few clicks was the Yahoo! city guide. The company launched the inaugural city edition, Yahoo! San Francisco, in June 1996. Yahoo! New York and Yahoo! Los Angeles followed in August. The city editions contained such vital information as local movie listings, restaurant guides, entertainment calendars, even pizza delivery numbers. The sites also contained information useful to visitors, like hotel and rental car information. Yahoo! designed the city guides with the intention of making the site more relevant to local consumers in those locations. The company also offered registered users the option of personalizing the content of a start page with My Yahoo!.

Among the services Yahoo! added in 1998 were Yahoo! Clubs, an online community, Yahoo! Calendar, an online calendar and Yahoo! Small Business, with content and services aimed at small business proprietors. The new business site featured package tracking services from a variety of shipping companies, as well as editorial content from publications such as *Fast Company*, *Entrepreneur Magazine* and *Inc*.

Strategic Partnerships

Yahoo! forged partnerships with print outfits such as Fodor's and the *Village Voice*. Yahoo! also licensed its name in unconventional ways. The company partnered with Ziff-Davis to create the Yahoo! Internet Life magazine, and backpack manufacturer Gregory Mountain Sports produced a Yahoo! branded computer bag. Other licensed products included Yahoo! baseballs, sunglasses, yo-yos, kazoos, surfboards, shoes, stationary, and a compilation CD. Yahoo! benefited from high-profile product placements on popular television shows and movies, which were often provided free of charge by studios. The Yahoo! logo appeared in NBC's primetime drama *ER* and in Ron Howard's comedy *EdTV*, among others. Yahoo! also paid for its logo to appear in affiliation with Bay Area sports teams. The San Jose Shark's Zamboni bore the Yahoo! logo, as did the scoreboard at 3Com Park where the San Francisco Giants and 49ers played.

Yahoo! added to its set of sports marketing opportunities in 1998 by signing on to be an official sponsor of Major League Soccer through 2002 in a multimillion-dollar deal. Yahoo! promoted the MLS with coverage on the web site and in chat rooms in return for television exposure. In September 2000, Yahoo! signed a deal with the NBA and WNBA to become a global sponsor. Yahoo! would provide on-line coverage of league games and other events in return for event sponsorship and television time. As a result of the agreement, Yahoo! Sports offered content such as video highlights, real-time game statistics and live audio broadcasts. Other sports content offered by Yahoo! Sports included football, hockey, baseball, soccer and golf coverage and broadcasts.

Yahoo! Advertising Developments

Compared with other dot-coms, Yahoo!'s media spending was restrained. In 1998, Yahoo!'s total television spending was $7.2 million, compared with $31.4 million by AOL, $26.7 by Internet holding company CMG, and $18.8 million by eTrade. Though Yahoo!'s TV spending tripled to $21.7 million in 1999, this outlay was dwarfed by eTrade ($96.9 million), Ameritrade ($79.4 million) and AOL ($45.8 million).

Despite its comparatively small marketing budget, Yahoo! earned honors from Advertising Age as the top marketer in the portal category for 1999. In the first nine months of 1998, Yahoo! led all other web publishers in advertising revenue, with $88 million. Despite leading the ad revenue category, Yahoo! was not among the top 25 Internet advertising spenders, preferring to execute much of its marketing strategy offline. For example, Yahoo! inked a $20 million cross-promotional advertising deal with the Fox television network. Yahoo! became a sponsor of the 1999 Super Bowl pregame show and of the animated sitcom "Family Guy." Yahoo! also garnered prime time and late night advertising slots on Fox's news and sports channels for nine months. In return, Yahoo! provided extensive coverage of the Super Bowl on its web site and promoted "Family Guy" for a six-week period. Ultimately, the deal involved cross-promotions in Fox Films, Fox Music, Fox Interactive, Fox Broadcasting and Fox cable channels. The promotional partnership resembled earlier deals between Internet portals and media companies such as the AOL/Time Warner merger and Walt Disney Co.'s equity investment in Infoseek Corp, except in the case of Yahoo! and Fox, neither company invested in the other. Rupert Murdoch, chairman of the Fox parent Company News Corp., said that while he saw "enormous potential [in the Internet]," he could not "see the profits coming soon enough" to warrant a merger.[19]

Yahoo! Enhances Its Marketing Services

On March 4, 1999, Yahoo! launched a marketing services business called Fusion Marketing Online. Fusion Marketing provided ad buyers with an integrated advertising package consisting of online advertising, online commerce, online events, offline promotion, and direct marketing. Yahoo!'s Fusion Marketing also offered permission marketing, web hosting, sponsorships, brand development and event marketing. Yahoo!'s direct marketing offerings were introduced as a result of its October 1998 acquisition of direct marketer Yoyodyne. The package of marketing services afforded companies advertising options beyond the decreasingly effective banner advertisements. The Fusion Marketing program also targeted Old Economy companies that had been reluctant to advertise online. Eddie

Bauer, Lowestfare.com and web retailer Bluefly were among the first clients of Yahoo! Fusion Marketing. Yahoo! Fusion Marketing also worked with Pepsi to develop Pepsistuff.com, a site where Pepsi drinkers purchased branded merchandise with points earned with Pepsi product purchases. More than 1 million users registered in the first month of the site's operation.

THINKING GLOBALLY

Yahoo! stock opened in January 2000 trading above $230. That year, awareness of the brand in the U.S. among Internet users reached 90 percent. Yahoo! had achieved a place among the best of the new economy dot-coms, and now its global aspirations had become a top priority for the company. "Make no mistake about it," said CEO Tim Koogle in a December 1999 article. "We are building a global branded network business."[20] In October 1999 Yahoo! was still trailing AOL in terms of unique users domestically, by a 53 million to 40 million margin. Abroad, however, Yahoo! was almost always ranked either first or second in every market it entered, while AOL often failed to rank among the top three. Yahoo! maintained specialized sites in 20 foreign countries, whereas AOL was present in 15 countries. Roughly one-third of Yahoo!'s registered users came from abroad. In October 1999, AOL had 4 million international subscribers, compared with 19 million domestic subscribers. Compared with other portals, Yahoo!'s lead was commanding. It averaged 33.4 unique visitors every month, while Lycos and Excite averaged 14.9 million and 14.1 million unique visitors per month, respectively. The two main areas for Yahoo!'s global growth where Europe and Asia.

Yahoo! Europe

Yahoo! first moved into Europe in summer 1996, when it partnered with Ziff-Davis International Media Group to form Yahoo! Europe. Initially, Yahoo! Europe offered home pages with specialized content for the United Kingdom, Germany and France. By 2000, Yahoo! was the portal with the largest audience in Europe, where 42 percent of all Internet users visited the site. In addition to city guides for major cities like London, Yahoo! had pages for eight individual countries.

Yahoo! biggest competitor domestically, AOL, also maintained a significant presence in Europe as the top Internet service provider (ISP) with 4 million subscribers and the third most popular portal in 2000. Aside from AOL, Yahoo!'s primary competition came from European media and telecom companies. In 2000, German ISP T-Online was the top ISP in Europe, and ranked second globally behind AOL with 5.2 million European subscribers. France Telecom offered an ISP called Wanadoo that attracted 2.2 million subscribers, while Spain's Tera Networks boasted 2 million subscribers. In this highly competitive atmosphere, Yahoo! emerged as one of the top three portals in every market it entered. In 1999, Yahoo! was the top portal in Great Britain, the second-ranked portal in Germany and France and in the top three in Italy, Spain, Norway, Sweden, and Denmark. This broad audience attracted advertisers, which numbered 1,500 by mid-2000. In 2000, ad sales in Europe contributed about $20 million, or about 10 percent, to Yahoo!'s total.

Yahoo! in Asia

Yahoo! and Japanese investment company Softbank, which held the largest minority stake in Yahoo!, launched Yahoo! Japan in April 1996. Yahoo! Japan soon attracted a significantly greater share of Internet traffic than any other Japanese directory. In November 1997, Yahoo! Japan became the youngest company ever to go public and saw its share price nearly triple in the first day, despite the sagging Japanese economy. The Japanese site brought in $4 million in advertising in 1997, which more than doubled 1996 revenue and was greater than 1997 ad sales for Yahoo! Europe. After its success in Japan, Yahoo! looked to provide specialized sites for other countries in Asia. The Asian region held enormous possibilities for a large Internet audience, which had already exploded from 3 million users in 1996 to 10 million in 1997. As part of a joint venture with Softbank, the company introduced native-language Yahoo! Korea in September 1997. Yahoo! followed its native-language ventures in Korea and Japan with an English-based site called Yahoo! Asia. Yahoo! Asia, which mirrored the U.S. home site, but afforded Asian users faster content retrieval by being based in Singapore, debuted in January 1997. By November of that year, the Yahoo! Asia site was attracting major advertisers. AT&T, Hewlett-Packard, Intel, Philips, and Sun Microsystems were among the first multinational corporations to advertise on Yahoo! Asia. The company also added a Chinese-language site in early 1998, targeting web surfers in China, Taiwan, Hong-Kong, Malaysia and Singapore.

In the first quarter of 1999, Yahoo! opened Yahoo! Hong Kong and Yahoo! Taiwan, followed by Yahoo! China during the third quarter. In May 2000, Yahoo! launched a television advertising campaign in China. The ads ran only in Hong Kong at first. The TV spot, which was produced in the U.S., features a balding man searching for hair treatments using Yahoo!. Yahoo! faced established local competition in China, where the top three portals, all domestic, accounted for roughly 70 percent of the country's online advertising budgets. By 2000, the U.S. version of Yahoo! was the most popular site in China, while Yahoo! China trailed local portal sina.com in the rankings. International Data Corp. estimated in 2000 that online spending coming from Asian countries other than Japan would total $87.5 billion by 2004, compared with $2.2 billion in 1999.

As it had in North America and Europe, Yahoo! became wildly popular among Asian Internet users. A survey of 30,000 people from nine Asian countries conducted in December 1999 by online survey company www.consult.com revealed that respondents cited Yahoo! as their favorite Internet directory. Yahoo! Japan, the most successful Asian portal, drew 100 million page views per day in July 2000, which contributed to a global total of 750 million page views daily. Over 85 percent of all Internet users in Japan visited the Yahoo! site each month in 2000. These remarkable numbers followed a year when advertising sales quadrupled to $47 million. In the first quarter of 2000, the number of ads on Yahoo! Japan jumped 40 percent. This success came partly from the fact that competition in Japan was almost nonexistent. Neither AOL or MSN had any presence in the country, and web efforts from Sony and Nippon Telegraph & Telephone had met with consumer disdain. This left Yahoo! "virtually alone"[21] in a major market.

Following print and television campaigns in Asian markets, Yahoo! added grass-roots marketing efforts in several key markets. This grass-roots approach was prompted by research that revealed word of mouth to be an especially important factor/decision variable for portal use in Asia. In Hong Kong, Yahoo! teamed with a local radio station in May 2000 to hold a contest that challenged university students to invent creative means of linking campuses online. The contest drew 25,000 entries, and the winner was invited to implement the strategy. In June, Yahoo! sponsored a computer camp in Singapore that was attended by 150 schoolchildren. The company also sought to reach other audiences in Singapore by holding an Internet workshop for readers of a women's magazine and planning outreach to "country clubs and senior citizens."[22] In China, Yahoo! distributed 15,000 free Yahoo! Messenger CDs containing software for instant messaging, e-mail and news alerts among eight universities in Beijing. An exam-week promotion at universities in Taiwan involved free massages and free Internet surfing at on-campus locations.

YAHOO! BROADENS ITS OFFERINGS

Going Wireless

In Europe and Asia, wireless technology gained an even stronger foothold than it had in the United States. Cell phone use in Western Europe rose to 41 percent in 2000, compared to 31 percent in the U.S. As wireless and mobile technologies emerged, Yahoo! sought ways to provide service for its customers on platforms beyond the desktop computer, such as cell phones, pagers and personal digital assistants. The company formed a business division, called Yahoo! Everywhere, to develop applications for the wireless web. After spending $80 million to acquire wireless software start-up Online Anywhere, Yahoo! was able to offer content and services formatted for non-PC devices. Mohan Vishwanath, the former CEO of Online Anywhere who became vice president of Yahoo! Everywhere, characterized the project as a logical growth mechanism:

> The Yahoo! Everywhere strategy is to extend the Yahoo! brand and services beyond the desktop. . . . It is a way for us to increase the number of touch points with our users in markets where we already have a strong presence. And in newer markets, it is a way for us to acquire new customers.[23]

To promote its technology, Yahoo! developed a strategic partnership in 1999 to provide content to Sprint PCS users. The company's success with Sprint led to deals with wireless carriers around the world, such as Palm Inc., Motorola and German mobile giant, D2 Mannesman Mobilefunk. By mid-2000, Yahoo! had worked out agreements with telecommunications companies in regions all over the world, including Scandanavia, Canada, Southeast Asia and Italy.

Since an equal number of web surfers were predicted to use wireless connections to access the Internet as would use home connections (300 million), one analyst described the mobile market as a "potential goldmine for Yahoo!"[24] Yet the company's earliest efforts in the wireless market were widely panned for their limited scope and unexceptional service. For example, though Yahoo! Everywhere offered to send its users the midday and closing price of any stock as part of its Yahoo! Alerts service, its competitor Strategy.com delivered extras such as an alert for any stock price change of as little as 5 percent.

At first, advertising on Yahoo! Everywhere products was limited to the Yahoo! Alerts. The company began developing voice ads and geographically targeted advertising for wireless users. The company employed non-traditional media to promote its Yahoo!

Everywhere strategy as well. In September 1999 the company unveiled a convoy of 10 Yahoo! branded taxis in San Francisco. The taxis were completely "wrapped" with the purple and yellow logo, so that even the side and rear windows contributed to the branded look. The taxis came equipped with Palm handheld computers that enabled passengers to access the Internet via wireless connection and Yahoo! software. The promotion ran in San Francisco through March 2000, and was followed by a similar campaign in New York City the following September. Brand manager Linda Bennett explained how the Internet-ready taxis related to Yahoo! Everywhere:

> Yahoo! Everywhere is a place you go to find anything, connect with anyone, and it doesn't mean being tethered to your home office or workplace. It's about getting information where you need it, even in the back of a taxi.[25]

New Acquisitions

Yahoo! purchased Internet service provider GeoCities for almost $5 billion in stock -- more than a 50 percent premium on GeoCities stock -- in January 1999. The deal gave Yahoo! an additional 18 million unique users. In April 1999, Yahoo! purchased streaming audio and video site Broadcast.com for about $5 billion. This acquisition gave Yahoo! the ability to offer sophisticated media content to its users, a fact which had some analysts comparing Yahoo! to a media company. Jeffrey Mallet, the company's president and COO, acknowledged that similarities exist between Yahoo! and traditional media companies, but added that unlike major media companies, Yahoo! derives all its content from outside sources. "We really are a pure-play online enabler,"[26] Mallet said at the time of the Broadcast.com purchase. Yahoo! added group e-mail and bulletin board services to its free Yahoo! Mail services when it acquired eGroups for $420 million in stock in June 2000. Yahoo! planned for the group e-mail services would complement some of its other offerings, such as Yahoo! Auctions and Yahoo! Clubs, by facilitating communication between groups of people with similar interests.

CHALLENGES FOR YAHOO!

Economic Troubles

By mid-2000, the economy had begun to falter and even an Internet blue-chip like Yahoo! was not immune to the effects of the dot-com crash. Analysts who considered Yahoo!'s stock overvalued (citing its high p/e ratio) saw their suspicions confirmed as the price fell 80 percent over the year. Since Yahoo! derived over 80 percent of its revenue from online advertising sales, and the bulk of its advertisers were Internet companies, their collective struggles would affect Yahoo!'s revenues. "It's only a matter of time before we see the impact on Yahoo!'s results," said one analyst in September 2000. "We continue to look for signs that traditional advertisers are embracing online advertising, but we are receiving little comfort."[27] The number of advertisers and merchants served by Yahoo! fell to 3,450 from 3,675 from the second to third quarter of the year. Of additional concern for ad-dependent Internet properties was the fact that growth in advertiser spending decreased six percent to $1.79 billion from the second to the third quarter while the average ad rate fell from $32.22 per thousand visitors to $30.53 from the winter to the summer. Contributing to this drop in advertising was the low click-through rate. Click-through rates plummeted from two percent in 1999 to below one percent, lower than the two percent response rate for junk mail. Yahoo! had a large share of the Internet advertising market -- of the approximately $8 billion spent on online advertising in 2000, Yahoo! received one out of every eight dollars -- but the market was not large enough to drive high-growth brands.

Yahoo! was quick to reassure Wall Street that profits would continue, citing a reduction in the percentage of pure-play Internet advertisers to 40 percent from 47 percent in the second quarter of 2000 and retention of 98 percent of its biggest advertisers. The company's CFO, Susan Decker, insisted that "financially questionable" customers contributed less than ten percent of Yahoo!'s total revenues.[28] The company also pointed to the fact that its top 200 advertisers, most of which were so-called traditional advertisers, contributed 60 percent of Yahoo!'s total revenue.

Despite its plummeting stock, Yahoo! did benefit from several positive indicators during the latter half of 2000. Yahoo! Japan doubled its profits in the fourth quarter with the help of strong advertising revenues, but warned that a slowdown similar to that in America was expected. Overseas sales through Yahoo! Shopping grew sixfold during the 2000 holiday shopping season. Domestically, though overall Internet spending by consumers during the holidays grew a disappointing 53 percent, Yahoo! managed to double the sales its shopping site directed to retailers. Yahoo! earned an estimated $30 million from its Yahoo! Shopping service during that period, when many other e-tailers failed to turn a profit. Yahoo!'s users also began spending more time online during the holiday season. AOL traditionally led the "user-minutes-online" category, but in December 2000 Yahoo! visitors spent an average of almost one-and-a-half hours on Yahoo! sites, better than second-place MSN by nearly 20 minutes. Overall, however, Internet users in December had five fewer sessions on average and spent three fewer minutes online compared to October of the same year. Yahoo!'s own marketing expenditure continued to increase compared with previous years (see Fig. 2). In 2000, the company spent $420 million on marketing and sales, up 46 percent from 1999. Online advertising sales for Yahoo! grew 74 percent, despite overall growth in ad spending of only 12 percent. For the year, Yahoo!'s $1.1 billion -- the first time it topped the billion-dollar mark -- revenue matched predictions.

Still, the forecast for 2001 was grim. The company's projected 2001 revenue of between $1.2 and $1.3 billion, which translated to 18 percent growth. Yahoo! grew 88 percent in 2000, and limited growth in 2001 would likely yield an earnings per share drop (33-43 cents). This news disappointed analysts and investors alike. Internet advertising was expected to decline, according to the Institute of Practitioners in Advertising, from three percent to two percent of total expenditures. Since Yahoo! was the last major portal to remain independent, after Excite merged with the @Home Network, Snap.com with NBC, Lycos with CMGI, Infoseek with Disney, and AOL with Time Warner, speculation about a possible takeover increased as its stock price plunged. Analysts figured a major global media company, such as Viacom, would be the most likely to pursue Yahoo!.

Executive Changes at Yahoo!

In January 2001, Yahoo! reported record revenues for the fourth quarter of 2000. The forecast for the first quarter of 2001, however, was bleak: Yahoo! expected revenues to fall 25 percent, to $230 million. After ad sales dropped further than anticipated, Yahoo! had to cut its forecast by an additional 25 percent, to $175 million. These reduced predictions followed dismal stock performance that saw Yahoo! share price drop from a quarterly high of $87 to a $25 low in the fourth quarter of 2000. At the February 27, 2001 board meeting, the board decided that CEO Tim Koogle would step down, but would retain his chairman title. After searching months for a replacement, on May 1, 2001 Yahoo! named Terry Semel, former co-CEO of Warner Bros. studio, as its new CEO. Semel, who ran Warner Bros. with partner Bob Daly between 1982 and 1999, had a formidable entertainment industry pedigree. He was responsible for major blockbusters like the *Batman* and *Lethal Weapon* franchises, and brought entertainment industry connections to Yahoo!. Semel expressed optimism for Yahoo!'s future:

> We are the Internet's most dominant brand. We have the largest and most loyal audience. When advertising spending picks up, Yahoo! will be well positioned to take a disproportionate share of the market. . . . There are three major worldwide portals, and we don't see a fourth. And therein lies the opportunity. We have a global franchise that simply cannot be replicated.[29]

YAHOO! LOOKS FOR SOLUTIONS

Yahoo! Alters its Approach

Yahoo! changed its strategy in order to generate more income from non-advertising sources. CEO Semel announced in November 2001 his intention to achieve a 50-50 split between revenue from advertising and revenue from other sources by 2004. In 2000, 90 percent of Yahoo!'s revenues came from advertising. This figure was reduced to 80 percent in 2001, but advertising revenues decreased by almost 40 percent that year. In order to find new revenue streams, the company began charging for some services that traditionally had been free, a move that many consumers bristled at. Yahoo! acknowledged the difficulty of getting consumers to pay for services they had come to expect would be free. "We have absolutely trained people to get things for free," said Yahoo! vice president of communication Geoff Ralston.

To attract more consumer dollars, Yahoo! targeted customers with Internet ads offering services as diverse as extra home-page space, personal domain names, enhanced e-mail, additional bandwidth, financial research, real-time stock quotes, auction listings and more, for a fee. The company increased the commission fee for sellers at its auction site Yahoo! Auctions to a fee ranging from 0.5 percent to 2 percent of the final value of an auctioned item. Previously, Yahoo! had only charged a listing fee of up to $2.25, not a commission based on the value of the item sold. To compensate for the new pricing scheme, Yahoo! reduced the listing fee to between five cents and 75 cents. Yahoo! also began charging players in its fantasy baseball league a $4.95 fee to be able to get their team results over a web phone.

Yahoo! kept segments of its traditionally free services out of this pricing scheme. For example, Internet personal ads cost nothing to post on Yahoo!, but consumers must pay $19.95 a month for the privilege of responding to an ad. The Yahoo! Mail e-mail service remained free, but starting in 2002 consumers had to pay for mail-forwarding features and extra storage space. In a controversial move, Yahoo! revised its privacy policy in March

227

2002 to allow the company to market its services and products and services of other companies unless users specifically tell Yahoo! not to. Users received e-mails where they could check 16 boxes on a web site and instruct Yahoo! not to send marketing materials via phone, postal mail or e-mail. Additionally, the revised policy allowed Yahoo! to share consumer data with other marketers for specific marketing campaigns. Srinija Srinivasan, Yahoo! vice president and editor in chief, commented that the number of responses to the e-mail was "very low" and that the company's "fundamental approach to privacy hasn't changed."[30]

Yahoo! also sought to change its relationships with advertisers. Yahoo! had garnered a reputation for neglecting the needs of corporate marketers. The company had grown accustomed to owning some of the most sought-after advertising space on the Internet, and could afford to be expensive, inflexible and even inattentive to potential advertisers. The shrinking of advertising budgets of the slowed economy forced Yahoo! to reevaluate its attitude. "Cooperative relationships will be the hallmark in our world, with both clients and agencies," said Wenda Harris Millard, chief advertising sales officer. "No 'my way or the highway.'" Yahoo! also reduced prices for its ad space by as much as 60 percent in an effort to entice more traditional marketers to buy advertising. Additionally, Yahoo! sought to improve the quality of its service to current advertisers and its recruitment of potential advertisers by adding experience to its sales team. In late 2001, the company hired 30 senior advertising salespeople with at least 10 years of experience. One Yahoo! executive explained the new hires, saying, "We needed more senior people, far more experienced people who have access to clients."[31]

Yahoo! also attempted to add more traditional marketers to its roster of Internet advertisers. The problem for Yahoo! was that many traditional marketers were still wary of large ad spends on the Internet. "Traditional marketers aren't really convinced that online advertising works," said an analyst with Forrester Research. "While they are spending money, it's still very slow and very tentative."[32] Yahoo! revamped its ad sales program by cutting prices, hiring more experienced marketing executives, and allowing new ad formats on its sites. An ad for the 2002 Ford Explorer was one such example of the new formats. The ad featured sound effects simulating an engine, animation that made the web browser appear to shake and a full-sized picture of the new SUV when consumers clicked on the ad. The Ford Explorer ad was the first animated ad allowed by Yahoo!. Another ad for the Explorer appeared when users visited Yahoo!'s homepage. An animated flock of birds flew onto the page and began pecking at a cluster of seeds at the bottom of the page. When the birds ate the seeds, they revealed the Ford Explorer logo. Yahoo! also began offering its advertising customers proprietary research. One example of this research is a Yahoo! offering called the Yahoo! Buzz Index, which tracks the number of web searches for a particular name or product.

Additionally, Yahoo! teamed with advertisers to produce specialty web sites, such as PepsiStuff.com. The site enabled consumers to collect points from certain Pepsi and Mountain Dew products and redeem them for downloads of music, e-books, coupons, and screensavers. During the promotion, Pepsi collected more than 3.4 million e-mail addresses. Yahoo! also teamed with Pepsi for the 2001 world premier broadcast of a Britney Spears video. The ad was first shown on a special site (pepsi.Yahoo!.com/britney) a full two hours before it was set to debut on television during the Academy Awards. Pepsi purchased a 48-

hour "roadblock" with Yahoo!, which meant Pepsi purchased every advertising unit on Yahoo!.com during the period. For the first week of availability, the Britney commercial was viewed by web surfers 1.1 million times.

Yahoo! Corporate Offerings

Utilizing streaming media capabilities from its Broadcast.com acquisition, Yahoo! used its Yahoo! Broadcast division to host web conferences, online training, and virtual corporate meetings. In the fourth quarter of 2000, Yahoo! hosted more than 1,000 online conferences. The company also established a unit called Corporate Yahoo! (changed to Yahoo! Portal Solutions in 2001) that specialized in building web site portals for corporations, including McDonald's, Pfizer and the state of North Carolina. Following the leads of other technology companies, Yahoo! developed a corporate services division in June 2000. The division, called Yahoo! Enterprise Solutions (YES), enabled corporations to customize Yahoo!'s web portal with the help of a package of software tools. By offering enterprise services, Yahoo! hoped to lessen its dependence on online advertising sales. As of early January 2001, YES had attracted 18 clients, including McDonald's Corp., Bayer AG and Janus Capital Corp. Still, this service contributed only 10 percent of the company's total revenue and only 32 corporations signed on by November of that year.

Yahoo! also began hosting on-line conferences for large corporations such as Procter & Gamble and Samsung Electronics. In December 2000, Yahoo! teamed with wireless carrier Motient to allow users of two-way wireless messaging service to access Yahoo! e-mail accounts. A few weeks later, Yahoo! partnered with Internet appliance maker VTech Connect to introduce two co-branded e-mail appliances. As with the Motient deal, this partnership allowed users to access existing Yahoo! e-mail accounts. In January 2001, Yahoo! added another corporate service, called Yahoo! Industry Marketplaces, which enabled technology professionals to research and purchase electronics, software and hardware from a variety of vendors. The format was similar to Yahoo! Shopping, where users could search for items and compare prices.

New Acquisitions and Partnerships

Yahoo! continued to add content through acquisitions. In 2001, it completed a $12 million acquisition of Launch Media, the 10th largest music web site that also possessed the biggest music video collection on the Internet. In a break from its traditional umbrella advertising strategy, Yahoo! allowed Launch to retain its own sales staff and its own brand. Rather than changing the brand to "Yahoo! Launch," the site remained Launch, and was billed as "Your Yahoo! music experience."

Yahoo! also established more partnerships with large media companies. In 2001, Yahoo! signed on to carry Pressplay, the online music service from Sony and Vivendi Universal. Yahoo! also partnered with Sony to jointly develop an Internet site. "More entertainment companies are coming to Yahoo! to make sure their content is distributed," said David Mandelbrot, Yahoo!'s vice president and general manager of entertainment. "We're becoming more of a marketing partner rather than a company that takes dollars for our advertising." In addition to accepting marketing campaigns for movies, such as Disney's 2001 blockbuster *Pearl Harbor*, Yahoo! used its integrated marketing programs to post movie show times at local venues, show animated commercials, and annotate Yahoo! users' Internet calendars with movie opening dates.

What To Do?

Industry experts offered differing recommendations for Yahoo!'s turnaround. Some insisted that Yahoo! needed to find a partner in a large media company in order to survive. Economist Jack Myers stated, "It seems almost inevitable that Yahoo! would have to ally itself with one of the media conglomerates." Such a partnership would potentially allow Yahoo! to capitalize on a media company's expertise in television or print. Others suggested that Yahoo! simply start charging for its services. *Fortune* magazine proposed a scenario in which 10 percent of Yahoo!'s 80 million registered users paid $10 a month for "e-mail, a calendar, a home page, access to chat rooms and the rest, the company would generate nearly $1 billion in annual revenues before it sold any ads."[33] Since users could still get all the proposed services for free from other sources, the question would be whether Yahoo! brand loyalty and popularity would be enough to entice consumers to pay.

In spite of its financial troubles, Yahoo! remained among the elite Internet brands in 2002. The company's vast network of sites and services extended into many corners of the globe and many aspects of business, entertainment, information and technology. Yahoo! had custom web sites for 24 countries and in 12 languages. It attracted more than 200 million unique visitors from around the world to its pages each month. The company had more than 5,800 advertising customers annually, as well as 14,000 merchants for the Yahoo! Shopping site. Yahoo! boasted the longest average time spent on its web site, ahead of both AOL and MSN (see Fig. 4). Still, Yahoo! management faced the daunting challenge of finding new sources of revenue while keeping the essence and equity of the brand intact.

DISCUSSION QUESTIONS

1. Describe the sources of equity for the Yahoo! brand. Did these sources change during Yahoo!'s history? If so, how?
2. How did Yahoo!'s marketing program contribute to the company's success? What changes, if any, would you recommend for the future?
3. What do you think of Yahoo!'s new strategy of selling services? What impact, if any, will it have on consumers' perceptions of the brand?

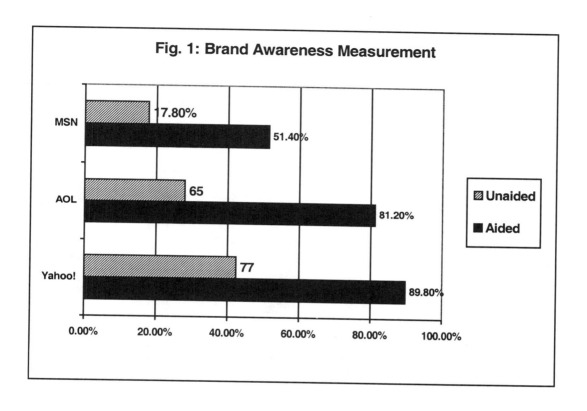

Fig. 1: Brand Awareness Measurement

MSN — Unaided 17.80%, Aided 51.40%
AOL — Unaided 65, Aided 81.20%
Yahoo! — Unaided 77, Aided 89.80%

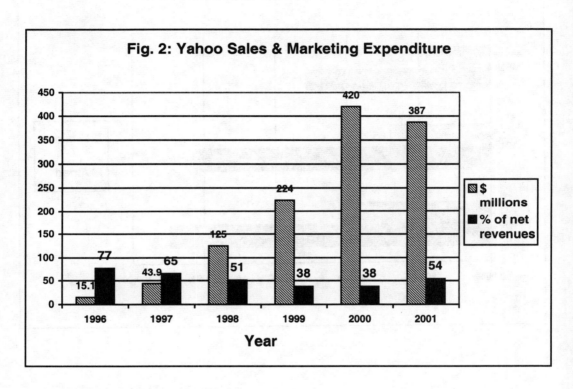

Fig. 2: Yahoo Sales & Marketing Expenditure

(Source: Yahoo! annual reports)
(Source: IDC, Internet Portal Brands Image Survey, September 2000)

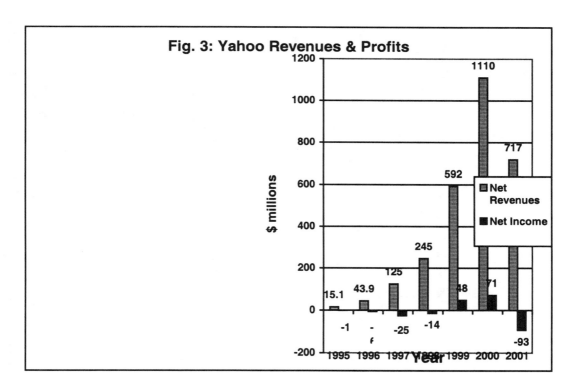

(source: Yahoo! annual reports)

Fig 4: Viewership Comparison, U.S.

	Time spent online/per person /month	Unique visitors (millions)
Yahoo!	1:25:15	59.4
AOL	39:30	64.8
MSN	1:11:52	54.6

(Source: Nielsen/NetRatings Audience Measurement Service, April 2002)

REFERENCES

[1] This case was prepared by Keith Richey under the supervision of Professor Kevin Lane Keller as the basis for class discussion.

[2] Kara Swisher. "Interview: Behind the Portal: What's Yahoo! Up To?" *Wall Street Journal*, April 17, 2000, p. R74.

[3] Kara Swisher. "Interview: Behind the Portal: What's Yahoo! Up To?" *Wall Street Journal*, April 17, 2000, p. R74.

[4] Kara Swisher. "Interview: Behind the Portal: What's Yahoo! Up To?" *Wall Street Journal*, April 17, 2000, p. R74.

[5] Joseph Nocera. "Do You Believe? How Yahoo! Became a Blue Chip." *Fortune*, June 7, 1999, p. 76.

[6] As quoted in "Directories Look For Ways to Build Brands." *Advertising Age*, June 1996

[7] As quoted in "Inside Yahoo! Search Party." *Adweek*, July 12, 1999.

[8] As quoted in "Inside Yahoo! Search Party." *Adweek*, July 12, 1999.

[9] As quoted in "Brandweek's Marketers of the Year: Yahoo!, Karen Edwards." *Adweek*, October 20, 1997

[10] As quoted in "Brandweek's Marketers of the Year: Yahoo!, Karen Edwards." *Adweek*, October 20, 1997.

[11] "What Is Yahoo!, Really?" *Fortune*, June 22, 1998.

[12] As quoted in "Inside Yahoo! Search Party." *Adweek*, July 12, 1999.

[13] As quoted in "Yahoo! Still Searching For Profits on the Internet." *Fortune*, December 9, 1996.

[14] Tobi Elkin. "The Interactive Future: Jerry Yang" *Advertising Age*, April 17, 2000, p. I56.

[15] As quoted in "Yahoo! Informs the World It's Now an E-Mall." *Wall Street Journal*, October 29, 1999.

[16] As quoted in "Brandweek's Marketers of the Year: Yahoo!, Karen Edwards." *Adweek*, October 20, 1997.

[17] Cover Story. Business Week, September 7, 1998.

[18] As quoted in "Yahoo! TV Ads Connect the Brand With Shopping." *Advertising Age*, November 1, 1999.

[19] As quoted in "Yahoo! Inc. to Spend $20 Million In Campaign on News Corp.'s Fox." *Wall Street Journal*, January 26, 1999.

[20] As quoted in "Yahoo!'s Koogle Has Global Aspirations." *Forbes*, December 13, 1999.

[21] As quoted in "Yahoo! Japan Wins Hoorays." *Business Week*, June 19, 2000.

[22] "Yahoo! Makes Grass-Roots Push in Asia." *Wall Street Journal*, August 1, 2000.

[23] "Interview: Wireless War." *Wall Street Journal*, September 18, 2000.

[24] "Yahoo! Everywhere Still Has to Find Its Way." *Business Week*, June 2, 2000.

[25] "Yahoo! Hits Streets With Internet Taxis." *B to B*, October 23, 2000.

[26] As quoted in "Yahoo! Finalizes Broadcast.com Purchase." *Redherring.com*, July 21, 1999.

[27] As quoted in "Heard on the Street." *Wall Street Journal*, September 1, 2000.

[28] As quoted in "Yahoo! Surges After Earnings Beat All Expectations." *FT.com*, July 12, 2000.

[29] Marc Gunther, "The Cheering Fades for Yahoo!" *Fortune*, November 12, 2001, p. 151.

[30] Mylene Mangalindan. "Users Flame New Yahoo! Privacy Plan." *Wall Street Journal*, April 12, 2002, p. A16.

[31] Tobi Elkin. "Yahoo! Goes for Old School Marketing." *Advertising Age*, November 19, 2001.

[32] Marc Gunther, "The Cheering Fades for Yahoo!" *Fortune*, November 12, 2001, p. 151.

[33] Marc Gunther, "The Cheering Fades for Yahoo!" *Fortune*, November 12, 2001, p. 151.

SNAPPLE:
REVITALIZING A BRAND[1]

INTRODUCTION

In the 1990s, Snapple Corporation was positioned to take advantage of the explosion of the New Age beverage segment. The company was one of the leading New Age beverage brands when the category was beginning to take off. With the combination of a unique product and package design and quirky advertising, the company had grown from a regional underground favorite to a nationally recognized brand. Snapple's rise in the beverage industry was crowned in 1994, when the Quaker Oats Company purchased Snapple for $1.7 billion. Quaker expected to make Snapple a major player in the industry, like it had done with Gatorade. The company was unable, however, to capitalize on the brand's previous success. Snapple languished for a period of three years in the hands of Quaker management. In 1997, Quaker sold Snapple to Triarc Beverage Group for $300 million. Triarc faced a number of challenges, including reversing the sales slide, revamping the distribution system and creating new products that would enable growth. Most importantly, Triarc had to find a way to reconnect the brand with consumers.

THE EMERGENCE OF SNAPPLE

The roots of Snapple Corporation date back to 1972 in Brooklyn, New York when brothers-in-law Leonard Marsh and Hyman Golden left their window-washing business, teamed up with Marsh's childhood friend and health food store owner Arnold Greenberg, and began selling pure fruit juice as "Unadulterated Food Products Co." In 1978, they created an apple soda that fizzled -- so much so that several bottles exploded -- inspiring the "snap" in the drink's eventual name. They bought the rights to the name from a man in Texas for what then seemed like a very expensive price of $500. Over time they established themselves as the "first company to produce a complete line of all-natural beverages," that were "Made from the Best Stuff on Earth."

In the 1980s, Snapple essentially created the non-carbonated segment of ready-to-drink beverages with its introduction of ready-to-drink fruit juices and iced teas. Also, Snapple was the first company to sell its drinks in single serving wide-mouthed glass bottles, rather than the ubiquitous aluminum cans. The company clad its bottles in unique, bright labeling and introduced a new process called "hot-packing" (filling bottles at 180°F liquid to sterilize the contents) that eliminated the need for preservatives, and enabled it to extend its "all-natural" claims to its entire line of products. Its goal was to "make a natural product and make sure it tastes good, smells good and looks good." Although Snapple remained a small niche brand throughout much of the decade, the strategy had begun to work. By the late 1980s, growing ranks of health-conscious consumers were snapping up Snapple products as an alternative to sodas. By 1991, Snapple emerged as a nationally-recognized brand.

In the spring of 1992, Snapple management raised capital by selling a majority stake of the firm to Thomas H. Lee, a Boston-based investment firm, for $140 million. Marsh, Golden, and Greenberg maintained control of the company and continued to improve operations. In December of the same year, the company went public by selling 4 million shares of common stock at a price of $20 per share. The offering was oversubscribed and, by the day's end, the share price had risen 45 percent. By the end of January, Snapple shares traded at $34. Overnight, the value of the company exceeded that of corporations such as National Semiconductor and Teledyne. By 1993, Snapple sales had exploded to $516 million, more than double the 1992 figures. The stock price had risen to five times its initial offering price, and Snapple had become a household name. Yet, operating costs were also on the rise. Sales, general and administration expenses had grown from $22.7 to $59 million from 1992 to 1993, and operating margins had fallen 2.3 percent.

THE SNAPPLE FORMULA

Over the two decades that they had been in the non-alcoholic beverage business, Marsh, Golden and Greenburg had developed a set of tactics that they believed helped to propel Snapple sales. First, they tried to differentiate the company from its competitors by continually offering customers new and exotic choices of ready-to-drink beverages. In 1993 alone, the company produced a dizzying 52 different flavors. In addition to offering diverse flavors, the company concentrated on providing quality flavors in its beverages. For example, 95 percent of Snapple teas came from India and a small percentage came from Sri Lanka. The extensive offering of new and exotic flavors generally helped stimulate consumer interest and support sales. Not all of Snapple offerings, however, were successful. Within the tea segment, for example, decaffeinated and unsweetened teas consistently performed below management's expectations. Yet, on balance, the team was able to bring more blockbuster flavors to market than unsuccessful introductions.

Second, the team elected to focus its early marketing efforts on the East and West coasts, where demand for New Age beverages was highest. Early sales to Midwestern states were not as strong, leading some to believe that Snapple's quirky urban advertising alienated middle America. International sales accounted for just 1 percent of total revenues and, despite the fact that faster growth would require a significant amount of capital, management planned to aggressively push into Europe, Central and South America and Asia.

Third, the company initially developed its own distribution channels, eschewing the traditional wholesaler-supermarket model used by its larger, established competition. Instead, Snapple sold "up-and-down-the-street" channels -- that is, in convenience outlets, sandwich shops, gas stations and delicatessens --using a system of independent distributors.

Fourth, in the high-growth, ready-to-drink beverage market, Snapple management found that it was able to price its unique products and positioning at a significant premium. In 1993, Snapple charged $1.00 to $1.25 for a 16-ounce bottle, a 30 percent to 38 percent margin. When asked to justify the beverage's relatively high price, Snapple marketers responded that it was a premium product that was "available to anyone", as opposed to traditional luxury goods, such as a Porsche automobile, which were out-of-reach of the average consumer. But could the company sustain this high price premium, especially in the iced tea segment? After all, unlike cola or fruit juice, home-prepared iced tea can be prepared in less time and much less cost than the store-bought, ready-to-drink equivalent. Consequently, many analysts believed that in order to successfully enter the supermarket business, Snapple management would have to reposition the brand and sell products in multi-packs, in cans and at a lower price.

SNAPPLE BRAND EQUITY

By 1994, Snapple was experiencing tremendous growth. According to Jude Hammerle, Snapple's Director of Advertising and Promotion: "The velocity at which the brand is growing now is so monumental that you could get dizzy just thinking about that." Said Michael Bellas, the President of Beverage Marketing, "Snapple has made us all believers."

Consumers loved Snapple -- they said so over and over again through fan clubs, testimonials and letter writing; some considered it a kind of Snapple cult. Snapple appeared on license plates and even became the middle name for a New Jersey baby boy. Consumer surveys suggested that the Snapple name was catchy and popular and engendered positive feelings in consumers. As Hammerle said, "The name is really one of the most user-friendly, consumer-friendly names that you can ever find." Although Snapple representatives were frequently quoted as saying their target market was "anyone with a mouth," the company's advertising focused on teens, the 18 to 30 year old age group and the "traditional iced tea consumer."

During the early 1990s, Snapple ran a series of very successful ad campaigns, and had a great deal of success advertising on national radio and television, using off-beat humor and consumer-composed jingles. For example, for one advertisement the company invited an art critic to analyze the Snapple label. Snapple also gained appeal through product placements in popular shows such as *Seinfeld*, movies such as *Sleepless in Seattle* and official sponsorship of well-known celebrities such as Rush Limbaugh, Howard Stern and Jennifer Capriati. Television commercials featured people such as New York's ex-Mayor Ed Koch defending his city and Snapple to a critical Kentucky farmer. Snapple also relied on "word-of-mouth" advertising and pursued unusual events throughout the country that Coke and Pepsi avoided, such as a Minnesotan Cherry Spitting and New Jersey Miss Crustacean contests.

The company's most successful ad campaign, however, starred Wendy the Snapple Lady. Wendy Kaufman, a woman with a thick New York accent, was a company employee in the order department. She took it upon herself to personally answer incoming consumer letters and became the drink's unofficial spokeswoman. She rocketed to stardom after starring in the television commercials where she read letters from Snapple fans. Capitalizing on the growing trend toward testimonial advertising, the Wendy ads projected a "real people" image in unscripted and spontaneous commercials with real Snapple customers. Wendy gained national recognition through appearances in places such as the Oprah Winfrey Show.

Snapple was now one of the leading brands in the exploding New Age beverage market, which had passed the fad stage and was a legitimate segment in the beverage industry.

THE NEW AGE BEVERAGE MARKET

For nearly two decades, the non-alcoholic beverage market had thrived and grown continuously. The soft drink sector reached a whopping $47 billion in retail sales in 1993, although growth in the segment was expected to be slow, at approximately two to three percent, for some years. With essentially flat sales forecast for the core soda segment, many of the large beverage companies looked to move into new categories to improve revenues.

Nevertheless, by the early 1990s, soda sales dominated other ready-to-drink categories by a factor of nearly 50 to 1.

During the late-1980s, however, a new trend -- the New Age movement of the non-alcoholic beverage market -- emerged and evolved in response to consumers' growing concerns over calories and artificial additives. New Age ready-to-drink (bottled and canned) beverages in the segment projected a "better for you" image and, by 1994, could be divided into eight distinct groups: 1) Ready-to-drink Tea, 2) Sports beverages, 3) PET (plastic) bottled water, 4) Single-serve fruit beverages, 5) All-natural soda, 6) Sparkling flavored water, 7) Sparkling fruit beverages, and 8) Ready-to-drink Coffee. The market shares were, respectively: 29.9 percent; 22.9 percent; 16.4 percent; 14.5 percent, with the other four categories making up the remaining 16 percent.

Market research about the New Age ready-to-drink segment suggested that customers generally selected beverages based on fashion-, taste-, and status-related considerations. Consequently, distinctive flavors, quality ingredients and clean labels were generally more important than price. Product, packaging and promotion considerations -- as they combined to form overall brand image -- played a critical role in the consumers buying decision.

The ready-to-drink tea group illustrates these points. As of October 1993, between 75 percent and 80 percent of all U.S. households drank iced tea, placing the product third to soft drinks and beer in the beverage consumption rankings. As the New Age movement gained momentum, the ready-to-drink iced tea segment grew at an amazing rate of 188.9 percent as health-conscious consumers embraced iced tea, with fewer calories and additives, as an alternative to soda and beer. In response, several beverage companies began to stress the importance of the high-quality ingredients in their advertising. For example, Perrier/Celestial Seasonings, Crystal Geyser and White Rock tried to build brand equity and product identity by stressing the quality of their respective brands of their spring water, which was used in their ready-to-drink tea products. Companies also stressed that their products were "real brewed", although it was unclear whether this meant "brewed from real tea leaves" or "made from concentrate or tea essence."

NEW COMPETITION

Although Snapple may have penetrated the ready-to-drink beverage market first, and precipitated the New Age category, few observers believed that it would continue to dominate the market for long. With flat sales in the soda segment, Snapple had begun to attract the attention of beverage industry behemoths such as Coca-Cola and Pepsi. It was just a matter of time before new players entered the market. A key question would be whether newer, larger players would create momentum in the ready-to-drink market and carry Snapple along with it.

Pepsi, along with Unilever, became the first major brand to challenge Snapple. In 1992, the two companies announced a joint effort to sell Unilever's Lipton iced tea in a ready-to-drink package. The new Pepsi/Lipton partnership first offered the bottled Lipton Original, "the only ready-to-drink iced tea brewed from real tea leaves," followed by the canned Lipton Brisk. In 1993, the companies launched a $30 to $35 million advertising campaign featuring Sports Illustrated swimsuit edition cover model Vendela drinking Lipton in front of a fascinated audience of both men and women. The joint venture also launched an especially aggressive radio campaign targeting Snapple, attacking the company for its use of reconstituted tea powders.

At the same time, English beverage giant Tetley licensed the rights to manufacture and distribute all ready-to-drink products bearing the Tetley trademark to A&W. Tetley planned to invest $35 million to market a new round tea bag and saw opportunities to cross-market to hot tea drinkers. The Tetley/A&W combination's advertising introduced "Pearle", a sandwich shop waitress who couldn't understand why the bags were round. Tetley also included coupons for the ready-to-drink product with every box of round bag tea.

In 1994, Coca-Cola entered the New Age beverage market with the introduction of a psychedelic fruit drink, Fruitopia, which was marketed using a retro peace-and-love ad theme. An early slogan was: "Fruitopia. For the mind, body and planet." The upstart brand totaled sales of $20.4 million in its first year on advertising spending of approximately $30 million. The new Fruitopia brand was able to piggyback on Coke's extensive distribution system, thus bypassing some of its competitors' logistical problems. In the iced tea market, Coca-Cola's Nestea brand revived the "Take the Nestea Plunge" theme for the introduction of its ready-to-drink iced teas. Ads featured good-looking people, but not models, and stressed brand equity and the "good for me" theme.

At the time, however, the ready-to-drink tea market was suffering for several reasons. First, slower growth rates naturally occurred as the sales base grew. Second, the three largest brands in the category could no longer count on domestic geographic expansion to increase sales. Third, fruit drinks were beginning to provide stiff competition. Snapple tea was not the only product line experiencing difficulty. Despite the hype surrounding Coke's launch of Fruitopia, sales for 1994 finished at only $60 million, far below the target of $400 million.

Further complicating things was additional competition. Soon after Quaker Oats completed its purchase of Snapple, Arizona Iced Tea entered the ready-to-drink iced tea market. Like Snapple, Arizona was founded by two New Yorkers, Don Vultaggio and John Ferolito. The two developed a canned iced tea that captured a nearly 17 percent market share and $2 billion in revenues in 1995, putting it squarely in competition with the larger players in the market. Priced similarly to Snapple, the new company also added a liquor-like 20-ounce bottle. Despite the fact that the company 1) gave their products practically no marketing support beyond the point-of-purchase, 2) was slow to develop a formal product development process, and 3) was plagued by lawsuits from numerous angry ex-distributors, Arizona moved into a strong position in the ready-to-drink category.

Before long, several other competitors followed Arizona into the ready-to-drink category. First, Redco began offering ready-to-drink iced teas under the Red Rose and Salada tea labels. Next, Perrier/Celestial Seasonings formed a joint venture to market herbal ready-to-drink teas similar to Celestial Seasoning's hot teas. The new product line featured water from Perrier's domestic springs in Northern California and New Hampshire, and was backed by a strong advertising campaign featuring TV and radio spots, billboards, special events and product samplings. Next, Crystal Geyser began importing Tejava-brand tea from Japan. It contained no sweeteners, preservatives or additives with label and was beautifully decorated with images of Japanese women tea-pickers. The company distributed the line through restaurants and hotels, primarily in California, and targeted an upscale and older consumer.

THE QUAKER OATS TAKEOVER

Despite the new competitors in the ready-to-drink tea market and plunging share prices in late 1994, Snapple executives remained bullish. Yet, Snapple's majority investors, Thomas H. Lee, were apparently less bullish about the company's long-term prospects and quickly accepted Quaker Oats' proposed $1.7 billion acquisition deal -- generating a gain of nearly $1 billion over a two year period. All told, the $1.7 billion deal represented a multiple of about 17 times earnings, significantly more than the 10 or 11 times earnings yielded by other recent transactions in the beverage category or by comparable publicly-traded companies. However, some analysts believed that the deal was a good one. "There are some significant synergies," suggested Michael Bellas, president of New York-based Beverage Marketing Corporation. "They are very professional, a big force on the horizon now. I'm sure that's being considered by both Atlanta [Coca-Cola] and Somers [Pepsi]."

Snapple Under Quaker Oats Management

New competitors aside, by 1995 many analysts felt that the market for New Age drinks was changing dramatically. Increasingly, the young, trendy consumers that had created the ready-to-drink category seemed to be getting bored and began to shift back to the more neutral flavors of colas and clear sodas.

Quaker Oats attempted to respond to these trends with new advertising and promotional tactics. Because Snapple was considered a brand whose popularity spread primarily by word of mouth, the company tried to be especially receptive to the consumer ideas. For example, it introduced a new flavor, Ralph's Cantaloupe Cocktail, when its namesake, Ralph Orafino, wrote to the company and requested a melon-flavored drink. Also, in August 1995, the company sponsored the "First Annual Snapple Convention" in Hempstead, New York for 3,000 of the drink's most hardcore fans. The idea for this "Snapple love fest" came from the brand's self-proclaimed "#1 Fan", 6 year-old Jennifer Murry, who wrote to the company:

> *Dear Snapple Woman,*
> *Shouldn't Snapple have some kind of special day or holiday or festival even. Because, you see people on TV, I mean, like the man that didn't believe Snapple was made of natural things or fruits. I think there should be a holiday or festival. Or a Snapple parade.*

Quaker sent announcements for the convention to the quarter-million Snapple devotees who had felt strongly enough about the product to send personal letters to the company. In exchange for a $5 admission fee and 20 Snapple labels, Quaker offered the fans "36,000 square feet of taste tests, a Wendy lookalike contest, TV commercials on video monitors, web surfing, a cooking demonstration, panel discussions featuring Wendy and the real-life 'stars' of Snapple TV spots, trivia contests, Snapple-inspired artwork and fashions, raffles, miniature golf and carnival games. Plus, each attendee received two free bottles of Snapple."

Despite the apparent success of the convention, Quaker made several critical errors in its first major selling season after acquiring Snapple. In a world where refreshment drink producers normally live for the summer season, Quaker neither followed a regular schedule for Snapple advertising, nor introduced new products quickly. As a result, supermarket sales were slacking off. June sales of Snapple iced tea were down 19 percent, fruit blends were down 25 percent and lemonades were down 32 percent from the year before.

Also, Snapple's reputation began to suffer when people began challenging the company's basic premise that it sold healthy products. Jane Hurley, of the Center for Science in the Public Interest, the same woman who exposed the nutrition fallacies of movie theatre popcorn and Chinese food, pointed out that the label's claim that most Snapple drinks are mostly sweetened water, containing less than 10 percent fruit juice. She said, "It's about the same as Hi-C, and no one ever called that a health drink...We're not saying to this stuff will hurt you. It's more of a rip-off than a health risk." Others pointed out that a bottle of Snapple iced tea contained more calories than a Coke.

Further complicating matters, Quaker had expected to use Snapple's extensive distribution network of 300 national distributors to push Gatorade into smaller retail outlets that Quaker had not traditionally used. Unfortunately, the company discovered too late that the Snapple distribution systems were not compatible with its existing Gatorade system. Quaker responded by trying to transfer big supermarket accounts from Snapple distributors to Gatorade distributors and encouraging the Snapple distributors to push the up-and-down-the-street channels harder -- however, the Snapple distributors refused. Even worse, Quaker encountered some unexpected production obstacles.

Quaker Attempts New Strategies

Quaker management responded with drastic changes. They installed new people in brand management positions, reduced the number of flavors offered from 50 to 35, reduced contract manufacturers, and tripled the ad budget. In addition, Quaker also made changes to the flavor line, including introducing seasonal products such as cider tea for Halloween. At the same time, they continued the push into supermarkets with new packaging: 12-packs, 4-packs and plastic 32- and 64-ounce bottles.

Additionally, Quaker worked on a system to process orders faster and make the bottling plants more efficient. This move cut inventory in half and enabled deliveries to be made within two days, instead of 21 days. In addition, Snapple announced plans to place highly visible coolers in supermarkets, just like Coke and Pepsi, and introduce a diet line of drinks.

SNAPPLE SALES DECLINE

In the end, however, the efforts to save the summer of 1995 were too little, too late, as Coke and Pepsi aggressively promoted new iced tea and fruit juice campaigns. Despite spending more than $40 million for a national summertime sampling campaign, Snapple's sales dropped another 20 precent for the quarter, supermarket tea sales were down 14 percent and juice sales fell 15 percent, prompting critics to question whether Quaker Oats had made a mistake in purchasing the company. Tom Pirko, President of Bevmark commented: "They bought the brand at a point when it was past its zenith". Despite the disappointing summer, Quaker Oats management continued to think otherwise. "Snapple is on the verge of a comeback," said Margaret Stender, Quaker Oats's Vice-President of Marketing. Despite the company's apparent optimism, Lipton overtook Snapple in volume sales in the ready-to-drink tea category in 1995, although Snapple maintained its number one position in dollar sales due to its premium pricing strategy.

In 1996, Quaker attempted to move Snapple back towards more traditional marketing approaches. First, it introduced an inside-the-bottle-cap game promotion for 1996 and began a $40 million nationwide give-away campaign during the summer. Backed by a TV and radio ad campaign touting how Snapple was "spreading taste all over the place," extensive "sampling brigades" passed out free Snapple at beaches, parks and on street corners. Consumers could also call a toll-free number to get coupons good for free bottles. Second, it launched a new advertising campaign to replace the "Wendy" ads. The ads had aired for years and some key Quaker Oats staff believed that the ads were losing steam and that Wendy's New York brashness might be hindering Snapple's acceptance in the Midwest. The company hired Spike Lee to direct several new spots such as "Threedom Equals Freedom" and "We want to be No. 3," which announced that Snapple knew it was running in third place behind Coke and Pepsi. The company also revived "The Best Stuff on Earth" theme.

Quaker's trouble with Snapple continued, however. Although revenues in the new diet drink segment grew 23 percent in 1996 to nearly 12 percent of total sales, the company continued to struggle. "We have no evidence that [Quaker is] closer to solving Snapple's problems," said Naomi Ghez, food-stock analyst for Goldman, Sachs & Co. Others were more pointed in their comments. "They can't even give Snapple away right," noted *Brandweek*. "What the hell *is* Snapple? No one knows what it means any more," stated Alan Brew, a corporate brand consultant.

TROUBLE IN THE CORPORATE SUITE

In January 1995, just one month after the Snapple buy-out, market rumors suggested that Coke was planning a hostile takeover of Quaker Oats. For the quarter ending December 1994, Quaker's net earnings fell to $34.4 million ($.25 per share) from $42.8 million ($0.31 per share) for the same period the previous year. While some speculated that PepsiCo might also be interested in the company, many assumed that the Federal Trade Commission would not allow it. Without a definite buyer on the horizon, few thought that Quaker made for an attractive investment opportunity and stock price declines were expected for at least the short-term future. The addition of $1.7 billion in debt from the Snapple purchase, coupled with the existing $1 billion in short and long term debt it already had, reduced Quaker's takeover appeal. Finally, should a rival become serious about buying the company, there would be little insiders could do to block it, as they owned a mere one percent of the company's shares. Although the company soon sold off its pet food and chili businesses, the stock price remained at $35 a share.

By the end of 1996, Smithburg had placed a ceiling on the amount of resources allocated to Snapple. Despite Smithburg's promises back in February of 15 percent to 20 percent gains in Snapple sales (which analysts dubbed "gulp fiction"), sales in fact dropped eight percent and losses for the year were expected to exceed $100 million with no turning-point in sight. He conceded, "We clearly do not yet have the momentum we need," especially in the single-serve market, the source of 80 percent of Snapple's business.

Rumors circulated on Wall Street that Quaker had received a multi-billion dollar bid for Gatorade, but that Quaker continued to insist that the purchaser also take Snapple.

Snapple's market share in the iced tea category dropped another 4.7 points to 16.7 percent in the first quarter of 1997. Although it continued to retain its number one position in the juice drink category, the brand had lost two share points to its competition. Quaker Oats also struggled, posting a $1.1 billion loss ($8.15 a share) on an optional accounting write-down for the Snapple acquisition. Smithburg announced he was leaving the company shortly thereafter. The market reacted by bidding Quaker's stock up $1.25 that afternoon.

TRIARC ENTERS THE PICTURE

In late March, just before leaving the company, Smithburg announced the company's decision to sell Snapple to the Triarc Beverage Group for $300 million. Triarc was a subsidiary of the Triarc Companies, a holding company run by two buyout specialists, Nelson Peltz and Peter May. Formed in 1929, the Triarc Companies and its predecessor had focused on the specialty chemical, natural gas and textiles industries. However, in recent years, the firm had begun to diversify by collecting assets in the food and beverage sectors. By 1996, it had acquired Mistic Brands, a producer of premium non-alcoholic beverages, Arby's Corporation, a national fast food franchise and Royal Crown, a producer of soft drinks such RC Cola and Diet Rite Cola.

"The decision to sell Snapple was reached after an extensive review of various shareholder value-building options by management," said Quaker Chairman William Smithburg. "After reviewing all possible options, we decided it was in the shareholders' interest to remove the financial burdens and risks Snapple brought to the portfolio and better focus on our value-driving businesses." Triarc Beverage Group CEO Michael Weinstein commented, "Well, we really think we bought...not a company, but a brand and not only the largest brand in the premium beverage category, but a brand that actually defines what the category is."

Market reaction to the sale was mixed. John McMillin, a food industry analyst at Prudential Securities, stated: "It was a fire sale price ... The bad news is the investment has been a disaster, the good news is they're trying to put it behind them." Michael Branca, a food industry analyst at Lehman Brothers, commented: "...Triarc's beverage management is highly respected in the beverage distribution business ... Snapple could well be reborn under Triarc."

TRIARC'S INITIAL MOVES WITH SNAPPLE

While beverage industry analysts predicted that the Snapple brand was doomed for phase-out, Triarc was confident that it could restore Snapple to its pre-Quaker market share and status. At the time of Triarc's purchase of Snapple, consumers had more choices between ready-to-drink beverages than ever before. By mid-1997, the New Age market had undergone yet another shake-up. Pepsi stopped distributing fruit drinks from Ocean Spray and launched its own FruitWorks brand. Other new brands like Nantucket Nectars, a line of 100 percent juice drinks packaged in unique bottles, and Campbell Soup Co.'s V8 Splash, a carrot-based blend of fruit juices targeting younger consumers, were entering the market rapidly and threatened to squeeze out even more market share from Snapple. To breathe life back into Snapple, Triarc had to invest heavily in new product development and employ dynamic marketing strategies that would differentiate Snapple from competitors and recapture the attention of consumers.

Amid much speculation, Weinstein, with the assistance of SVP-marketing Ken Gilbert, immediately began the process of rebuilding the brand. Triarc soon announced that it would apply the same marketing principles to Snapple that it used to turn around its successful Mistic beverage line: edgy advertising, strong distributor relationships, colorful labels and focused street sales. When asked whether Triarc would use Mistic spokesman and quirky basketball player, Dennis Rodman, Weinstein commented: "No, no. Dennis is the Mistic guy." Within weeks, Weinstein -- much to the delight of the press -- met with former Snapple spokeswoman Wendy Kaufman. "If we can just get the brand back to where it was, we've done a great job," said Weinstein. He admitted that bringing Wendy back would not turn Snapple around, but he felt it would signal the return of "speed, fun, innovation and quirkiness." The first set of Snapple ads under Triarc's direction featured Wendy's reappearance on a desert island and the labels of several of Snapple's products featured Wendy's face to symbolize the return of Snapple to its core values. "Wendy, this year, is going to do lots of local appearances," said Steve Jarmon, VP-communications. "We're getting her involved with grass-roots kinds of activities. She draws well."

New products

Intensive development of new Snapple products that appealed to the ever-changing demands of the consumer beverage market was one of Triarc's most significant moves to revive the brand.

Whipper Snapple. Perhaps the most innovative and important development to emerge out of Triarc's product development efforts was the Whipper Snapple, a fruit smoothie beverage introduced in the summer of 1998. Whipper Snapple aimed at capitalizing on the growing popularity of juice bars and in so doing, offered the first bottled fruit smoothie to hit the beverage market. Whipper Snapple was touted as a breakthrough product for Snapple because of its unique bottle design and eye-catching labeling, the product's creative name and the variety of flavors offered including a lineup of "power smoothies" containing popular herbal ingredients such as bee pollen, gingko bilboa, and wheat grass aimed at capturing health conscious consumers.

Sweet Tea. Triarc also undertook efforts to revive Snapple's sluggish sales of bottled juice and tea beverages, and to explore new opportunities within these bottled beverage categories. To create greater appeal of Snapple among Southerners, Snapple introduced its Sweet Tea product line, which added cane sugar and other sweeteners to traditional Snapple tea recipes to create a Snapple version of the popular Southern beverage. The development of variations of a lemonade iced tea to compete with a similar beverage marketed by Nantucket Nectars was begun and expected to reach consumers by 1999.

Snapple Farms. Furthermore, Triarc launched Snapple Farms, a 100 percent pure juice drink with potential to enter the lucrative school lunch market. The fresh and natural approach of the Snapple Farms line was aimed at changing consumer impressions of Snapple as a sugary, unnatural beverage.

Triarc continued to innovate its products beyond the 1998 introduction of Whipper Snapple and Snapple Farms:

Snapple Hydro. Snapple Hydro thirst quenchers were re-launched in April 1999 after an unsuccessful try in 1998 under the Refresher's brand name. The range is composed of several fruit juices and two real-brewed sun teas. Snapple Hydro has all the characteristics of a sport beverage. As with Gatorade, it contains sodium electrolytes, which enable the body to replenish the chemicals lost during exercise, and has less sugar than regular sodas. Hydro was not positioned necessarily to attack Gatorade core consumer base of athletes. Nevertheless, the marketing strategy supporting the new brand was ambitious: Snapple Hydro aimed to conquer the "motion market" or in other words, to capture a "stomach's share" of a large base of active consumers. Hydro wanted to be seen as the ideal beverage for health-conscious consumers looking for easy-to-drink refreshment during leisure activities or simply when they were "on the go." Hydro relied on Snapple's keys of success: It offers all-natural ingredients and punchy fruit flavors in an innovative 20-ounce PET plastic bottle.

Snapple Elements. Also launched in April 1999, Snapple Elements is a range of 6-flavor herbal-enhanced fruit drinks and teas, which was positioned in the fast-growing Wellness Beverage Category along with SoBe. These new functional drinks were intended to offer more than refreshment. For example, Elements offered health-conscious consumers the benefits of guarana or gingko biloba, for energy and digestibility respectively, combined with the pleasure of great tasting fruit juice or tea.

With product names such as Fire, Moon, Sun or Earth and a "refresh your natural resources" positioning, the new Element lineup was a means to enhance the healthy-product side of Snapple's brand image. Elements was designed to build on Snapple's core values: attractive quirky flavor's names, such as Dragonfruit or Starfruit, a voluptuous shaped proprietary bottle and great tastes. Apart from being an all-natural beverage, the health-promise of Elements was limited to the listing of herbal additive dosage on the label and balanced by a clearly claimed refreshment benefit.

REJUVENATING SNAPPLE'S MARKETING

Marketing these new product innovations as well as Snapple's existing products was another central focus of Triarc's revitalization of the brand. Many of Triarc's marketing efforts aimed to recapture the "feel" Snapple had before it was purchased by Quaker -- e.g., using off-the-wall marketing techniques such as nationwide contests and unusual bottle labeling. The company continued to sponsor two controversial personalities: shock jock Howard Stern for Snapple and conservative talk-show host Rush Limbaugh for Diet Snapple.

In addition to enlisting the help of Wendy Kaufman, "the Snapple lady," in the brand's marketing program, Triarc sought the attention of consumers through imaginative nationwide promotion campaigns and contests. The "Win Nothing Instantly" contest was a popular 1998 marketing program in which Snapple consumers won unique cash prizes such as "free rent for a year" or "no car payments for six months." Subsequent promotion campaigns focused on using Snapple's packaging and labeling to emphasize the renewed quirkiness of the brand. The $1 million "The Joke's On Us" promotion featured the faces of 23 average looking Snapple employees appearing on various product labels throughout 1999 in an effort to convey Snapple's appeal to ordinary people who value the "best stuff made on earth." Brand icon Wendy Kaufman embarked on a national joke tour as support.

247

Consumers could also save labels for discounts on logoed gear offered via Snapple's revamped web site, the brand's first merchandise push.

Triarc's marketing team hoped that these unusual marketing campaigns would restore "attitude" to the brand and give it the creative buzz it once benefited from while still a leading beverage brand earlier in the decade. As one Triarc executive explained, "This brand is not about marketing b.s., but about having fun, being quirky, having the best stuff--including real people." Recognizing the importance of packaging and labeling of its products to capture the attention of consumers, Snapple executives redesigned the theme of the brand's labels to reflect a woodcut motif to emphasize Snapple's purity. Triarc also began exploring new methods of labeling so as to maximize color quality and reduce the occurrence of label damage.

Triarc's innovative efforts paid off. Despite the continued fierce competitiveness of the beverage market, Triarc slowed Snapple's downslide by boosting sales across the board. In its first year operating Snapple, Triarc sold 100 million more bottles of Snapple than Quaker would have if Quaker's 22 percent first-half sales decline had continued. In fiscal 1998, Triarc Inc. increased annual sales for the first time since 1995. Sales of Snapple rose eight percent in 1998 and contributed significantly to Triarc's 50 percent increase in premium beverage sales that year. "This is a fashion business," commented Havis Dawson of Beverage World. "Snapple is coming back into fashion because it's once again asking the question: What's new?"

TRIARC'S PLANS FOR FURTHER GROWTH

With the Snapple brand "back on its feet," Triarc now needed to implement new marketing plans to ensure its continued growth and prosperity. Snapple's marketing program for 1999 was a mixture of traditional and more innovative elements. Snapple's objective was to re-assert the brand values that helped to build Snapple's success, as well as to keep the brand on a cutting edge and moving forward. Back-to-the-roots advertising campaigns and sponsorship programs, combined with the launch of Snapple's web site and an innovative outdoor campaign, were also key points of Snapple's marketing program.

Television advertising

Created by Deutsch N.Y. as part of a $27 million TV and radio campaign, two new commercials advertising Snapple's core fruit juice and iced-tea came on air April 1999. They both highlighted a strong product-focused message aimed at strengthening the key differentiating asset of Snapple's core products against lower-end competitors. The spots stuck to the premium and all-natural positioning of the brand and in particular emphasized the fact that Snapple was made from real juice. The ads presented the "Little Fruits" characters -- actors dressed as bananas, strawberries, lemons and other Snapple ingredients. One ad played on the idea of Snapple as a "safe home" for "at-risk" fruit. As a narrator informs the audience "At Snapple, we know the pressure facing young fruit today, and how easy it is to go bad," the ad shows some of the Little Fruits committing crimes against other fruit. These scenes are contrasted with footage of fruit playing music and playing in the grass at the safe home with narration stating "That's why . . . we've created a place where good fruit can come and get even better." This product focus was presented in a quirky, off-kilter, not too adversarial tone, as summarized in the tagline, "The Best Stuff Is in Here." The ad was honored by *Adweek* magazine as one of the best television ads of 1999.

A $30 million media budget helped to support the new campaign, including TV, radio and outdoor media. Snapple's $30 million media budget also included a new and innovative communication vehicle by which Snapple Iced Tea was advertised on beaches across the U.S in the summer of 1999 through a new process of creating impressions on the sand.

Sponsorship

In 1999, Snapple Iced Tea became the official Iced Tea of the New York Yankees, an appropriate match for the brand given Snapple's Brooklyn roots. A fully integrated marketing program enhanced the local significance and impact of this program. Apart from traditional vending and signage, the newly-launched Sun-Tea and Diet Sun-Tea brands were specially promoted, commercials were aired during the games and a donation of Yankees home game tickets was organized through a charity. Triarc also signed on Tara Lipinski as a Snapple spokesperson, promoting the sponsorship with a humorous ad spoofing the association.

Web site

Snapple launched its own web site in May 1999. Designed by SF Interactive, the site was intended to be an active part of Snapple's integrated marketing program. It provided an innovative vehicle to support on-going promotion programs, as well as to relive Snapple's advertising campaign or to unveil novelties. The tone of the web site was designed to fit Snapple's brand character, enhancing the humorous side of the brand image and leveraging the graphic look and feel of Snapple equities.

Following these new marketing measures, sales of Snapple cases rose 14 percent during the second quarter of 1999. Snapple continued to be the leading brand in the "New Age" beverage category, which grew by 15 percent in 1999, with volume growth of six percent for the year. Snapple's performance in 2000 surpassed its strong growth from 1999. For the year, Snapple maintained a 40 percent share of supermarket alternative beverage sale.

Snapple introduced its first brand extension in July 2000 in the form of four new candy products – Snapplets hard candy, Beans jelly beans, Fruits chewy candy, and Whirls gummies. The candies all bore the Snapple trademark, but were created and manufactured under license by Cody-Kramer Imports. During the development of these new promotions and products, Snapple's financial performance continued to improve. In the first six months of 2000, Snapple volume increased 27 percent compared with overall juice industry growth of only 11 percent. For that period, Snapple's revenues rose seven percent to $349.4 million from the same six months the previous year.

THE SALE OF SNAPPLE

Following this success, Triarc Inc. spun off the Snapple Beverage Group into its own business unit and made an initial public offering that would raise $115 million for the company. In addition to Snapple, the Snapple Beverage Group owned and marketed Triarc's other beverage brands, comprised of Mistic, Royal Crown, Diet Rite, Stewart's and

Nehi. Triarc Beverage Group CEO Michael Weinstein became the new Snapple Beverage Group CEO. On June 22, 2000 Triarc announced that its board of directors had approved the IPO and expected to complete the offering during the third quarter of 2000. The IPO never occurred, however, because Triarc found a buyer for Snapple in Cadbury Schweppes PLC.

On September 18, 2000, Cadbury announced plans to purchase Snapple Beverage Group for $1.45 billion. Triarc expected to gain $700 million from the sale. Careful to avoid making the same mistakes as Quaker Oats, Cadbury kept Snapple management intact, preserved the company's headquarters in Long Island, NY, and maintained the existing distribution system. Michael Weinstein remained as CEO of the Snapple Beverage Group, which Cadbury administered separately from its Dr. Pepper/Seven Up unit. The acquisition of the Snapple Beverage Group gave Cadbury a two percent boost in its share of the overall (carbonated and non-carbonated) refreshment beverage market.

The purchase of Snapple Beverage Group also made Cadbury a leader in non-carbonated premium New Age beverages, which according to Cadbury COO John Brock, "Put [Cadbury] in an outstanding position to compete."[2] Considering that Triarc bought Snapple from Quaker in 1997 for $300 million, its sale to Cadbury represented the final step in Snapple's turnaround in the hands of Triarc management.

NEW ADVERTISING

Snapple added some "edge" to its advertising in 2001. The company retained the "Little Fruits" characters, and cast them in ads themed around reproduction and jail. One ad showed the fruit attending a sex-education seminar where the instructor reads from "The Joys of Ripening." Footage of a lime studying a centerfold in *Peeled* (the fruit equivalent of *Playboy*), a raspberry and lemon discovered in a compromising position in a closet and a banana and strawberry locked in an embrace along the shore of a beach plays before the ad concludes, "With fruit joined together, it's a very special thing -- at Snapple." Another spot featuring a prison was titled "Where Bad Fruit Go." Also in 2001, Snapple introduced advertising based loosely on *The Wind in the Willows* for its Elements line of juices. Four offbeat animated 30-second television spots featured the characters Grumpy Gopher, Sinister Rabbit, Mr. Weasel, and Happy Squirrel interacting in their shared apartment. In one ad, the four characters evade their landlord on rent day by sneaking out via the fire escape.

In Summer 2001, Snapple introduced a new energy beverage called Venom, designed to compete with the likes of Red Bull, Coca-Cola's KMX, and Anheuser-Busch's 180. Venom contained the equivalent of one cup of coffee's caffeine dose and was flavored with a blend of citrus and juniper. Like other energy drinks, Venom was priced above $2 for a slender eight-ounce can. Venom initially received no advertising support.

In 2002, Cadbury developed a new advertising campaign to replace the "Little Fruits" spots, which had been running since 1998. The new campaign, aimed at 18-24 year-olds, features an anthropomorphized Snapple bottle in a number of real-life situations. The campaign also involved a promotion, called "What's your story?" that asked consumers to share humorous anecdotes from their lives. Winning entries were then "acted out" by animated Snapple bottles in nationally-televised commercials. These included a performance of a boy band made from dressed-up Snapple bottles, and a wild house party filled with Snapple bottle teens that comes to a halt when the parent Snapple bottles come home.

DISCUSSION QUESTIONS

1. How would you characterize Snapple's brand image and sources of brand equity? What are the strengths and weaknesses of the brand's existing personality and image?
2. Where did Quaker go wrong? What could they or should they have done differently?
3. How effective and appropriate do you think Triarc's marketing program was? What changes, if any, would you recommend Cadbury make to Snapple marketing?
4. How might Snapple's sale to Cadbury affect its equity? What are the dangers of the brand's association with a large corporation?
5. What do you think Cadbury's next moves with Snapple should be? Should the company attempt to expand or reposition Snapple?

Fig. 1: Snapple Family of Beverages

<u>Snapple</u>
Iced Tea
Juice
Diet Drinks

<u>Snapple Elements</u>
Fruit Drinks
Enhanced Water
Venom

REFERENCES

[1] This case was made possible through the cooperation of Snapple and the assistance of Michael Weinstein, Jack Belisto and Ken Gilbert. Eric Free prepared this case under the supervision of Professor Kevin Lane Keller and with research assistance from Peter Gilmore, Emmanuelle Louis Hofer, and Keith Richey.

[2] As quoted in Beverage Digest, September 18, 2000.

ACCENTURE:
REBRANDING AND REPOSITIONING A GLOBAL BRAND[1]

INTRODUCTION

Andersen Consulting was established in 1989 when the consulting practice of the accounting firm Arthur Andersen separated to form an independent business unit. Andersen Consulting faced the extremely difficult task of positioning itself in the Information Technology market space while simultaneously forging a separate identity from its accounting heritage. The business challenge was to retain the positive aspects of the brand equity developed over decades as Arthur Andersen, yet break away from the limitations associated with an accounting brand. What was notable was that before its inception, Andersen Consulting was generating almost $1 billion annually in revenue, yet wasn't well known in the information technology marketplace. And to those who did know them, they were often thought of as accountants, and not up to the task of delivering innovative technology solutions.

In order to bridge this gap, Andersen Consulting used extensive market research to create a brand and naming strategy that would establish immediate credibility in the "consulting" arena, while at the same time leveraging all of the positive aspects with the Arthur Andersen brand. Market research also helped form the strategy for successfully launching the new name and positioning.

In order to build a new identity, Andersen Consulting set a groundbreaking precedent by using sophisticated marketing strategies coupled with the professional services industry's first large-scale advertising campaign to promote its name, positioning and brand image.

Andersen Consulting's expertise in marketing and communications quickly set it apart from its consulting competitors, making a name for itself amidst a crowded competitive field ranging from hardware/software providers like IBM to strategy consulting firms like McKinsey. Over the next decade, Andersen Consulting grew from an accounting firm's offshoot into the world's largest management and technology consulting organization.

Despite this success, the relationship between Arthur Andersen and Andersen Consulting became strained over time, leading Andersen Consulting to seek its independence as a separate company from Arthur Andersen. In August 2000, following a successful arbitration against Andersen Worldwide and Arthur Andersen, Andersen Consulting was granted its independence. Now the firm faced a new challenge. As part of the ruling granting its independence, the license to use the Andersen Consulting name was to expire December 31, 2000. After spending an estimated $7 billion[2] building the Andersen Consulting brand over a decade, the company now had to find, implement and introduce to the world a new name in a matter of months. Never before had a rebranding of such scope been implemented over so short a timeframe. Moreover, this rebranding also coincided with a new positioning that reflected the organization's further growth and broadened set of capabilities. The case study that follows tells the evolution of Andersen Consulting to the newly rebranded and repositioned Accenture.

COMPANY HISTORY

In 1913, at the age of 28, Northwestern University economics professor Arthur Andersen founded the accounting firm Arthur Andersen & Co. Arthur Andersen envisioned an accounting firm that offered more than the standard certifications of corporate balance sheets. In his mind, a "thoroughly trained accountant [possessed] a sound understanding of the principles of economics, of finance and of organization."[3]

Arthur Andersen & Co. created an early version of the consulting unit when it formed the Administrative Accounting group in 1942. The Administrative Accounting practice was charged with developing accounting systems, methods and procedures for Arthur Andersen clients. In the 1950s, Arthur Andersen began offering consulting services to companies wishing to implement information systems, and renamed the unit the Administrative Services Division. Consultants from the company programmed and installed the world's first business computer for General Electric in 1954. Demand for information systems rose and by the 1970s the Administrative Services Division broadened the scope of its business beyond "the design and implementation of systems" to include "the conduct of studies to produce the information needed by management to direct the activities of its organization."[4]

By the late 1970s, Arthur Andersen's business was becoming increasingly global. A new business structure was needed to address legal, tax and competition issues in several markets. In 1977, the company created Arthur Andersen & Co. Societe Cooperative to govern the different divisions of the company, to maintain the one firm concept and to deliver seamless services across the world. This entity was later to be coined the Andersen Worldwide Organization, finally being shortened to Andersen Worldwide in 1996. In 1979, what was once the Administrative Services Division of Arthur Andersen became the Management Information Consulting Division (MICD). MICD performed a range of consulting services defined as "Information Business -- providing information to people who run things."[5]

CONSULTING TAKES OFF

The consulting business boomed in the 1980s, particularly because a national recession forced companies to rethink their strategies -- with the help of consultants -- in order to stay competitive. As a result, MICD began generating significant profits for the accounting firm. Though MICD operated as a professional services firm, it functioned as a unit of Arthur Andersen. However, an important distinction should be made, when MICD went to market, they went to market as Arthur Andersen, not as MICD. Consequently, MICD's identity was directly linked to Arthur Andersen. This link did not necessarily benefit MICD. The qualities typically associated with accounting firms, such as risk-aversion and conservatism, did not match the traits essential for a consulting organization -- innovative, creative, dynamic and strategic. As a result, Arthur Andersen's MICD division suffered low visibility and suffered from the perception it was not perceived to be a major player in the consulting market. A 1982 recruiting image study conducted by Decision Research advised MICD that its recruiting efforts "must convince recruits that the Consulting Division is not primarily an accounting function." A 1984 study by Decision Research concluded that MICD's "image among non-clients [was] undifferentiated from the remainder of the Big 8."[6]

Image Initiative

To respond to this image crisis, MICD decided to embark on an "Image Initiative" in 1987 to generate awareness and to differentiate itself in the information technology services market space, as well as to distance itself from its accountancy heritage image. A critical component of the Image Initiative was the selection of a new name for MICD. For the renaming project, MICD enlisted the advice of select senior Partners who provided strategic direction and name recommendations. MICD also secured the strategic and brand counsel from the advertising agency Young & Rubicam. To help devise a naming strategy, research was conducted among Fortune 500 senior executives and confirmed "that the audit and tax heritage of Arthur Andersen hamper[ed] the competitiveness of the MICD practice."[7] The research revealed that although the link to Arthur Andersen provided credibility for MICD, many consulting buyers had reservations about employing a unit of an accounting firm that they viewed as "stodgy," "inflexible" and "old-fashioned."

The strategy and development of a new name sparked spirited internal debate among the partnership, as there were divergent views on brand equity and its impact on future business opportunities. Basically there were three modes of thought. Those who thought MICD should completely distance itself from its heritage with a distinct and new name. A name such as "Systems Technology Group" appealed to this group. A second group thought it best to borrow equity from Arthur Andersen, yet create a distinct position in the market space. Advocates of this strategy preferred names such as "The Andersen Consulting Group" or "Andersen Consulting." Finally, others preferred a complete alignment with Arthur Andersen in a name choice, preferring name choices with Arthur Andersen as the cornerstone of the new name.

In the end, relying on the benefits of sound market research, and the counsel of its marketing advisors, MICD chose the succinct "Andersen Consulting" name -- thus providing separation from Arthur Andersen while at the same time benefiting from its equity. The name also created a clear positioning in the market space with the "consulting" descriptor. When the logo appeared in print, "Andersen Consulting" was followed by the subscript tagline "Arthur Andersen & Co., S.C;" thus the firm retained a link to Arthur Andersen. The association with Arthur Andersen lent credibility and name-recognition to the firm at first, but became a liability as Andersen Consulting encountered greater competition in the consulting market. An article in *The Economist* noted, "The 'safety-first' image so vital to accountancy began to hurt the consulting business, which competed in a market where a reputation for innovation was the key to success."[8]

EMERGENCE OF ANDERSEN CONSULTING

The consulting business experienced tremendous growth in the 1980s, ballooning to an estimated $30 billion annual business globally in 1990 from just $3 billion in 1980. While a U.S. recession in the 1980s had driven growth, a similar recession in the early 1990s was not as beneficial to consulting firms. The latter downturn affected consulting firms more severely than the companies they counted on for revenue, partly because the business climate of the previous decade had fostered corporate distrust of consultancies. Additionally, corporations wanted changes implemented, not merely suggested, and not every consulting firm was able to execute the strategy it recommended. Numerous consulting firms posted losses for the first time in years, and many were forced to heed their own advice and downsize. Bain Consulting layed off 17 percent of its staff in 1990, KPMG Peat Marwick cut back on the number of consulting partners in the firm during 1991. Andersen Consulting grew, however, even as the consulting industry faltered. In 1991, the company's revenues rose 20 percent to $2.26 billion. Andersen Consulting's revenues grew by 19 percent to $2.7 billion in 1992, a year when the IT consultancy segment grew by under seven percent.

Systems Integration
Andersen Consulting rode the wave of this consulting boom, and during its first few years as a separate business unit, Andersen Consulting emerged as one of the premier IT consultancies. In addition to offering standard business consulting, Andersen Consulting offered a range of IT services, from designing complex computer networks that integrated a company's databases to developing and installing financial trading systems. The IT business yielded high profit margins, which in turn fueled Andersen Consulting's accelerated growth. The company's systems integration capabilities were responsible for much of this growth. Systems integration refers to defining, designing, building and implementing complex packaged application or custom technology-based business solutions required to support critical enterprise operations.

Systems integration represented the latest trend in the larger category of Information Technology Services. Andersen Consulting focused on providing systems integration services to a wide range of key industries, including products, financial services, communications, government, health care and utilities among others.

The company also found success with traditional outsourcing avenues as well. In July 1990, Andersen Consulting opened a data processing center. Soon, Andersen Consulting established a strong presence in the outsourcing market, posting strong increases on an annual basis.

ROLE OF MARKETING
The newly formed Andersen Consulting set a new standard for marketing a professional services company. Andersen Consulting is widely credited as being the first professional services firm to advertise aggressively. As Jim Murphy, Global Managing Director of Marketing & Communications said, "In 1989, Andersen Consulting not only created a new management and technology organization, but also created with the help of our communications agency Young & Rubicam, a new advertising category for professional services." The professional services category historically had formal rules that prevented advertising, but by 1989 this restriction was no longer in place. Still, most professional services firms chose not to advertise feeling it was inappropriate or unprofessional. In 1989, in a bold and unprecedented step, in 1989 the firm began marketing itself as an organization that helped companies apply technology to create business advantage. The marketing and communications campaign was devised to create awareness of the brand and to communicate a leadership position for Andersen Consulting in the marketplace. A small group of partners knew that marketing activities would be invaluable in Andersen Consulting's quest to forge an independent identity. Teresa Poggenpohl, Partner and Director of Global Advertising and Brand Management, explained that the group of partners

"understood marketing in a strategic sense and had the courage to create the brand and invest in it" at a time when branding was not a priority for professional services firms.

Breakthrough Approaches

The brand was officially launched with a New Year's campaign featuring a television commercial that stressed Andersen Consulting's technology expertise, positioning them as a leader in empowering organizations and individuals to effectively apply technology to their business advantage. The commercial also demonstrated the differentiation that Andersen Consulting sought by its clever tone and manner, thus personifying the organization as creative, driven, far-sighted and innovative. As the camera panned a computer-animated cityscape where the 2000 New Year was being counted down, a voiceover intoned:

> One night, not too many years from now, some companies will have cause for celebration. They'll be the ones who used information and technology not merely as a way to compute, but as a way to compete. Andersen Consulting would like to help you be one of them.

The campaign also featured print advertising to complement the broadcast commercials. One such print ad entitled "Map" consisted of a completely reconfigured map of the United States, with the headline "Sometimes success requires a little reorganization." The copy offered information technology as a means of overcoming the restrictions or limitations of geography. Andersen Consulting spent approximately $5 million in advertising during its first year, which at the time was a full 50 percent of all media expenditures for the entire consulting category. This level of expenditure, combined with the use of flighted media schedules (alternating periods of high advertising activity with inactivity to create the illusion of a more ambitious advertising program), was highly unorthodox within the consulting industry. The vast majority of consulting companies favored business relationships, trade shows and credentials brochures to image advertising.

Andersen Consulting's break with tradition had been the subject of an internal debate, with many partners opposing what they regarded as a costly risk. Once the marketing program was in place, however, it turned out to be instrumental in Andersen Consulting's early success. Teresa Poggenpohl, Partner and Director of Global Advertising and Brand Management, credited the early image work with being "the catalyst to get senior executive registration of the Andersen Consulting brand, serving as a critical door opener for partners and business development."[9] Complementing its extensive advertising program, the firm also initiated an aggressive and targeted media relations program. A team of media specialists within Andersen Consulting partnered with Burson-Marsteller, a leading public relations firm to influence industry analysts, leading industry publications and the tier-one business press to position Andersen Consulting as a thought leader in the market space, and to increase awareness among its target audience to support its brand building activities.

Metrics to Drive Performance

From the beginning, Andersen Consulting sought consistency in its marketing activities. The firm's commitment to advertising exceeded other consulting firms in terms of annual investment, and this ad spending drove awareness of the brand. By supplementing the topline advertising with media and analyst relations, thought leadership publications and other image development activities, Andersen Consulting maintained a consistent and integrated marketing program well in advance of competing firms. Andersen Consulting measured the effects of this advertising with annual tracking studies and regular measures of the senior executive target audience's perceptions of the brand. Market research was critical in obtaining valuable input from its key target audience, while also measuring the success of its initiatives.

The partners continually demanded proof that the results of the advertising warranted the expenditures. Since the advertising investment was drawn directly from the partners' potential profits, they needed assurance that their money was well spent. This led to the development of efficient and effective marketing techniques as well as metrics to gauge the effectiveness of the marketing.

From its inception, Andersen Consulting conducted extensive market research focusing on five factors: (1) marketplace awareness -- the measure of brand awareness in each of the major countries across brand attributes, personality traits and service offerings; (2) client satisfaction -- the measure of Andersen Consulting's performance with its global client base; (3) buyer values -- the measure of the key values of its global target audience to understand and stay ahead of market trends; (4) advertising copy testing -- the pre and post testing measuring the effectiveness of all print, poster and television advertising concepts and (5) media monitoring -- the measure of the number and type of media hits in the leading business and industry press. In 1988, Andersen Consulting initiated a tracking study of market awareness of its name. At that time, on an unaided basis only six percent of respondents nationally knew of Andersen Consulting as a systems integration consultancy, a number that would climb to 37 percent globally in five years (see Figs. 2-4). For comparison, IBM had a 90 percent awareness in the same arena. The firm also conducted annual surveys of its senior executive target audience and tested for advertising effectiveness. Teresa Poggenpohl, Partner and Director of Global Advertising and Brand Management said, "Research is critical to all of our programs. Research and insights evolve our strategy, some enable people to react to our creative, others to measure how we're doing in terms of driving awareness and perception gains in the marketplace."[10]

Global Reach

In 1992, Andersen Consulting spent approximately $10 million globally on advertising. That same year, the firm implemented an integrated marketing model, thus integrating its marketing and communications strategies on a global scale. The program involved three different but related areas of focus: image development, market development and business development. Image development entailed research, positioning, advertising, communications, media/industry analyst relations, events and other activities that strengthened the firm's personality and global brand. Market development involved database marketing, business development centers, market research and other activities that provided an industry market focus, defined best clients and articulated what the firm could offer these clients. For example, in order to facilitate development of new ideas to help clients, the firm established a number of Business Integration Centers, Technology Centers and Solution Centers around the world. According to Jim Murphy, Global Managing Director of Marketing & Communications, these centers "not only . . . fostered innovation for Andersen Consulting, they also built and solidified relationships and enhanced the firm's brand and positioning in the marketplace."[11]   The final aspect of Andersen Consulting's integrated marketing program -- business development -- involved market management, client management, relationship selling and opportunity management.   All aspects of the model were supported by marketplace research to gain marketplace insight as well as to measure communications effectiveness.

The Changing Marketplace

A significant portion of Andersen Consulting's annual revenue came from its systems integration business. Still, Andersen Consulting executives foresaw further growth beyond computer networking projects. The company wished not only to grow into other consulting disciplines, such as corporate strategy, but also sought to bundle their diverse services together and become "the world's first and foremost full-service consulting emporium."[12] The use of this combination of services to improve a company's operations was known as "business integration."

Andersen Consulting exhibited its business integration expertise during a consulting engagement with the U.S. pharmaceuticals company Merck.   Merck enlisted Andersen Consulting in 1991 to help it market medicines manufactured by the Swedish drug company Astra, makers of the anti-ulcer medication Prilosec. A team of Merck employees and Andersen Consulting consultants created a marketing department made of 31 decentralized business units.   Andersen Consulting designed and installed a computer network that enabled salespeople from every unit to exchange information with every other unit. Astra Merck's marketing department achieved almost immediate success, as sales of Prilosec grew 50 percent in the first nine months of 1993 and revenues for the year topped $600 million. Though Andersen Consulting was first brought in for a one-time IT consulting engagement at Astra Merck, by 1993 the pharmaceutical company "consider[ed] the consultancy a strategic partner and credit[ed] Andersen Consulting with molding much of Astra Merck's business plan."[13] Astra Merck CEO Wayne Yetter explained the partnership: "I started this [relationship] as an IT project, but you can't really separate IT from strategy, people and business processes."[14] Andersen Consulting's managing partner at the time, George Shaheen, defined business integration as:

> There is no such thing as an IT project. There is only a business project with an IT content. Certainly IT was . . . key in transforming [the organization]. But success came from using the technology to link the strategy with the operations and the people to obtain real business advantage.[15]

Shaheen added in another interview:

> I think we've been able to proceed expeditiously because for years we realized that experience in and around the business side of the equation is very important along with the technology side.[16]

Capitalizing on Business Integration

As the marketplace continued to change, Andersen Consulting anticipated and moved with it, taking a major step in global branding by developing a globally integrated

261

advertising program in 1994. Prior to that year, Andersen Consulting advertising either originated in the U.S. for export to different international markets, or select markets were responsible for creating their own advertising campaigns. As the firm's business focus became more global, Andersen Consulting began developing an advertising program that projected globally consistent images and messages across all mediums and was powerful in all local markets. The firm conducted rigorous focus group testing in the U.S., Europe, Japan and Australia to determine which ad concepts would help Andersen Consulting achieve the desired image, positioning and messaging. Due to this diligent research approach, many advertisements earned the company and its advertising agency, Young & Rubicam many awards over the years, including *The Wall Street Journal* top scoring advertising award, the *Business Week* Award for Excellence in Corporate Advertising and the Forbes Advertising Excellence Best in Category award.

To allow for maximum transferability across cultural boundaries, much of Andersen Consulting's advertising was metaphor-based. One such metaphorical based ad was called "Shark." In this advertisement, a school of fish swam in hazardous, predator-laden waters. As the fish swam, they collectively formed together in the image of a shark. The unspoken message emphasized the power that a skillful, team-oriented organization can yield. Most importantly, the ad conveyed that different parts of an organization must be linked and properly aligned to achieve business success.

For efficiency and to ensure a highly targeted strategy for its global campaign, Andersen Consulting sought advertising paths that targeted key prospects and clients where they lived and worked, targeting business publications and business and news television programming. A classic example of Andersen Consulting's effective and efficient advertising was the company's development of airport billboard advertising. Andersen Consulting was the first consulting company to embrace airports as a marketing opportunity in the mid-1990s, and, as such, its message stood out, placing billboard style advertisements in prominent, high-traffic areas near airline executive lounges in over 30 airports worldwide. The airport advertising strategy complemented traditional print and television advertising, surrounding a captive audience of key prospects and clients where they lived and worked.

The firm's advertising appeared in 18 countries in 1994, up from just five the previous year. Also in 1994, another significant development for Andersen Consulting was their international sports sponsorships strategy, becoming a sponsor for the Williams Formula One racing team. In 1994 they also became the title sponsor of the then titled Andersen Consulting World Championship of Golf. This event evolved into its present day form being one leg of the World Golf Championships entitled the Accenture Match Play Championship.

Measurable Results

In just half a decade, Andersen Consulting's marketing and communications program achieved noticeable results. Awareness had increased by 75 percent in approximately three years in Europe, with the United States increasing its awareness from six percent to 50 percent. Additionally, between 1990 and 1993, total global awareness of Andersen Consulting grew from 32 percent to 79 percent. Awareness levels for the firm as a business reengineering services provider increased from 26 percent in 1993 to 43 percent in 1997. A study conducted in 1997 by industry analyst IDC found that Andersen Consulting and IBM enjoyed the greatest familiarity among technology buyers. The study also ranked Andersen Consulting together with IBM as the two IT consulting firms with the strongest set of attributes.

Clearly, Andersen Consulting's status as an IT leader was a source of equity that aided the company in its growth during the early 1990s. Other associations for clients and prospects included "creative and innovative in developing applications," "visionary" and "leader." Thus, the firm was known not only for its technological capabilities, but also for its strategy consulting. In little over half a decade, with the help of effective advertising and a proven record for results, Andersen Consulting had earned a reputation as one of the premier consultancies in the world. By 1998, Andersen Consulting was the market leader in four major categories in consumer rankings of consulting firms: 1) management and technology consulting, 2) operational strategy consulting, 3) systems integration and 4) business reengineering.[17]

CONFLICTS WITH ARTHUR ANDERSEN

As Andersen Consulting continued to prosper, Arthur Andersen was also changing as an organization. A 1990 agreement allowed the accounting unit of the parent company Andersen Worldwide to establish a non-computer consulting practice for businesses with annual revenue under $175 million. The consultants and accountants agreed that each company would provide "separate, complementary services with minimal overlap"[18] in order to limit competitive crossover. As Arthur Andersen expanded its business capabilities over the next several years to include consulting services similar to those offered by Andersen Consulting, the distinction between the two companies was further eroded. This overlap was creating confusion in the marketplace.

Exploring Marketplace Confusion

Over time, Arthur Andersen also began using marketing as a tool to build business. Thus, in 1993, Andersen Consulting hired the OmniTech Consulting Group to research client and potential client perceptions of the confusing relationship between Arthur Andersen and Andersen Consulting. OmniTech concluded that by developing a willfully ambiguous advertising campaign, Arthur Andersen was attempting to leverage Andersen Consulting's brand image. A different study, also conducted by OmniTech, discovered that respondents were capable of differentiating the two brands to a satisfactory extent until Arthur Andersen advertisements were introduced to the group, at which point the differentiation lessened. Ultimately, OmniTech concluded "despite the favorable brand identity for Andersen Consulting, brand confusion is a major and growing issue for Andersen Consulting."[19]

Since this confusion resulted in loss of potential clients, and could therefore damage Andersen Consulting's business, the firm kept a close watch on the issue after the OmniTech report. A domestic awareness tracking study from 1994 reported that 41 percent of senior-level executive respondents and 81 percent of CEOs surveyed expressed confusion about the relationship between Arthur Andersen and Andersen Consulting.

Arthur Andersen Business Consulting

Arthur Andersen combined several practices within the firm to create Arthur Andersen Business Consulting in 1994. In compliance with the Securities and Exchange Commision's auditor-independence rules, Arthur Andersen stated in its SEC filing that its consulting practice "does not perform, or hold itself out as performing, systems integration consulting services, which account for the bulk of Andersen Consulting's business."[20] Soon after its formation, however, Arthur Andersen Business Consulting began targeting companies above the $175 million ceiling and offering computer-systems consulting. A memo from an Arthur Andersen partner stated, "With business consulting, we'll have the ability to sustain our commitment to segments of the middle market -- under $200 million and over -- and parts of the larger global market."[21]

A research report from the Gartner Group remarked, "If this expansion of services by AA continues, we could see these two organizations becoming direct competitors. This would confuse clients and the market."[22] Adding to the confusion was the fact that the media at times referred to both Arthur Andersen Business Consulting and Andersen Consulting as "Arthur Andersen Consulting." Mistakes such as these were made in such major publications such as *The Wall Street Journal* and *Dow Jones News*, as well as in Associated Press articles.

In a 1994 study commissioned by Andersen Worldwide, the research firm Decision Research concluded that the relationship between Arthur Andersen and Andersen Consulting was "unclear to most buyers, even clients of the firm." A similar study conducted by Landor Associates found "that the existing degree of linkage between the two business units is confused and/or not well understood in the marketplace." Arthur Andersen commissioned a Global Reputation Study, which reported that Andersen Consulting enjoyed a stronger image than Arthur Andersen, and consequently Arthur Andersen benefited from confusion with Andersen Consulting. Further proof of this benefit to Arthur Andersen was evidenced by awareness tracking studies from 1994 and 1995 (see Fig. 6). Not only did awareness levels for Arthur Andersen move consistently with Andersen Consulting levels, but also the accounting unit enjoyed relatively high levels of awareness for service categories in which the firm had little market presence compared to Andersen Consulting. For example, Arthur Andersen achieved a high awareness score in the "strategy consulting" category despite the fact that the company had almost no corporate strategy practice. Analysts attributed Arthur Andersen's elevated reputation in this category to confusion with Andersen Consulting. Arthur Andersen's managing partner at the time, Dick Measelle, agreed that his company benefited from the confusion when discussing an Andersen Consulting ad in a 1994 interview:

> If you ask 100 people, "Whose ad that was, who sponsored the golf tournament?" about 40 percent of them would say "Arthur Andersen." The point is that we benefit from the market image that they have.[23]

A troublesome problem resulting from the confusion was the potential loss of brand equity for Andersen Consulting. If potential clients mistakenly thought Arthur Andersen managed Andersen Consulting, then they would be likely to attribute qualities of one business unit to the other. This meant that in many cases, Andersen Consulting was taking on associations resulting from customer experiences with Arthur Andersen, and vice versa. As noted above, the association with an accounting firm was not beneficial for Andersen Consulting. Conversely, given the amount of time and money Andersen

Consulting spent building its brand into a premier global consulting firm, the association with Andersen Consulting aided the brand equity of Arthur Andersen Business Consulting (which was in some areas a competitor of Andersen Consulting).

CAPITALIZING ON SUCCESS

The mid-1990s was a time of great success for Andersen Consulting. From 1994 to 1997, consumer perceptions of Andersen Consulting improved considerably. The percentage of survey respondents that agreed with a characterization of Andersen Consulting as "visionary" increased from 39 percent in 1994 to 54 percent in 1997. The percentage that agreed that the firm was "creative" grew from 44 percent in 1994 to 58 percent in 1997 and the percentage of respondents who considered the firm a "leader" rose from 48 percent in 1994 to 68 percent in 1997. The firm's client retention percentage rose from 55 percent to 70 percent between 1993 and 1997 (see Fig. 5). Andersen Consulting reaped financial successes as well. From 1993 to 1998, the firm's billings grew an average of 20 percent annually, reaching $8.2 billion in 1998. The firm's revenues continued to grow until they topped $11 billion in 2001.

The positioning of Andersen Consulting's print and television advertising evolved slightly over time, but the personality of the ads still relied on a clever tone and manner, using a central metaphoric image that suggested a problem businesses often faced, which was reinforced by a question underneath. For example, one advertisement contained a picture of an elephant crossing a precipitous drop by walking on a log placed over the gap. The question: "Who says you can't be big and nimble?" The ad copy explains that Andersen Consulting possesses the skills to help a "massive, far-flung organization . . . have the balance of a small one."

"A-to-the-Power-of-C" Rebranding

In an effort to evolve and stay ahead of the marketplace, an 18-month comprehensive review of the company was undertaken in 1998. The review included a global audit of current practices, a competitive analysis and client surveys. This analysis produced a revised positioning to reflect the move to an eCommerce business environment. Andersen Consulting also sought to extend and strengthen its brand image by updating the corporate logo. Previously, the company had removed the "Arthur Andersen & Co., S.C." tagline from its name and all related materials to emphasize the distinction and separation from Arthur Andersen. Now, the firm wished to overhaul its logo to reflect its new brand positioning and further distance it from Arthur Andersen in look and feel. The new logo used the initials "AC" in a unique way, with a lower-case "c" resting above and to the right of the upper-case "A." This graphic identity was drawn from the exponential notation in mathematics, so the logo communicated "A" raised to the "c" power. In television spots, the logo would be illuminated by animated beams of light. This lighting effect was intended to symbolically communicate Andersen Consulting's "energy and vision."[24] To convey the lighting effect in print advertising, the letters appeared in either white or silver. Other aspects of the revised branding and logo included the concept of a "foundation line," which represented a firm business foundation and stability in a changing world, a 24-color palette demonstrating their range of capabilities for diverse application across all marketing and communications materials and a new musical "aural signature" for use in television, video and multimedia applications.

To inform its global audience of its new image, Andersen Consulting committed to expanding and strengthening its global marketing efforts. Midway through 1998, (and continuing over the next two years) Andersen Consulting boosted its global marketing and communications commitment significantly, two-thirds of which was slated for use outside the U.S. The campaign included print and airport poster advertising in 30 countries, with the more expensive television advertising appearing in the major global markets. Half of the budget went towards corporate sponsorships, which included events such as a Van Gogh exhibit in Washington D.C. during the fall of 1998, the 1998 Andersen Consulting Match Play Championship and Formula One auto racing.

In 1999 Andersen Consulting announced a new $44 million advertising campaign aimed at further differentiating the firm from its competitors. The general theme of the print, TV, Internet and airport poster campaign advertised Andersen Consulting's business integration approach, with particular emphasis on unleashing an organization's full potential, also reflecting the move into the eCommerce environment. In a digitally animated television spot developed for the campaign by Young & Rubicam, the constellations Sagittarius, Hercules and Taurus joined forces to harness the moon as a voice-over intoned, "Every organization has many stars. But Andersen Consulting can help you integrate all your diverse talents. So that when you reach for the moon, you might actually get it." An ad appearing in print during 1999 exhibited an letter "e" carved out of ice melting in the middle of a desert. The ad asked the viewer, "Is your eCommerce strategy built to last?" and explained that Andersen Consulting had the expertise to help businesses succeed in e-commerce.

SPLITTING FROM ARTHUR ANDERSEN

In mid-December 1997, Andersen Consulting sought to split from Arthur Andersen. Citing "breaches of contract and irreconcilable differences," Andersen Consulting filed arbitration with the International Court of Arbitration in Paris that would force the two business units to formally separate.

At issue were the annual payments Andersen Consulting had to yield to Arthur Andersen under the terms of their 1989 agreement and the expansion by Arthur Andersen as a direct competitor into information-technology consulting. When the two firms split in 1989, they agreed that the more profitable of the two would pay the other a portion of annual profits no greater than 15 percent. As the more profitable company, Andersen Consulting transferred over $450 million to Arthur Andersen from 1989 to 1997, with payments for 1997 totaling $173 million. By 1996, Arthur Andersen Business Consulting was offering a range of IT services and directly competing with Andersen Consulting for clients. That year, Arthur Andersen's chief executive Richard Measelle expressed his firm's intention of working with clients with sales of up to $2 billion, well above the $175 million limit established after the 1989 separation agreement. Measelle also declared technology would be a "core competency" of the company, and later restated Arthur Andersen's core objectives:

> To pursue unconstrained growth; to provide consulting services, either directly or indirectly to all markets and to have the technology we need to compete.[25]

After several failed attempts by parent company Andersen Worldwide to reconcile the differences between the two competing business units, Andersen Consulting filed arbitration seeking official separation from Arthur Andersen. Arthur Andersen was willing to part with Andersen Consulting if the consulting firm paid upwards of $14 billion in compensation for use of the Andersen name and use of technology developed by the accounting group. Andersen Consulting countered by demanding return of the transfer payments and seeking damages for Arthur Andersen's negative effect on the consulting firm's brand equity.

REPOSITIONING ANDERSEN CONSULTING

Measuring Brand Equity

As the arbitration process advanced, Andersen Consulting developed plans to reposition itself. Andersen Consulting had distinguished itself from its competition over the last several years, and the firm wished to capitalize on this momentum with a new brand positioning. To evaluate the value of the Andersen Consulting brand, the company undertook a brand equity measurement study. The study focused on numerous aspects of Andersen Consulting's brand equity: corporate image and awareness, personality traits and perceived capabilities, plus client consideration and preference. Using data collected by the research firm BPRI, the study compared public perceptions of Andersen Consulting with four competitors: IBM, Ernst & Young, McKinsey and EDS. In terms of perceived capabilities, McKinsey emerged as the foremost business strategy services company while IBM led the IT services segment. Andersen Consulting however had a strong position in "both" business strategy and Information Technology services which enabled it to post very strong consideration scores, and ultimately lead on brand equity. An overall brand equity model was applied to rank the companies by assigning each company a score in each of four categories (image, awareness, consideration, preference) and averaging the scores. Andersen Consulting staked out a leadership position, achieving the highest score on the brand equity scale (see Fig. 1).

A different study conducted by Harris Research ranked U.S. consulting firms using a different set of competitors. Compared with McKinsey, Booz Allen, BCG, and A.T. Kearney, Andersen Consulting ranked first in the following categories: share of mind, value for money, uniqueness and momentum. Based on a 1998 survey of 500 executives conducted by Landor, Andersen Consulting ranked as the 14th strongest brand in the U.S., ahead of Holiday Inn, Kodak and Citibank.

The study revealed that not only did Andersen Consulting possess favorable qualities and attributes that combined to provide strong overall brand equity, but also the company occupied a unique position in that it offered valued strategic business services *and* well-regarded IT solutions. Based on results from both studies, Andersen Consulting leadership concluded that the company was "the company that combines strategic insight, vision and thought leadership with IT expertise in developing client solutions."[26] This unique combination of skills enabled Andersen Consulting to establish points of parity with both technology and strategy firms, while at the same time achieving points of difference. For example, Andersen Consulting's technology capabilities were a point of parity that enabled the firm to compete for clients with IBM. Since clients viewed IBM as a technology consultant and not a business strategist, Andersen Consulting's reputation for insight and vision constituted a point of difference.

Developing a New Positioning

Over the years, Andersen Consulting had evolved its positioning to better meet the needs of its clients and marketplace opportunity (see Fig. 9). In this sense, Andersen Consulting fostered a fluid and evolving positioning. This evolutionary model came not just from the demands of the marketplace. According to Jim Murphy, Andersen Consulting's Global Managing Director of Marketing & Communications, the business leadership of Andersen Consulting was "historically uneasy with the status quo. There is a hunger for pushing the next horizon."[27]

In the months before the arbitration decision, Andersen Consulting was developing a new positioning that sought to formalize its position as a leader in the new economy. To distinguish Andersen Consulting from its competition, the firm developed a positioning platform that captured the company's vision and strategy -- positioning Accenture as a bridge builder helping companies bridge the gap from the old economy to the new. It also positioned the company as one who helped companies transform trends into business opportunities using its deep global knowledge, its unique vantage point and its breadth and depth of resources and relationships. Behind this idea of partnering with clients was Andersen Consulting's vision statement: "To help our clients create their future."

In July 2000, the firm tested its new positioning with employees, partners, clients, potential clients, dot-coms and recruits in key markets worldwide. The response was very positive, and the company forged ahead with the repositioning. [28]

Underpinning this positioning was the company's vision "to become one of the world's leading companies, bringing innovations to improve the way the world works and lives."[29] Andersen Consulting executives saw the firm as a leader in the new economy capable of creating value for companies in innovative ways, of broadening the accepted definition of a consulting firm. The firm's new positioning was intended to capture that essence. This change in business strategy was realized through extensive market research with senior executives coupled with input from a team of brand experts.

Andersen Consulting's new positioning included four attributes: agile, visionary, well-connected and passionate. From the point of view of Andersen Consulting, agility referred to the ability to move quickly and in synch the with rapid pace of business in the New Economy. This trait was exemplified by the firm's speed to value strategy in which Andersen Consulting helped companies deliver business ideas to the marketplace faster. The firm's reputation for strategic and innovative thinking contributed to the development of the visionary trait. To encourage its people to promote strategic thinking and thought leadership on current business issues and trends, Andersen Consulting published *Outlook* magazine and frequently contributed to other magazines, such as *Chief Executive*. Andersen Consulting also sponsored the Andersen Consulting Customer Contact Forum for the telecommunications industry, The International Utilities & Energy Conference and was an active participant in the World Economic Forum. Andersen Consulting was well-connected due to its global reach and its vast network of partners and proprietary businesses. Finally, a passion for helping companies succeed had long been a cornerstone of Andersen Consulting's mission.

Target Markets
One key difference of the new positioning was Andersen Consulting's new focus on serving two markets, "Today's most important businesses as well as tomorrow's aspiring leaders."[30] Demonstrating this unique two-fold approach was the fact that as of 2000, Andersen Consulting worked with 91 of *Fortune* magazine's 1999 Global 100 companies, as well as over half of the *The Industry Standard*'s 100 most important companies of the Internet economy. For example, Andersen Consulting helped Motorola employees self-manage their human resources processes and transactions through Enet, an intranet-based virtual HR system that was integrated with Motorola's back-end HR system.

Emerging technology companies, such as ETrade, represented "aspiring leaders" whose business Andersen Consulting sought. To attract future e-commerce leaders, in fiscal 1999 Andersen Consulting developed 25 Business Launch Centres across the globe that offered "everything you need to speed from startup to initial public offering." The Launch Centres possessed a variety of capabilities, including business model strategizing, organizational structuring, marketing, web site construction and post-launch support such as operations scaling.

A Network of Businesses
Strengthening Andersen Consulting's new positioning was the recent shift in the company's strategy toward a "network of businesses."[31] This strategy enhanced Andersen Consulting's ability to deliver fully integrated and innovative solutions to its clients. The idea was to use its network of businesses approach to strengthen its core consulting and outsourcing expertise through alliances, affiliated companies and other capabilities.

Andersen Consulting's capability as a strategic partner was exemplified by the creation of an affiliated company with Microsoft called Avanade, formed in March 2000. Avanade was designed to help companies integrate Microsoft technology, particularly Windows 2000 software. Andersen Consulting provided roughly three-quarters of the initial 1,000-member Avanade employee base, which was trained with the skills necessary to understand and implement new Microsoft technology.

OFFICIAL SEPARATION FROM ARTHUR ANDERSEN

Arbitrator's Ruling
On August 7, 2000, the arbitration ruling from Columbian lawyer Dr. Guillermo Gamba released Andersen Consulting from any further obligation to Arthur Andersen or Andersen Worldwide -- financial, professional or otherwise. Although the arbitrator's decision required Andersen Consulting to forfeit the annual transfer payments the firm had placed in escrow since 1997 (totaling $530 million) in addition to the $300 million transfer payment for fiscal 1999, this payment was significantly less than the $14.5 billion asked for by the accounting firm. In justifying his decision to award separation to Andersen Consulting, Gamba faulted Andersen Worldwide for improperly supervising the two units since their separation in 1989. Gamba stated in an interview after the ruling:

Andersen Consulting was right in my opinion when they claimed that [Andersen Worldwide] was not performing its coordinating obligations. That's the reason the decision favored Andersen Consulting.[32]

In return for its independence, Andersen Consulting did have to make one concession. The license to use the Andersen Consulting name was to expire December 31, 2000. Actually, the organization had begun to explore changing their name in advance of the arbitration decision. Many in the leadership team felt the label "consulting" was somewhat limiting to the future role of Andersen Consulting as an organization. Nonetheless, the challenges would be numerous: Andersen Consulting had to quickly create a new name, effectively transfer equity of the old name to the new one, raise awareness of the new name globally, decisively eliminate confusion between itself and Arthur Andersen and reposition the firm in the marketplace to reflect its new vision and strategy. Never in history had such a large scale rebranding occurred in such a short time frame (see Fig. 8). Within 147 days of the ruling, the company had to unveil a name that was trademarkable in 47 countries, effective and inoffensive in over 200 languages, corresponded with an available URL and was acceptable to employees and clients.

THE REBRANDING AND REPOSITIONING PROCESS

Though the execution of the rebranding and repositioning process was a daunting task, Andersen Consulting executives embraced the opportunity to create a new image for their company. Joe Forehand, Managing Partner of CEO of Andersen Consulting, explained in a press release:

> We are a very different organization today than we were when we formed Andersen Consulting back in 1989, so adopting a new name and brand identity is a logical next step in our growth strategy.[33]

Andersen Consulting was well-prepared for a rebranding project of such scope because, just two years prior, the business had overhauled its visual identity as part of the "A-to-the-power-of-C" rebranding. In looking back, Jim Murphy referred to the 1999 rebranding as in some ways being "a rehearsal of a global brand change."

To carry out the global rebranding and repositioning, Andersen Consulting supplemented its annual $75 million marketing & communications budget with an additional $100 million. To create interest around the effort, Andersen Consulting tapped the advertising agency Young & Rubicam to develop a teaser advertising campaign in support of the rebranding and repositioning effort. The homepage of the corporate web site was also updated to reflect the upcoming rebranding and repositioning effort. The ads and corporate web site featured a graphic of a partially "torn" Andersen Consulting logo which revealed the message: "Renamed. Redefined. Reborn. 01.01.01." The firm also developed a series of teaser television advertisements that the company introduced during the Sydney Olympics, which took place in September 2000.

Positioning

In advance of the name change in order to meet changing marketplace demands, Andersen Consulting had completed rigorous testing to develop a new strategic positioning. Once Andersen Consulting determined its new positioning, all that remained was finding a name that reflected the positioning. Teresa Poggenpohl, stated, "The timing [was] excellent because we had just spent several months developing a new brand positioning that support[ed] the firm's new business strategy and vision."[34]

Andersen Consulting had a strong reputation from which to launch the new brand. James Murphy, felt that the target audience and general public would readily adopt the new name. "It's not like we don't have the credentials," said Murphy. "Now, we want to transfer the equity that we have built into that name and brand it to a new name."[35] The short amount of time Andersen Consulting had in which to execute the change was, in the minds of many inside the firm, the major challenge.

Finding a New Name

Led by Andersen Consulting's marketing and communications department, the search for a new name began immediately following the arbitrator's ruling. With the help of outside branding experts, Landor Associates, as well as through an internal Andersen Consulting name-generation initiative dubbed "Brandstorming," thousands of name candidates were generated.

From these names, 550 candidates were selected to undergo research based on specific criteria: how well the name fit with the organization's strategy, how distinctive or unique it was and the name's potential for longevity. The research entailed a preliminary round of trademark and URL availability research in the United States, where the majority of the company's business was generated. Timing was of the essence as the company had a little over 80 days to come up with a new name and logo. This would allow enough time to rebrand all aspects of the organization by the December 31, 2000 deadline.

After this legal review, fifty-one names were still viable. These candidates were then subjected to more rigorous research, including native speaker review and linguistic analysis in 47 countries, against 200 languages, to screen for cultural sensitivities and ensure the name carried positive connotations in each market. All the while, these names continued to go through trademark and URL availability searches in the remaining 47 countries where the company operated. The tight deadline compounded the already complex global trademark check.

In addition to time, another challenge was the recent increase in volume of registered Internet domain names. Registration had increased 46 percent over Year 2000 levels and from May to September 2000 only, the number of registered domains had nearly doubled to 17 million, practically one registration per second. As a result, when the 51 names were found to be available globally, the firm began purchasing the URLs for these name candidates in the U.S. After the final name selection, it would purchase the URLs in each country.

The overall name development and search for Accenture was unprecedented -- not only because of the 81 days in which it was conducted, but also because of its scale and scope. For example, typically, any external client or consumer research is limited, if conducted at all during name searches. But, Andersen Consulting wanted to gain its clients' perspectives on the name candidates. So it tested the 51 name candidates across eight key markets with its senior executive target audience. The objective of the research was to gauge: their overall reaction, the fit with the company's vision and positioning and measure the name's uniqueness.

In addition, legal review is typically done with less than 10 lawyers from two law firms across eight countries. For Andersen Consulting, over 70 attorneys from 25 law firms were engaged across 47 countries. All of these additional challenges had to be met and overcome given the incredibly short timeframe the company had to work within.

At the conclusion of this research, the name candidate list was down to 10 names, which were presented to Andersen Consulting's executive committee for final selection. The executive committee chose the name "Accenture," which had been submitted by a consultant named Kim Petersen, who worked in Andersen Consulting's Oslo office. The name rhymes with "adventure" and connoted "an accent on the future." Petersen explained his submission:

> When trying to come up with a new name for the firm, I thought of things like bold growth, operational excellence and a great place to work. Accenture seemed to capture all those things.[36]

The executive committee selected the name Accenture because it clearly fit the firm's positioning and vision, in addition, they thought the name was catchy and distinctive. Since an employee created the name, the executives hoped it would build consensus within the firm and speed the adoption of the Accenture name. One Landor Associates executive who worked closely with Andersen Consulting during the name selection process, provided further justification for the selection:

> A name must reflect a company accurately, and it must bring that essence into clear, sharp focus. In this instance, Accenture is the optimal solution for this client, because it does reflect their rebranding and repositioning and their future direction by suggesting placing an accent on the future, directly tying into the brand essence.[37]

Announcing Accenture

Following the specified launch schedule, Andersen Consulting announced its new name on October 26, 2000. The company held an internal global webcast to announce the Accenture name and to answer questions about the name change with its Partners and employees. Managing Partner and CEO, Joe Forehand commented on the new name at the time of the announcement:

> Accenture expresses what we have become as an organization as well as what we hope to be – a network of businesses that transcends the boundaries of traditional consulting and brings innovations that dramatically improve the way the world works and lives.[38]

External activities included an announcement press release, followed by a teleconference with leading media to launch the name to the marketplace. Until the official changeover on midnight of December 31, 2000, the firm retained the Andersen Consulting name and logo, and continued to globally heighten awareness and interest of the new name, through the "Renamed. Redefined. Reborn. 01.01.01" print, poster and television effort.

As a second step in the renaming process, in mid-November, Andersen Consulting launched a new logo to represent Accenture visually. The logo consisted of the word "Accenture" written in lowercase letters, with a "greater-than" symbol above the letter "T" serving to accent the word. The greater-than symbol was included in the design as a means of symbolically pointing forward to the future. The lower case "a" demonstrated that Accenture was approachable and accessible. Once the logo was revealed, the challenging task of rebranding the organization really began.

ACCENTURE LAUNCH

On midnight, December 31, 2000, Andersen Consulting officially adopted the Accenture name. Accordingly, on January 1, the company's corporate web site was changed from **www.ac.com** to **www.accenture.com**. Accompanying the announcement was a massive global marketing program designed to raise awareness of the new name. The program targeted senior executives at Accenture's clients and prospects, all Accenture Partners and employees, the media, leading industry analysts, potential recruits and academia.

Internal Launch

Launching the new Accenture name internally was an equally important and daunting task. Accenture needed to execute a complete and monumental changeover throughout all levels of the organization and ensure that all employees and clients understood the new brand and the new positioning. This process was managed and realized by 55 teams of nearly 2,000 employees across the organization, as well as many more outside individuals and agencies. The firm had achieved 1,200 milestones to make the Accenture name change happen. The new name had to be reflected by the company's 178 offices in 47 countries, by its 70,000 employees and their 7 million business cards, by its 1,200 proprietary software applications, and by all other documents (including signage and stationary) and 20,000 databases. To keep employees apprised of the rebranding and repositioning process, Accenture began distributing internal newsletters and e-mails, along with special issues of the internal magazine *Dialogue* beginning in August 2000. Throughout the process Joe Forehand kept everyone informed from the arbitration announcement to the selection of the new name with periodic global webcasts.

On January 3, 2001, Joe Forehand welcomed the new year and the new company, "Accenture," with a global webcast from Australia, the site of the Accenture Match Play Championship. Additionally, when employees returned to work after New Year's, they found Accenture launch packages which included a letter from Joe Forehand, a brand book that explained the new brand and new positioning and special launch-themed issues of *Dialogue* and *Dialogue Online*, the company's internal communications web site and magazine. Throughout January, Accenture executed a series of open houses and celebratory events to recognize the new brand at local offices around the world.

External Launch Efforts: Phase One

Accenture planned a two-phased marketing strategy for introducing Accenture to its global audience. The aim of both phases was to surround the company's target audience -- including 40,000 clients and prospects and Accenture's 70,000 employees, as well as 1.5 million recruits -- with messages informing them about the new name and new positioning. The first phase was a high impact launch on January 1, 2001 using extensive global advertising. In addition to continued media and analyst relations, the launch utilized television, print, poster and Internet placements that linked the Accenture name with the New Year, a linkage that harkened back to Accenture's first ever advertisements from 1989.

The campaign also included print and airport poster advertising. The ads were intended to introduce the new name and transfer equity from its former brand. Additionally, they positioned Accenture as offering a broad range of capabilities across: Consulting, Technology, Outsourcing and Alliances. These capabilities reflected Accenture's broadened breadth of services. By highlighting each of Accenture's core capabilities, the firm hoped to illustrate it offered far more than just strategy or IT consulting.

In the U.S., Accenture television spots appeared during College Bowl games on New Year's Day. Accenture commercials also debuted at this time across other international markets. This repositioning recast Accenture as a company who could bridge boundaries to create the future -- helping their clients bridge the gap from the old economy to the new.

One such television ad opened with the sounds of a New Year's Eve celebration in Times Square over the backdrop of a mountain range. The camera soon reveals that the celebration is being viewed on a personal digital assistant by a climber perched on the side of a remote mountain. As the camera pans back to the mountain range, a voiceover says, "To everyone, everywhere, celebrating the future: Happy New Year from Accenture."

An Accenture branded airship was introduced at the January 2001 Accenture Match Play Championship (formerly the Andersen Consulting Match Play Championship) event in Melbourne, Australia. Since the event coincided with the rebranding launch, the company substantially increased its investment in the Accenture Match Play Championship. Over the course of the five-day tournament coverage, Accenture ran some 300 commercials in its international markets and 100 commercials in the U.S. Print advertisements publicizing the event appeared in major newspapers, business periodicals and golf magazines in the U.S.

As evidenced by the success of the Accenture Match Play Championship, Accenture utilized its sponsorships of other major global sporting events to achieve a high impact internationally. High-profile global advertising opportunities included the Formula 1 Racing Series, several European skiing events, the Six Nations Rugby tournament, the Asian PGA tour, the Accenture Dream Soccer Match in Japan and the Italian Football Championship. By January 2001, television, print, Internet and poster advertisements touting the Accenture name appeared in each of 47 different countries where the company did business. Between January and March, over 6,000 total television commercials spots aired in markets globally. This ad schedule was supplemented by over 1,000 global print ads.

The company utilized innovative print and billboard advertising in addition to television. In Australia, the company placed a "cover wrap" on the magazine Business Review Weekly and placed advertising on bus stops and park benches in Sydney's business district. The company adorned its Paris office building with gigantic Accenture branding, and several Air France buses bore the new logo. Andersen Consulting placed large-scale outdoor ads in Milan's Oberdan Square and Rome's Obelisk, and coated 10 taxis in London with Accenture signage.

In addition to the high profile advertising program, over 43,000 clients received a launch mailing which included creative packaging to announce the new name and positioning, a capabilities brochure outlining the companies service offerings, *Outlook* magazine (the company's thought leadership publication) and a letter from Joe Forehand the Managing Partner and CEO. Further, the Accenture Match Play Championship golf tournament hosted 450 clients and Partners. The impact of the launch was noticeable in other ways. Traffic to accenture.com was up 72 percent over a typical week with 27,700 visitors daily. Finally, the media touted the launch impact as the largest rebranding initiative ever undertaken by a professional services company, and the "01.01.01" launch garnered approximately 120 news items globally in just the first two weeks alone.

External Launch Efforts: Phase Two

The second phase of the advertising program began in late January 2001 with high-profile television spots debuting in the United States during the Super Bowl on January 28. Provocative print ads were also a part of the mix. The new series of ads presented the viewer (or reader) with a striking fact regarding the future in the form of an unexpected headline, followed by the phrase "Now it gets interesting." For example, in one print ad a headline appearing as if torn from newsprint and reading "Bacteria Tested As a Digital Circuit: Use In Chips May Dwarf Silicon" was superimposed over a microscope-view of a bacteria colony. "Now it gets interesting" appeared between brackets under the newsprint headline. Jim Murphy explained the purpose of the ads:

> Our goal was to make target audiences take notice of dramatic global changes in the marketplace in a way that positions Accenture as the organization that can help clients take advantage of these changes and turn them into opportunities.[39]

The advertisements were innovative and striking. They were also interactive as they were integrated with the corporate web site where users could find out more information on how Accenture could help them capitalize on the marketplace opportunities identified in the ad.

Although the Super Bowl television spots were not seen as typical for the broadcast, a study conducted by the Zyman Marketing Group pointed out their beneficial effects. Specifically, the study measured advertising effectiveness by tracking purchase intent before and after consumers viewed the ads. Accenture's "Bacteria" spot garnered a 77 percent increase in purchase intent, the most of any 2001 Super Bowl ad. Other Accenture spots -- "Birthday Cake," "Sports Car," and "Surgery" -- ranked third, eighth, and twelfth, respectively. Sergio Zyman, founder of the Zyman Marketing Group, said

> I believe they were able to accomplish what they set out to do with [the ads] because they focused on their most fundamental need during this launch phase of their brand - to convert a new name into a brand.[40]

The ads had the desired effect of generating interest in the company. Traffic to accenture.com increased dramatically in the days following the Super Bowl. On that Sunday, overall traffic to the web site doubled. In the week that followed the broadcast, traffic to the advertising section of the web site rose 2,100 percent.

These television spots also aired during several major golf tournaments including The Players Championship in March and the U.S. Open in June.

RESULTS AND RESEARCH

After the launch, the company executed an evaluation of the rebranding and repositioning program as part of its its global awareness tracking study with senior executives, its annual brand equity assessment, and its biannual recruitment awareness tracking study. At the end of 2001, one year after the launch of the new brand, the awareness for the Accenture name remained at, or above, previous levels for Andersen Consulting in most countries. Teresa Poggenpohl credited the advertising campaign with driving these levels, saying "We would never have achieved this awareness so quickly on a global basis around the world . . . without advertising."[41]

According to research, the results of the advertising, marketing and communications campaigns were impressive. For example, the advertising effect on "consideration" to purchase Accenture's services increased 350 percent following the campaign. The measurable "brand value" of Accenture also increased by seven percent over Andersen Consulting. Brand equity increased an impressive 11 percent. Awareness of Accenture's breadth and depth of services had achieved 96 percent of its previous level. Globally, awareness of Accenture as a provider of Management & Technology consulting services was 76 percent of its former level. With a few exceptions, the Accenture name registered immediately with clients, prospects and recruits.

Accenture IPO and Financial Results

In July 2001, once again Accenture looked to the future by offering shares of its stock in a $1.7 billion initial public offering. By making this bold move, Accenture wished to create increased opportunities for growth for its clients, shareholders and people around the world. Through the IPO Accenture believed it was better able to deliver a broader range of capabilities and solutions for its clients. The IPO climate at the time of the offering was not favorable, but Accenture outperformed many of the companies in its market space. By the end of the year, Accenture stock was up almost 80 percent from its IPO price of $14.50. Comparatively, consulting competitor KPMG Consulting's stock closed down more than 20 percent on the year.

The Need to Update the Positioning

The marketplace underwent dramatic changes as a result of the fallout from the dot-com crash and the general slowdown of the U.S. economy. Money evaporated from the venture capital pool. Companies looked for ways to cut costs as consumer spending declined. Businesses grew hesitant to turn to consulting companies for strategy that they could develop themselves. Derek Young, Accenture's Australia managing director, said at the time:

> The days when you got paid to give advice are finished. Our client management now want outcomes and they want to tie your remuneration to the value you deliver.[42]

Accenture now sought to "partner" with companies and help them execute their ideas. Accenture also scaled back its marketing during the summer of 2001 as it typically did during the summer holiday season. At this time, Accenture focused its energy towards developing an evolved positioning that better suited the marketplace and client demands.

Refining the Positioning

In 2002, Accenture unveiled an evolved positioning summarized succinctly by the brand essence "Innovation Delivered." The brand essence was supported by the positioning statement:

"From innovation to execution, Accenture helps accelerate your vision."

According to surveys conducted by the company, senior executives from a diverse group of industry sectors and countries identified their ability to execute and deliver on their ideas" as the number one barrier to success. The respondents expressed a need for external assistance from consulting firms to help them bring their ideas to life. Furthermore, senior executives named Accenture as the only company positioned to provide this assistance. Additionally, the survey revealed that executives considered consulting companies as a source of validation for innovative ideas generated within a company. The new positioning and brand essence came from these findings.

Accenture stressed that the innovation could come from either the consulting firm or the client, as explained by CEO Joe Forehand:

> We don't want to back away from being seen as someone who brings the best consulting, innovation, and ideas to clients, but our clients are telling us they have a lot of smart people with good ideas, too. They just need execution. We are uniquely positioned to fit into this intersection of business and technology capability to drive shareholder value for clients. . . . There's nobody in the industry that can be the best at everything across the whole spectrum of hardware, software, technology services and consulting. Our clients value [a company] that is an independent services organization that can make sure their interests are put first and foremost, but also one that has a network of alliance partners it can bring together.[43]

With the new positioning, the company targeted senior executives of global companies "with the ability to drive change in their organizations." The type of executive that Accenture targeted understood the importance of moving rapidly to capitalize on emerging opportunities in the ever-changing marketplace. This group of executives also recognized that the pursuit of competitive advantages sometimes required difficult decisions on their part. Accenture would ensure that such decisions were implemented successfully with the right execution, as described by the company's role with respect to its new positioning:

> [Accenture is a] catalyst to accelerate innovation to results. We spur ideas, put plans into action and help provoke significant change.

Accenture believed its global network of employees and alliance partners, as well as its breadth of services (i.e., Consulting, Technology, Outsourcing, Alliances), represented unparalleled resources to provide clients with innovative solutions.

Furthermore, the company identified personality traits as part of the positioning to be: innovative, smart, collaborative and passionate. Accenture saw itself as an innovator in ideas, technology, execution and collaboration. The company felt it typified a smart company because of its tradition of thought leadership and ability to rapidly develop strategies and execute them. Since it partnered with clients and shared its knowledge and expertise, Accenture viewed itself as collaborative. The company retained the passionate trait from its previous positioning, since it remained driven to help clients succeed and embrace challenges. Finally, research revealed that the passionate personality trait was the best way for Accenture employees to "live" the positioning and bring it to life everyday.

Further building on the "Innovation Delivered" idea, the Accenture signature had been updated to include the phrase "Innovation Delivered" to the existing Accenture logo. Going forward the Accenture "Innovation Delivered" signature would serve as the company's primary logo, reinforcing how Accenture collaborated with its clients to bring ideas to life.

Bringing "Innovation Delivered" to Life: "I Am Your Idea" Advertising Campaign

The new Accenture global advertising campaign, "I am your idea," was launched on February 20, 2002 -- the first day of the 2002 Accenture Match Play Championship. The campaign provides a clever and unique perspective. "I am your idea," speaks from the point of view of the idea itself, giving the idea its own voice and personality. Situations are depicted in which the ideas constantly present themselves, allowing the viewers and readers to see how ideas can take on a voice and personality of their own. In addition, the campaign drives the new "Innovation Delivered" positioning message by illustrating "whether it's your idea or Accenture's, we'll help you turn innovation into results." The advertisements were in response to one of the leading frustrations cited by senior executives -- that great ideas may go unrealized, be it the ideas of clients or Accenture.

One of the television commercials, called "Train," shows an executive writing his ideas on a luminous slip of paper as he is riding in a high-speed train. When he sees other business people on the train and in the station with similar pieces of paper, he is reminded that there are many other ideas out there. It is then that his idea reassures him with a message of, "You're actually going to do something with me."

A print ad from the campaign entitled "Highway" features a highway scene in which the reader has to make a choice. A central sign above the highway reads "I am your idea" with two additional signs underneath. One sign provides direction to a straight path and says "Use me," and another sign points towards a highway turn-off saying "Lose me." The copy reads "It's not how many ideas you have. It's how many you make happen. So whether it's your idea or Accenture's, we'll help you turn innovation into results. See how at accenture.com"

"The campaign was received very positively during testing with senior executives," said Teresa Poggenpohl, "Bringing a client's ideas to life was viewed to be extremely relevant and clear to the senior executives we spoke with. In addition, they found our acknowledgement of clients having ideas to be refreshing and differentiating."

The advertising campaign appeared in 31 countries and was seen on leading business and television news programs and in leading business publications. It was also supported by airport posters and outdoor advertising.

CONCLUSION

Following a decade of prosperity and growth, Accenture staked a new direction and forged a new identity at the turn of the 21st century. After successful arbitration against Andersen Worldwide and Arthur Andersen the company was able to recast itself under a new name, coinciding with the launch of a new positioning. The rebranding and repositioning of Accenture was unprecedented in scope and timeframe -- the largest rebranding initiative ever undertaken by a professional services firm, being successfully implemented across 47 countries in just 147 days. Accenture launched this rebranding and repositioning to its global audience with a multi-phase global marketing campaign that began before the official changeover occurred on January 1, 2001. The challenge was daunting, but the objectives clear: To reposition the company, transfer brand equity to Accenture, raise awareness of Accenture globally and to eliminate residual confusion with Arthur Andersen. Changes in the business climate in 2001 prompted a refinement to their positioning, one that delineated Accenture's ability to help companies capitalize on their marketplace opportunities by bringing their ideas to life.

DISCUSSION QUESTIONS

1. How would you characterize Andersen Consulting's brand equity in the late-1990s? What factors and decisions contributed to the building of this equity?
2. Compare the characteristics of Accenture's brand equity to those of Andersen Consulting. Do you think the rebranding and repositioning of the company successfully transferred the equity from the old name to the new one?
3. How should Accenture follow up on its image and awareness campaign? What should be the next steps in the company's marketing program?

Fig. 1: Overall Brand Equity Index

	Image	Awareness	Consideration	Preference	Average
Andersen Consulting	6.5	10	9.1	5.8	7.9
McKinsey	7.2	8.4	9.2	6.4	7.8
IBM	5.3	4.9	3.6	1.2	3.8
Ernst & Young	3.8	3.2	5.3	1.9	3.6
EDS	1.9	0.0	1.6	0.0	0.7

(source: *Brand Equity Measurment Initiative*, Andersen Consulting, November 1999)

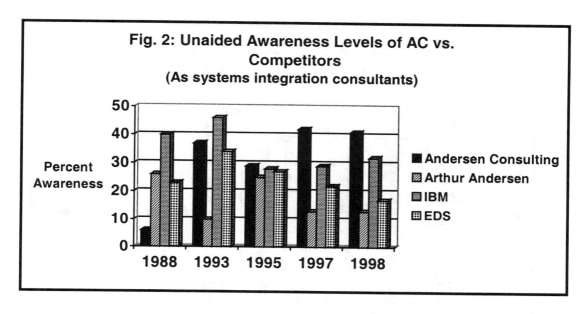

Fig. 2: Unaided Awareness Levels of AC vs. Competitors
(As systems integration consultants)

(Fig. 2 sources: Image Awareness Tracking Study (1998 & 1993), National Awareness Tracking (1993 & 1995) and Global Awareness Tracking (1997 & 1998))

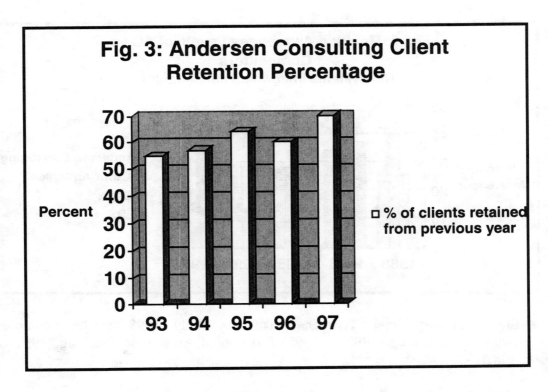

Fig. 3: Andersen Consulting Client Retention Percentage

Percent

□ % of clients retained from previous year

(Source: Andersen Consulting Marketing and Communications Department)

Fig. 4: Awareness Tracking: Andersen Consulting vs. Arthur Andersen

1994 Unaided Awareness

	Business Re-engineering	Strategy Consulting	Systems Integration	Organizational Change
Andersen Consulting	24%	18%	19%	10%
Arthur Andersen	27%	17%	18%	12%

November 1995 Unaided Awareness

	Business Re-engineering	Strategy Consulting	Systems Integration	Organizational Change
Andersen Consulting	35%	32%	29%	23%
Arthur Andersen	31%	22%	25%	18%

(source: 1995 Global Awareness Tracking Study)

Fig. 5: Top 10 IT services providers

Rank	Brand	Share of Market	
		1999	1998
1.	IBM Corp.	8.6	9.2
2.	EDS	6.1	6.6
3.	First Data Corp.	3.1	3.1
4.	Computer Sciences Corp.	3.1	3.1
5.	Automatic Data Processing	2.8	2.7
6.	Andersen Consulting	2.7	2.8
7.	Hewlett-Packard	1.8	2.1
8.	Deloitte Touche Tohmatsu	1.7	1.2
9.	PriceWaterhouseCoopers	1.6	1.0
10.	Oracle Corp.	1.6	1.3

(Source: *Advertising Age*, September 25, 2000)